Intelligence Agencies, Technology and Knowledge Production

This volume examines intelligence services since 1945 in their role as knowledge producers.

Intelligence agencies are producers and providers of arcane information. However, little is known about the social, cultural and material dimensions of their knowledge production, processing and distribution. This volume starts from the assumption that during the Cold War, these core activities of information services underwent decisive changes, of which scientisation and computerisation were essential. With a focus on the emerging alliances between intelligence agencies, science and (computer) technology, the chapters empirically explore these transformations and are characterised by innovative combinations of intelligence history with theoretical considerations from the history of science and technology, and the history of knowledge.

At the same time, the book challenges the bipolarity of Cold War history in general and of intelligence history in particular in favour of comparative and transnational perspectives. The focus is not only on the Soviet Union and the United States but also on Poland, Turkey, Germany and Brazil. This approach reveals surprising commonalities across systems: time and again, the expansion and use of intelligence knowledge came up against the limits that resulted from intelligence culture itself. The book enriches our global understanding of knowledge of the state and contributes to a historical framework for the past decade of debates about the societal consequences of intelligence data processing.

This book will be of much interest to students of intelligence studies, science and technology studies, security studies and international relations.

Rüdiger Bergien is Professor of Intelligence History at the Federal University for Applied Administrative Sciences, Germany.

Debora Gerstenberger is an Assistant Professor of Latin American History at the Institute for Latin American Studies, Freie Universität Berlin, Germany.

Constantin Goschler is a Professor of Contemporary History at the Ruhr-Universität Bochum, Germany, and is currently directing a research group on 'Security, Democracy and Transparency'.

Studies in Intelligence

General Editors: Richard J. Aldrich and Christopher Andrew

The CIA and the Congress for Cultural Freedom in the Early Cold War
The limits of making common cause
Sarah Miller Harris

Understanding Intelligence Failure
Warning, response and deterrence
James J. Wirtz

Intelligence Elites and Public Accountability
Relationships of Influence with Civil Society
Vian Bakir

Intelligence Oversight in the Twenty-First Century
Accountability in a changing world
Edited by Ian Leigh and Njord Wegge

Intelligence Leadership and Governance
Building Effective Intelligence Communities in the 21st Century
Patrick F. Walsh

Intelligence Analysis in the Digital Age
Edited by Stig Stenslie, Lars Haugom, and Brigt H. Vaage

Conflict and Cooperation in Intelligence and Security Organisations
An Institutional Costs Approach
James Thomson

National Security Intelligence and Ethics
Edited by Seumas Miller, Mitt Regan, and Patrick F. Walsh

Intelligence Agencies, Technology and Knowledge Production
Data Processing and Information Transfer in Secret Services during the Cold War
Edited by Rüdiger Bergien, Debora Gerstenberger and Constantin Goschler

For more information about this series, please visit: www.routledge.com/Studies-in-Intelligence/book-series/SE0788

Intelligence Agencies, Technology and Knowledge Production

Data Processing and Information Transfer in Secret Services during the Cold War

Edited by Rüdiger Bergien, Debora Gerstenberger and Constantin Goschler

LONDON AND NEW YORK

First published 2022
by Routledge
4 Park Square, Milton Park, Abingdon, Oxon OX14 4RN

and by Routledge
605 Third Avenue, New York, NY 10158

Routledge is an imprint of the Taylor & Francis Group, an informa business

© 2022 selection and editorial matter, Rüdiger Bergien, Debora Gerstenberger and Constantin Goschler; individual chapters, the contributors

The right of Rüdiger Bergien, Debora Gerstenberger and Constantin Goschler to be identified as the authors of the editorial material, and of the authors for their individual chapters, has been asserted in accordance with sections 77 and 78 of the Copyright, Designs and Patents Act 1988.

All rights reserved. No part of this book may be reprinted or reproduced or utilised in any form or by any electronic, mechanical, or other means, now known or hereafter invented, including photocopying and recording, or in any information storage or retrieval system, without permission in writing from the publishers.

Trademark notice: Product or corporate names may be trademarks or registered trademarks, and are used only for identification and explanation without intent to infringe.

British Library Cataloguing-in-Publication Data
A catalogue record for this book is available from the British Library

Library of Congress Cataloging-in-Publication Data
A catalog record for this book has been requested

ISBN: 978-0-367-70639-5 (hbk)
ISBN: 978-0-367-70641-8 (pbk)
ISBN: 978-1-003-14732-9 (ebk)

DOI: 10.4324/9781003147329

Typeset in Times New Roman
by Apex CoVantage, LLC

Contents

List of figures	vii
Acknowledgements	viii
List of contributors	ix

The knowledge of intelligence agencies in the Cold War world: an introduction 1

RÜDIGER BERGIEN, DEBORA GERSTENBERGER
AND CONSTANTIN GOSCHLER

1 **Compromised cooperation: scholarly experts on Eastern Europe in the service of West German intelligence in the early Cold War** 18

THOMAS WOLF

2 **Dogma versus progress: KGB's technological and scientific (in-)capacities from the 1960s to the 1980s** 37

EVGENIA LEZINA

3 **Sublimation without domination: exploring the knowledge of U.S. strategic intelligence during the Cold War** 65

ANDREAS LUTSCH

4 **American security databases and the production of space, 1967–1974: enhancing or obscuring patterns?** 85

JENS WEGENER

5 **Knowledge transfer and technopolitics: the CIA, the West German intelligence service and the digitisation of information processing in the 1960s** 101

RÜDIGER BERGIEN

vi *Contents*

6 **Information technology is power: the intelligence service's grab for the IT sector in Brazil** 121

MARCELO VIANNA

7 **The computer as document shredder: video terminals and the dawn of a new era of knowledge production in Brazil's Serviço Nacional de Informações** 140

DEBORA GERSTENBERGER

8 **Turkish intelligence, surveillance and the secrets of the Cold War: blocked modernisation?** 164

EGEMEN BEZCI

9 **Solid modernity: data storage and information circuits in the communist security police in Poland** 184

FRANCISZEK DĄBROWSKI

10 **Eliminating the human factor? Perceptions of digital computers at the German domestic intelligence service** 206

CHRISTOPHER KIRCHBERG

11 **Global war academies: intelligence schools during the civil-military dictatorship in Brazil** 231

SAMANTHA VIZ QUADRAT

12 **Intelligence for the masses: the annual reports on the protection of the constitution in West Germany between Cold War propaganda and government public relations** 249

MARCEL SCHMEER

Conclusion 274

RÜDIGER BERGIEN, DEBORA GERSTENBERGER
AND CONSTANTIN GOSCHLER

Index 285

Figures

2.1	The building of the former KGB Main Computing Center in Lubyanskaya square today houses the Information Security Center (TsIB) of Russia's Federal Security Service (FSB)	49
6.1	ACE documents subsystem screen, as illustrated in a 1984 SARDI user's manual	127
6.2	Report and sample of cryptography of the Prólogo project (1978–1979)	129
6.3	Caricature by Hilde Weber published in the daily newspaper *O Estado de S. Paulo* in January 1980 on CSN's ambitions to control strategic areas	130
6.4	CISA/SNI's reports from December 26, 1977, about APPD activities	132
7.1	Illustration of IBM 3270 display terminals taken from an advertising brochure	141
7.2	List of destroyed and digitised documents	150
7.3	Model of a *Folha Auxiliar* containing the data that would be digitised	155
7.4	Network of different databases at SNI, as envisioned in 1981	157
8.1	White Book on Greece's War Preparedness	171
10.1	Cover of Postel's autobiography published in 1999	207
12.1	"Reception Area of the German Television Broadcasting Corporation in the Federal Republic" as published in the weekly journal *Aus Politik und Zeitgeschichte*	257
12.2	"Explosive attack on the car of a federal judge in Karlsruhe" and "RAF 'baby bomb'" as published by the German Ministry of the Interior in 1972	262

Acknowledgements

This volume is essentially the result of a conference organised by Rüdiger Bergien, Debora Gerstenberger, Constantin Goschler and Christopher Kirchberg at the Leibniz Centre for Contemporary History Research (Zentrum für Zeithistorische Forschung, ZZF) in Potsdam in June 2019. The conference took place under the title "The Knowledge of Intelligence. Scientification, Data Processing and Information Transfer in Secret Services, 1945–1990" and was decidedly designed as an international workshop in which different national and regional experiences could be discussed comparatively. We would like to thank all those who participated in the conference with great commitment and filled it with intellectual content. We also want to thank all those who helped organise the conference.

Special thanks go to the institutions that made this fruitful academic meeting possible: the Fritz Thyssen Foundation, which generously sponsored the conference; the Institute for Latin American Studies at Freie Universität Berlin, which covered travel costs for participants from Brazil; and the Leibniz Centre for Contemporary History Research, which took over the organisation of the conference and provided the conference facilities.

When the conference took place in Potsdam in the summer of 2019 in beautiful sunshine and a relaxed atmosphere, no one had any idea that nothing less than a worldwide pandemic would stand between the start of our project and the completion of the edited volume. It was exceedingly difficult for everyone involved to write, edit, correct, proofread and format the contributions for this volume under these conditions. We are all the happier that we nevertheless managed to bring the volume to a good end. All have shown great dedication, patience and perseverance.

For copyediting, we thank Francesca Bondy, Ivo Komljen and Karim Elawar. For matching bibliographies and formatting the layout of endnotes, we thank Lara Backhaus and Stefan Pulte.

Finally, we would like to thank the staff of Routledge, especially Andrew Humphrys and Bethany Lund-Yates, and the series editors of the Routledge series Studies in Intelligence, Richard Aldrich, Christopher Andrew and Claudia Hillebrand, for their professional support, their patience and for their trust in us and our project.

Contributors

Rüdiger Bergien is Professor of Intelligence History at the Federal University of Applied Administrative Sciences, Berlin, and specialises in the history of digitalisation in intelligence and security agencies.

Egemen Bezci holds a PhD in politics from the University of Nottingham. He is a Fellow of the Royal Historical Society and author of *Turkish Intelligence and the Cold War: The Turkish Secret Service, the US, and UK* (2019).

Franciszek Dąbrowski is an archivist in the Archives of the Institute of the National Remembrance in Warsaw, deputy editor-in-chief of the "Institute of National Remembrance Review" and a history lecturer with the War Studies University in Warsaw.

Debora Gerstenberger is Assistant Professor of Latin American History at the Institute for Latin American Studies at Freie Universität Berlin and is currently working on a monograph about the computerisation of the institutions of state security (intelligence, military, police) in Latin America. ORCID: https://orcid.org/0000-0002-2214-1619

Constantin Goschler is Professor of Contemporary History at the Ruhr- Universität Bochum and is currently directing a research group on "Security, Democracy and Transparency." ORCID: https://orcid.org/0000-0001-7577-1342

Christopher Kirchberg is a research assistant with the "Security, Democracy and Transparency" research group at the Ruhr- Universität Bochum. ORCID: http://orcid.org/0000-0003-4417-8778

Evgenia Lezina is a research fellow at the Leibniz Centre for Contemporary History Potsdam, currently working on a research project on "The Soviet State Security's Political and Power Resources. KGB Structures, Practices and Methods in the Last Decades of the Soviet Union."

Andreas Lutsch is Junior Professor of Intelligence Analysis at the Federal University of Applied Administrative Sciences, Berlin

Samantha Viz Quadrat is Associate Professor of Contemporary History of America at the Universidade Federal Fluminense (Brazil) and coordinator

x *Contributors*

of the research project "Transnational violence and dictatorships in Latin America: a study regarding SNI (CNPq-Brazil)." ORCID: https://orcid.org/0000-0003-1547-1000

Marcel Schmeer is a researcher at the Center for Intelligence and Security Studies (CISS) at Universität der Bundeswehr München and a PhD candidate at Ruhr-Universität Bochum focusing on security history, especially the history of the German police and intelligence services. ORCID: https://orcid.org/0000-0001-6237-4700

Marcelo Vianna is Director of Research at the Federal Institute of Education, Science and Technology of Rio Grande do Sul and co-author of *Professions, Bureaucracies and Knowledge: Historical Perspectives* (2020). ORCID: https://orcid.org/0000-0002-3687-3474

Jens Wegener is a postdoctoral researcher with the "Security, Democracy and Transparency" research group at the Ruhr-Universität Bochum.

Thomas Wolf was Research assistant of the Independent Historians' Commission on the History of the Federal Intelligence Service (UHK BND). He is the author of *Die Entstehung des BND. Aufbau, Finanzierung, Kontrolle* (2018).

The knowledge of intelligence agencies in the Cold War world

An introduction

Rüdiger Bergien, Debora Gerstenberger and Constantin Goschler

In the 1960s, heads of intelligence in the West, the East and the South often described their agencies as scientific and technological enterprises. Central Intelligence Agency (CIA) director William F. Raborn explained in a 1966 interview that the main purpose of a modern intelligence organisation was scientific data analysis.[1] In the same year, the president of the West German Federal Intelligence Service (Bundesnachrichtendienst, BND), Reinhard Gehlen, described the future of his service to a parliamentary committee as developing into "a kind of research institute" (*eine Art wissenschaftliches Institut*).[2] In the following year, the Soviet Committee for State Security (Komitet gosudarstvennoi bezopasnosti, KGB) chairman Yuri Andropov began his term of office with a twofold agenda for reform: the introduction of new technologies and the "intellectualization" of the KGB.[3] And in 1968, the Brazilian military dictatorship began the large-scale build-up of a "National Information System" (Sistema Nacional de Informações, SISNI) with the main intelligence service, the Serviço Nacional de Informações (SNI), as its centrepiece.[4]

The intelligence services' growing attention to science and technology also influenced public and popular representations on both sides of the Iron Curtain. In the Hollywood film *Three Days of the Condor* (1975), the protagonist, a CIA employee impersonated by Robert Redford, resembles a social analyst when he states: "I am not a spy, I just read books." And in in the spy novel *Avakoum Zahov vs. 07* by Bulgarian author Andrei Gulyashki, published in 1966, the KGB employee Avakum Zahov, who has a PhD in archaeology, defeats a dissolute James Bond with his brain power.[5]

The remarkable parallels in these images of secret services allow for several interpretations. First, the development "from espionage to intelligence"[6] could be highlighted: the technologisation of intelligence gathering and the increase in data processing fundamentally changed the character of intelligence services. These went from spy organisations that stole secrets from human sources to institutions that prioritised the processing of information (some but not all of which was secret).[7] A second interpretation might emphasise the fact that the aforementioned praise of science and technology as a valuable tool of intelligence was deeply embedded in contemporary modernisation discourses. The acquisition of cutting-edge information technology both served to overcome the "cloak and dagger"

DOI: 10.4324/9781003147329-1

2   *Bergien/Gerstenberger/Goschler*

image of intelligence agencies and helped to justify the enormous increase in their budgets, not least through the acquisition of expensive electronic data processing (EDP).[8] A third interpretation might stress the possibilities and the political consequences of the alliance between science, technology and intelligence activities. In popular representations of the Cold War, the combination of secret services, scientific methods and (information) technology appears particularly powerful and also particularly dangerous, even dystopian. After all, the alliance described here emerged at a time when the nuclear annihilation of the world seemed a real possibility.

All of these interpretations must be taken with caution. While at first glance they fit perfectly into the familiar narrative "rise of information societies,"[9] the question how self-representations and popular cultural projections during the Cold War world related to the actual development within the intelligence agencies remains. Contrary to what literary scholar Eva Horn argues in her thought-provoking book *The Secret War*,[10] we believe that the realities of the secret services cannot be inferred exclusively or primarily from (literary) fictions. Instead, empirical historical research is needed in order to reveal the actual transformations of intelligence techniques and intelligence knowledge during the Cold War. Since historical interpretations should not remain trapped in the vocabulary and the concepts of the period under scrutiny, the very concept of "information society," which emerged as an important aspect of self-interpretation in our period of investigation, also needs to be historicised.[11] What role did the tendencies of scientisation as well as the increasing use of EDP play in intelligence practice and in the resulting knowledge, and to what extent did this, in turn, possibly influence the political status of intelligence knowledge?

A historical perspective on the intertwinement of intelligence agencies and science and computer technology during the Cold War will contribute to a better understanding of how specific ways of state surveillance and control have evolved, how epistemologies of state knowledge (which relied at least partly on the "secret knowledge" of the respective intelligence providers) shifted and consequently how governmentalities of states changed. Since the rise of "information societies" is often interpreted as the prehistory of *big data*, historical research can also illuminate the complex problems that institutions face when applying new (scientific) methods and artefacts as well as the tensions and problems associated with the change, thus drawing a more realistic picture of what intelligence agencies can and cannot do with cutting-edge information technology. Analyses of the disparities between old and new techniques and practices during the Cold War can also cast light on contemporary processes.

We start from the "cultural turn in intelligence studies" (Simon Willmetts) and thus from the premise that intelligence agencies were never isolated from the outside world, as they occasionally claimed to be. Rather, they were "shaped and suffused by extrinsic cultural values" and, in turn, themselves shaped those cultural values.[12] However, cultural values and technical and scientific developments are closely intertwined, and this also affects secret services. Kristie Macrakis stated that during the Cold War, "technophilia" had become a cure-all for numerous problems in the United States, including the "intelligence problem of a closed society."[13] In this context, scientisation of intelligence services presumably took place in several ways: science and scientific methods helped handle the "information flood," but above all, they provided "context and meaning" for the data.[14] Yet the belief in science and the tendency of information services to see technology as the solution to all problems needs further investigation. "Much work," Macrakis rightly said in 2010, remained to be done to assess "technological espionage during the Cold War more fully, particularly from the perspective of the history of science and technology."[15]

We agree with Macrakis on the need to explore the scientific and technological sides of intelligence work during the Cold War. However, her thesis that during the Cold War the United States developed an espionage style that "reflected its love affair with technology," whereas the Soviet Union and the Eastern Bloc "continued a tradition of using humans to collect intelligence,"[16] narrows down the scope of investigation to the aspect of *information-gathering*. While this undoubtedly constituted an important part of intelligence activity, our volume is primarily concerned with intelligence agencies' *information processing* and *information storing* – in short, with the *production of intelligence knowledge*. According to our hypothesis, the production of intelligence was in multiple ways entangled with the dynamics of computerisation and scientisation not only in the United States but in almost the entire Cold War world.

By shifting the focus to the production of intelligence knowledge, we draw in particular on insights from the history of knowledge. Proponents of a history of knowledge argue that knowledge is formatted and shaped in different media and also mutates while travelling through diverse environments, not least in the course of transitions between different modes of representation. Knowledge is conceived not as a solid entity but rather as elements of cultural production which are constantly changing while moving across social, institutional and cultural borders.[17]

Philipp Sarasin and Andreas Kilcher pointed out that a political history of the circulation of knowledge needs to look at "impediments, diversions, bottlenecks and blockades."[18] The knowledge of intelligence agencies is by its very definition restricted knowledge:[19] it can even be considered the last refuge of the *arcana imperii* of the modern state. Thus, important questions include "How is the circulation of intelligence knowledge restricted or facilitated, by whom and for what purposes?" Our understanding of the circulation of knowledge therefore assigns a decisive role to actors and practices, something that at times is lacking in the frequent use of circulation metaphors in global history studies.[20]

From the history of knowledge perspective, the question whether intelligence agencies were able to produce "true knowledge" seems somewhat inappropriate. The interesting issues rather are as follows: how does the knowledge of intelligence agencies undergo transformations while circulating between different contexts, especially as a result of increasing international cooperation? How is it shaped and altered by storage methods, technical infrastructures and other material and immaterial aspects? Who were the actors of knowledge production and knowledge transfer, and what was their role in the production and refashioning

4   *Bergien/Gerstenberger/Goschler*

of intelligence knowledge? How was intelligence knowledge selected, remoulded and used in public and political spheres?

And finally, we intend not only to bring intelligence history and the history of science and technology closer together but also to question the traditional bipolarity in intelligence history, which is mostly focused on the United States and the Soviet Union. Even during the Cold War, the world did not consist exclusively of two monolithic blocs. Perspectives from smaller allies, non-aligned states and states from the Global South will help to put supposedly universal trends – or else trends that are clearly associated with a particular ideological orientation – into perspective. Both transnational history and global history on the one hand and contemporary history of technology (which has strong links with science and technology studies) on the other show us that looking only at the most powerful centres in the world is not enough to understand larger processes and contexts.[21] Eden Medina has argued that historians of science have invoked "decentering as a way to draw attention to different forms of knowledge production around the world and move away from privileging forms of knowledge classifiable as Western science."[22]

With our broader geographical horizon that encompasses not only the United States and the Soviet Union but also Poland, Turkey, the two German states and, prominently, Brazil, we can gain diverse and more nuanced insights into the history of intelligence. To what extent did it matter that the scientisation and digitisation of intelligence services took place under diverse political conditions, ranging from Western liberal democracy to Eastern state socialist regimes and authoritarian regimes in Latin America? Will a comparison lead to an Agambian perspective where capitalist and socialist, liberal and non-liberal intelligence agencies ultimately become indistinguishable? Or were there in fact quantitative and qualitative changes in the production and handling of intelligence knowledge that can be directly linked to the political environment? Will a comparison lead back to a Mertonian perspective, according to which modern science can only flourish within the framework of a liberal democracy – from which it might be concluded that intelligence services could only successfully combine with science in democracies? And consequently, were liberal states in the industrialised centres ahead in the production of intelligence knowledge, as modernisation theory would suggest? Or was Western *technophilia*, as Macrakis describes for the United States, ultimately inferior to old-school methods of knowledge production that were pursued elsewhere?

***

Although intelligence agencies are commonly seen as knowledge producers par excellence, the investigation of social, technical and material dimensions of the collection, processing and distribution of information – as well as the effects these proceedings had – has just begun. The status quo reflects both intelligence history's lack of interconnections with other historiographic fields and contemporary historiography's indifference towards the history of intelligence.[23] While current

Knowledge of intelligence: An introduction 5

and future effects of globalisation, information "explosion" through the Internet, digital surveillance, big data and so forth are intensively discussed in intelligence studies,[24] historical perspectives on these issues are largely lacking.[25] However, there are some relevant contributions that help establish a research perspective that could be labelled *global history of intelligence knowledge.*

Intelligence studies and contemporary history are in agreement that the intelligence services changed decisively during the Cold War. Yet so far only a few studies have addressed the growing interaction of intelligence agencies with science during the Cold War. An outstanding example is David C. Engerman's monograph *Know Your Enemy* about the creation of the interdisciplinary Soviet studies in the United States, where he showed that the needs of the Cold War conjoined academic work and political projects, and that academic knowledge and intelligence knowledge first fertilised each other and then separated again.[26] In contrast, considerably more attention has been paid to the role of digitisation, especially in the wake of 9/11 and after the Snowden leaks in 2013.[27] Michael Warner has linked today's cybersecurity culture, the entirety of technical and judiciary measures to protect computer systems, digital data and networks, to political interventions of intelligence services that started as early as the late 1960s.[28] Richard Aldrich has traced current media's "revelation culture" regarding secret intelligence back to the 1960s.[29] Contemporary historians as well as intelligence scholars have also turned to the history of the conflict between state arcane spheres and public quests for transparency. Lisa Medrow, Daniel Münzner and Robert Radu have traced the origins of the modern constellation of espionage, secrecy and the public sphere between 1870 and 1940.[30] Special attention has also been paid to the tension between the growing databases of the secret services and public demands for transparency in Western societies.[31]

Improved access to intelligence agencies' records has enabled historians to write comprehensive general accounts about services such as the British MI5 or the West German Federal Intelligence Service, covering fields that were previously omitted, such as knowledge production practices, academisation and professionalisation, organisational culture and subculture.[32] Studies such as Uwe Krähnke's praxeology of the East German state security service[33] and Władysław Bułhak's approach to the professionalisation of the Polish secret police in the 1970s[34] laid the foundations for a comparative view of intelligence services in different political systems. Existing research has focused on information flows between intelligence services and centres of power but has failed to explore concrete practices of information *production* and *processing.* Often, the question whether a certain piece of intelligence information in a specific political situation was true or not prevails.[35] Some intelligence scholars have looked at "intelligence failures" or organisational deficiencies and a lack of communication channels between intelligence services and policymakers.[36] A few studies have even approached the field of collective mentalities and organisational culture. Starting from socio-psychological perspectives, they included ideological distortions and phenomena such as "group think" and "house views" in their analysis.[37] Richard S. Heuer has contributed to an anatomy of intelligence knowledge with his often-quoted *Psychology of*

6 *Bergien/Gerstenberger/Goschler*

Intelligence Analysis,[38] but this study lacks (micro) analyses of organisational day-to-day-routines.

On the other hand, in the field of surveillance studies, intelligence services are usually dealt with as main users and driving forces of the development and extension of data-generating techniques, ranging from finger printing to population registration and biometrics.[39] In most of these studies, intelligence agencies appear as "black boxes" of an overarching repressive state structure, whose inner workings remain obscure and whose data processing practices are described with references to public guessing.[40] While surveillance studies often have been inclined to expose the hidden dark sides of liberal societies, historians investigating dictatorships or authoritarian regimes have analysed the impact of state security surveillance on certain social and political groups, with the educational aspect of exposing the crimes of newly overthrown regimes often in the foreground, at least initially. After the end of the Eastern European communist dictatorships and the Latin American authoritarian military regimes, the respective services were rightly considered as central pillars of overarching repressive state structures. Historians who address the East German Secret Police Staatssicherheit (Stasi) or Brazil's SNI thus aimed to analyse the atrocities and human rights violations of the systems of state security within the respective political regime and the responsibilities for crimes such as arbitrary imprisonment, torture and murder.[41] Some researchers have provided organisational histories of the repressive apparatuses with a focus on the operative units in charge of fighting the inner enemy.[42] The history of intelligence has thus contributed to the societal quest to come to terms with a dictatorial past.

Altogether, organisational cultures, routine practices or information processing techniques so far have not been privileged topics in intelligence studies and intelligence history. Intelligence knowledge production has rarely been studied as complex, socially and culturally embedded, often precarious practices that heavily depend on material and technical conditions and circumstances. The difficulties experienced by British MI5 and East German state institutions in adopting their paper card indexes to a perceived information explosion in the 1950s, for instance, have been seen in the context of organisational deficiencies or reform backlogs and not in the context of broader societal trends.[43] A similar reticence is evident with regard to comparisons between "the East" and "the West." Secret police information processing and Western intelligence's information processing are usually seen as being fundamentally different. This is partly due to the fact that many Cold War authoritarian and dictatorial regimes are associated with technological backwardness; the technical skills of the respective intelligence agencies have often been derided. German Democratic Republic (GDR) historians, for instance, had become so accustomed to ridiculing GDR microelectronics that it took two decades to ask whether the hundreds of *Robotron* computers used by the Stasi in the late 1980s actually made a qualitative difference for state surveillance.[44]

Intelligence historians have an even clearer opinion on the quality of communist foreign espionage. The analytical capabilities of the KGB, Stasi and other services are considered drastically inferior to Western, that is US and British, services. Christopher Andrew has emphasised that in the 1970s, many foreign KGB

Knowledge of intelligence: An introduction   7

operations were not about information-gathering but instead consisted to a large degree of surveilling and, occasionally, harming Soviet dissidents, in clear continuity with the NKVD's hunt for inner enemies abroad in the 1920s and 1930s.[45] Raymond Garthoff has argued that communist intelligence services did not achieve the independent thinking expected by US analysts due to ideologically distorted "house views" and to the Politburo's habitual rejection of any perceptions of reality that contradicted their own world views.[46]

The contrasting of ideological (and irrational) Soviet espionage with American intellectual freedom clearly refers to Cold War patterns of perception.[47] We must question the assumption that "foreign intelligence is the first and foremost task of any intelligence agency"[48] and the treatment of domestic surveillance – the undisputed focus of any communist or other authoritarian secret service – as a negligible, secondary task. The East German Stasi started to store the personal data of hundreds of thousands of travellers who crossed the border to West Germany in electronic databases as early as 1978 – years before West German authorities began comparable measures. The fact that the Stasi used this data quite efficiently[49] gives reason to question some of the biases usually held by intelligence scholars against secret police data processing and domestic surveillance.

Comparative perspectives do not presuppose that intelligence services were all the same regardless of the political system. Rather, they suggest that intelligence services in liberal (Western) societies as well as intelligence services (and secret police) serving dictatorial regimes are producers of secret state knowledge and must be considered a structural element of statehood in the twentieth century. Their respective knowledge production can thus provide an "axis of comparison between outwardly diverse individual cases."[50] Such an approach not only sheds new light on a service's particular history; it may also enrich our understanding of the knowledge of the state and its transformations during the Cold War.[51]

***

Intelligence knowledge is dynamic, multifaceted, susceptible to faults and contradictory results, and shaped by culturally determined frameworks of perception as well as by technical infrastructures. Consequently, this volume takes several approaches to the topic, illuminating the changes in intelligence knowledge in the context of practices, discourses and representations in various fields. Furthermore, intelligence services will be examined in different political systems and cultures, which were at the same time interwoven in many ways in the Cold War world. The aim of our undertaking is to make visible analogous and divergent patterns and development trajectories in order to provide an understanding of intelligence knowledge and its evolution that is more comprehensive than separate approaches would allow.

Our volume promotes four analytical perspectives which are entangled in different ways in the individual contributions. The *first* perspective focuses on the intensifying relationship of intelligence services with science, more precisely on the implementation of scientific methods and standards. In the twentieth century, the idea that social developments could be controlled scientifically became increasingly important. In this context, the term *scientisation* is used to describe the diffusion of scientific categories, methodologies and practices into state and society; it manifests itself in the rise of experts and in the preference given to systematic knowledge production over immediate experience.[52] The 1960s in particular saw the euphoric exaggeration of the potential of science and research in solving the problems facing humanity. At first glance, there is much to suggest that this technical and scientific post-war optimism also influenced intelligence services' expectations and perceptions. In our volume, we address the following questions: did *scientisation* of intelligence agencies actually occur, and if so, how and to what degree? How did scientific insights, methods and standards affect practices of intelligence knowledge production?

A characteristic of the 1950s–1970s was also the change in data processing brought on by computers. Our *second* analytical perspective thus focuses on the introduction of digital tools into intelligence agencies. The digitisation of the "secret state" began during the Second World War with the use of the world's first digital computers in the context of signals intelligence (SIGINT). The second phase started in the late 1950s and 1960s with the attempts by the services to digitise their own information stores, which were until then mainly based on paper index cards. A third phase followed a few years later with the establishment of information associations based on remote data transmission.[53] The contributions in this volume are primarily devoted to the second and third phases, which covered the services as a whole rather than just SIGINT. Digitisation changed the way information was procured as well as the analysis, transfer and materiality of knowledge, and it also produced a number of unintended effects upon knowledge production in organisations:[54] staff with IT expertise were employed, large numbers of existing staff were put through IT courses and further training, work routines, schedules and organisational structures were subject to constant revision in the name of digitisation. But the question remains: how exactly did digitisation affect the actual practices of knowledge production?

The *third* perspective aims at the institutionalisation of *inter-service knowledge transfer*. How has this changed the possibilities and consequences of as well as the barriers to knowledge circulation? The Cold War prompted an increase in intelligence liaison and international intelligence cooperation. The common threat each bloc perceived enabled intelligence cooperation at a scale unseen in the years prior to 1945.[55] From the 1970s onward, a development described as the internationalisation of threats took place.[56] Richard Aldrich has argued that this development led to a fundamental change in intelligence service practices, which he described as "deterritorialisation." The oft-discussed blurring of the boundaries between domestic and foreign intelligence can be understood as part of this development.[57] This increase in cooperation and interaction is tantamount to an increase in knowledge transfer between services. On the one hand, knowledge possesses many authors. It does not travel unidirectionally, nor is it immutable. It is permanently transformed and reinterpreted. On the other hand, there are – and

Knowledge of intelligence: An introduction   9

this holds especially true for intelligence knowledge – blockades and restrictions that need to be considered.[58]

Finally, the *fourth* perspective focuses on the *communication* of intelligence knowledge to other societal fields and to a wider public. In what ways was there an attempt to "translate" intelligence knowledge for the public in order to achieve certain political goals and increase political power? Philip Sarasin argues that "media of knowledge" are fundamental parts of "power relations and themselves exert effects of power."[59] Thus, the communication of intelligence knowledge to other societal fields cannot be conceived as pure revelations of state secrets but must also be considered as a part of the game in complex power relations. Of course, intelligence knowledge is *transformed* through communication. The effects of intelligence information depend on *how* and *what exactly* is communicated as well as on how the public *perceives* what is communicated.

***

The contributions in this volume approach the questions raised here in different ways. The search for the significance of the scientisation of intelligence agencies yields ambivalent findings on the extent to which science was considered useful for "knowing the enemy" during the Cold War. In his contribution about the so-called *Ostforschung* (German research on Eastern Europe), *Thomas Wolf* (Chapter 1) asks if scientisation actually occurred in the case of the West German Federal Intelligence Agency and its predecessor, the Gehlen Organization, in the first decade after the Second World War. The Gehlen Organization devoted many resources to establishing connections with protagonists in the field of *Ostforschung*. However, Wolf claims that the intention behind these efforts was not for the sake of the researchers as academic scholars. Rather, these were seen as potential networkers through whom connections to Soviet centres of power could be established. Notably, research subjects and results were of little interest to the intelligence agency. Since there was no intellectual connection to be made, in fact no scientisation took place.

The case of the KGB during the 1970s and 1980s was different, as *Evgenia Lezina* (Chapter 2) shows in her contribution on the KGB's counterintelligence. According to official discourse, it was absolutely necessary for a successful fight against the enemy to obtain intimate knowledge about the enemy on a scientific basis. In fact, Soviet state authorities invested significant resources in the professionalisation and mechanisation of their intelligence service, to some positive effect. However, according to Lezina, the development into an institution fully equipped for analytic rigor was not successful, as it collided with the ideological belief system that was integral to the secret police culture of the organisation.

So while the example of the KGB seems to support the assumptions that the alliance between intelligence and science can only flourish in liberal democracies, the example of the CIA contradicts such conclusions: even though CIA intelligence analysis was largely established by scientific researchers (including historians) and shaped by an explicit orientation on methodology and a certain degree

10 *Bergien/Gerstenberger/Goschler*

of self-reflection, it was not highly appreciated by CIA practitioners, as *Andreas Lutsch* reveals (Chapter 3). While intelligence as a political resource grew increasingly important in US decision-making processes, the question about methodological rigour and empirical density was not important for the estimation of its political value. The politicisation of intelligence knowledge in the United States apparently went hand in hand with the elevation or even mythification of the "intellectual core" of the intelligence service.

While the relationship between intelligence agencies, politics and science seems to have been rather ambivalent in the United States, the technological field apparently served as an effective mediator between politics and intelligence. *Jens Wegener* (Chapter 4) examines the influence that the military and security policy agendas of various US governments had on mechanisation and digitisation of intelligence knowledge production. He interprets the development of intelligence databases as the rise of a spatial technology. In times of political and social change and the blurring of borders between friend and foe, technology was employed to enable political domination of spaces – whether in warfare in Indochina or in US metropolises witnessing civil unrest. By linking spatial to individual biographical information, digital security databases were now new elements in a long tradition of human geography. Through the information these databases generated, politicians wanted to gain better control over space, especially over national borders. The new counterintelligence technology had broader implications beyond its narrow field of application: since the new (intelligence) technology was developed by US companies, this industry was henceforth more strongly determined by the interests of the US government.

Wegener's question whether EDP and, more specifically, security databases became the most important spatial technology in the "American Century" is taken up by several other contributions and answered in different ways. *Rüdiger Bergien* (Chapter 5) underlines the importance of the pioneering technological role of the United States, even though he offers differentiated answers to the question of "technopolitics." Whereas the CIA provided the BND with "digital development aid" on several levels, the 'machine hegemony' sought by the CIA only provided a limited "payback" in the form of digitised intelligence knowledge collected by the BND. In addition, digitisation produced a number of unexpected side effects. For example, the BND, which had made its own compartmentalisation a dogma, was forced to work much more closely with civilian computer manufacturers such as IBM than it had planned. Digitisation ultimately led to a growing diversity and a greater "civilianisation" of the intelligence organisations (IT experts were mostly civilians and not members of the military or other state institutions). Subsequently, the wartime image of older, conservative, military-savvy upper-class white men was fading.

There were various attempts to address the technological superiority of the United States. Both the Federal Republic and the GDR were oriented towards US technology but tried to escape the associated technopower in different ways. Brazil took a different path, as *Marcelo Vianna* (Chapter 6) reveals: in the late 1970s, there were attempts by the government (especially the Ministry of Planning) to

Knowledge of intelligence: An introduction   11

develop a Brazilian national computer industry to counter the dominance of companies like IBM. But this initiative was soon sidelined by Brazil's SNI. SNI was not only concerned with its own digitisation (built on IBM mainframes) from the late 1970s on but became directly involved in IT policies and politics. Vianna demonstrates how SNI's modernisation was accompanied by the military's interest in influencing information technology. Ultimately, the process culminated in SNI's surveillance and control of the technical-scientific community. SNI served as an actor and driving force in the digitisation of society as a whole in the 1970s and 1980s – similarly to the National Security Agency (NSA) in the United States in the 1950s.[60]

Common sense holds that the introduction of digital computers into institutions of state security goes hand in hand with an enormous increase in data. However, the installation of IBM video terminals in Brazil's SNI in 1978 at first had the opposite effect: *Debora Gerstenberger* (Chapter 7) shows that up to 95 per cent of the existing intelligence documents (mostly containing detailed information about "subversive" individuals) were eliminated in the course of digitisation. The stock of knowledge on which the analysts based their intelligence information melted down to a fraction. At the same time, external databases provided by other institutions (vehicle registration office, criminal police, geographical institutes) were connected to the intelligence agency. The intelligence knowledge so created was not only more encompassing but also more interconnected. When digital tools were established at the intelligence service, re-democratisation was already being envisioned. Thus, computers went hand in hand with a new governmentality of the state.

While secret services in the GDR struggled to import prohibited Western hardware and Brazilian secret services ultimately stopped the techno-nationalists' efforts to build a competitive domestic computer industry, Turkey enjoyed the privilege of being equipped with US technology for surveillance purposes. However, *Egemen Bezci* (Chapter 8) demonstrates that the progressive increase in technical and scientific capabilities did not necessarily have a positive impact on the evolution of Turkish intelligence. Rather, domestic political turbulences, bureaucratic rivalry, frequent military coups and the politicians' disdain for the intelligence agency limited the importance of intelligence knowledge. The Turkish experience during the Cold War shows that regime type, nature of security threats, civilian-military relations and domestic socio-economic conditions are crucial for the actual effects of technological development in intelligence communities. At the same time, Bezci contradicts the assumption that states that relied on direct technical support from the United States automatically benefited to a high degree from advanced technology.

In countries that belonged to the Warsaw Pact rather than to NATO, the will to use science and technology was strong, but the actual possibilities were limited. In his contribution on the computerisation of the Polish secret police, *Franciszek Dąbrowski* (Chapter 9) shows how digitisation was accompanied by an effort to channel knowledge circulation, introduce access descriptions and thus establish new knowledge hierarchies. The communist security police developed

12   Bergien/Gerstenberger/Goschler

multiple systems of card indexes and registries that up to 1972 underwent several major enhancements. The electronic systems were supposed to enhance and speed up access to data resources and enable the quick and efficient evaluation of information. However, a multitude of databases corresponded simultaneously to a multitude of different computer platforms. This led to considerable technical fragmentation. Even though the specific rules for the registration and processing of data underwent several major transformations (some of which were later withdrawn), the paramount duty to maintain the secrecy of the data and their own operations ultimately turned out to be incompatible with efficient reporting and the evaluation of information. It turns out that the gains of electronic systems were undone by internal secrecy rules that thwarted the compatibility of the systems.

A recurring pattern in the digitisation of the intelligence services across state and ideological boundaries was that efficiency did not automatically increase – what increased instead was always the institutional complexity, which usually caused new problems. This is also shown by *Christopher Kirchberg* (Chapter 10), who describes the introduction of the computer network system Nachrichtendienstliches Informationssystem (NADIS) in the West German domestic intelligence service Federal Office for the Protection of the Constitution (Bundesamt für Verfassungsschutz, BfV). With the establishment of the new computer system, the BfV had hoped to be able to compensate for human weaknesses and to overcome dependency on certain experts. Instead, digitisation led to unforeseen path dependencies. The dependency on agents that provided (often false) human interpretations, which digitalisation was supposed to overcome, was replaced by the dependency on highly qualified IT personnel. The importance of the human factor shifted but did not decrease.

Samantha Viz Quadrat (Chapter 11) turns our attention to the circulation of intelligence techniques and practices. Since Brazil's authoritarian regime (1964–1985) was based on (intelligence) information and repression, a powerful state structure was maintained to train the civilian and military personnel who would work in espionage and in the persecution of political opponents. Quadrat's article focuses on two of the most relevant institutions in this context: the Superior War College (Escola Superior de Guerra, ESG), established in 1949, and the National Intelligence College (Escola Nacional de Informações, EsNI), created in 1971. Both institutions fostered centralisation, standardisation and internationalisation of intelligence knowledge; these were strategies that Brazilian actors employed to keep their intelligence services up to date in the context of an authoritarian military regime. Due to the good functioning of the intelligence schools, they were not only recipients of relevant knowledge from the industrialised centres but also producers and distributors within a global network of intelligence training. The chapter once again underlines that a perspective focused on the pre-eminent powers of the great alliances of the Cold War tends to overlook important processes of knowledge formation.

Marcel Schmeer (Chapter 12) addresses the popularisation of intelligence knowledge for the purpose of informing – or rather *disinforming* – the public. In his chapter, he examines the West German *Reports on the Protection of the*

Constitution that have been published and presented and thus made available to civil society annually since the early 1960s. This unique media policy tool was initially produced in the wake of the competition of the system with the GDR. Originally conceived as a mere counter-propaganda instrument, the reports changed in their form and objectives during the détente period. Against the background of social trends towards liberalisation and burgeoning demands for transparency in state arcana, the reports attempted to sensitise the public to the work and the importance of the German domestic intelligence service. Its findings, the corresponding knowledge of intelligence, were henceforth increasingly presented in a scientific and professionalised manner. The popularised threat perception of the "guardians of the state" has shaped the German security culture to this day.

Notes

1 Apud Bułhak, "Similar But Not the Same," 19.
2 Dülffer, *Geheimdienst in der Krise* . . .
3 See Evgenia Lezina's contribution in this volume. KGB stands for "Komitet Gosudarstvennoye Bezopastnosti," the Soviet secret police.
4 See Marcelo Vianna's contribution in this volume.
5 McCrisken and Moran, "James Bond, Ian Fleming and Intelligence," 808.
6 Warner, *Rise and Fall of Intelligence*.
7 See here in particular Warner, "Reflections on Technology and Intelligence Systems."
8 Bergien, "Programmieren."
9 Weller, *Information History*.
10 Horn, *The Secret War*.
11 The term was used by social scientists from the 1960s onwards as an attempt to grasp fundamental changes linked to the spread of new information technologies and microelectronics. Castells, *The Information Age*. On the handling of social science concepts in contemporary history, see Graf and Priemel, "Zeitgeschichte in der Welt der Sozialwissenschaften."
12 Willmetts, "Cultural Turn," 803.
13 Macrakis, "Technophilic Hubris," 380.
14 Ibid., 381.
15 Ibid., 384.
16 Ibid., 378.
17 Sarasin and Kilcher, "Zirkulationen," 9 f.; cf. also Östling et al., "The History of Knowledge," 9, with reference to Secord, "Knowledge in Transit."
18 Sarasin and Kilcher, "Zirkulationen," 10.
19 Cf. the workshop "Restricting Knowledge: Channeling Security Information in Recent History" at the German Historical Institute & Woodrow Wilson International Center for Scholars, 8–9 December 2016. <www.ghi-dc.org/events-conferences/event-history/2016/conferences/restricting-knowledge-channeling-security-information-in-recent-history.html?L=0> (last accessed September 19, 2019).
20 See the thoughtful critique of the use of the concept of circulation in global history by Gänger, *Circulation*.
21 Global history has become one of the most dynamic areas of historical scholarship. Scholarly contributions are numerous and diverse but all united by the conviction that Eurocentric or "Western" views must be overcome. Central organs of global history in Europe are, for example, the European Network in Universal and Global History (ENIUGH) and the journals *Journal of Global History* and *Comparativ*. For a specific focus on the connection between global history and the history of technology (and

14 *Bergien/Gerstenberger/Goschler*

actor-network theory), see Gerstenberger and Glasman, eds., *Techniken der Globalisierung*. For a specific focus on the inclusion of Latin America in the "general" history of technology, see Medina et al., eds., *Beyond Imported Magic*.

22 Medina, "Decentered Computer History," S103–S104.

23 Andrew, "Reflections," 51.

24 Lowenthal, *The Future of Intelligence*; Shiraz, "Globalisation and Intelligence."

25 See the critical accounts about intelligence studies' status quo in Willmetts, "Cultural Turn"; Hoffmann, "Why Is There No IR Scholarship." Pioneering studies mainly focus on domestic security and police work, not intelligence. See, for example, Gugerli and Mangold, "Betriebssysteme"; Mangold, *Fahndung*; Springer and Jedlitschka, eds., *Gedächtnis der Staatssicherheit*.

26 Engerman, *Know Your Enemy*.

27 Aldrich and Moran, "Delayed Disclosure"; Melley, *Covert Sphere*; Moran, *Classified: Secrecy and the State*; Dover et al., *Handbook of Security*.

28 Warner, "Cybersecurity."

29 Aldrich, "Regulation."

30 Medrow et al., eds., *Kampf um Wissen*.

31 Frohman, *Politics of Personal Information*; Goschler et al., "Sicherheit, Demokratie und Transparenz."

32 Andrew, *Defence*. See also Aldrich, *GCHQ*; Dülffer et al., *Veröffentlichungen*.

33 See, for example, Krähnke et al., *Im Dienst*.

34 Bułhak, "Similar but Not the Same."

35 Such questions are, for instance, asked about 1967/68 Viet Cong assault preparations, about Soviet nuclear missile armament in the 1970s or about Al Quaida assassination plans in the late 1990s.

36 Gardiner, "Squaring the Circle."

37 Of particular interest was also the so-called mirror-imaging – for example, the tendency of authors of the US National Intelligence Estimates in the last two decades of the Cold War to interpret Soviet policy in ways that reflected American policy. Fischer, "We May Not Always Be Right."

38 Heuer, *Psychology of Intelligence Analysis*.

39 See, for example, the contributions in Ball et al., eds., *Routledge Handbook of Surveillance Studies*.

40 Gordon, *Justice Juggernaut*.

41 See for the KGB, Andrew and Mitrochin, *Sword*, for Brazil: Fico, *Como eles agiam*.

42 See the contributions in Kaminski et al., eds., *Handbuch*.

43 Andrew, *Defence*.

44 A first approach has been made by Booß, *Scheitern*; see also Bergien, "Programmieren."

45 NKVD stands for "People's Commissariat of Internal Affairs." Andrew, "Intelligence."

46 Garthoff, *Soviet Leaders and Intelligence*. See also Maddrell, ed., *Image*; Maddrell, "Achieving."

47 Willmetts, "Cultural Turn."

48 Hoffmann, "Why," 6.

49 Bergien, "Programmieren."

50 In the words of Philip H. J. Davies, in intelligence "one must acquire information, figure out what it means, and make sure that it gets to the places and people who need it. . . . It makes relatively little difference if the information is about drug cartels. . . , foreign trade negotiations. . . , or uncovering putative counterrevolutionary conspiracies." Davies and Gustafson, "An Agenda for the Comparative Study," 7.

51 See, for example, the contributions in Collin and Horstman, *Wissen*.

52 Raphael, "Verwissenschaftlichung."

53 Agar, "What Difference"

54 See Büchner, "Digitalisierung und Organisation."

Knowledge of intelligence: An introduction 15

55 On the eve of the Second World War, however, effective cooperation was already established between the Polish, French and British services, among others, which succeeded in breaking the German Enigma encryption. Warner, *The Rise and Fall*.
56 Richard Aldrich illustrates this development with the example of the comparatively small Danish domestic intelligence service PET, which currently maintains relations with 80 services from 50 countries. Aldrich, "US – European Intelligence Co-Operation," 35.
57 Aldrich, "Intelligence Co-Operation," 27 f.
58 Sarasin and Kilcher, "Zirkulationen," 9 f.
59 Sarasin, "Wissensgeschichte?," 172.
60 Agar, "Putting the Spooks Back in."

Bibliography

Agar, J. 2006. "What Difference Did Computers Make?" *Social Studies of Science* 35, no. 6: 869–907.

Agar, J. 2016. "Putting the Spooks Back in? The UK Secret State and the History of Computing." *Information & Culture: A Journal of History* 51, no. 1: 102–124.

Aldrich, R. J. 2009. "US–European Intelligence Co-Operation on Counter-Terrorism: Low Politics and Compulsion." *The British Journal of Politics and International Relations* 11, no. 1: 122–139. https://doi.org/10.1111/j.1467-856x.2008.00353.x.

Aldrich, R. J. 2010. *GCHQ: The Uncensored Story of Britain's Most Secret Intelligence Agency*. New York: HarperPress.

Aldrich, R. J., and Moran, C. R. 2019. "'Delayed Disclosure': National Security, Whistle-Blowers and the Nature of Secrecy." *Political Studies* 67, no. 2: 291–306. https://doi.org/10.1177/0032321718764990.

Andrew, C. M. 2004. "Intelligence, International Relations and 'Under-theorisation'." *Intelligence and National Security* 19, no. 2: 170–184. https://doi.org/10.1080/0268452042000302949.

Andrew, C. M. 2009. "Reflections on Intelligence Historiography since 1939." In *National Intelligence Systems: Current Research and Future Prospects*, ed. G. F. Treverton, 38–57. Cambridge: Cambridge University Press.

Andrew, C. M. 2009. *The Defence of the Realm: The Authorized History of MI5*. London: Allen Lane.

Andrew, C. M., and Mitrochin, V. N. 1999. *The Sword and the Shield: The Mitrokhin Archive and the Secret History of the KGB*. New York: Basic Books.

Bergien, R. 2019. "Programmieren mit dem Klassenfeind: Die Stasi, Siemens und der Transfer von EDV-Wissen im Kalten Krieg." *Vierteljahrshefte für Zeitgeschichte* 67, no. 1: 1–30. https://doi.org/10.1515/vfzg-2019-0001.

Booß, C. 2021. *Vom Scheitern der kybernetischen Utopie. Die Entwicklung von Überwachung und Informationsverarbeitung im MfS*. Göttingen: Vandenhoeck & Ruprecht.

Büchner, S. 2018. "Zum Verhältnis von Digitalisierung und Organisation." *Zeitschrift für Soziologie* 47, no. 5: 332–348. https://doi.org/10.1515/zfsoz-2018-0121.

Bułhak, W. 2014. "Similar but Not the Same. In Search of a Methodology in the Cold War Communist Intelligence Studies." In *Need to Know: Eastern and Western Perspectives*, ed. ibid. and T. Wegener Friis, 1–25. Odense: University Press of Southern Denmark.

Davies, P. H. J., and Gustafson, K. C. 2013. "An Agenda for the Comparative Study of Intelligence. Yet Another Missing Dimension." In *Intelligence Elsewhere: Spies and Espionage Outside the Anglosphere*, ed. P. H. J. Davies and K. C. Gustafson, 3–12. Washington, DC: Georgetown University Press.

16   *Bergien/Gerstenberger/Goschler*

Dülffer, J. 2018. *Geheimdienst in der Krise: Der BND in den 1960er-Jahren*. Berlin: Ch. Links.

Dülffer, J., Henke, K.-D., Krieger, W., and Müller, R. D., eds. 2013–2021. *Veröffentlichungen der Unabhängigen Historikerkommission zur Erforschung der Geschichte des Bundesnachrichtendienstes 1945–1968*, 13 volumes. Berlin: C. Links.

Engerman, D. C. 2009. *Know Your Enemy: The Rise and Fall of America's Soviet Experts*. Oxford: Oxford University Press.

Fico, C. 2001. *Como eles agiam. Os subterrâneos da ditadura militar; espionagem e polícia política*. Rio de Janeiro: Editora Record.

Fischer, B. 2015. "'We May Not Always be Right, But We're Never Wrong' US Intelligence Assessments of the Soviet Union, 1972–1991." In *The Image of the Enemy: Intelligence Analysis of Adversaries since 1945*, ed. P. Maddrell, 93–128. Washington, DC: Georgetown University Press.

Frohman, L. 2020. *The Politics of Personal Information: Surveillance, Privacy, and the Politics of Personal Information in West Germany, 1965–1990*. New York: Berghahn.

Fry, M. G., and Hochstein, M. 1993. "Epistemic Communities: Intelligence Studies and International Relations." *Intelligence and National Security* 8, no. 3: 14–28. https://doi.org/10.1080/02684529308432212.

Gänger, S. 2017. "Circulation: Reflections on Circularity, Entity, and Liquidity in the Language of Global History." *Journal of Global History* 12: 303–318.

Gardiner, K. L. 1991. "Squaring the Circle: Dealing with Intelligence-policy Breakdowns." *Intelligence and National Security* 6, no. 1: 141–153.

Garthoff, R. L. 2015. *Soviet Leaders and Intelligence: Assessing the American Adversary during the Cold War*. Washington, DC: Georgetown University Press.

Gerstenberger, D., and Glasman, J., eds. 2016. *Techniken der Globalisierung: Globalgeschichte meets Akteur-Netzwerk-Theorie*. Bielefeld: transcript.

Gordon, D. R. 1990. *The Justice Juggernaut: Fighting Street Crime, Controlling Citizens*. New Brunswick: Rutgers University Press.

Goschler, C., Kirchberg, C., and Wegener, J. 2016. "Sicherheit, Demokratie und Transparenz. Elektronische Datenverbundsysteme in der Bundesrepublik und den USA in den 1970er und 1980er Jahren." In *Wege in die digitale Gesellschaft. Computernutzung in der Bundesrepublik 1955–1990*, ed. F. Bösch, 64–85. Göttingen: Wallstein.

Graf, R., and Priemel, K. 2011. "Zeitgeschichte in der Welt der Sozialwissenschaften. Legitimität und Originalität einer Disziplin." *Vierteljahrshefte für Zeitgeschichte* 59, no: 4: 479–508.

Gugerli, D., and Mangold, H. 2016. "Betriebssysteme und Computerfahndung. Zur Genese einer digitalen Überwachungskultur." *Geschichte und Gesellschaft* 42, no. 1: 144–174. https://doi.org/10.13109/gege.2016.42.1.144.

Heuer, R. S. Jr. 1999. *Psychology of Intelligence Analysis*. Washington, DC: US Government Printing.

Hoffmann, S. 2019. "Why is There No IR Scholarship on Intelligence Agencies? Some Ideas for a New Approach." *ZMO Working Papers* no. 23. https://nbn-resolving.org/urn:nbn:de:101:1-201909121056392418564 0.

Horn, E. 2013. *The Secret War: Treason, Espionage, and Modern Fiction*. Evanston, IL: Northwestern University Press.

Kaminski, L., Persak, K., and Gieseke, J., eds. 2009. *Handbuch der kommunistischen Geheimdienste in Osteuropa 1944–1991*. Göttingen: Vandenhoeck Ruprecht.

Krähnke, U., Finster, M., Reimann, P., and Zschirpe, A. 2017. *Im Dienst der Staatssicherheit: Eine soziologische Studie über die hauptamtlichen Mitarbeiter des DDR-Geheimdienstes*. Frankfurt and New York: Campus Verlag.

Lowenthal, M. M. 2018. *The Future of Intelligence*. Cambridge, UK and Malden, MA: Polity.

Knowledge of intelligence: An introduction   17

Macrakis, K. 2010. "Technophilic Hubris and Espionage Styles during the Cold War." *Isis* 101, no. 2: 378–385.

Maddrell, P. 2015. "Introduction. Achieving Objective, Policy-Relevant Intelligence." In *The Image of the Enemy: Intelligence Analysis of Adversaries since 1945*, ed. P. Maddrell, 1–27. Washington, DC: Georgetown University Press.

Mangold, H. 2017. *Fahndung nach dem Raster. Informationsverarbeitung bei der bundesdeutschen Kriminalpolizei, 1965–1984*. Zürich: Interferenzen.

McCrisken, T., and Moran, C. 2018. "James Bond, Ian Fleming and Intelligence: Breaking Down the Boundary between the 'Real' and the 'Imagined'." *Intelligence and National Security* 33, no. 6: 804–821. https://doi.org/10.1080/02684527.2018.1468648.

Medina, E. 2018. "Forensic Identification in the Aftermath of Human Rights Crimes in Chile: A Decentered Computer History." *Technology and Culture* 59, no. 4 Supplement: S100–S133.

Medina, E., Marques, I. da Costa, and Holmes, C., eds. 2014. *Beyond Imported Magic: Essays on Science, Technology, and Society in Latin America*. Cambridge, MA: MIT Press.

Medrow, L., Münzner, D., and Radu, R., eds. 2015. *Kampf um Wissen. Spionage, Geheimhaltung und Öffentlichkeit 1870–1940*. Paderborn: Ferdinand Schöningh.

Melley, T. 2012. *The Covert Sphere: Secrecy, Fiction, and the National Security State*. New York: Cornell University Press.

Moran, C. 2013. *Classified: Secrecy and the State in Modern Britain*. Cambridge: Cambridge University Press.

Östling, J., Larsson Heidenblad, D., Sandmo, E., Nilsson Hammar, A., and Nordberg, K. H. 2018. "The History of Knowledge and the Circulation of Knowledge. An Introduction." In *Circulation of Knowledge: Explorations in the History of Knowledge*, ed. J. Östling, E. Sandmo, D. Larsson Heidenblad, A. Nilsson Hammar, and K. Nordberg, 9–36. Lund: Nordic Academic Press.

Raphael, L. 1996. "Die Verwissenschaftlichung des Sozialen als methodische und konzeptionelle Herausforderung für eine Sozialgeschichte des 20. Jahrhunderts." *Geschichte und Gesellschaft* 22: 165–190.

Sarasin, P. 2011. "Was ist Wissensgeschichte?" *Internationales Archiv für Sozialgeschichte der deutschen Literatur* 36: 159–172. https://doi.org/10.1515/iasl.2011.010.

Sarasin, P., and Kilcher, A. 2011. "Editorial. Zirkulationen." *Nach Feierabend. Zürcher Jahrbuch für Wissensgeschichte* 7: 7–11.

Secord, J. A. 2004. "Knowledge in Transit." *Isis* 95: 654–672. https://doi.org/10.1086/430657.

Shiraz, Z. 2017. "Globalisation and Intelligence." In *The Palgrave Handbook of Security, Risk and Intelligence*, ed. R. Dover, H. Dylan, and M. S. Goodman, 265–280. London: Palgrave Macmillan UK.

Springer, P., and Jedlitschka, K., eds. 2015. *Das Gedächtnis der Staatssicherheit: Die Kartei- und Archivabteilung des MfS*. Göttingen: Vandenhoeck & Ruprecht.

Warner, M. 2012. "Cybersecurity. A Pre-history." *Intelligence and National Security* 27, no. 5: 781–799. https://doi.org/10.1080/02684527.2012.708530.

Warner, M. 2012. "Reflections on Technology and Intelligence Systems." *Intelligence and National Security* 27, no. 1: 133–153. https://doi.org/10.1080/02684527.2012.621604.

Warner, M. 2014. *The Rise and Fall of Intelligence: An International Security History*. Washington, DC: Georgetown University Press.

Weller, T. 2008. *Information History: An Introduction*. Oxford: Chandos.

Weller, T. 2010. *Information History in the Modern World: Histories of the Information Age*. Basingstoke: Palgrave Macmillan.

Willmetts, S. 2019. "The Cultural Turn in Intelligence Studies." *Intelligence and National Security* 34, no. 6: 800–817. https://doi.org/10.1080/02684527.2019.1615711.

1 Compromised cooperation

Scholarly experts on Eastern Europe in the service of West German intelligence in the early Cold War

Thomas Wolf

Introduction

In the aftermath of the Second World War, when the Cold War antagonism that would shape the following decades began to emerge more clearly, it became apparent to political decision-makers in the West that sound knowledge about what would henceforth be their most important opponent was lacking. A few months after the end of the war, George T. Robinson, chief of the USSR Division at the wartime intelligence agency Office of Strategic Services (OSS), emphasised that knowledge about the Soviet Union had now become one of the most important foreign policy resources. At the same time, he drew attention to the fact that the level of expertise in this particular field left something to be desired. "Never before," he worried, "had so many known so little about so much."[1] Indeed, at the time of writing, the fledgling academic field of American Soviet studies was just beginning to emerge; with the help of government and private sector funding, it gradually gained momentum with the establishment of the "Russian Institute" (RI) at Columbia University in 1946 and the "Russian Research Center" (RRC) at Harvard University in 1948.[2] In Great Britain and France, the situation was a similar one: despite a longer research tradition, the field of Soviet studies also remained in its infancy and comprised only a small group of scholars.[3]

The situation in West Germany, on the other hand, was a rather different one. Here, there were long, though problematic, legacies to draw upon. Already before the beginning of the Second World War and then increasingly during the war, various institutions and branches of research in Germany had been involved in the production of knowledge about the Soviet Union and other states of Eastern Europe. The so-called *Ostforschung* (Eastern studies) rose to particular prominence within this context. *Ostforschung*[4] refers to a multidisciplinary research field with Eastern Europe as its object of study. Its scientific contributions were characterised by a heavy emphasis on the historical German influence in these regions, which served as a means to justify the "struggle for Germanisation" within them. Accordingly, *Ostforschung* has been closely linked to expansionist political programmes from its early beginnings in the 1920s. Numerous scholarly experts on Eastern Europe benefited considerably during the period of National Socialist rule and had, to a large extent, willingly served the regime. Many actively participated in the

DOI: 10.4324/9781003147329-2

Compromised cooperation 19

development and subsequent implementation of the genocidal National Socialist New Order in Eastern Europe with its racist agenda.[5] Thus, in West Germany after 1945, the problem was less a dearth of contemporary scholarly experts on Eastern Europe (as in the case of the United States) but rather the question to what extent the field and the associated research institutes should draw upon this personnel and continue earlier approaches.

In the United States, good relations and close cooperation with the Armed Forces and the intelligence community were integral to the emergence of Soviet studies. Prior research conducted during the war had been carried out in close coordination with the wartime intelligence service OSS.[6] In the early Cold War period, when Soviet studies began to take root, the relationship also remained a close one. The newly established academic institutions sought to build and maintain personal relationships, not least for the purpose of securing essential financial resources from state authorities to fund their research. The rise of American Soviet studies was therefore tethered to political interests and those of the intelligence community in particular. Even though the full extent of the relationship with the intelligence services remains unclear due to the limited availability of primary sources, the existence of these connections and their significance for the early history of American Soviet studies are beyond dispute.[7]

This chapter will examine the relationship between intelligence work and *Ostforschung* in West Germany during the early Cold War from a comparative perspective. There has been speculation for many years about the degree of cooperation between the German foreign intelligence service BND or its forerunner organisation and scholars on Eastern Europe after the end of the war.[8] However, due to access restrictions in the relevant archives, this relationship could not be examined in detail for a considerable period of time. Only recently, key BND documents have been made available for historical research.[9] Based on these documents, previously available sources can now be reinterpreted: in particular, the correspondence of scholars can be evaluated in terms of what types of relationships existed between individuals – many of whom can now be clearly identified and named as intelligence officials – and the information that was shared among them. This makes it possible to analyse the extent to which cooperation and exchanges of knowledge took place and, last but not least, gain a deeper understanding of the intellectual legacies of *Ostforschung* and their influence on the production of knowledge in an intelligence context.

The chapter is divided into three sections: the first section focuses on the major players at the nexus of academic research and intelligence work. Who were the scholars in the employ of the intelligence service? What were the intentions behind their employment? What were their actual missions? In a second section, the re-emerging scientific landscape comes into view, along with questions pertaining to the influence of the BND and its predecessor on the establishment of research institutes after the Second World War. Did the intelligence services actively contribute to the institutional (re-)establishment of a research landscape, as it had been the case in the United States? Finally, in the third section, the specific processes of exchange are examined: what kind of knowledge about Eastern Europe circulated

20   *Thomas Wolf*

between intelligence services and *Ostforschung*? What types of obstacles were encountered, and where did synergistic effects come into play?

Scholars of Eastern Europe in the service of the Gehlen Intelligence Organization, 1946–1949

The relationship between scholars and the intelligence community is typically shrouded in secrecy. This also applies to the relationship between the research field of *Ostforschung* and the Gehlen Intelligence Organization (which later became the Bundesnachrichtendienst, or BND) in the Federal Republic of Germany. The intelligence gathering agency based in Pullach was staffed with former Wehrmacht officers and a considerable number of former members of the SS, in addition to individuals who had previously served in other organisations belonging to the security and terror apparatus of the National Socialist regime. It was established by the US Army in 1946, turned over to the CIA in 1949 and then recast into the Federal Intelligence Service, the BND, in 1956.

To put the early relations between the Gehlen Organization and scholars of Eastern Europe into perspective, it is first necessary to briefly outline the prehistory of this cooperation: As already mentioned, *Ostforschung* and politics had entered into an ominous liaison before and during the Second World War when various academics involved themselves in the development and implementation of National Socialist war aims and annihilation policies. Particularly in the military intelligence service, the so-called *Abwehr*, scholars found an institutional focal point to contribute with their concepts and have put them into practice. Agricultural experts and academics, including Theodor Oberländer, Hans Koch, Werner Markert and Otto Schiller, participated in the preparation of plans for the occupation of Eastern European and also witnessed first-hand their subsequent execution.[10] Oberländer, for instance, had already been working for the Abwehr since 1937, and during the war he served on the staff of the Ukrainian "Nachtigall Battalion," a volunteer unit accused of participating in the Lviv massacre in 1941.[11] Church historian Hans Koch provides another case in point: a professor of East European history at Königsberg, Breslau and Vienna, Koch worked for German military intelligence during the war and utilised his contacts to the right-wing extremist Organisation of Ukrainian Nationalists (OUN) to mobilise Ukrainian collaborators for the German war effort.[12]

After the war, during the formative years of the Federal Republic of Germany, both West German research on the East and the foreign intelligence service exhibited a considerable degree of continuity in terms of their personnel. This raises the question of whether the cooperation continued in the altered political landscape of the early Cold War era, and, if so, how extensive this cooperation was and what kinds of objectives were pursued.

In 1946, a group of economists, historians and social scientists began working for the Gehlen Organization. Known among their contemporaries within the organisation as the "professors' group," these scholars were tasked with providing analyses on the economy and population of Soviet Bloc countries. In large part, this group consisted of scholars who had already worked for military intelligence during the war, such as Oberländer, Schiller, Markert and Koch. Professional or academic credentials were not the decisive criterion for inclusion in the group. What mattered, first and foremost, was that the researchers were acquainted with each other – some were related, while others had served together during the war.[13]

The "professors' group" was headed by Peter-Heinz Seraphim. In addition to authoring a racist and anti-Semitic book on *Judaism in Eastern Europe*, he also held various important positions in the field of *Ostforschung* during the period of National Socialist rule. Among other things, he was a prominent contributor of publications for the Institut für Deutsche Ostarbeit (IDO, Institute for German Work in the East), a research centre founded by the National Socialists in occupied Kraków, which was called into existence to help assert German rule in Poland. He was also editor of the in-house journal of the Institut zur Erforschung der Judenfrage (Institute for the Study of the Jewish Question) in Frankfurt (Main), which was the most important anti-Semitic research centre established in Germany during the war.[14] Seraphim had been taken to the United States in 1945, whereupon he wrote reports for the US military and intelligence agencies. Seraphim himself described his work for the Americans as a "scientific activity in my eastern specialty," which, in his view, also found "some resonance" among the authorities who had commissioned these reports.[15]

Most of the members of the "professors' group" had thus been connected with the intelligence service in various contexts prior to 1945, and now, as a kind of "brain trust"[16] for the Gehlen Organization, they came to revive these former ties. In the service of the Gehlen Organization, however, their assignment now changed in qualitative terms. Instead of complex issues and expertise pertaining to practical measures, they were tasked with preparing concise studies on various economic and demographic subjects relating to the USSR. For this purpose, they mainly relied on old or publicly available research materials.[17]

It is difficult to determine the extent to which their studies contributed to the overall intelligence mission of the Gehlen Organization. None of the aforementioned studies have been preserved for posterity in the existing archival collections of files and documents of the foreign intelligence service. This alone strongly suggests that the research itself was deemed to be of limited value and therefore hardly processed further within the Gehlen Organization. Other documents also support the conclusion that the analyses bore the hallmarks of contemporary historical studies: One of Seraphim's colleagues, who had received papers that were clearly prepared by the "professors' group," praised their quality and readability, and accordingly expressed his regrets that they "have to be kept secret," since "there is nothing in them that could not be published now, whereas it might not have been possible in the past."[18] Explanations that did not concern the current state of the Soviet Union's economic and political development predominated. In other words, the main focus was evidently on analyses involving historical issues rather than current affairs. To a certain degree, this approach was commensurate with the research traditions of *Ostforschung*, which sought to trace the long-term historical developments of the regions of Eastern Europe.

22   *Thomas Wolf*

The US intelligence community's own reception of these studies also supports this conclusion: in June 1947, personnel of the CIA's predecessor complained that the studies of the "professors' group" were characterised by "a strong German point of view," which meant they lacked objectivity and were thus unsuitable for American intelligence purposes.[19] One of the most likely explanations for this is that the studies largely drew upon concepts from the *Ostforschung* research tradition. The perceived lack of political relevance as well as biased views thus reduced their inherent value for American intelligence. Thus, in the fall of 1949, when the takeover of the Gehlen Organization by the CIA was completed, American funding of the "professors' group" was withdrawn.[20]

Patterns of cooperation between scholars on Eastern Europe and the Gehlen Organization can be observed in yet another example. Recently declassified documents show that there has been at least one other case, comparable to that of the "professors' group," which sheds further light upon the character of contacts between scholarly experts and the intelligence community in West Germany after the war. From 1948 onwards, another group of academics began working for the Gehlen Organization. This project initially bore the name Institut für Ostforschung (IfO, "Institute for Eastern Studies"). In November 1949, it counted at least nine staff members who, in contrast to the "professors' group," were mostly younger and had been less prominently active in the context of *Ostforschung* before 1945. As of now, it remains difficult to ascertain which factors were decisive for the composition of this particular group. What is striking, however, is that the majority were Baltic Germans, who had spent at least a part of their lives in states that were now under Soviet rule. Conceivably, personal relationships were established during this period, which came to play a significant role in the recruitment process.

Among the IfO's scholars was Walter Meder, for instance. Born 1904 in Reval (now Tallin), Meder had attended Estonian elite schools and received his PhD in law from the University of Tartu in 1927. He then worked as a research assistant in Tartu and later as a lecturer in Poznań. After the Second World War, during which he served as a soldier in the Wehrmacht, he settled in West Germany and resumed his academic career. From 1954 onwards, he held the chair of Eastern European Law at the Free University of Berlin.[21] Another IfO member was Boris Meissner: born 1915 in Pskov (Estonia), he later became a senior foreign service official in West Germany and then professor of Eastern European law at the University of Cologne.[22] Georg von Rauch, who like Meder and Meissner had studied in Tartu and also worked at the Reichsuniversität Posen during the war, was also a member of the group. During the war, Rauch had worked for Foreign Armies East, the military intelligence analysis department of the High Command of the German Army under the leadership of Reinhard Gehlen.[23] The Gehlen Organization spent 5,000 German Marks per month to pay for the salaries of the group.[24]

A closer look at the activities of its members reveals numerous structural similarities between the IfO project and the "professors' group." Thus, some patterns can be identified which point to the limits of knowledge transfer between the Gehlen Organization and the scholars on the intelligence agency's payroll: the Gehlen Organization also requested smaller studies on specific economic topics,

Compromised cooperation 23

such as the state of extraction and processing of tin, tungsten and other metals, or the performance of the energy sectors in the Soviet Union and the People's Democracies in Eastern Europe.[25] The scholars intended to supplement secret intelligence information with information gleaned from open sources and to jointly evaluate all the material. When increasing budgetary constraints in 1950 meant there were insufficient funds for research-related travel, the Gehlen Organization refocused the mission: henceforth, IfO members should only evaluate the intelligence material and refrain from adding publicly available documents, which would have had to be consulted in special libraries in West Germany.[26] This highlights the obstacles affecting and hampering the transfer of knowledge between the intelligence agency on the one hand and the scholars on the other. Whenever possible, the Gehlen Organization placed particular emphasis on information obtained through intelligence channels and methods as the main foundation of the knowledge it produced. This information was prioritised over openly available information. The scholars, in turn, principally organised their work according to prevalent criteria pertaining to the production of scientific knowledge. In this particular case, norms regarding the systematic use of available information for the explanation of a phenomenon and the embedding of new information within the context of existing, proven knowledge were of particular relevance. The decisions made by the senior leadership in Pullach demonstrate that the IfO members were thus unable to decisively shape the internal processes of knowledge production in the Gehlen Organization. Given these conceptual differences, it is not surprising that the IfO eventually shared in the same fate as the "professors' group" and was also disbanded without much resistance or even regret during the handover process of the Gehlen Organization from the Army to the CIA. In the wake of the takeover, the organisation's finances were subjected to a comprehensive review and further streamlined, which led to an increasing focus on the activities and functions that were perceived to be at the core of intelligence gathering.

This exemplifies a key difference in the relationship between scholars of Eastern Europe and the intelligence services in Germany and the United States: after the war, the US military and intelligence community not only consistently drew on the expertise of Sovietologists who, at least up until about the mid-1950s, were also involved in the analysis of overarching and complex issues. They were "desiring not operational intelligence but good social science."[27] In Germany, the work that the Gehlen Organization tasked scholars with was more limited in terms of scale and scope. This difference is probably due to the very different foreign policy options and objectives of West Germany and the United States, which invariably led to divergent information interests: the United States as the leading nation in the West, pursuing a foreign policy doctrine of containing and rolling back communism worldwide;[28] the Federal Republic of Germany, on the other hand, as a firmly integrated state that was not yet sovereign in foreign policy terms until the mid-1950s. These conditions resulted in very different demands on the intelligence services to contribute to the foundation of knowledge upon which foreign policy decisions were made. The Americans were interested in obtaining social science-based knowledge about the political and social stability of the Soviet Union in the

24   *Thomas Wolf*

belief that this would give them the ability to base foreign policy decisions on this knowledge. For the Federal Republic, with its much narrower foreign policy focus, such knowledge was less relevant.

Furthermore, the habitus of the senior staff members in the agencies may have also played a role. In the United States, the intelligence services were staffed by personnel with a wide range of different professional backgrounds. The Gehlen Organization, on the other hand, was dominated by former general staff officers without academic credentials.[29] These different mindsets invariably had an impact on the willingness to draw on scholarly experts and rely on their research.

The different task profiles, in turn, likely influenced the fact that the scholars' motivation to carry out intelligence missions also varied widely. The demanding tasks of the CIA and other military and intelligence agencies were willingly accepted by the US research institutes.[30]

In Germany, other reasons were decisive for the scholars to join the intelligence service in the immediate post-war years. In all likelihood, the most important point was a rather obvious one, namely the opportunity to earn a living. Their academic careers were interrupted, and most of the major institutes, namely those in Gdańsk (Danzig), Wrocław (Breslau), Kaliningrad (Königsberg) and Poznań (Posen), had been lost. In this situation, the Gehlen Organization provided the scholars with financial and material support in return for their expertise and research. Additionally, some of these *Ostforscher* also enjoyed certain advantages during their denazification trials. Their work on behalf of an agency financed and directed by the American occupation forces served as a compelling argument for their political discharge, and as such it had a positive impact on the courts' decision-making.[31] Some of the scholars, especially those who were under considerable pressure on account of their well-known personal involvement with the Nazi system, even provided with legal assistance for the preparation of their trials. With this support, Peter-Heinz Seraphim and Theodor Oberländer, for example, passed through their denazification proceedings and were categorised as acquitted ("entlastet").[32] As a result, the latter was able to pursue a stellar political career in later years: in 1953, Oberländer became Federal Minister for Displaced Persons, Refugees and Victims of War. Conversely, the intelligence work itself, on the other hand, rarely represented a strong motivational factor for the scholars to cooperate. Thus, almost all members of the "professors' group" perceived of their jobs as an interim solution, and from 1947 onwards, most were able to revive their academic careers and leave the intelligence service.[33] A few years later, this same process could be observed among the personnel of the IfO project.

The Gehlen Intelligence Organization and the re-establishment of *Ostforschung* in West Germany since 1949

In the United States, the first institutes of Russian studies emerged with the direct support of government agencies and, not least, the intelligence community. The groundwork had already been laid during the war, when George T. Robinson, who

Compromised cooperation   25

later became the first director of Columbia University's Russian Institute, headed the USSR Division of the OSS. This professional experience proved to be decisive in 1946, when he was entrusted with the directorship of the RI: not so much his academic reputation, but these practical qualifications, which probably also served as evidence that productive cooperation between the research institute he was in charge of and government agencies would be possible in the future.[34]

In post-war West Germany, interdisciplinary research institutes for Eastern European studies were also established with government assistance. But since the knowledge generated there was hardly of critical importance to the West German government as a basis for political decision-making, the main intention was to develop arguments for the already established foreign policy guideline of calling for the return of Germany's former eastern territories.[35] Until today, however, the question of whether or to what extent the intelligence community played a role in the re-establishment of these research institutes remains an open one. Did the German foreign intelligence service, like its American counterpart, the CIA, support the establishment of these institutes for the express purpose of conducting research there?

Indeed, the scholars working for the Gehlen Organization attempted to set up research institutes of their own, which built on their previous work for the intelligence service. In 1950, Seraphim drew up plans for the establishment of a central institute for Eastern studies in West Germany, based on the material and the expertise gathered by the "professors' group."[36] However, for various reasons, he ultimately failed to obtain the necessary support for his plans: on the one hand, his biography until 1945 disqualified him from prominent, high-ranking positions, even in the eyes of his academic colleagues.[37] On the other hand, his concept clashed with the intentions of other leading scholars in the field, who in the meantime had revived their academic careers and therefore had better opportunities to obtain support for their concepts from the wider scientific community and funding for their projects.[38]

The IfO project ended in a rather similar manner. After the Gehlen Organization withdrew its financial support, the group approached the federal government in the spring of 1950 with a plan to create a Federal Institute for Eastern Studies that would succeed the IfO. As with Seraphim's approach, these plans focused on the idea of coordinating all West German research on Eastern Europe.[39] The IfO concept reflects many of the most important developments and orientations of the re-emerging *Ostforschung* in West Germany. However, the priorities of IfO scholars differed from those of most of the other academics involved in the institutional re-establishment of the scientific landscape. With regard to the intellectual direction of the planned institute, the IfO concept placed particular emphasis on research about the Soviet Union. Studies on other regions of Eastern Europe under Soviet rule, especially the GDR and the former eastern territories that had once been part of Germany, were to be carried out by subsidiary institutes, whose research would be coordinated by the new Federal Institute.[40] In other words, research on the Soviet Union, with a focus on contemporary political, social and economic questions, would have taken centre stage. IfO members thus called for a "fundamental reorientation of German research on the East," which should henceforth no longer focus primarily on German historical legacies.[41] In this respect, the scholars explicitly mentioned political consulting as being among the most valuable contributions made by the new institute, which entailed providing expert advice and analysis to interested ministries and federal security authorities, and the emerging West German domestic security agency (BfV) in particular. Results in the form of "periodic reporting on political and economic developments in the Soviet sphere of power," which was considered to be of value for political decision-makers, were envisaged as the main product of the Federal Institute's research activities.[42]

But the IfO's plans never came to fruition.[43] While the reasons for failure are not entirely clear, these developments further highlight the conditions that shaped the relations between intelligence services and Eastern studies in West Germany during the early Cold War. The academic and political context in which research institutes emerged was a different one from that in the United States. In West Germany, the kind of knowledge about the East that was deemed to be politically relevant was primarily the kind that would prove useful for keeping the question of German reunification alive, rather than reports which sought to provide an accurate picture of the current economic situation in the Eastern Bloc.

The intelligence service in Pullach had also clearly recognised this interest. In this respect, it is not surprising that the Gehlen Organization did not take any steps on its own initiative to support the plans of Seraphim and the IfO – in fact, it did the exact opposite. While Seraphim was assured by the leadership of the Gehlen Organization that they would support his plan in principle,[44] he received no financial or political assistance towards this end. The IfO project faced a similar situation: its members requested financial support from Pullach until they received payments from the federal government.[45] After several requests, however, they were merely granted a final "shutdown sum for the work which had once been so commendable."[46] These words of gratitude clearly amounted to little more than lip service and were hardly a reflection of sincere appreciation for the work that had been done in the past. This much can be gleaned from the fact that a mere 4,500 Marks were granted to the whole group, whereas requests for additional support were denied and any expansion of the financial assistance was clearly ruled out. "Ongoing payments are out of the question," as Gehlen succinctly commented on this final decision.[47]

The only plausible explanation for the fact that Seraphim and the experts of the IfO developed two independent concepts for the establishment of a central institute for research on Eastern Europe in such quick succession is that their approaches were not coordinated and obviously did not originate from the Gehlen Organization itself but rather from ambitious scholars who tried to earn a living and pursue their careers. Thus, Pullach was more of an instrument than an actor in the academic landscape in the post-war period because the scholars used the intelligence service as a vehicle with which to (re)gain a foothold – at least they hoped that the Gehlen Organization would fulfil this function for them.

Knowledge about the economies of Eastern Europe in *Ostforschung* and the intelligence community

Whereas the general tendency in the discussion thus far has been to highlight the constraints and limits of cooperation, it must be noted that the number of contacts that the Gehlen Organization maintained with eminent scholars in the late 1940s was remarkably high: in September 1956, a compilation on "German research on Eastern Europe since the Second World War" was prepared for the Federal Foreign Office by Werner Markert. Now a professor of history in Tübingen, Markert himself had once been a member of the "professors' group." In the latter part of his compilation, which provided a thematic overview of the research institutions with their leading members, Markert listed 37 scholars as the currently most important practitioners of Eastern European studies. At least seven of them (almost 20 per cent) had previously worked for the intelligence service in Pullach, either as full-time staff or as "freelance research fellows."[48]

Against this backdrop, the final question to be asked is to what extent knowledge was exchanged between *Ostforschung* and the West German foreign intelligence service, and how these processes ultimately influenced the production of intelligence knowledge about the East. The BND and its predecessor, the Gehlen Organization, are particularly suitable for such an examination because the aforementioned relationships also resulted in close ties in other respects: in the 1950s, leading members of the Gehlen Organization respectively of the BND's economic analysis department wrote and published academic papers. In other words, they acted as intelligence analysts and scholars on Eastern Europe at the same time.

A key actor within this context was Helmut Klocke, who had distinguished himself as a social scientist with agricultural studies on Hungary in the 1920s and 1930s. After the war, he joined the "professors' group" and subsequently worked for the Gehlen Organization as a full-time staff member. He immediately became head of the economic analysis department. After assuming his new position, Klocke recruited other young researchers focused on Eastern Europe, such as Karl Günzel, who was a student of Hans Freyer. Thus, in contrast to all other branches of the nascent BND, Klockes department came to develop a strong academic profile.[49]

In addition to their full-time work for the intelligence service, Klocke and his colleagues published papers in academic journals and textbooks in the field of Eastern Europe research.[50] The leadership of the Gehlen Organization was fully aware of these activities, and granted the authors permission to publish their contributions using their real names.[51] Their work as intelligence analysts, on the other hand, was not disclosed as a matter of course. This notwithstanding, most of their peers in academia knew about the work with which they earned their keep.[52]

The fact that Klocke and his colleagues were active in two fields dealing with the same subject – namely the economy of Eastern Europe – allows us to examine whether knowledge was exchanged between these two spheres and to what extent the transferred knowledge changed in the process. Furthermore, this constellation and the close cooperation with other scholars in the context of the scientific

28 *Thomas Wolf*

publications make it possible to work out more precisely whether the processes of knowledge production within the intelligence service were influenced by these relations.

The general picture that emerges in this regard following an examination of their open correspondence remains an ambivalent one. On the one hand, Klocke exhibited an interest in the efforts of Eastern studies and in the maintenance of steady, long-term contacts with its associated institutes and scholars.[53] In return, Werner Markert, with whom Klocke was in touch most regularly, also sought to ensure that representatives of the Gehlen Organization were kept abreast of the latest discussions, for instance by inviting them to conferences and actively encouraging them to attend.[54] On the other hand, however, there is hardly any evidence of concrete information having been requested or even exchanged: Despite the lack of detailed information about the economy of the Soviet Bloc in the scientific community, BND personnel were never approached by other scholars with requests to include information obtained through intelligence gathering methods in their papers. By the same token, they did not offer such contributions themselves either. It is unlikely that considerations revolving around security and secrecy were the decisive factors. In some other cases, confidential topics were discussed, such as the recruitment of young academics for the Gehlen Organization.[55] It is more probable that the separation between intelligence work and scholarship was due to the fact that the scientific papers written by the BND analysts were handled by their academic colleagues first and foremost on the basis of scholarly categories. This became apparent, for example, when Karl Günzel was harshly criticised by the editor of the *Poland Handbook* for not having consulted all the available research literature. Instead, Günzel had provided empirical data that did "not satisfy scientific standards,"[56] meaning they were either outdated or demonstrably false.

Thus, the available open correspondence provides no clear evidence of a circulation of knowledge. However, in light of the fact that Klocke and his co-workers wrote their scientific publications in accordance with the research paradigms of the sub-discipline of *Ostforschung*, a comparison of their BND analyses with regard to these paradigms opens up another broader perspective.

The concept of totalitarianism was of crucial importance in this regard. Originally conceived as an approach to the analysis of political systems, the function of the concept changed within the context of the Cold War, especially in West Germany, where it served as a dichotomous model with which to denote certain values and beliefs. The emphasis on the fundamental difference between the Soviet Union as a state detached from (Western) European "normal development," characterised by an unrestricted, ideology-driven claim to power of the communist party, was thus always combined with a specific attribution: under the totalitarianism approach advocated in West German *Ostforschung*, the Soviet Union was described as somewhat backward yet dangerous and expansionist at the very same time. All efforts to contain communism thus received an intellectual foundation and justification and the fear of a Soviet expansion to the West was nourished.[57]

The academic publications of the BND analysts were commensurate with the totalitarianism paradigm. They focused primarily on economic transformation in the Soviet-controlled areas of Eastern Europe, in particular the forced industriali-sation and collectivisation as central objectives. These, they argued, were consid-ered by the Kremlin to be both an ideological imperative and a practical necessity in the face of economic backwardness compared to the West, and therefore con-sistently pursued in all people's democracies; only minor adjustments in terms of pace and prioritisation in individual cases were deemed permissible. Ultimately, the Soviet Union would "impose completely uniform political, economic, and cultural traits on the people's democracies," as Klocke wrote in 1953.[58] In the years that followed, he would remain steadfast in his opinions. Six years later, for instance, his concluding analysis of the social structure in the people's democracies was decidedly unambiguous:

> Russia's detachment from the European Middle since the October Revolution, its development into an independent power centre, the Soviet Union, its claim to totality, had to result in the reshaping of the social structure according to the Soviet model in the case of a Soviet victory in defeated states.[59]

The BND reports written by Klocke and his colleagues also adhered to the paradigm of totalitarianism. This is borne out by an evaluation of the BND's com-prehensive analyses of the Eastern European economy, which are available for this period from 1955 and 1959.[60] They provided detailed descriptions of various struc-tural deficits of the centrally administered economy and concentrated on concrete measures taken by the Soviet Union to align the various economies of the Eastern Bloc to its own advantage. In particular, the setbacks of the "New Course" were widely discussed.[61] The overarching objective of the measures, namely the attain-ment of economic superiority over the West, was always the basic premise behind all these considerations. Given the limited economic potential of the territory cur-rently under Soviet rule, the BND analysts headed by Klocke concluded that the Soviet Union would therefore have to "extend its domination to Western Europe and other parts of Asia" in order to achieve this goal.[62] Four years later, Klocke and his colleagues remained persistent on this point in their analysis. While the Soviet Union would initially focus its activities to expand their power "primarily on the developing countries," the overriding goal of achieving economic supremacy on a global scale, however, still remained: "in the long run, the rest of the world must be involved in achieving this ultimate goal."[63] Despite the absence of any concrete evidence for an immediate threat to Western Europe, they emphasised the expan-sionist intentions of the Soviet Union as a key finding in their BND reports, fully in line with the view of the theory of totalitarianism. The paradigmatic conformity of their intelligence work and their scholarship most likely stems not least from the fact that they carried the concept of totalitarianism from the context of Eastern European studies over to their intelligence reports.

At the same time, this approach led to a rather unspecific assessment of the con-crete economic situation and scope for political action in the people's democracies. For example, analyses focused on Poland lacked a comparison of the developments intended by the Soviet Union with the specific political reform conditions in the

30   *Thomas Wolf*

country. Indeed, the BND report contained a detailed picture of the economic situation in Poland. It also correctly identified the insufficient supply of goods, poor working and living conditions in many regions and missed plan targets in terms of labour productivity as serious economic problems.[64] The overarching perspective of describing economic processes according to the paradigm of totalitarianism, however, caused the BND analysts to overlook the potential for public protest and the greater willingness within Poland's party elite to pursue a path distinct from that of other Eastern Bloc countries.[65] Accordingly, the reader of the BND report, which had been published in August 1955, found no indicators or considerations that pointed to sociopolitical crisis symptoms. Under this approach, any predictions about political riots, as it became apparent in Poznań about ten months later, were ruled out from the outset.

To better contextualise such assessments, a brief comparison with developments in other departments of the BND, where scientific methods and appropriately trained personnel were also employed, may provide some valuable insights. Efforts on behalf of the intelligence agency to systematically institutionalise scientific research under its umbrella in the late 1950s and 1960s are particularly noteworthy in this regard. From 1962 onwards, an Institute for Ionospheric Research was integrated into the BND. This was a scientific department that conducted geophysical research for radio transmission but also some space research, which entailed the monitoring of satellites and other spacecraft. The integration caused some problems as a result of clashing mentalities.[66] Ultimately, however, it proved to be a successful endeavour, not least because the institute was able to retain a relatively high degree of autonomy. The potential for conflict between internal logics and requirements of the two fields of technical research and intelligence was thus reduced, and the intelligence service consciously drew on the institute's technical expertise. In practical terms, these developments actually boosted the "scientization of the technical sector"[67] of the BND.

Although it is difficult to compare these two very different scientific disciplines and their value for intelligence work, the contrast between the rather problematic and deficient interaction with Eastern studies on the one hand and ionospheric research on the other is quite striking. In the latter case, there was no political context regarding the demands for usable knowledge. Rather, it was essentially a matter of improving the technical capabilities of intelligence work. Unlike the field of Eastern studies, dependencies with other actors that produced knowledge on the same subject area did not feature as prominently here.

Conclusion

Through newly accessible archival sources and an approach informed by the history of knowledge, it becomes possible to draw a complex picture of the relations between the Gehlen Organization and scholars of Eastern Europe in West Germany after the end of the Second World War. First and foremost, it becomes readily apparent that contacts between the two spheres, especially in the late 1940s, were far more extensive than has previously been assumed. In two concrete cases,

Compromised cooperation   31

groups of scholarly experts conducted research for the Gehlen Organization. Prior to 1945, some of the individuals involved were prominent exponents of völkisch-nationalist *Ostforschung*; after the war, almost all scholars became important figures in the (re)emerging scientific landscape in West Germany.

Based on a detailed examination of the nature and extent of cooperation between these scholars and the intelligence community, however, this relationship was anything but unproblematic and free of limitations. To adequately account for these issues, an analysis based on categories that allow for a comparison with the cooperation of intelligence and Soviet studies in the United States is of value. Through this comparative approach, characteristic features of the cooperation in Germany become clear. In the case of the United States, the first major research institutes were established after the end of the Second World War through close collaboration with and funding from government agencies, including the intelligence community in particular. There is no evidence of anything like this for West Germany regarding the foreign intelligence service BND or its predecessor, the Gehlen Organization. Here, the financial resources were limited, and the willingness to support the establishment of additional proposed research institutions was lacking. This is particularly remarkable, since such proposals were made by researchers who had worked as a "brain trust" for the Gehlen Organization. Cooperation with these institutes would therefore have continued under the best possible circumstances.

If we now look at the reasons for the lack of available support, the second major difference regarding the degree of cooperation between intelligence services and Soviet studies in the United States and West Germany comes into focus. The US agencies, at least in the early post-war years, were interested in high-quality social science results, which in turn had to be viable for policy-making. These types of demands were largely absent in the German case. In all likelihood, the two most important reasons for this are, on the one hand, the habitus of the leadership in the organisation, which was not particularly receptive to comprehensive scientific knowledge. On the other hand, there were implicit or explicit assumptions regarding the expectations of the West German government, which had little use for this knowledge in light of its limited foreign policy options. Thus, the kind of knowledge that combined social science analyses and policy recommendations, as it had been prepared for government agencies by the American Russian Institute,[68] was not produced.

This demonstrates that certain contexts had a profound effect on the production of knowledge regarding the Soviet Union in the case of the BND. The aim was to present a detailed but not overly analytical and differentiated assessment of economic conditions in the Eastern Bloc, which largely ignored the social and political consequences thereof. The essential paradigm under which the available information was interpreted came from the intellectual framework informing the approach of the economic analysts working for the BND: the theory of totalitarianism and a rendition that was specific to West Germany within the context of the early Cold War. Intelligence knowledge about the economy in the Eastern Bloc was generated through this particular approach; phenomena that did not fit into this framework were left out.

32 Thomas Wolf

With this in mind, it can be concluded that the generally assumed "scientisation" of intelligence evaluation during the Cold War can obviously not be written as a linear history of improvement. At least in the case of the economic analyses conducted under the aegis of the BND, the knowledge produced by academics shows no significant progress with regard to more scientifically rigorous methods of information processing. Hence, a line of argumentation that presupposes that scientisation necessarily leads to better results and thus offers policymakers more valuable information for their decision-making can be a misleading one. However, a history of intelligence knowledge with a particular focus on relations between intelligence agencies and other social actors and institutions can yield valuable new insights if it keeps these contexts and boundaries in mind.

In the case of the relationship between *Ostforschung* and the intelligence service, at least, it is evident that *both* the exchanges between these two spheres and the apparent obstacles encountered during their interaction led to specific problems. The prevalent apprehension and scepticism towards scholarly research among intelligence personnel, in conjunction with the ideology-driven premises that were uncritically adopted, meant that the BND analyses appeared scientific on the surface, yet failed to adequately grasp complex political realities of the East.

Notes

1 See Engerman, *Know Your Enemy*, 29.
2 See ibid., chapter 1.
3 See Desjardins, *Soviet Union through French Eyes*, 5; Hutchings, "Russian Studies in UK Universities."
4 There is no universally accepted definition of the term *Ostforschung* (*Eastern Studies*). A distinction is often made between *Ostforschung* and *Osteuropaforschung* in Germany. The former is considered an umbrella term for various disciplines which, prior to 1945, were highly politicised, informed by völkisch-nationalist ideology, and geared towards justifying German claims to rule in Eastern Europe through their findings. *Osteuropaforschung*, on the other hand, is regarded as a more serious science, which considered societies and politics in the regions of Eastern Europe as discrete objects of research. (Burgleigh, *Germany Turns Eastwards*, 20). After 1945, the term *Ostforschung* persisted and was widely used to summarize all research on the former German Eastern territories as well as East Central and Eastern Europe. Although völkisch components now receded, revisionist tendencies remained strong in the discipline (Unger, *Ostforschung in Westdeutschland*, 34). It is in this understanding, keeping in mind the substantive distinctions before and after 1945, that the term is used in this chapter.
5 See Burgleigh, *Germany Turns Eastwards*, 32; Krzoska, "Ostforschung."
6 See Engermann, *Know Your Enemy*, 28.
7 Ibid.; Diamond, *Compromised Campus*.
8 See for example Ritzer and Winkler, "Jäger."
9 The Independent Historians' Commission on the History of the Federal Intelligence Service (UHK BND) was given unrestricted access to the classified files covering the period from 1945 to 1968. Furthermore, the BND released several relevant documents: see BArch B 206.
10 Gerlach, "Agrarreform," 14.
11 For a detailed overview, see Wachs, *Theodor Oberländer*, 354–360.
12 Brandon, "Biography Hans Koch," 351–352; Struve, *Deutsche Herrschaft*, 166–168; Fahlbusch, *Wissenschaft*, 520–521, and Wachs, *Theodor Oberländer*, 73.

Compromised cooperation 33

13 Fahlbusch, *Wissenschaft*, 521; Petersen, *Bevölkerungsökonomie*, 49; Wachs, *Theodor Oberländer*, 58.
14 Petersen, *Bevölkerungsökonomie*, 161–166; 194–211; Klingemann, *Soziologie und Politik*, 82–84.
15 Seraphim to Hoffmann, 21 August 1946, GStA PK, XX. HA. Rep. 99c, No. 79.
16 Bossard, Recommendations drawn up at request of Gen. Chamberlain for the attention of Gen. Walsh, 27 August 1947. In *Forging an Intelligence Partnership: CIA and the Origins of the BND, 1945–1949. A Documentary History. Vol. I*, ed. Kevin C. Ruffner. Washington 1999, p. 399.
17 Müller, *Reinhard Gehlen*, 509.
18 Hoffmann to Seraphim, 17 November 1947, GStA PK, XX. HA. Rep. 99c, No. 79.
19 Bossard, Recommendations drawn up at request of Gen. Chamberlain for the attention of Gen. Walsh, 27 August 1947. In *Forging an Intelligence Partnership: CIA and the Origins of the BND, 1945–1949. A Documentary History. Vol. I*, ed. Kevin C. Ruffner. Washington 1999, 399.
20 Wolf, *Die Entstehung des BND. Aufbau, Finanzierung, Kontrolle*, 73–74.
21 Stegelmann, *Das Berliner Osteuropa-Institut. Organisationsbiografie einer interdisziplinären Hochschuleinrichtung 1945–1976*, 126–136.
22 On Meissner's diplomatic career, see Redecker, „Boris Meissner und das Auswärtige Amt"; for an overview of Meissner's scholarship, see Eisfeld, „Boris Meissner und der Göttinger Arbeitskreis, seine Nachwirkungen in Wissenschaft und Politik."
23 Schaller, *Die "Reichsuniversität Posen" 1941–1945*, 101–102; Höhne and Zolling, *General*, 13.
24 C, Übersicht über die Verwendung des Abschaltbetrages für IfO, 19 November 1949, BArch B 206, 3018.
25 31/W1 to C, Arbeiten von "IFO," 9 March 1950. In BArch B 206, 3018.
26 31,0 to C, Ifo, 23 March 1950, BArch B 206, 3018; C to Leiter 31, Ifo, 24 March 1950, BArch B 206, 3018; 31/W1 an GV C, Ausarbeitung Ifo, 27 April 1950, BArch B 206, 3018.
27 Engerman, *Know Your Enemy*, 6.
28 See Stöver, "Rollback. An Offensive Strategy for the Cold War."
29 See Wolf, *Entstehung des BND*, 105–111; Rass, *Sozialprofil des BND*, 185–213.
30 Engerman, *Know Your Enemy*, 47–48
31 Meldebogen auf Grund des Gesetzes zur Befreiung von Nationalsozialismus und Militarismus, Theodor Oberländer, 3 September 1946, Staatsarchiv München, 357, Spruchkammerakte Theodor Oberländer; see further Nerlich 2015, 392; Petersen, *Bevölkerungsökonomie*, 257.
32 Wolf, *Entstehung des BND*, 69–71.
33 Ibid., 72.
34 Engerman, *Know Your Enemy*, 25–26.
35 Unger, *Ostforschung in Westdeutschland*, 130.
36 Wolf, *Entstehung des BND*, 73.
37 Petersen, *Bevölkerungsökonomie – Ostforschung – Politik. Eine biographische Studie zu Peter-Heinz Seraphim (1902–1979)*, 288–289.
38 Ibid., 282–286.
39 Arbeitskreis für Ostfragen, Denkschrift über die Möglichkeit des Aufbaus eines Bundesinstituts für Ostforschung in Marburg, 18 April 1950, BArch Z 35, 14–23, esp. 17.
40 Other concepts, in particular the finally implemented approach advocated by Hermann Aubin, were based on a tripartite and equal ranking institutional structure, according to which (1) North- and East German, (2) Russian and (3) South-Eastern European Studies were to be conducted by different institutes. See Kleindienst, *Die Entwicklung der bundesdeutschen Osteuropaforschung*, 36–37.
41 In particular, they emphasized the model example of recent US research on Eastern Europe, which could serve as a reference point for the re-emerging West German

34 *Thomas Wolf*

scientific community both in thematic and methodological terms. See Arbeitskreis für Ostfragen, Denkschrift über die Möglichkeit des Aufbaus eines Bundesinstituts für Ostforschung in Marburg, 18 April 1950, BArch Z 35, 16.

42 Ibid., 22.

43 Meissner to Markert, 5 January 1951, University Archive Tübingen, 792, No. 139.

44 Circular letter Seraphim, 20 December 1949, Nachlass Theodor Oberländer.

45 C to Leiter 30, Bestand des IfO, 20 January 1950, BArch B 206, 3018.

46 Leiter 31 to GV C, 14 April 1950, BArch B 206, 3018.

47 30,0 to Leiter 31, 2 March 1950, BArch B 206, 3018; see further C to Leiter 31, Abschaltung IfO, 19 November 1949, BArch B 206, 3018; Leiter 31 to GV C, 14 April 1950, BArch B 206, 3018.

48 Specifically, this group consisted of Gustav Hilger, Gunther Ipsen, Werner Markert, Reinhart Maurach, Walter Meder, Boris Meissner and Otto Schiller. See Markert, W. 1956. „Die deutsche Osteuropaforschung seit dem zweiten Weltkrieg." *University Archive Tübingen*, 792, no. 97.

49 Wolf, *Entstehung des BND*, 128–129.

50 In the 1950s Klocke published articles, sometimes in serial form, such as in the renowned journal *Osteuropa,* as well as shorter monographs and various book reviews. In addition, he appeared as a speaker at conferences of associations for Eastern European Studies. Klocke's most important publications in the 1950s include: Klocke, "Wandlungen"; Klocke, „Wirtschaft und ihre Entwicklung"; Klocke, "Nationalbewusstsein in Osteuropa"; Klocke, *Phasen der sowjetischen Wirtschaftsordnung*. His colleagues in the economic analysis department also published in prominent journals, Law-Robinson, "Transportwesen," Law-Robinson, "Eisenerzbasis."

51 Klocke to Markert, 3 September 1951, University Archive Tübingen, 792, no. 320.

52 See, for example, the correspondence between Werner Markert, Hans Schwalm, Klocke, Gerhard Czybulka and Karl Günzel, University Archive Tübingen, 792, no. 99, 127, 135 and 160.

53 Klocke to Markert, 8 June 1953, University Archive Tübingen, 792, no. 127; Klocke to Markert, 13 September 1953, University Archive Tübingen, 792, no. 127.

54 Markert to Klocke, 10 September 1953, University Archive Tübingen, 792, no. 127.

55 Klocke to Markert, 2 November 1951, University Archive Tübingen, 792, no. 320; Klocke to Markert, 4 February 1957, University Archive Tübingen, 792, no. 160.

56 Schwalm to Günzel, 24 August 1956, University Archive Tübingen, 792, no. 99.

57 See Unger, *Ostforschung in Westdeutschland*, 192–196.

58 Klocke, "Ostwirtschaftsblock," 397.

59 Klocke, "Wandlungen," 91.

60 BND, Das Wirtschafts- und Rüstungspotenzial des Ostblocks, August 1955, BArch B 206, 51121; 1–145; BND, Die Wirtschafts- und Rüstungslage des Ostblocks. Langfristiger Rück- und Ausblick. Teil I: Wirtschaft, BArch B 206, 51126, 2–17.

61 BND, Das Wirtschafts- und Rüstungspotenzial des Ostblocks, August 1955, BArch B 206, 51121, 95–96; BND, Die Wirtschafts- und Rüstungslage des Ostblocks. Langfristiger Rück- und Ausblick. Teil I: Wirtschaft, BArch B 206, 51126, 5–6, 13–14.

62 BND, Das Wirtschafts- und Rüstungspotenzial des Ostblocks, August 1955, BArch B 206, 51121, 110.

63 BND, Die Wirtschafts- und Rüstungslage des Ostblocks. Langfristiger Rück- und Ausblick. Teil I: Wirtschaft, BArch B 206, 51126, 16.

64 See ibid., 62–64, 95–98.

65 See Brus "1953 to 1956," 54.

66 See Müller, *Reinhard Gehlen*, 276–278.

67 Ibid., 278.

68 Engerman, *Know Your Enemy*, 49–50.

Bibliography

Brandon, R. 2017. "Biography Hans Koch." In *Handbuch der völkischen Wissenschaften. Akteure, Netzwerke, Forschungsprogramme*, ed. M. Fahlbusch, I. Haar, and A. Pinwinkler, 347–358. Berlin and Boston: De Gruyter.

Brus, W. 1986. "1953 to 1956: The 'Thaw' and the 'New Course'." In *The Economic History of Eastern Europe 1919–1975. Vol. III*, ed. M. C. Kaser and E. A. Radice, 40–69. Oxford: Clarendon Press.

Burgleigh, M. 1988. *Germany Turns Eastwards: A Study of Ostforschung in the Third Reich.* Cambridge: Cambridge University Press.

Desjardins, R. 1988. *Soviet Union through French Eyes, 1945–85.* New York: St. Martin's Press.

Diamond, S. 1992. *Compromised Campus: The Collaboration of Universities with the Intelligence Community, 1945–1955.* New York: Oxford University Press.

Eisfeld, A. 2018. "Boris Meissner und der Göttinger Arbeitskreis, seine Nachwirkungen in Wissenschaft und Politik." In *Ein Jahrhundert Ost-West-Beziehungen. Zum 100. Geburtstag von Boris Meissner*, ed. G. Goring and M. Pabst, 23–47. Lüneburg: Carl-Schirren-Gesellschaft.

Engerman, D. C. 2009. *Know Your Enemy: The Rise and Fall of America's Soviet Experts.* Oxford: Oxford University Press.

Fahlbusch, M. 1999. *Wissenschaft im Dienst der nationalsozialistischen Politik? Die "Volksdeutschen Forschungsgemeinschaften" von 1931–1945.* Baden-Baden: Nomos.

Forging an Intelligence Partnership: CIA and the Origins of the BND, 1945–1949. A Documentary History. Vol. I, ed. Kevin C. Ruffner. 1995. Washington: CIA History Staff.

Gerlach, C. 1995. "Die deutsche Agrarreform und die Bevölkerungspolitik in den besetzten sowjetischen Gebieten." In *Besatzung und Bündnis. Deutsche Herrschaftsstrategien in Ost- und Südosteuropa*, ed. C. Gerlach and C. Dieckman, 9–60. Berlin: Verl. der Buchläden.

Höhne, H., and Zolling, H. 1972. *The General was a Spy: The Truth about General Gehlen and His Spy Ring.* New York: Coward, Mcann & Geoghegan.

Hutchings, S. 2002. "Russian Studies in UK Universities." *Subject Centre for Languages, Linguistics and Area Studies.* www.llas.ac.uk/resources/gpg/386.html (accessed February 3, 2021).

Kleindienst, T. 2009. *Die Entwicklung der bundesdeutschen Osteuropaforschung im Spannungsfeld zwischen Wissenschaft und Politik.* Marburg: Herder-Inst.

Klingemann, C. 2009. *Soziologie und Politik. Sozialwissenschaftliches Expertenwissen im Dritten Reich und in der frühen westdeutschen Nachkriegszeit.* Wiesbaden: Springer.

Klocke, H. 1952. *Die Phasen der sowjetischen Wirtschaftsordnung in der Union und in den Satellitenstaaten.* Stuttgart: Deutsche Gesellschaft für Osteuropakunde.

Klocke, H. 1953. "Der Ostwirtschaftsblock als Wirtschaftsunion." *Zeitschrift für Geopolitik* 24: 387–397.

Klocke, H. 1956. "Nationalbewusstsein in Osteuropa." *Osteuropa* 6: 29–36, and 375–386.

Klocke, H. 1958. "Die Wirtschaft und ihre Entwicklung." In *Sowjetbuch*, ed. H. Koch, 2nd expanded edition, 129–160. Cologne: Dt. Industrieverl.

Klocke, H. 1959. "Wandlungen der Sozialstruktur im europäischen Vorfeld der Sowjetunion seit 1945." *Osteuropa* 9: 91–100, 360–373, and 792–805.

Krzoska, M. 2017. "Ostforschung." In *Handbuch der völkischen Wissenschaften. Akteure, Netzwerke, Forschungsprogramme*, ed. M. Fahlbusch, I. Haar, and A. Pinwinkler, 1090–1102. Berlin and Boston: De Gruyter.

36   Thomas Wolf

Law-Robinson, H. 1952a. "Transportwesen." *Osteuropa Sonderheft: Der 19. Parteitag der KPdSU* 2: 442–446.

Law-Robinson, H. 1952b. "Eisenerzbasis des Kusnezker Kombinats." *Osteuropa* 2: 52–55.

Müller, A. 2017. *Agentenfunk und Funkaufklärung des Bundesnachrichtendienstes 1945–1960*. Berlin: Ch.Links.

Müller, R.-D. 2017. *Reinhard Gehlen. Geheimdienstchef im Hintergrund der Bonner Republik. Die Biografie. Teil 1: 1902–1950*. Berlin: Ch.Links.

Nerlich, V. 2015. *"A Baltico ad Euxinum." Reinhart Maurach und die Frühzeit der deutschen Ostrechtsforschung*. Berlin: Schmidt.

Petersen, H.-C. 2007. *Bevölkerungsökonomie – Ostforschung – Politik. Eine biographische Studie zu Peter-Heinz Seraphim (1902–1979)*. Osnabrück: fibre.

Rass, C. 2016. *Das Sozialprofil des BND. Von den Anfängen bis 1968*. Berlin: Ch.Links.

Redecker, N. v. 2018. "Boris Meissner und das Auswärtige Amt." In *Ein Jahrhundert Ost-West-Beziehungen. Zum 100. Geburtstag von Boris Meissner*, ed. G. Goring and M. Pabst, 11–21. Lüneburg: Carl-Schirren-Gesellschaft.

Ritzer, U., and Winkler, W. 2017. "Jäger, Sammler, Vogelfreund." *Süddeutsche Zeitung*, December 2, 2017. https://gfx.sueddeutsche.de/apps/e868059/www/ (accessed February 3, 2021).

Schaller, H. W. 2010. *Die "Reichsuniversität Posen" 1941–1945*. Frankfurt am Main: Lang.

Stegelmann, U. 2015. *Das Berliner Osteuropa-Institut. Organisationsbiografie einer interdisziplinären Hochschuleinrichtung 1945–1976*. Frankfurt am Main: PL Academic Research.

Stöver, B. 2004. "Rollback. An Offensive Strategy for the Cold War." In *The United States and Germany in the Era of the Cold War, 1945–1990. A Handbook. Volume 1: 1945–1968*, ed. D. Junker, 97–102. Cambridge: Cambridge University Press.

Struve, K. 2015. *Deutsche Herrschaft, ukrainischer Nationalismus, antijüdische Gewalt. Der Sommer 1941 in der Westukraine*. Berlinand and Boston: de Gruyter.

Unger, C. R. 2007. *Ostforschung in Westdeutschland. Die Erforschung des europäischen Ostens und die Deutsche Forschungsgemeinschaft, 1945–1975*. Stuttgart: Steiner.

Wachs, P.-C. 2000. *Der Fall Theodor Oberländer (1905–1998). Ein Lehrstück deutscher Geschichte*. Frankfurt am Main: Campus.

Wolf, T. 2018. *Die Entstehung des BND. Aufbau, Finanzierung, Kontrolle*. Berlin: Ch.Links.

2 Dogma versus progress

KGB's technological and scientific (in-)capacities from the 1960s to the 1980s

Evgenia Lezina

Introduction

After the death of Stalin in 1953, the Soviet Party leadership initiated an ideological shift, announcing that the period of class struggle was over. The Third Programme of the Communist Party of the Soviet Union (CPSU), adopted during the 22nd Party Congress in 1961, concluded that in the new stage, "the state, which arose as a state of the dictatorship of the proletariat" "has become a state of the entire people (*obshchenarodnoye gosudarstvo*)."[1]

This alteration in the Party policy inevitably entailed a shift in the Soviet secret police's functioning. In this period mass terror gave way to a system of mass social control and manipulation.[2] Yet the repressive function continued in new forms providing for the perpetuation of what John Dziak termed "a counterintelligence state."[3] According to Dziak, a major characteristic feature of the Soviet system was "an overarching concern with 'enemies,' both internal and external," and as a result, "security and the extirpation of real or presumed threats" became the regime's "premier enterprise."[4]

Terminating mass terror while maintaining the intensity of police control in the post-Stalin era required a constant adjustment of the state security structures to the changing circumstances or "operating environment" (*operativnaya obstanovka*) in the Chekist terminology. "Operating environment," explained the long-time chief of the Soviet Committee for State Security (Komitet gosudarstvennoi bezopasnosti, KGB)[5] Yuri Andropov,

> represents a combination of such conditions as the activity of the enemy, our own abilities, and common for both sides social and natural environments. It includes such important components as the objects of the enemy's aspirations and the groups of people that the enemy is counting on in its covert and subversive operations.[6]

From the 1960s onwards the Soviet KGB struggled to adapt to the changing social and political situation through improving management and training of personnel, but, above all, through taking advantage of modern technologies of data collecting, processing and storage. These efforts, resulting in

DOI: 10.4324/9781003147329-3

38 *Evgenia Lezina*

the substantial expansion and diversification of the internal security structures, were shaped and directed by the complex ideological framework superimposed by the CPSU Central Committee. Both in terms of operation and self-perception, the Soviet secret police might be regarded as "domestic intelligence": it not only served purely repressive aims but also functioned as a vast information-gathering apparatus able to generate images of the society's inner "enemies."

One can highlight roughly four main periods of the operating environment before the collapse of the USSR in 1991 and four varying but closely interrelated priorities of the secret police's self-development. It is noteworthy that the period in which the KGB managed to finally deploy its encompassing control structures was the final one, when it tried to hold its grip over the processes unleashed due to the policies of *glasnost'* and *perestroika.*

This chapter will probe into these transformations, focusing on the specific knowledge-producing capacities of the Soviet secret police in the context of what is known as the "Information Age" and exploring how the KGB handled data analysis in its work. It starts with an overview of the four periods of the operating environment's evolution, highlighting the Soviet political police's technologisation and scientisation endeavours at each phase. It further elaborates on the overall consequences and impacts of these attempts, enquiring how the KGB's intentions to modernise interacted with the inner restraints of the whole Soviet system. My primary interest is how the ever-growing piles of collected data were eventually processed and analysed and to what extent they affected the operational practice of the Soviet state security bodies.

Phase one: "the state of the entire people" stage

Despite the official proclamation that at a new historical stage "the state security organs became the organs of the state of the entire people," the internal "enemy" figure central to the Soviet authoritarian mindset remained intact in the post-Stalinist Soviet Union.[7] As one of the top KGB officers Fillip Bobkov formulated it in 1960, "the imperialists, no longer having the social base for the deployment of broad subversive work against our country" were "trying to intensify the subversive activities of individual anti-Soviet elements."[8] This implied that a smaller and finer netting was required to catch these "elements," whose anti-Soviet stance was allegedly foreign-inspired. Eventually, new secret police methods were introduced during the late 1950s and the early 1960s, and were particularly well professed under Yuri Andropov, who chaired the KGB between 1967 and 1982. The new modus operandi focused on preventive measures or social prophylaxis, more capillary control of citizens through the networks of agents and trusted persons, and so forth – an approach which Oleg Kharkhordin defined as "relentless and rational system of preventive surveillance."[9]

The Soviet internal security structures or the counterintelligence units of the KGB established in March 1954 were accordingly strengthened and diversified adjusting to the new challenges of time. The Scientific-Technological Revolution or "STR" was, as Susan Reid succinctly summed up,

> a central term in official pronouncements already of the Khrushchev era, which made it a defining characteristic of socialist modernity. The Third Party Programme adopted in 1961 – the definitive ideological statement of the Khrushchev period – identified social progress with scientific and technological progress.[10]

In 1959, the KGB set up the Operational and Technical Directorate (O&T) and relevant departments in its regional branches to improve the level of technical equipment of the state security agencies.[11] The following year the Committee enhanced its counterintelligence structures by combining several directorates under a unified Second Chief Directorate in charge of counterintelligence and internal political control.[12]

In 1967, one of Andropov's first moves as a chairman was to institute the Fifth Directorate for Ideological Counterintelligence to oversee the realms of culture, education, religion, science, sport, health care, mass media and so forth.[13] The formation of the Fifth Directorate and the continued criminalisation of the "anti-Soviet agitation and propaganda" (in the new Criminal Codes of the Soviets republics adopted in 1960) represented a reaction to the growing sophistication and development of society, triggered by the appearance of various uncontrolled channels of information (like *samizdat*, foreign radio "voices") and increase in the educational level of employees (due to investments by the state in the military–industrial complex and endeavours to create its own intellectual, albeit predominantly technocratic, elite).[14] In this context, the introduction of new technologies of suppression and their justification as well as the fight against "anti-Soviet slander" rendered an attempt to neutralise the process of the growing complexity in society.[15]

Phase two: the "détente"

The emergence of a qualitatively different operating environment was linked with the relaxation of tension in US–Soviet relations in the late 1960s and the early 1970s known as détente (*razryadka*).[16] Since the late 1960s, the state security agencies were increasingly focused on improving their counterintelligence technological base as well as control structures, particularly those ensuring surveillance over foreign visitors and any Soviet citizens' contacts with foreigners, including correspondence. Also, in this context, one of the main tasks of the KGB counterintelligence units became securing state secrets.[17]

During this period, it turned up that effective and quick processing of the growing amount of information by traditional means was impossible. "Even our opponents point out that 'the KGB's disadvantage is the inability "to digest" the information it extracts, which is often not properly analyzed,'" the authors of one the KGB internal publication admitted in 1969.[18] "Tentatively," continued General

40   *Evgenia Lezina*

Major Aleksandr Evdokushin and Lieutenant Colonel Boris Kurashvili in their contribution to *Sbornik KGB SSSR* journal,

> we can say that the traditional information system has ceased to satisfy the needs of counterintelligence since the mid-1950s, when the USSR's international relations expanded significantly and the number of foreigners entering our country from capitalist states and our citizens traveling abroad increased sharply.[19]

To overcome the situation where "a constantly increasing volume of accumulated information and its insufficiently effective accounting and analysis negatively affect[ed] the solution of specific issues within the competence of the KGB," supernumerary (*vneshtatnye*) information and analytical groups were organised in counterintelligence units across the country in the second half of the 1960s.[20]

When the Fifth Directorate was set up in 1967, its Sixth Division was put in charge of information and analytical work. The same tasks were set before the newly created Directorate "A" of the Second Chief Directorate.[21] In May 1967, the KGB chairman issued the "Temporary Regulation on the Organization of Analytical Work in the Second Chief Directorate" and released a Unified classification table of operational information (also used by the Fifth Directorate with some modifications).[22] Since then, information work was carried out on the basis of classification tables as an information language of counterintelligence. To effectively gather the data, a punch card system was launched in most of the KGB territorial bodies.[23]

Almost two years later, in March 1969, the KGB chairman ordered the inauguration of separate regular in-house (*shtatnye*) Information and Analytical (I&A) units which would serve the needs of both Second and Fifth counterintelligence divisions.[24] According to the Interim Regulation governing them, I&A units were in charge of producing information service systems (*sistemy informatsionnogo obsluzhivaniya*, SIO) and ensuring their smooth function.[25] Within a year, I&A subdivisions appeared in most of the KGB in the Soviet republics and regions.[26]

In May 1969, the Scientific Research Information and Analytical Institute (NIIAI) was set up "to introduce electronic computers in the KGB for mechanization and automation of analytical work and the creation of an automated information support system of counterintelligence activities (*avtomatizirovannaya sistema informatsionnogo obespecheniya kontrrazvedyvatel'noi deyatel'nosti*, ASIO KD)."[27] Five years later, in July 1974, the NIIAI branch was instituted in Kiev in the KGB of the Ukrainian SSR, the second-largest union republic.[28]

Also, in the late 1960s plans were announced to gradually put into operation the Unified Information Support System for Counterintelligence (Edinaya sistema informatsionnogo obespecheniya kontrrazvedki, ESIOK).[29] Behind this project was the idea of mechanisation and automation of information processes as well as eventual computerisation. "The establishment of the ESIOK is planned in three stages," the Deputy Head of Directorate "A" of the KGB Second Chief Directorate Colonel Shamilov explained at a meeting of I&A staff held in Kiev in 1968.

Dogma versus progress 41

At the first stage, according to Shamilov, information retrieval systems for collecting, storing and simple statistical processing of operational information were to be formed. At the second stage, these subsystems were to be combined into a single complex

> capable of processing large amounts of operational information, solving some logical problems, in particular, determining the degree of belonging of foreigners who arrived in the USSR through various channels to the enemy's special services, and identifying new trends in tactics and methods of enemy subversive activities, etc.[30]

At the third stage, the arrangement should evolve into an automated control system (ACS), with the help of which "perspective and current planning, as well as control and operational management would be carried out."[31]

The 24th Congress of the CPSU convened in the spring of 1971 set "the all-round improvement of planning and management of the systems based on the wide use of modern mathematical methods, electronic computing and communications" as an overriding priority.[32] In November of the same year, the KGB chairman announced the development of the ESIOK (with the code-name "Delta"), which was to accumulate information of interest for counterintelligence, obtained by the Committee's units, as well as data received by the KGB from ministries, departments, institutions and organisations. The latter included the Ministry of Internal Affairs, Ministry of Foreign Affairs, the USSR State Committee on Science and Technology (GKNT), press-agencies TASS and Novosti (APN), "Intourist" travel agency and other state bodies.[33] For the elaboration, implementation and operation of the system, KGB officials set up a new Scientific-Operational Directorate (Directorate "N") within the Second Chief Directorate in 1971.[34] In December 1972 the instruction guiding the procedure for gradual introduction of the ESIOK ("Delta") was released.[35]

In August 1973, one of the major subsystems of the ESIOK "Fort-67" was put into effect. It was an information system for accumulating, processing and issuing data about foreigners' contacts with Soviet citizens and other persons permanently residing in the USSR. After this point, Directorate "N" conducted the centralised electronic registration (*uchet*) of the relevant data upon receiving filled-in unified operational questionnaires from the I&A units of the KGB local bodies. In the regional branches, the information on identified contacts with foreigners was processed and issued, as it was put in the relevant order, "using the available capabilities and office equipment (*sredstva orgtekhniki*)."[36]

Alongside systematisation and accumulation of data, another focus during this period was on education and academic enhancement. In fact, during the 1960s and 1970s, special resolutions of the Party and government stressed that the level of training of specialists did not "correspond to the increasing requirements of science and production."[37] The KGB internal directives and orders also reveal the efforts to improve the cadre.[38] As Victor Yasmann formulated it, "the KGB's invasion of the sphere of ideology, dealing with sophisticated social issues, and

42 *Evgenia Lezina*

the 'necessity' of controlling scientific and creative intelligentsia had prompted Andropov's other step: 'intellectualization' of the KGB."[39]

In the training of the cadre and academic work, the central institution for internal state security bodies and "the principal educational and training institute for the entire KGB realm" was the Red Banner Higher School of the Committee for State Security, named after Felix Dzerzhinsky in 1962, the former Higher School of the Ministry for State Security.[40] It became an institution of higher education only in 1952. By the beginning of the 1950s, the Higher School offered three special disciplines. By the early 1960s, it offered seven. However, its major transformations took place in the 1970s and 1980s. They were largely governed by the decision of the KGB Collegium of June 14, 1972, which emphasised the need to introduce modern methods and forms of training, as well as the need for a serious restructuring in the educational process.[41] As a result, by 1980 the Higher School possessed 10 faculties, 42 departments, a preparatory division, a number of special courses and had several thousand students enrolled in classes simultaneously.[42]

Thus, by the end of the 1960s and the early 1970s, in a situation of relatively greater openness generated by the détente, the KGB leadership clearly indicated their intention to strengthen and expand the KGB control structures, to improve counterintelligence technological base and to enhance staff training. However, development and implementation of specific solutions fell on the periods of fundamentally different operating environment to which we now turn.

Phase three: "a second Cold War" period

The Soviet invasion of Afghanistan and the United States' response to it, including the boycott of the 1980 Moscow Olympics and the technology embargo, put an end to détente and marked a period known as the Second Cold War.[43] This new state of affairs affected the operating environment for the Soviet state security once again. KGB chairman Andropov emphasised while speaking at the National Consultation Meeting of the Leadership of the KGB in May 1981:

> The enemy, having confirmed for itself the fruitlessness of activities of individual anti-social elements, is now trying to influence wider groups of population with the objective to create so-called "pockets of social agitation" in order to ultimately achieve the "ideological erosion" of the Soviet society.[44]

The talk was no longer about the foreign-inspired individuals but about potential disloyalty of a wider variety of groups in the USSR.

Andropov also singled out "the enemy's subversive activities in the economic area" as a distinctive characteristic of the new operating environment. According to the KGB chief, these diversions manifested "themselves in attempts to cause difficulties for our country's national economy, to hamper the industry development rates, to conceal from us the most important results of the scientific and technological revolution."[45] Based on this premise, the KGB established two new counterintelligence directorates – one for Transport Counterintelligence

Dogma versus progress   43

(Fourth Directorate) in 1981 and another for Economic Counterintelligence (Sixth Directorate) in 1982.[46] Through the Sixth Directorate, which was put in charge of counterintelligence at all industrial enterprises of the USSR, including the "military-industrial complex," the KGB became more deeply embedded in the Soviet economy in a situation of growing economic crisis and further stagnation.[47]

During this period, several preparatory steps were undertaken, and some segments of the ESIOK became fully functional. In October 1979, the automated ESIOK's subsystem "Delta-Potok" (Delta-Stream) for overseeing the entry of foreigners, their stay in the country and departure from the USSR was put into operation. The introduction of this centralised registration of foreign visitors was timed with the beginning of the 1980 Moscow Summer Olympic Games.[48] In the lead up to the Olympics, another ESIOK's subsystem "Personalia-NSI" was launched, a reference subsystem for foreigners and Soviet citizens that organised the data regularly collected in all counterintelligence directorates.[49] The implementation of the Olympic Information Complex of the KGB provided for monitoring and processing of data on approximately 550,000 foreigners who either had planned to visit or actually visited the Soviet Union in 1980. Most importantly, during the Olympics KGB bodies were permanently "armed" with the interacting automated information systems "Delta-Potok" and "Personalia-NSI."[50]

In this way on the eve of *perestroika* the KGB basically finished preparations to placing a full-scale "cupola of control" over Soviet society and foreigners having any links to the Soviet state. Ironically, as will be shown in the next section, these surveillance structures capable of gathering, storing and processing data at a qualitatively new level were largely brought into force at the height of Gorbachev's liberalisation campaign.

The fourth and the last phase: *perestroika* and beyond

The policies of *perestroika* and *glasnost'* proclaimed by the General Secretary of CPSU Mikhail Gorbachev in 1985 signified a brand new challenge for the secret police. As it was explicitly put in one of the KGB orders, "as a result of *perestroika*, a fundamentally new political and operating environment for the activities of Soviet counterintelligence emerged."[51] This gave rise to "the insistent need to take additional measures to deepen the restructuring of the operational and service functions of state security agencies, to improve their quality and efficiency."[52] Additionally, the increasing role of information and analytical work in counterintelligence was underlined.

Although the implementation of the ESIOK was announced already in 1971, it took almost 15 years until all counterintelligence units in the centre and in the regions switched to a unified procedure for selection, accumulation, processing and use of information, as well as to a unified system of documents. The development of common programming language which provided for a single standard for information made it possible to "fill in" the system with the data satisfying the operational needs of the KGB counterintelligence branches.[53]

The permanent regulation on the KGB Information and Analytical subdivisions put into effect in March 1986 authorised these structures to create standard projects

44 *Evgenia Lezina*

of automated or non-automated information systems. They were used to select, accumulate, logically process and issue data necessary for solving tasks of protecting state and military secrets, detecting, preventing and suppressing intelligence and subversive activities, as well as "organizing and maintaining the selection of information to be accumulated in the ESIOK information systems."[54]

Due to the high cost, complexity of elaboration and commissioning of the ESIOK, it was introduced in stages. In the initial phase, those territorial KGB bodies that did not possess computer facilities were provided with manual circuit (*neavtomatizirovannyi kontur*) of the ESIOK (code "Delta-NK") "as an intermediate link for subsequent transfer to a higher level of technical support using computers."[55]

In September 1986, the major component of the ESIOK, the Central Bank of Operational Data (Tsentral'nyi bank operativnykh dannykh, CBD), which stored information about the facts and signs of intelligence and subversive activities, entered into permanent operation. The most important data of interest to all operational units of the central office and of the KGB territorial bodies were subject to centralisation and accumulation in the CBD. The latter and the previously initiated "Delta-Potok" and "Personalia-NSI" subsystems constituted the central network or element of the ESIOK. These changes signalised the first operational phase of the ESIOK ("Delta").[56] Its structure thus consisted of "a set of interconnected subsystems of the central level, specialized segments, data banks on the lines of counterintelligence work and information systems of the KGB-UKGB."[57]

The "periphery" of the ESIOK comprised of a set of automated information systems of the KGB in the centre and in the field, built on the basis of a single procedure for the selection of data, common input documents and the rules for filling them out. The composition of data selected for the ESIOK was determined by the Thematic List of Information first released in 1981.[58] The data grouping in the system incorporated four elements (conditionally entitled "system objects"), which formed four basic functional blocs of the ESIOK: "Action," "Personality," "Organization" and "Event."[59]

According to the Thematic List of Information, the ESIOK was to collect, process and issue data relating to the following:

- Intelligence and subversive actions of the enemy, their participants, time and location, as well as methods and means of obtaining this information by operational units ("Action");
- Foreigners and some citizens of the USSR who represented the operational interest, on whom counterintelligence measures were being carried out in order to identify their possible belonging to the foreign special services and organisations used in subversive activities against the USSR, as well as individual citizens who bore hostile intentions or were preparing to commit highly dangerous state offenses ("Personality");
- Organizations, the constant study of which was linked with the tasks of unveiling the intelligence and subversive activities of the enemy ("Organization");

Dogma versus progress   45

- The incidents and events which the enemy might have been involved in or which the enemy could use to undertake subversive actions against the USSR and other countries of the socialist community, which took place in the territory of the republic, region or district, or in the facilities under the KGB-UKGB operational service ("Event").[60]

In accordance with the Thematic List, employees elaborated specialised vocabularies (43 in all), which "served for the unambiguous description and coding of the information selected for accumulation."[61] Though Thematic List and vocabularies were generally intended for all KGB units across the country, they were normally adjusted to local operating environments.[62]

To give an example: in the case of Lithuania, the indicators used to collect data regarding subversive actions of the enemy (Vocabulary No. 1) were grouped in 22 sections which combined 1,110 characteristics. One section of classification focused on "Signs of Anti-Soviet Activity and Ideological Subversion by the Enemy." Among 114 of the enumerated characteristics by which such a diversion was to be singled out, one could be tagged with "discrediting Marxist-Leninist theory as the scientific and philosophical basis of Soviet society," "falsification of the class essence of the Soviet state," "the spread of slanderous information about the place and role of the Communist Party in the system of socialist society," and so forth. "Intentionally creating an unhealthy work environment" could testify to preparation for wrecking and was to be registered in the ESIOK as well. Among "facts and signs that could testify to the preparation for and committing high treason in the form of flight abroad or refusal to return from abroad to the USSR" were "expressing dissatisfaction with one's life situation at home" and "the manifestation of a negative attitude towards the socialist system with elements of worship of the Western way of life and bourgeois democracy" (61 items in all). "Demonstrative withdrawal" from the ranks of the CPSU and its youth branch – the *Komsomol*, refusal to work and participate in elections, going on a hunger strike, appeal to foreigners and foreign organisations for help, "dragging into the art of bourgeois ideas" and "into the scientific works of anti-Marxist concepts," expression of intentions to involve minors in a religious group and to create a school for teaching religious dogma to youngsters were "facts and signs that could testify to preparations for anti-Soviet agitation and propaganda" (83 positions in all).[63]

In fact, any operatively significant information (or any information subject to operational accounting) was to be accumulated. Abstract cards on people who fell into the sight of KGB in connection with operational records, signals, materials of special and nomenclature cases (*liternye i nomeklaturnye dela*) were filled out by field officers, as the Chekists from the city of Sverdlovsk described in their contribution to *Sbornik KGB SSSR*. Special groups of employees fulfilled these tasks based on the materials of the Tenth (Accounting and Archival) department and the O&T department.[64] The authors also pointed out that "the information available in the passport division of the Sverdlovsk regional police (*militsiya*) directorate was taken into account for persons travelling abroad on private business, as well as for foreign nationals and stateless persons residing in the USSR."[65]

46 *Evgenia Lezina*

After switching to the ESIOK in 1986, the existing subsystems were transferred to the central and republican banks of operational data. In the case of Ukraine, for instance, this referred to the following arrays of information stored in the republican data bank as well as in the reference and information funds of the I&A units: "Fort-67" (contacts of Soviet citizens with foreigners), "Ftor-74" (international correspondence of Soviet citizens), "Filter" (international telephone conversations), "Rubikon" (registration of foreigners), "Nakip'" (data related to seizure or hijacking of Soviet or foreign vehicles), "Fregat" (trips of Soviet citizens abroad and admission of foreigners in the USSR), "Fakel-U" (outdoor surveillance), as well as some locally specific clusters.[66]

By April 1985, these information systems and operational information arrays in the KGB of the Ukrainian SSR accumulated operatively significant information on 184,598 foreigners and 92,036 Soviet citizens. Besides, the reference and informational funds of I&A units in the Ukrainian regions contained operatively significant data on 241,430 Soviet citizens. Additionally, "the "Delta-U-Signal" system, designed to control the verification of the received primary (signal) information, preserved data on 4,800 persons."[67]

In 1986, the first deputy chairman of the KGB of the USSR Nikolai Emokhonov specified that the all-union ESIOK ("Delta") at that moment incorporated about 40 subsystems, including over 30 ones in the KGB regional branches. According to Emokhonov, these funds annually prepared more than 10,000 information materials and fulfilled over 50,000 requests of operational workers. He also underscored that by 1991 the number of the system's elements in the territorial bodies and structures of military counterintelligence would reach 140, and by 1996 – up to 220. Emokhonov further explained that the central elements of ESIOK would be concentrated in a single computer centre with a total data bank of more than 3 billion characters.[68]

So, as the Unified Information Support System evolved, new thematic clusters or functional blocs were added to accumulate operational data. For instance, in December 1985, the KGB Collegium ordered Directorate "N" to provide collecting and integrated processing of data on the "Enemy intelligence and subversive activities carried out from the standpoint of firms in capitalist states, their representative offices and specialists" in a separate ESIOK cluster.[69] In 1988, a block "Silhouette" was designed to solve information problems linked with the search for authors and distributors of anonymous anti-Soviet documents.[70] The block on "Emergency situations" was added to the ESIOK in November 1989.[71] Since May 1991 the CDB ESIOK was to gather data on the joint ventures with the participation of Soviet and foreign firms and companies, the total number of which had reached more than 3,200 by then.[72]

In the last year of the Soviet rule, when the withdrawal of the Soviet forces from the Eastern and Central Europe had started, the KGB's Third Chief Directorate was tasked with ensuring "reception, analysis, processing and use in the ESIOK of the data contained in the information systems of military counterintelligence bodies by groups of forces abroad."[73] Additionally, the military counterintelligence had to be equipped with an automated databank "Inspection" for systematic accumulation and analysis of evidence related to organisation and coordination of the activities of the state security agencies in the field of disarmament.[74]

With the elaboration of the technical base of the KGB and improvement of software within the framework of ASIO KD ESIOK ("Delta") and based on the previous experience of operating a number of systems in a manual mode, several automated functional blocks were introduced in the second half of the 1980s. Among them were, for instance, the blocs "Signal" and "Control" (designed to monitor the implementation of decisions and plans).[75] Another automated cluster was intended for improving the manoeuvring of the undercover apparatus and gathering information about residents, agents, and holders of safe apartments.[76]

Some territorial branches, including the UKGB for the Sverdlovsk region, worked out subsystems meeting their own needs.[77] In the late 1980s the UKGB for Moscow and the Moscow region even endeavoured to devise a new method of informational and analytical support for the process of checking primary signals, conducting operative checks and operative processes (block "Tsikl") on the basis of its ASIO KD "Delta-Moscow" system.[78]

Thus, the ESIOK functional blocks and information clusters tended to multiply. In 1989, the automated circuit of the Lithuanian KGB reference information fund, for example, consisted of 23 clusters, while the manual circuit included ten blocks and two information arrays.[79] Already in 1986 the head of Directorate "N" Major General Georgii Pipia reported that the ESIOK funds were "performing significant work in information support for counterintelligence units."[80] He specified that during 1985 alone

> "1,175,000 foreigners who either entered the country or were issued visas for entry into the Soviet Union were checked with the help of the central network of the ESIOK" and that among them "163 persons were identified whose entry into the USSR had been blocked: 9,875 persons who were put on control of entry, 41,000 persons on whom the operational materials were available, and 135 were identified as intelligence agents and agents of the enemy special services."[81]

During the same period, "over 1,500 of various information and reference, statistical and logical tasks" were resolved at the request of the operational subdivisions of the KGB counterintelligence directorates and regional branches. As the report further underscored, "the results were used in work on cases and signals, in investigative work and analytical studies, in the preparations of the KGB normative acts, orientations along the lines and directions of counterintelligence activities."[82]

By the end of 1986, the segments of "the central network of the ESIOK alone concentrated data extracted from 500,000 operational documents" and "arrays of these subsystems included over 3 million descriptions of system objects."[83] A "Delta-Potok" information block on individuals from capitalist and developing countries who had visited the Soviet Union between 1973 and 1986 contained 12 million descriptions.[84]

48 *Evgenia Lezina*

In terms of the hardware, three standard projects of information systems were elaborated and adopted to be used at large, small and microcomputers ("Delta-ES," "Delta-SM" and "Delta-MK" correspondingly) at the KGB's 164 main territorial bodies. By 1988,

> based on a typical mathematical and programming software, three subsystems in the centre (CBD, "Delta-Potok," "Personalia-NSI") and the automated systems in the KGB of Ukraine and Latvia as well as in the KGB Directorates of the Leningrad and Sverdlovsk regions apt to work at large "ES"-type computers were built.[85]

A standard project in the regional KGB offices for mini "SM"-type computers required up to 60 automated information systems (*avtomatizirovannye informatsionnye sistemy, AIS*); a "Delta-micro" standard project required more than a hundred. It was officially prescribed to give priority to domestic over foreign equipment.[86]

Nevertheless, full-fledged computerisation of regional structures was evidently a long way to go. Answering in April 1989 a question about the approximate time frame for resolving the issue of computerising counterintelligence processes of the entire Committee, the then head of the KGB Vladimir Kryuchkov (1988–1991) frankly acknowledged that "it won't be soon."[87] Lieutenant Colonel Valentin Korolev, who until February 1987 held the post of a deputy head of the department for combating espionage of the Second Service of the UKGB for Moscow and the Moscow region, openly confessed in 1990 that Soviet counterintelligence officers "saw computers only in magazines and on TV, that is, not more often and not much closer than the bulk of the population" of the USSR.[88] However, according to the available official data, by the late 1980s, the central unit of the ESIOK and over 60 automated systems in the subdivisions of the central office and in the KGB regional branches were commissioned.[89]

In March 1988, the Main Computing Center (Glavnyi vychislitelnyi tsentr, GVTs) of the KGB was built in Dzerzhinskaya (since 1990 – Lubyanskaya) Square in Moscow, next to the Committee's headquarters (see Figure 2.1). It was put into operation as a new technical base for the ESIOK. Possessing "a set of computer equipment (computing power), communications, preparation and transmission of data, subscriber stations, service and other auxiliary equipment," the Main Computing Centre was destined to transfer the automated systems of counterintelligence and other units to a new technological base.[90] Automation of information chains with subdivisions of the KGB central apparatus was realised with the help of subscriber stations (*abonetskiye punkty*) located at the subdivisions' facilities around Lubyanskaya square and linked to the Main Computer Center. Data connections between the KGB territorial bodies and GVTs were organised using the "Rodnik-Istok" data transmission system.[91]

Starting from 1989, the KGB directorates as well as regional counterintelligence units could gain their own EDP systems (*avtomatizirovannaya sistema obrabotki dannykh*, ASOD) which likewise operated at the GVTs. ASOD accumulated the

Dogma versus progress 49

Figure 2.1 The building of the former KGB Main Computing Center in Lubyanskaya square today houses the Information Security Center (TsIB) of Russia's Federal Security Service (FSB).

Source: Photograph by the author.

specific data meeting interests and needs of operational departments – the data that was not subject to submission to the segments of the central link of the ESIOK. And yet, ASOD possessed a software integrated into and compatible with the ESIOK CBD, ASIO KD and an automated databank (*avtomatizirovannyi bank dannykh*, ABD) on the lines of the work of counterintelligence directorates.[92] Additionally, the Main Computing Center provided a technical base for the Scientific Research Information and Analytical Institute of the KGB of the USSR.[93] Among other things, NIIAI created and distributed the algorithms and programmes for computers within the whole KGB's realm.[94]

At the regional level, specifically trained "information officers" were put in charge of preparing data for the ESIOK and other automated systems as well as of obtaining from them information necessary for the operational staff.[95] However, the crucial question would be how this ever-growing mountain of data was actually processed and interpreted and in what way it affected the practice of operational activities. The following section will focus on these issues.

50   Evgenia Lezina

Making use of accumulated data: secret police and data analysis

Despite all the achievements reported by the KGB operational staff and management, organisation of information and analytical work in the Soviet state security structures was not unproblematic. In fact, the shortcomings lamented from the very start seemed to persist until the end of the Soviet rule.

At the regional level, a basic problem was that many city and most district apparatuses did not have employees specifically assigned for analytical work. In this situation, operational officers represented the primary link between the field work and operational analysis.[96] Highly limited in resources and constantly overloaded with work, they were often unable to provide the necessary level of data accumulation and processing. As the head of the KGB district section in the Lithuanian Trakai reported during one of the meetings in the early 1980s,

> the operational staff of the unit is always very busy and simply not able to do all this in a timely manner. Therefore, sometimes they postpone it to a later time, and then completely forget it. As a result, we do not take into account all the contacts that deserve operative attention.[97]

In 1982, the Chekists from the Kazakh SSR acknowledged that the study of the operating environment in their republican KGB had significant flaws. The head of I&A department, Kubash Tastaibekov and his co-worker Nikolai Nelidov wrote in an internal publication stating that until then, there had been "no clear system of analysis, approaches to the formulation of the researched problem had differed, and the issues that should be studied had been poorly worked out."[98] As a result, the authors concluded,

> the analysis by a number of regional bodies poorly took into account the identified intelligence and other aspirations . . . which sometimes led to its superficial assessment, got reflected on the quality of planning and implementation of the Chekists' activities.[99]

The problems with the information and analytical work in the KGB branches appeared to continue throughout the 1980s. "Despite the fact that considerable efforts and resources are spent on organizing I&A work, it is often the case that operational materials are scattered, processed unskillfully, at best, they are accumulated without appropriate generalization and analysis," admitted in late 1988 Major General Gennadii Grishanin, First Deputy Head of the KGB's Inspection Directorate in charge of supervision over the territorial KGB bodies.[100]

In late September 1985, the Collegium of the KGB of the Ukrainian SSR issued a special decision in which it strongly criticised the development of I&A work in the regional offices of the republic. Underscoring the following, the Collegium drew attention to the major flaws that reigned in the I&A realm:

> [A] significant part of the leading and operational staff of counterintelligence units has not yet been imbued with an understanding of the significance of

Dogma versus progress   51

I&A work as an important means and a meaningful reserve for improving the organization of intelligence and operational activities.

Among the flaws, for instance, were a shallow study of the ESIOK Thematic list of information and vocabularies of the SIO KD "Delta-U" as well as their inept use in training of agents, assessing and selecting information for accounting in the system; untimely introduction of the obtained operatively significant information into the regional systems, and long delays in sending it for processing to the republican and central banks of operational data of the ESIOK "Delta"; neglect of "thematic processing, improvement of analysis and issuance of data accumulated in the system"; not making the most of the operational data concentrated in information systems, letter-coded and other cases in analytical work and so on.[101]

Writing for *Sbornik KGB SSSR* as late as in 1989, the head of the KGB Kabardino-Balkarian Autonomous Republic Major General Stanislav Pyatakov and his co-author also confessed that "despite the relatively large volume of . . . operatively significant data and the available capabilities of electronic computer technology, the level of information and analytical work as a whole have not yet satisfied the needs of operational practice."[102] According to the Chekists from Nalchik, primary reasons for this were that "many of the chiefs and operational staff have . . . clearly not examined and correctly used the Thematic List of the ESIOK in practice, which leads to loss of data or poor and incomplete accounting of them."[103] Additionally, Pyatakov stated that frequently information was not reported in a timely fashion in the CBD and agent cards were updated too late. Some operational officers sabotaged data entry into the ESIOK under the pretext of "secrecy" of information. Entries were also made without evaluating their relationship to previous data. Thus, evidence on the operating environment appeared disrupted and was impossible to make use of.[104]

Likewise, field officers from several locations criticised the very organisation of I&A work in their regional directorates (they even expressed mutual solidarity on this in a few contributions to *Sbornik*). As the operatives from Smolensk put it in their 1991 article, "the capabilities of the information-analytical groups (IAG) of the KGB were not adapted to meet the needs of priority lines."[105] According to the authors, "the obstacle was a certain isolation of IAG from the problems of operational units, insufficient flexibility of information bookmarking programs, statistical approaches and quantitative criteria of work, as well as significant difficulties in their staffing."[106] Due to these problems, some of the regional KGB bodies chose to set up supernumerary analysis teams within their Second departments to better obtain and analyse the data.[107]

Another continuous problem was that of analysis in the KGB central apparatus. Clearly, accumulated piles of data were to be processed and taken advantage of in decision-making processes. Despite the expansion of the KGB's information-gathering functions manifested in the emergence of large centralised databases and surveillance systems, its analytical activity lagged behind considerably, which secret police leadership also admitted.

52 *Evgenia Lezina*

Back in 1969, one of the leading officers at the central office complained that operative staff "poorly used the collected information in solving operative tasks and that they contact I&A units rarely."[108] He proceeded, admitting that

> a careful examination of some analytical reports shows that they do not meet the requirements for such documents. At best, they are only a good generalization of operative information. The conclusions presented in them, as a rule, do not contain a substantiation supported by a profound analytical study of the issues under consideration.[109]

The problems of this sort persisted until the late 1980s.

In fact, for many years the all-union KGB did not possess an analytical apparatus of its own. There were some proto-structures, but it was not until September 1989 that a comprehensive Service of Operational Analysis and Information (SOAI) was finally set up.[110] It can be assumed that this was due to the fact that the Soviet secret police, fixated on "internal enemies," "antisocial elements," "subversive activities" and "ideological diversion," was unable to seriously focus on analytical work that goes hand in hand with critical thinking (which represented a sedition or *kramola*, in Soviet official mindset).

Nevertheless, by the end of *perestroika*, due to the growing instability and uncertainty, the need for analysis of internal data in the central apparatus ostensibly became an absolute necessity and an overarching priority admitting no delay. In August 1990, the KGB Collegium issued the decision "On Measures to Improve Information and Analytical Work in Counterintelligence," which recognised that "the centralized analysis and forecast of aspirations, forms, methods and tactics of subversive activities of foreign special services" was not performed and that "the quality of prioritization, planning, and coordination of analytical studies and the implementation of their results in practice remain[ed] low."[111] The KGB Collegium concluded that "the reasons for these and a number of other shortcomings consist[ed] primarily in the absence of a modern scientific outlook and the system of information and analytical work in the KGB of the USSR."[112]

The KGB Collegium's decision provided for the inauguration of the Analytical Directorate of the KGB of the USSR, which came to replace SOAI on October 19, 1990 – that is less than one year before the Soviet regime's collapse.[113] The last KGB chief Vadim Bakatin wrote in 1992 that before joining the Committee in the fall of 1991, he had been "confident of the enormous intellectual and analytical capabilities of this organization."[114] "Frankly," confessed Bakatin, "I was disappointed. . . . Thinking in broad political categories was allowed only in the Old Square, and the role of the KGB was mainly to formulate primary data and carry out the decisions already taken."[115]

Partly the source of the problem might have been the low quality of I&A staff. After the KGB Analytical Directorate was established in late 1990, its boss Nikolai Leonov, who had previously headed the foreign intelligence I&A Directorate in 1971–1983, in an interview to *Sbornik KGB SSSR* highlighted the customary approach to the selection of personnel for the counterintelligence I&A units. "If

Dogma versus progress   53

someone messed up, appeared lazy, and not capable of anything, it meant that he was quite 'ripe' to be transferred [to I&A section]. As a result, we have what we have,"[116] stated Leonov, simultaneously drawing attention to the fact that "analysts are not trained in the educational institutions of the Committee. Nor are they trained in civilian universities" of the USSR.[117]

Another part of the problem in the field of analysis might be the inadequacy of the KGB's own educational approach. Numerically, the expansion of educational capacities looked impressive. From 1930 to 1952 (in 22 years until the emergence of the Higher School as the higher educational institution), about 20,000 operational workers were trained and underwent advanced training at the Dzerzhinsky Higher School.[118] In 1986, the then KGB chairman Viktor Chebrikov (1982–1988) announced that in the following five years alone, they planned to train 22,300 people at the KGB schools and another 53,500 were supposed to undergo advanced training.[119]

Likewise, the expansion of academic work was substantial. The postgraduate studies were launched in 1954 and over 26 years until 1980, 474 dissertations were defended (440 graduates got "candidates of science" (*kandidatskaya*) degrees and 34 doctoral degrees). In the next five years, between 1981 and 1985, 231 graduates received academic titles (including 13 doctors and 218 candidates of science).[120] In 1986 the KGB chief stated that the next 12th Five-year plan would bring about 598 graduates with academic degrees – 27 doctors and 571 candidates of science.[121]

Yet the available documents make it clear that the Chekist education of cadre was unable to meet the challenges of time. In fact, during the *perestroika* period it became common ground within the KGB leadership and academic staff to admit that "the level of education of graduates of the Higher School d[id] not quite correspond to the needs of modern practice."[122] More so, in one of the orders issued by the KGB chairman in December 1988, every aspect of the Higher School's activity was severely criticised: methods of teaching and educational work, advanced training, instructional materials, work with permanent staff, the system of training scientific and pedagogical personnel and so forth. Furthermore, KGB officials recognised that "the organization of scientific research and the introduction of its results into the educational process and operational practice require[d] a radical restructuring."[123]

Documentary sources reveal that the "Chekist science" was intellectual hostage to its own ideological bias, such as the class-struggle concept and other postulates of Marxism-Leninism. As Victor Yasmann correctly underscored:

> In reality, the Dzerzhinskiy Higher School was . . . kind of an academy of "Chekist sciences and practice," a collective bearer of "esprit de corps," and the bulwark of a distinct totalitarian ideology known to the specialists as "Chekism".[124]

There is a high probability that for this exact reason, that is due to ideological limitations, the KGB's internal structures did not manage to obtain a scientifically

54   *Evgenia Lezina*

grounded view of the Soviet society and to generate scientifically based social analysis, despite the attempts to do so.

Conclusion

In the post-Stalin era, the communist party was trapped in an escalating tension between the restrictions contingent upon ideological dogmas and the pressures of scientific and technical progress. This conflict turned the history of the KGB into a story of paradoxes. The second half of the Soviet rule was marked by the diversification of the internal intelligence structures and the expansion of its information-gathering function as well as by the efforts to intellectualise and professionalise the operational staff and to improve the training of cadre. Despite a constant emphasis on academic and personnel enhancement and improvement of technological base, the implemented measures turned out inadequate.

Since the mid-1980s, the Soviet secret police found itself in permanent instability. It started with warnings of the emergence of "new pockets of agitation" in the early 1980s and ended up facing a brand new reality by the end of the decade. The appearance of totally new social phenomena such as "national fronts," mass protests, independent deputies, harder-to-control media, and so forth posed a serious challenge to the KGB. This new environment explains many attempts of belated reforms and action taken in an emergency order, like the creation of the analytical service or the restructuring of the educational system.

The role of the internal security structures in the Soviet state appears significantly different from that in Western democracies. The overall concern of the Soviet political police with "ideological subversion" by internal and external "foes" entailed an almost unlimited expansion of ideologically unacceptable behaviour subject to registration and further sanctioning. This led to a considerable overstretching of criminalisation and a continuous expansion of the range of application of criminal law.[125] Such an approach burdened the system and threatened an exhaustion of resources and fatigue from the constant race.

The sources available in the archives of the former Soviet republics seem to support the argument that the Soviet secret police was "far worse at intelligence analysis than at intelligence collection."[126] Based on the new findings, it can also be argued that an eventual academisation of the KGB did not, in fact, foster scientisation, as analytic thinking grounded in critical thinking was largely alien to the state security agencies. The fact that a comprehensive analytical service was not formed in the KGB central apparatus until the end of the 1980s testifies to avoidance rather than lack of resources or necessity. Interestingly, in one *Sbornik* article published as early as in 1965, the author quite eloquently described the achievements in analytical work by the West German counterintelligence structures, emphasising that between 20 and 50 per cent of the central office's staff were employed in the analytical divisions.[127]

The Soviet Chekists could neither create their own science nor use the borrowed scientific resources from other disciplines. Hostage to its own ideological tenets, the strange brainchild of the Soviet system the "Chekist science" was incapable of

Dogma versus progress   55

undistorted knowledge-production. In fact, an "operating environment" which the Chekists relentlessly endeavoured to fathom was for them above all a "class category."[128] "Its research and evaluation," according to the internal KGB regulations, required "strict adherence to the principles of partisanship (*strogogo soblyudeniya prinitsipov partiinosti*)" and "assessments of the international and internal political situations, trends in their development, the activities of forces hostile to our country, elaborated by the CPSU Central Committee."[129]

Although the Soviet secret police made efforts to react to changes in the social and political environment with modernisation and scientisation, the outcome of these attempts amounted to the launching of vast databases with compromising materials to track potentially disloyal citizens and either sanction them whenever deemed necessary or put them under stronger surveillance. Thus, digitisation and unified data accumulation allowed for placing "a cupola of control" over Soviet society and foreign visitors but did not ultimately generate scientifically valid knowledge able to offer a solution for overcoming the system's stalemate.

Notes

1 Hodnet, *Resolutions*, 234. This chapter was prepared as part of a research project funded by the German Research Foundation (Deutsche Forschungsgemeinschaft; DFG) – Projektnummer 403506742.
2 See, for instance, Baberowski, "Wege aus der Gewalt."
3 Dziak, *Chekisty* 2–3.
4 Ibid., 1.
5 Created in 1954 as a union-republic state committee, the KGB was transformed from a body under the Council of Ministers of the USSR into the central body of state administration of the USSR with the rights of a state committee – the KGB of the USSR – on 5 July 1978. As of January 1990, the all-union KGB had state committees in 14 republics (KGB of the Russian SFSR was created only in May 1991) and in 20 autonomous republics (ASSR). Below the republican level existed 121 KGB directorates (*upravleniya*) in the regions (*oblasti*). At the lower levels in autonomous regions and areas (*okruga*) as well as some cities there existed KGB departments (*otdely*) and at level of districts there were sections (*raiotdeleniya*). The total number of *gorraiorgany* reached 1,810 as of 1990. To add to this, the state security agencies ran the system of special departments (*osobye otdely*) in the armed forces. The KGB functioned as a military structure, so the relationships between its central apparatus and territorial bodies were that of rigid centralization and tough subordination. See: Prikaz Predsedatelya KGB pri SM SSSR No. 229–102 ot 2.3.1959 "Polozheniye o KGB pri SM SSSR." Galuzevii derzhavnii arkhiv Sluzhbi bezpeki Ukraini (GDA SBU) f. 9, spr. 28-sp, ark. 20–28. Ukazaniye Predsedatelya KGB SSSR No. 4s ot 1.1.1990 "O napravlenii spiska okruzhnykh, gorodskikh i rayonnykh otdelov-otdelenii KGB-UKGB (v t.ch. otdelov KGB-UKGB v avtonomnykh oblastyakh), otdelov-otdelenii KGB-UKGB po gorodam (rayonam) i transportnym ob'yektam, a takzhe otdelov UKGB po promyshlennym ob'yektam." GDA SBU, f. 9, spr. 371-sp, ark. 103–128ob. Knight, *The KGB*, 120–125.
6 Yuri Andropov, "O zadachakh organov gosudarstvennoĭ bezopasnosti v svete reshenii 26-go s'yezda KPSS," 25.5.1981, in: *Deyatel'nost' organov gosudarstvennoi bezopasnosti SSSR na sovremennom etape. Sbornik dokumentov i materialov. V. 2.* (M.: Vysshaya Krasnoznamennaya shkola KGB SSSR imeni F. Dzerzhinskogo (VKSh), 1983), 37.
7 Chebrikov, "Istoriya sovetskih organov gosudarstvennoi bezopasnosti," 534, 546.

56 *Evgenia Lezina*

8 F. Bobkov, "Ideologicheskaya diversiya imperializma protiv SSSR i deyatel'nost' organov KGB po bor'be s nei." Lietuvos Ypatingasis Archyvas (LYA), f. K-51, ap. 1, b. 325, l. 25.

9 Kharkhordin, *The Collective and the Individual*, 299. See also Hornsby, *Protest, Reform and Repression*, 197–221.

10 Reid, "The Khrushchev Kitchen," 290.

11 Prikaz Predsedatelya KGB pri SM SSSR No. 00182 ot 2.7.1959 "Ob organizatsii Operativno-Tekhnicheskogo upravleniya KGB pri SM SSSR." GDA SBU, f. 9, spr. 273-sp, ark. 49.

12 Prikaz Predsedatelya KGB pri SM SSSR No. 0026 ot 11.2.1960. "O vnesenii izmenenii v strukturu KGB pri SM SSSR i yego organov na mestakh i sokrashchenii ikh shtatnoi chislennosti." GDA SBU, f. 9, spr. 280-sp, ark. 14–24.

13 Prikaz Predsedatelya KGB pri SM SSSR No. 0097 ot 25.7.1967 "O vnesenii izmenenii v strukturu Komiteta gosbezopasnosti pri SM SSSR i yego organov na mestakh." GDA SBU, f. 9, spr. 28-sp, ark. 75–76.

14 W. Tompson quotes data by the Soviet Central Statistical Administration (TsSU) as of 1985: "Between 1959 and 1984, the proportion of Soviet adults with a full higher educational qualification more than tripled, to 8.2 per cent. A further 1.6 per cent had incomplete tertiary education, while 36.4 per cent had completed secondary education (specialized or general), as compared with just 15.8 per cent in 1959," Tompson, *The Soviet Union*, 87.

15 See: Criminal Code of the Russian Soviet Federated Socialist Republic enacted in 1960. <https://chronicle-of-current-events.com/the-rsfsr-criminal-code/Soviet-laws/>

16 Chebrikov, "Istoriya sovetskih organov gosudarstvennoi bezopasnosti," 591. On détente see Stevenson, *The Rise and Fall*; Bowker, *Brezhnev*.

17 Resolyutsiya TsK KPSS i SM SSSR ot 1.10.1970 "O merakh po usileniyu rezhima sekretnosti." Cited in: ibid, 575. See also Lezina, "Soviet State Security."

18 Evdokushin and Kurashvili, "O dal'neishem razvitii informatsionnoi," 22.

19 Ibid.

20 Prikaz Predsedatelya KGB pri SM SSSR No. 0072 ot 10.5.1965. Cited in: Gorshkov and Pikulev, "Organizatsiya informatsionno-analiticheskoi raboty," 31.

21 Evdokushin and Kurashvili, "O dal'neishem razvitii informatsionnoi," 22.

22 Prikaz Predsedatelya KGB pri SM SSSR No. 0115 ot 17.5.1967 "Ob o'yavlenii Vremennogo polozheniya ob organizatsii analiticheskoi raboty vo Vtorom glavnom upravlenii KGB i v mestnykh organakh KGB-UKGB-OKGB." Cited in: Gorshkov and Pikulev, "Organizatsiya informatsionno-analiticheskoi raboty," 31.

23 In the late 1960s the regional KGB bodies mostly used P80-6 or PD-45 punchers with 80-column or 45-column punched cards or edged-punched cards of K-5 format (207x147 mm) as well as corresponding sorting machines (C80–5 and C45–5). On the early experiences of organizing information and analytical work in the KGB regional bodies see: Gorshkov and Pikulev, "Organizatsiya informatsionno-analiticheskoi raboty," 31–36 (Gorky); Dichenko, "Iz praktiki organizatsii informatsionno-analiticheskoi raboty," 36–43 (Kiev); Rodionov and Kuznetsov, "Nekotoryi opyt sozdaniya informatsionno-poiskovoi sistemy," 36–40 (Sverdlovsk); Barzhin, "Perfokartnyi uchet operativnoi informatsii," 43–44 (Tyumen'); Bakhirev, "Ob organizatsii informatsionnogo massiva v oblastnom Upravlenii KGB," 103–110 (Smolensk); Dmitriyev, "Analiz v khode operativnoi proverki i razrabotki," 95–98.

24 Prikaz Predsedatelya KGB pri SM SSSR No. 0395 ot 10.10.1969 "O sozdanii informatsionno-analiticheskikh podradelenii v KGB soyuznykh, avtonomnykh respublik i UKGB po krayam i oblastyam." GDA SBU, f. 9, spr. 32-sp, ark. 24–30.

25 Ibid., 27.

26 Spravka No. 15/1957 ot 31.12.1970 po itogam raboty informatsionno-analiticheskogo otdeleniya KGB pri SM Litovskoi SSR za 1970 god. LYA, f. K-1, ap. 3, b. 790, l. 1–2.

27 Prikaz Predsedatelya KGB pri SM SSSR No. 0046 ot 5.5.1969. Cited in: Soldatov, "Analitika v organakh gosudarstvennoi bezopasnosti." At first the NIIAI functioned

Dogma versus progress 57

within the Eighth Chief (Encryption and Decryption) Directorate and later within Sixteenth Directorate (electronic reconnaissance, radio interception and decryption) created on 21 June 1973. Afterwards it became part of the O&T Directorate. See: Prikaz Predsedatelya KGB SSSR No. 00161 ot 16.8.1982 "Ob utverzhdenii Ustava Nauchno-issledovatel'skogo informatsionno-analiticheskogo instituta OTU KGB SSSR." GDA SBU, f. 9, spr. 30-sp, ark. 80–84.

28 Prikaz Predsedatelya KGB pri SM SSSR No. 0072 ot 4.7.1974 "Ob utverzhdenii i vvedenii v deistviye Polozheniya o filiale NIIAI 16 Upravleniya KGB v gorode Kiev." GDA SBU, f. 9, spr. 28-sp, ark. 175–182.

29 Evdokushin and Kurashvili, "O dal'neishem razvitii informatsionnoi," 26. Edinyi slovar' chekistkoi terminologii. Chast' II. Kontrrazvedka. M.: VKSh, 1988. GDA SBU, f. 13, spr. 696, ark. 94–95, 255.

30 Materialy seminara zamestitelei nachal'nikov upravlenii i rukovoditelei informatsionno-analiticheskikh podrazdelenii oblastnykh upravlenii KGB respubliki. Kiev, 2–3.12.1968. GDA SBU, f. 13, spr. 622, ark. 70.

31 Ibid.

32 Prikaz Predsedatelya KGB pri SM SSSR No. 00109 ot 1.11.1971 "O razrabotke i sozdanii Edinoi sistemy informatsionnogo obespecheniya kontrrazvedki (shifr "Delta")." GDA SBU, f. 9, spr. 91-sp, ark. 102.

33 Ibid., 102ob. On obtaining data from Visa and Passport Departments (OVIR) of the Ministry of Internal Affairs, the Ministry of Foreign Affairs of the Union Republics and diplomatic agencies of the Ministry of Foreign Affairs of the USSR see: Prikaz Predsedatelya KGB SSSR No. 0632 ot 22.10.1986 "O poryadke podgotovki i peredachi v sistemu 'Delta' informatsii o inostrannykh grazhdanakh i litsakh bez grazhdanstva dlya obespecheniya kontrolya za ikh prebyvaniyem v strane i vyezdom iz SSSR." GDA SBU, f. 9, spr. 122-sp, ark. 78–141.

34 Ibid., 102ob.-103. Prikaz Predsedatelya KGB SSSR No. 0153 ot 12.3.1988 "O perestroike informatsionno-analiticheskoi raboty v KGB SSSR v svyazi s vvodom v ekspluatatsiyu Glavnogo vychislitel'nogo tsentra KGB SSSR." GDA SBU, f. 9, spr. 34-sp, ark. 330.

35 Ukazaniye Predsedatelya KGB pri SM SSSR No. 84s ot 7.12.1972 "O vvedenii v deistviye Instruktsii o poryadke razrabotki i vvedeniya Edinoi sistemy informatsionnogo obespecheniya kontrrazvedki (shifr "Delta")." GDA SBU, f. 9, spr. 111-sp. Spravka po informatsionnym sistemam "Delta" i "Delta-U" ot 2.9.1976. GDA SBU, f. 9, spr. 367, ark. 192–196. The order provided for the following major stages of the ESIOK implementation: "1. Pre-design survey of KGB units carrying out counterintelligence activities (1972–1974). 2. Development of a preliminary design of the system and assignments for the technical design of the operational information part, information base, mathematical and engineering support, as well as the introduction of specialized systems "Fort-67" and "Fregat" (1975–1976). 3. Development of the technical design of the system, i.e. organizational and functional structure, information language of the "Delta" system (1976–1977). At this stage, methods of solving information problems using modern technical means, transferring, storing and processing information, switching on electronic computers, means and equipment for transmitting data for the central office and local KGB bodies, are determined. 4. Development of a working project of the system. At this stage, documentation for the operation of technical means and equipment is prepared, instructions, plans for the implementation and development of the system are drawn up, personnel are completed and trained, technical means and equipment are purchased and placed (1977–1978). 5. Implementation and development of the system (1979–1980)."

36 Prikaz Predsedatelya KGB pri SM SSSR No. 0326 ot 7.4.1973 "O vvode v deistviye v kontrrazvedyvatel'nykh podrazdeleniyakh KGB informatsionnoi sistemy 'Fort-67' i utverzhdenii Instruktsii po eye ekspluatatsii." LYA, f. K-51, ap. 3, b. 9, l. 184–187. Ukazaniye Predsedatelya KGB pri SM SSSR Ukrainskoi SSR No. 3s ot 7.4.1973 "Ob organizatsii raboty po sistemam 'Fort-67' i 'Fregat'." GDA SBU, f. 9, spr. 150-sp, ark. 60–65.

58   *Evgenia Lezina*

37 Telyatnikova, "Nekotorye actual'nye problemy perestroiki," 397.
38 See, for e.g.: Prikaz Predsedatelya KGB pri SM SSSR No. 0158 ot 8.4.1970 "Ob o'yavlenii resheniya Kollegii KGB pri SM SSSR ot 30.1.1970 "O sostoyanii i merakh po uluchsheniyu raboty s molodymi sotrudnikami operativnykh podrazdelenii organov gosbezopasnosti." The document is part of the "KGB Documents Online" collection.
39 Yasmann, *The KGB Documents: Part II*, 9.
40 Ibid.
41 Ragozin, "Vysshei shkole kontrrazvedki," 27–57.
42 Ibid. In 1960 Counterintelligence Faculty for preparation of operative staff with the knowledge of Western languages (No. 2) and Faculty of Special Technical Services (since 1962 – Technical Faculty No. 4) were introduced. In 1962 Military Counterintelligence Faculty (No. 1) was set up. In 1971 Faculty No. 6 for training of graduates and advanced training of operational and management personnel of the security agencies of friendly countries was organized. In 1973 Faculty No. 3 for training of operational staff with knowledge of Oriental languages was launched. In 1976 correspondence training was introduced (Faculty No. 8) and a preparatory division was set up to attract mostly young workers (by 1980 25–30 per cent of students of counterintelligence faculties went through it). In 1979 Faculty No. 5 for advanced training of senior staff as well as Investigation Faculty No. 10 (on the basis of the department for training of investigators) were opened. In 1980 the Higher School got Faculty No. 9 for training of operational staff with knowledge of the languages of the Middle East and Africa. See: Sever, *Istoriya KGB*, 84–85; Postnikov, *Kratkii ocherk istorii Vysshei shkoly KGB SSSR imeni F. Dzerzhinskogo* (M.: VKSh, 1990). Ragozin, "Vysshei shkole kontrrazvedki," 53–54.
43 Tompson, *The Soviet Union under Brezhnev*, 50.
44 O zadachakh organov gosudarstvennoi bezopasnosti v svete reshenii XXVI s'yezda. Doklad Predsedatelya KGB SSSR Yu. V. Andropova na Vsesoyuznom soveshchanii rukovodyashchego sostava organov i voisk KGB SSSR, 25.5.1981. In: *Deyatel'nost' organov gosudarstvennoi bezopasnosti SSSR na sovremennom etape. Sbornik dokumentov i materialov. V. 2.* (M.: VKSh, 1983), 38.
45 Ibid.
46 Ibid., 127–128.
47 Prikaz Predsedatelya KGB SSSR No. 00210 ot 16.4.1982, "Ob o'yavlenii resheniya Kollegii KGB SSSR ot 25.10.1982 "O merakh po usileniyu kontrrazvedyvatel'noi raboty po zashite ekonomiki strany ot podryvnoi deyatel'nosti protivnika." GDA SBU, f. 9, spr. 72-sp, ark. 392–401.
48 Prikaz Predsedatelya KGB SSSR No. 0495 ot 6.8.1979 "O vvode v ekspluatatsiyu avtomatizirovannoi informatsionnoi sistemy "Delta-Potok" i utverzhdenii Instruktsii o poryadke postanovki na tsentralizovannyi kontrol'nyi uchet v avtomatizirovannoi informatsionnoi sisteme (AIS) "Delta-Potok" v'yezzhayushchikh v SSSR inostrantsev i zakrytiya im v'yezda v Sovetskii Soyuz." LYA, f. K-51, ap. 3, b. 19, l. 157–167.
49 Ustinov et al., "Osnovnye itogi raboty," 154–155.
50 Ibid. As it was stated, "In order to increase the reliability of the functioning of the automated information systems that are part of the complex, the NIIAI of the 16th Directorate of the KGB of the USSR used four "Minsk-32" computers and three "ES-1022" computers (third generation), temporarily relocating them from solving other tasks."
51 Prikaz Predsedatelya KGB SSSR No. 0598 ot 19.9.1990 "Ob o'yavlenii resheniya Kollegii KGB SSSR ot 3.8.1990 'O merakh po sovershenstvovaniyu informatsionnoi i analiticheskoi raboty v kontrrazvedke'." LYA, f. K-51, ap. 3, b. 64, l. 88–88atv.
52 Ibid.
53 Pipia, "K voprosu ob otsenke," 18–37.
54 Prikaz Predsedatelya KGB SSSR No. 0151 ot 18.3.1986 "Ob utverzhdenii Polozheniya ob informatsionno-analiticheskikh podrazdeleniyakh KGB soyuznykh i avtonomnykh respublik, UKGB po krayam i oblastyam." GDA SBU, f. 9, spr. 127-sp, ark. 171–176.

Dogma versus progress 59

55 Ukazaniye Predsedatelya KGB SSSR No. 18s ot 19.3.1984. Cited in: "O perekhode na edinyi poryadok otbora, nakopleniya, obrabotki i vydachi informatsii v KGB Litovskoi SSR. Informatsionno-analiticheskoye upravleniye KGB Litovskoi SSR, 30.10.1984. LYA, f. K-1, ap. 56, b. 58, l. 1.

56 Pipia, "K voprosu ob otsenke," 18.

57 Pipia and Seletkov, "Printsipy postroeniya ESIOK," 323.

58 Prikaz Predsedatelya KGB SSSR No. 00238 ot 31.12.1981. Cited in: Pipia and Seletkov, "Printsipy postroeniya ESIOK," 319. See also: Ukazaniye Predsedatelya KGB SSSR No. 26s ot 5.4.1985 "O dal'neishem sovershenstvovanii poryadka otbora, nakopleniya v informatsionnykh sistemakh kontrrazvedki i ispol'zovaniya v operativnoi deyatel'nosti svedenii na lits iz chisla grazhdan SSSR." GDA SBU, f. 9, spr. 71-sp, ark. 332–334. Prikaz Predsedatelya KGB SSSR No. 0136 ot 14.3.1990 "Ob utverzhdenii Perechnya svedenii, podlezhashchikh otboru dlya nakopleniya v ESIOK." GDA SBU, f. 9, spr. 102-sp, ark. 66–74.

59 "O perekhode na edinyi poryadok otbora, nakopleniya, obrabotki i vydachi informatsii v KGB Litovskoi SSR." Informatsionno-Analiticheskoye upravleniye KGB Litovskoi SSR, 30.10.1984. LYA, f. K-1, ap. 56, b. 58, l. 3–4.

60 Ibid., L. 4–5.

61 Ibid., L. 3.

62 See, for instance, Pis'mo nachal'nika 6-go Upravleniya KGB USSR No. 7193 ot 31.8.1984 s predlozheniyami po vneseniyu dopolnenii v slovari informatsionnoi sistemy "Delta-NK." GDA SBU, f. 31, op. 1, spr. 3, ark. 188–192.

63 See: Vypiska iz perechnya svedenii, podlezhashchikh uchetu i nakopleniyu v sisteme "Delta-Litva." LYA, f. K-1, op. 56, d. 80, l. 1–121.

64 Rodionov and Kuznetsov, "Nekotoryi opyt sozdaniya informatsionno-poiskovoi sistemy," 37.

65 Ibid.

66 Among locally specific clusters in Ukraine were, for e.g., "Final-51" (subversive activities of the Organization of Ukrainian Nationalists abroad, their leaders, members, emissaries and like-minded persons in the territory of the Ukrainian SSR) and "Slavutich" (intelligence and subversive activities of foreigners). See: Predlozheniya No. 4/745 ot 13.5.1985 po obespecheniyu vypolneniya ukazaniya Predsedatelya KGB SSSR No. 26s ot 5.4.1985. GDA SBU, f. 31, op. 1, spr. 6, ark. 55–56. Godovyye plany raboty IAS KGB USSR i otchety ob ikh vypolnenii. T. 2, 1981–1983. GDA SBU, f. 32, op. 1, spr. 6, ark. 168, 274, 312.

67 Predlozheniya No. 4/745 ot 13.5.1985 po obespecheniyu vypolneniya ukazaniya Predsedatelya KGB SSSR No. 26s ot 5.4.1985. GDA SBU, f. 31, op. 1, spr. 6, ark. 55–56.

68 N. Emokhonov. Osnovnye napravleniya sovershenstvovaniya tekhnicheskoi osnashchennosti operativnykh podrazdelenii i tekhnicheskikh sluzhb organov KGB, in: *Deyatel'nost' organov gosudarstvennoi bezopasnosti SSSR na sovremennom etape. Sbornik dokumentov i materialov. V. 3.* (M: VKSh, 1986), 269.

69 Prikaz Predsedatelya KGB SSSR No. 00224 ot 30.12.1985 "Ob o'yavlenii resheniya Kollegii KGB SSSR ot 17.12.1985 'O merakh po usileniyu bor'by s razvedyvatel'no-podryvnoi deyatel'nost'yu spetssluzhb protivnika, osushchestvlyayemoi s pozitsii firm kapitalisticheskikh gosudarstv, ikh predstavitel'stv i spetsialistov'." GDA SBU, f. 9, spr. 31-sp, ark. 25.

70 Matyunin and Grachev, "Ob informatsionnom obespechenii," 173–174.

71 Prikaz Predsedatelya KGB SSSR No. 0735 ot 27.11.1989 "Ob o'yavlenii resheniya Kollegii KGB SSSR ot 27.10.1989 'O dal'neishem sovershenstvovanii gotovnosti organov i voisk KGB SSSR k deistviyam v chrezvychainykh situatsiyakh'." LYA, f. K-1, ap. 46, b. 183, l. 35.

72 Prikaz Predsedatelya KGB SSSR No. 0346 ot 18.5.1991 "O dopolnitel'nykh merakh po obespecheniyu gosudarstvennoi bezopasnosti v sfere deyatel'nosti sovmestnykh

60 *Evgenia Lezina*

predpriyatii s uchastiem sovetskikh i inostrannykh firm i kompanii." LYA, f. K-51, ap. 3 b. 68, l. 98, 102.

73 Prikaz Predsedatelya KGB SSSR No. 0078 ot 22.5.1991 "O zadachakh i merakh organov KGB v svyazi s vyvodom sovetskikh voisk iz-za granitsy." LYA, f. K-51, ap. 3, b. 68, l. 121atv.

74 Prikaz Predsedatelya KGB SSSR No. 0033 ot 28.2.1991 "O merakh po sovershenst-vovaniyu organizatsii i koordinatsii deyatel'nosti organov gosudarstvennoi bezopas-nosti v sfere razoruzheniya." LYA, f. K-51, ap. 3, b. 67, l. 5.

75 Prikaz Predsedatelya KGB Litovskoi SSR No. 0199 ot 11.10.1986 "Ob utverzhdenii Instruktsii po organizatsii i ekspluatatsii funktsional'nogo bloka 'Signal' informatsion-noi sistemy 'Delta-Litva' KGB Litovskoi SSR i vvoda etogo bloka v deistviye." LYA, f. K-51, op. 4, d. 5, l. 45–52b. On the early use of the "Signal" system see: Lantsov and Kuznetsov, "Informatsionnaya sistema 'Signal' v deistvii," 29–31. (Astrakhan'). Prikaz Predsedatelya KGB Litovskoi SSR No. 0230 ot 26.11.1986 "Ob utverzhdenii Instruktsii po organizatsii i ekspluatatsii funktsional'nogo bloka 'Kontrol' informat-sionnoi sistemy 'Delta-Litva' KGB Litovskoi SSR i vvoda etogo bloka v deistviye." LYA, f. K-51, op. 4, d. 5, l. 54–58.

76 Prikaz Predsedatelya KGB Litovskoi SSR No. 0116 ot 16.7.1987 "Ob utverzhdenii Instruktsii po organizatsii i ekspluatatsii funktsional'nogo bloka 'Luch-1' informat-sionnoi sistemy 'Delta-Litva' KGB Litovskoi SSR i vvoda etogo bloka v deistviye." LYA, f. K-51, op. 4, d. 7, l. 83–93.

77 The UKGB for Sverdlovsk region started the creation of an information complex ASIO KD "Delta-Sverdlovsk" with a number of local subsystems on a leased "Minsk-32" computer. Since March 1986 it switched to ES-1045. See: Kornilov and Fevralev, "Vozmozhnosti elektronno-vychislitel'noi tekhniki,"49–50. (Sverdlovsk)

78 Lugovets, "Tvorcheskomu poisku," 13–18. (Moscow)

79 Prikaz Predsedatelya KGB Litovskoi SSR No. 0197 ot 12.4.1989 "Ob ob'yavlenii Instruktsii po organizatsii i ekspluatatsii avtomatizirovannoi sistemy informatsionnogo obespecheniya kontrrazvedyvatel'noi deyatel'nosti KGB Litovskoi SSR (shifr "Delta-Litva")." LYA, f. K-51, op. 4, d. 11, l. 44–45.

80 Pipia and Seletkov, "Printsipy postroeniya ESIOK," 327–328.

81 Ibid.

82 Ibid.

83 Pipia, "K voprosu ob otsenke," 33.

84 Ibid.

85 Ibid., 28–29.

86 Ibid. As of 1990 in ASIO KD for the three standard projects of information systems computers of the following types were used: ES-1045, ES-1060, SM-4, SM-1420, SM-1425, "Iskra-226M," ES-1841, ES-1845. See: Prikaz Predsedatelya KGB SSSR No. 0463 of 25.7.1990 "Ob utverzhdenii Instruktsii o poryadke priobreteniya EVM otechestvennogo proizvodstva." GDA SBU, f. 9, spr. 78-sp, ark. 79–82.

87 Perestroika i rabota chekistov. Doklad chlena TsK KPSS, Predsedatelya KGB SSSR V. A. Kryuchkova na seminare-soveshchanii sekretarei partiynykh organizatsii tsentral'nogo apparata KGB SSSR 15.4.1989," *Sbornik KGB SSSR*, (133) 1989:25.

88 Korolev, "Sekrety sekretnykh sluzhb," 29.

89 Prikaz Predsedatelya KGB SSSR No. 0153 ot 12.3.1988 "O perestroike informatsi-onno-analiticheskoi raboty v KGB SSSR v svyazi s vvodom v ekspluatatsiyu Glavnogo vychislitel'nogo tsentra KGB SSSR." GDA SBU, f. 9, spr. 34-sp, ark. 319.

90 Ibid.

91 Ibid., 323ob.

92 Ibid., 324–324ob. Prikaz Predsedatelya KGB SSSR No. 0576 ot 11.9.1989 "Ob utverzhdenii Polozheniya ob avtomatizirovannoi sisteme obrabotki dannykh kontrrazvedyvatel'nogo podrazdeleniya." LYA, f. K-51, ap. 3, b. 56, l. 169–174atv.

Dogma versus progress 61

93 Prikaz Predsedatelya KGB SSSR No. 0153 ot 12.3.1988 "O perestroike informatsionno-analiticheskoi raboty v KGB SSSR v svyazi s vvodom v ekspluatatsiyu Glavnogo vychislitel'nogo tsentra KGB SSSR." GDA SBU, f. 9, spr. 34-sp, ark. 323–326.
94 Prikaz Predsedatelya KGB SSSR No. 0219 ot 18.4.1988 "Ob utverzhdenii Polozheniya o fonde algoritmov i programm dlya personal'nykh EVM v organakh KGB." GDA SBU, f. 9, spr. 100-sp, ark. 232–237.
95 Prikaz Predsedatelya KGB SSSR No. 28-dsp ot 1.6.1991 "Ob o'yavlenii Instruktsii po organizatsii deyatel'nosti operativnykh sotrudnikov, vedushchikh informatsionnuyu rabotu v kontrrazvedyvatel'nykh podrazdeleniyakh tsentral'nogo apparata KGB SSSR i KGB-UKGB." LYA, f. K-51, ap. 3, b. 69, l. 1–4.
96 E. Andriatis, "O putyakh sovershenstvovaniya analiticheskoi raboty v gorraiapparatakh v svete trebovanii prikaza KGB SSSR No. 0060–1979." KGB Litovskoi SSR. Informatsionno-analiticheskoye podrazdeleniye. Vilnius, 19.11.1980. LYA, f. K-1, ap. 56, b. 192, l. 46.
97 Ya. Radionov, "Vyyavleniye, organizatsiya raboty po izucheniyu i postanovke na uchet po sisteme 'Fort-67' svyazei inostrantsev iz chisla sovetskikh grazhdan." In: Materialy kustovogo seminara KGB Litovskoi SSR. April 1982–November 1982. LYA, f. K-1, ap. 56, b. 58, l. 61–65. Likewise, in the UKGB for the Lviv region, out of the 34 contacts of Soviet citizens with foreigners in 1974 not a single one was registered in the "Fort-67" system as of May 30. See: Prikaz Predsedatelya KGB pri SM Ukrainskoi SSR No. 0121 ot 17.6.1974 "O neudovletvoritel'nom sostoyanii ucheta operativnoi informatsii v UKGB pri SM USSR po L'vovskoi oblasti." GDA SBU, f. 9, spr. 351, ark. 37–39.
98 Tastaibekov and Nelidov, "Iz opyta provedeniya," 312.
99 Ibid.
100 Grishanin, "Perestraivat' i uglublyat' kontrol'," 23.
101 Resheniye Kollegii KGB Ukrainskoi SSR ot 30.9.1985 "O khode vypolneniya ukazaniya Predsedatelya KGB SSSR No. 18s ot 19.3.1984 'O perekhode KGB-UKGB na edinyi poryadok otbora, nakopleniya, obrabotki i vydachi informatsii v KGB-UKGB' i merakh po dal'neishemu sovershenstvovaniyu informatsionno-analiticheskoi raboty v organakh KGB respubliki." GDA SBU, f. 9, spr. 420, ark. 55–63.
102 Pyatakov and Yakovenko, "Nasushchnaya problema," 35. (Nal'chik).
103 Ibid.
104 Ibid.
105 Tseberganov and Panov, "Problemy analiza v operativnom podrazdelenii," 158–159, 64–68. (Smolensk).
106 Ibid.
107 Ibid. See also: Stepanov, "Chtoby 'podavlyat' protivnika," 20–22. (Rostov-on-Don).
108 Proskurin, "Informatsionno-analiticheskaya rabota," 180.
109 Ibid.
110 Prikaz Predsedatelya KGB SSSR No. 00133 ot 15.9.1989 "Ob organizatsii neshtatnoi informatsionno-analiticheskoi gruppy." GDA SBU, f. 9, spr. 93-sp, ark. 167–169. On the proto-structures see: Soldatov, "Analitika v organakh gosudarstvennoi bezopasnosti."
111 Prikaz Predsedatelya KGB SSSR No. 0598 ot 19.9.1990 "Ob o'yavlenii resheniya Kollegii KGB SSSR ot 3.8.1990 "O merakh po sovershenstvovaniyu informatsionnoi i analiticheskoi raboty v kontrrazvedke." LYA, f. K-51, ap. 3, b. 64, l. 88–88atv.
112 Ibid.
113 Prikaz Predsedatelya KGB SSSR No. 00136 ot 19.10.1990 "O sozdanii Analiticheskogo upravleniya KGB SSSR, utverzhdenii ego shtata i Vremennogo polozheniya ob etom Upravlenii, vnesenii izmenenii v shtaty KGB SSSR." LYA, f. K-51, ap. 3, b. 64, l. 176–190.
114 Bakatin, *Izbaleniye ot KGB*, 44–45.
115 Ibid.

62   *Evgenia Lezina*

116 "Sposobnost' prognozirovat'. Interv'yu s nachal'nikom Analiticheskogo upravleniya KGB SSSR N. S. Leonovym," *Sbornik KGB SSSR*, 156 (1991): 5, 7.
117 Ibid.
118 Ragozin, "Vysshei shkole kontrrazvedki," 34.
119 Zapiska Predsedatelya KGB SSSR V. Chebrikova v TsK KPSS No. 89-ch ot 30.1.1986 "O merakh po sovershenstvovaniyu podgotovki i povysheniya kvalifikatsii kadrov KGB SSSR." <https://nsarchive2.gwu.edu//rus/text_files/Perestroika/1986.01.30.pdf>
120 Konokotov, "Ob itogakh nauchno – issledovatel'skoi raboty," 425–438.
121 Zapiska Predsedatelya KGB SSSR V. Chebrikova v TsK KPSS No. 89-ch ot 30.1.1986.
122 See, for example, Telyatnikova, "Nekotorye actual'nye problemy perestroiki," 394.
123 Prikaz Predsedatelya KGB SSSR No. 0752 ot 16.12.1988 "Ob o'yavlenii resheniya Kollegii KGB SSSR 'O merakh po perestroike podgotovki i povysheniya kvalifikatsii chekistskikh kadrov v Vysshei shkole KGB SSSR imeni F. Dzerzhinskogo'." LYA, f. K-51, ap. 3, b. 55, l. 246.
124 Yasmann, *The KGB Documents*, 1.
125 Andrew, "Intelligence," 180.
126 Ibid.
127 Kurchatov, "Analiticheskaya rabota v kontrrazvedke FRG," 159–162.
128 "K voprosu ob izuchenii operativnoi obstanovki territorial'nymi organami KGB," *Sbornik KGB SSSR*, 91 (1981): 37.
129 Ibid.

Bibliography

Andrew, Ch. 2004. "Intelligence, International Relations and 'Under-Theorisation'." *Intelligence and National Security* 19: 170–184.

Baberowski, J. 2012. "Wege aus der Gewalt. Nikita Chruschtschow und die Entstalinisierung 1953–1964." In *Gesellschaft – Gewalt – Vertrauen*, ed. U. Bielefeld, H. Bude, and B. Greiner, 401–437. Hamburg: Hamburger Edition.

Bakatin, V. 1992. *Izbavleniye ot KGB*. Moskva: Novosti.

Bakhirev, M. 1972. "Ob organizatsii informatsionnogo massiva v oblastnom Upravlenii KGB." *Sbornik KGB SSSR* 53: 103–110. (Smolensk)

Barzhin, P. 1969. "Perfokartnyi uchet operativnoi informatsii." *Sbornik KGB SSSR* 42: 43–44. (Tyumen')

Bowker, M. 2002. "Brezhnev and Superpower Relations." In *Brezhnev Reconsidered*, ed. E. Bacon and M. Sandle, 90–109. New York: Palgrave Macmillan.

Chebrikov, V. 1977. *Istoriya sovetskih organov gosudarstvennoi bezopasnosti. Uchebnik*. Moskva: VKSh.

Dichenko, A. 1969. "Iz praktiki organizatsii informatsionno-analiticheskoi raboty v organakh gosbezopasnosti Ukrainy." *Sbornik KGB SSSR* 42: 36–43. (Kiev)

Dmitriyev, P. 1965. "Analiz v khode operativnoi proverki i razrabotki." *Sbornik KGB SSSR* 27–28: 95–98.

Dziak, J. J. 1988. *Chekisty*. Lexington: Lexington Books.

Evdokushin, A., and Kurashvili, B. 1969. "O dal'neishem razvitii informatsionnoi i analiticheskoi raboty kontrrazvedyvatel'nykh apparatov." *Sbornik KGB SSSR* 44: 22.

Gorshkov, M., and Pikulev, V. 1968. "Organizatsiya informatsionno-analiticheskoi raboty v UKGB." *Sbornik KGB SSSR* 40: 31.

Grishanin, G. 1989. "Perestraivat' i uglublyat' kontrol'." *Sbornik KGB SSSR* 129: 23.

Hodnet, G., ed. 1974. *Resolutions and Decisions of the Communist Party of the Soviet Union. Vol. 4. The Khrushchev Years 1953–1964*. Toronto: University of Toronto Press, 234.

Hornsby, R. 2013. *Protest, Reform and Repression in Khrushchev's Soviet Union*. Cambridge: Cambridge University Press.

Kharkhordin, O. 1999. *The Collective and the Individual in Russia: A Study of Practices*. Berkeley University of California Press.

Knight, A. W. 1988. *The KGB: Police and Politics in the Soviet Union*. Boston: Unwin Hyman.

Konokotov, S. 1987. "Ob itogakh nauchno – issledovatel'skoi raboty Vysshei Shkoly KGB SSSR 1981–1985 g. i nekotorykh putyakh sovershenstvovaniya eye organizatsii." *Trudy vysshei shkoly* 41–42: 425–438.

Kornilov, Yu., and Fevralev, V. 1988. "Vozmozhnosti elektronno-vychislitel'noi tekhniki – na sluzhbu operativnoi praktike (Opyt i razmyshleniya)." *Sbornik KGB SSR* 122: 49–50. (Sverdlovsk)

Korolev, V. 1990. "Sekrety sekretnykh sluzhb." *Ogonek* 43: 29.

Kurchatov, A. 1965. "Analiticheskaya rabota v kontrrazvedke FRG." *Sbornik KGB SSSR* 27–28: 159–162.

Lantsov, A., and Kuznetsov, B. 1973. "Informatsionnaya sistema 'Signal' v deistvii." *Sbornik KGB SSSR* 57: 29–31. (Astrakhan')

Lezina, E. 2020. "The Soviet State Security and the Regime of Secrecy: Guarding State Secrets and Political Control of Industrial Enterprises and Institutions in the post-Stalin Era." *Securitas Imperii* 37: 38–69.

Lugovets, R. 1988. "Tvorcheskomu poisku – vsemernuyu podderzhku." *Sbornik KGB SSSR* 126: 13–18. (Moscow)

Matyunin, V., and Grachev, Y. 1988. "Ob informatsionnom obespechenii kontrrazvedyvatel'noi raboty po rozysku avtorov i rasprostranitelei anonimnykh antisovetskikh dokumentov." *Trudy vysshei shkoly* 44: 173–174.

Pipia, G. 1988. "K voprosu ob otsenke effektivnosti funktsionirovaniya AIS kontrrazvedki." *Trudy vysshei shkoly* 43: 18–37.

Pipia, G., and Seletkov, S. 1986. "Printsipy postroeniya ESIOK. Eye sostoyaniye i perspektivy razvitiya." *Trudy vysshei shkoly* 39: 323.

Proskurin, V. 1986. "Informatsionno-analiticheskaya rabota i ispol'zovaniye eye rezul'tatov v bor'be s ideologicheskoi diversiyei protivnika." In *Problemy bor'by organov gosudarstvennoi bezopasnosti s ideologicheskoi diversiyei protivnika. Sbornik materialov nauchno-prakticheskoi konferentsii*. Moskva: VKSh, 177–182.

Pyatakov, S., and Yakovenko, S. 1989. "Nasushchnaya problema." *Sbornik KGB SSSR* 138: 35. (Nal'chik)

Ragozin, A. 1980. "Vysshei shkole kontrrazvedki – 50 let (Obrazovaniye, razvitiye i zadachi Vysshei shkoly KGB im. F. Dzerzhinskogo v podgotovke chekistskikh kadrov)." *Trudy vysshei shkoly* 21: 27–57.

Reid, S. E. 2005. "The Khrushchev Kitchen: Domesticating the Scientific-Technological Revolution." *Journal of Contemporary History* 40: 289–316.

Rodionov, Yu., and Kuznetsov, B. 1969. "Nekotoryi opyt sozdaniya informatsionnopoiskovoi sistemy." *Sbornik KGB SSSR* 41: 36–40. (Sverdlovsk)

Sever, A. 2008. *Istoriya KGB*. Moskva: Algoritm, 84–85

Soldatov, A. 2003. "Analitika v organakh gosudarstvennoi bezopasnosti." *Agentura.Ru*. www.agentura.ru/dossier/russia/fsb/analysis.

Stepanov, S. 1991. "Chtoby 'podavlyat' protivnika." *Sbornik KGB SSSR* 155: 20–22. (Rostov-on-Don)

Stevenson, R. W. 1985. *The Rise and Fall of Détente: Relaxations of Tension in US-Soviet Relations 1953–84*. London: Palgrave Macmillan.

· 64 *Evgenia Lezina*

Tastaibekov, K. T., and Nelidov, N. I. 1982. "Iz opyta provedeniya analiticheskikh issledovanii operativnoi obstanovki v Kazakhskoi SSR." *Trudy vysshei shkoly* 25: 312.

Telyatnikova, E. 1987. "Nekotorye actual'nye problemy perestroiki v Vysshei shkole imeni F. Dzerzhinskogo." *Trudy vysshei shkoly* 41–42: 397.

Tompson, W. J. 2003. *The Soviet Union under Brezhnev*. Harlow: Pearson Education Limited.

Tseberganov, Yu., and Panov, V. 1991. "Problemy analiza v operativnom podrazdelenii." *Sbornik KGB SSSR* 158–159: 64–68. (Smolensk)

Ustinov, I., et al. 1982. "Osnovnye itogi raboty po sozdaniyu i ekspluatatsii Olimpiiskogo informatsionnogo kompleksa KGB SSSR." *Trudy vysshei shkoly* 27: 154–155.

Yasmann, V. J. 1998a. *The KGB Documents and the Soviet Collapse: A Preliminary Report.* Washington, DC: The National Council for Eurasian and East European Research.

Yasmann, V. J. 1998b. *The KGB Documents and the Soviet Collapse: Part II.* Washington, DC: The National Council for Eurasian and East European Research.

3 Sublimation without domination

Exploring the knowledge of U.S. strategic intelligence during the Cold War

Andreas Lutsch

Introduction

In the process of knowledge production within any intelligence community, evaluating "raw" intelligence, crafting analytic products and transmitting "finished" intelligence to policymakers in a timely fashion are highly crucial aspects. Strategic intelligence is at the top of the analysis agenda. In the United States of America during the Cold War, strategic intelligence analysis was overwhelmingly concentrated on observing all dimensions, especially military dimensions, of the "Soviet threat."[1] US policymakers judged it imperative to establish a permanent and huge intelligence enterprise, with a prominent role assigned to the CIA. One core function of this enterprise was to detect and hence help decision-makers prevent a potential surprise nuclear attack by the Soviet Union.[2] Since 1950, the "National Intelligence Estimate" (NIE) had become the signature product of all-source based and coordinated national strategic intelligence.[3] Of those, 41 NIEs, presented more or less annually until the end of the Cold War, examined Soviet strategic nuclear forces. Those forces represented the core of the Soviet Union's surprise attack potential.[4]

In general, not all strategic intelligence is coordinated national strategic intelligence, though. Strategic intelligence – "the knowledge vital for national survival"[5] – focuses on most consequential (including existential) medium- to long-range threats which a state faces. Within this body of knowledge, coordinated strategic intelligence, based on all-source assessment, is an elevated layer. This implicates high "customer" expectations regarding knowledge quality and usefulness of estimates.

This explorative chapter examines broad contours of the production of top-level coordinated US strategic intelligence over the course of the Cold War. It focuses on two sweeping questions: how were production processes organisationally structured and methodologically oriented? And in contributing to the analytic basis for US strategic planning and policy, what stature as a body of knowledge did national strategic intelligence develop over time within the broader process of strategic assessment which was also shaped by decision-makers, policymakers, diplomats, and military officers?

The chapter builds on the conceptual outline provided by the introduction to this edited volume which considers the history of secret services as a history of

DOI: 10.4324/9781003147329-4

66   *Andreas Lutsch*

knowledge production. The chapter views the production of strategic intelligence as a social process.[6] It unfolds within ever-changing historical "constellations."[7] And the circulation of secret knowledge relates to complex questions about the degree to which those in government who have the power to decide are adept or at least open to use intelligence power to inform their decisions.[8]

The chapter can only highlight outlines of answers based mostly on scholarly literature and published accounts from selected US intelligence practitioners. It posits that the knowledge of US strategic intelligence during the Cold War was produced in a complex and disaggregated intelligence system and, though the latter was distinguished since 1950 by a robust function for coordinated strategic analysis, strategic intelligence, including coordinated strategic intelligence, sublimed but never dominated strategic assessment within the US government.

The chapter first outlines why the US intelligence system may be viewed as a complex disaggregated intelligence system which was distinguished since 1950 by a robust function for coordinated strategic analysis. Then the chapter discusses factors which inhibited the rise of a potential stature of strategic intelligence knowledge as the ultimate analytic basis for US strategic policy and planning during the Cold War.

A complex and disaggregated system . . .

How processes in intelligence assessment are conducted may fundamentally vary between states, between intelligence agencies within those states, and between such agencies and other sectors, bureaus or units in government that are not typically associated with intelligence collection, considering their hybrid function in government. Considering the variability in the way states can configure intelligence assessment processes, one can conceptually categorise them in organisationally fused, all-source analysis processes, on the one hand, and such analytic processes, on the other hand, which are, or must necessarily be, performed on the basis of disaggregation or even segregation of distinct analytic strands.

Of course, size matters. The bigger an intelligence community is, the more complex and the more specialised its organisational structures will be. Thus, in any large intelligence enterprise, aggregation will remain a great challenge also, but not just, when it comes to assessments. Moreover, the disaggregated system corresponds to a greater degree of compartmentalisation, if not diffusion, of intelligence production, processing and circulation. It also induces a competitive dynamic between analysts from different agencies or units, their products, arguments and views. This dynamic can be productive. It evokes a constant need to compare, balance and synchronise analytic perspectives whether or not synchronisation is supposed to result in products which are to some degree coordinated on an interagency basis.

In the case of the intelligence system of United States of America which developed since the Second World War, processes of intelligence assessment were not fused in the sense that a single intelligence agency was responsible for them. To this day, this idea was neither deemed feasible nor desirable. The organisational model which crystallised after the Second World War was hence not disestablished or substituted while US national intelligence capacities – agencies, members of agencies, collection and analysis capacities – grew massively throughout the Cold War.[9] The US intelligence community was recreated on the basis of the National Security Act of 1947 and with it the CIA.[10] But the CIA never became the central clearinghouse which its title may have insinuated. Besides other specialised intelligence agencies such as the *National Security Agency*, there also remained the cluster of channels through which military intelligence branches from the services – such as the US Army or the US Navy – injected their expertise into the intelligence process. And a guiding principle remained that also top-level decision-makers in the national security field would be best served if they received intelligence products tailored to their specific needs and – besides the CIA – produced by intelligence organisations close or subordinate to them. Such organizations were, for example, the Bureau for Intelligence and Research (INR) in the US Department of State (DoS) or the Defense Intelligence Agency (founded in 1961) within the US Department of Defense.[11] In addition, also "hybrid" units contributed which are often not too directly associated with the US IC. The Office of Net Assessment (ONA) in the US Department of Defense (DoD) (established in 1973), for example, produced highly classified strategic-level assessments for DoD leaders. These assessments transcended the typical division between intelligence and planning in that they offered integrated, descriptive and comparative "Red-Blue" strategic assessments within a frame of reference that focused on long-term security competition between the United States and the Soviet Union. In general terms, the lack of centralisation and hence also the tendency of appreciating competition in intelligence assessment may have appeared beneficial to avoid "lowest common denominator" assessments that would "hew closely to a safe middle line" or "avoid risky but potentially spot-on judgments."[12] This cornucopia of intelligence assessment suggested that the idea of approaching "truth by way of free competition"[13] continued to impregnate the ways in which secret knowledge was produced within the US intelligence system.

Besides the issues mentioned earlier – complexity, disaggregation of strands of the analytic process, compartmentalisation, competitive dynamics and the need to synchronise – a related aspect of the US way of organising processes related to intelligence analysis was that it tended to "impede integration and collaboration among analysts."[14] Analysts were, after all, embedded in agencies and units throughout the US IC. This limited the extent to which one could generally speak of one US IC with one consolidated view pertaining to an issue. In fact, this characteristic survived the Cold War: "analysis in the IC often more resembles cooperation among feudal baronies than collaboration among members of a professional community."[15]

Complexities and disaggregation were compounded by hiring and education patterns. Leaving the issues aside of how personnel with active-duty military backgrounds became intelligence analysts and how officials rotated within government, civilians often joined the IC after undergraduate or graduate studies in various fields, usually without having planned to become members of a specific

68   *Andreas Lutsch*

intelligence organisation before they commenced their studies. Most regarded themselves as specialists in something – economists, historians, regional specialists, Sovietologists and so on – rather than as specialists in intelligence analysis or as belonging to a profession called "intelligence analysis."[16]

Education and on-the-job training made the community of analysts even more diverse. Various organisations created their own programmes, "tradecraft" courses and institutions over time to educate and train their cadres to better meet the specific requirements of their organisations. The CIA, for example, created separate schools for operators and analysts in 1950 which were merged into the CIA University in 2002. DIA's Defense Intelligence School, founded in 1962, became the National Intelligence University.[17]

... with a robust function for coordinated strategic analysis ...

Despite this side-by-side production of strands of secret intelligence knowledge within the US IC during the Cold War, at least one measure with the aim of achieving greater analytic consolidation stands out – namely, in the field of strategic intelligence analysis, the establishment of the Office of National Estimates (O/NE) within the CIA in 1950, out of which grew the National Intelligence Council (NIC) in 1979. The NIC continues to be the highest-ranking strategic intelligence analysis unit within the US government.

This crucial step in 1950 had to be seen against the background of a novel constellation. The bipolar Cold War system crystallised throughout the late 1940s and the early 1950s. The United States assumed a new world political role as security provider in Europe and Asia. It emerged "as an intelligence superpower."[18] The United States forged the "first global peacetime intelligence alliance" with the United Kingdom, Canada, Australia and New Zealand, and this permitted path-breaking advances in collecting signals intelligence.[19] The IMINT revolution of the late 1950s and 1960s (reconnaissance aircraft like the U-2 and then satellite imagery) also ensured that the significance of strategic intelligence increased.[20] Thus, especially the technical collection capacities of the US intelligence apparatus grew massively. But an expectation of linearity appeared to be unwarranted if one correlated the growth of intelligence capacities and the degree of modernity in collection with success in the intelligence mission to reduce the indissoluble uncertainty which decision-makers faced. To the extent that historical experiences continued to shape the present, it was worth considering the recent past, the great powers' experiences during the first half of the twentieth century. The great powers' experiences with strategic threat assessment before both world wars did not

> supply confidence that more data, more analysts, or more investment in intelligence collection and analysis will yield shrewder assessments. . . . Like people growing old, governments may have been acquiring more and more powerful glasses but nevertheless becoming able to see less and less.[21]

Increases in the size of a government apparatus, including the IC, also made it more demanding to reconcile the analytic perspectives of government offices, while increases in the size of an opponent's government apparatus made it harder to figure out, for example, who dominated and who marginally influenced decision-making on the other side.[22] In other words, if applied to the situation of 1950, this view suggested that the mere creation of O/NE as an additional intelligence office would not per se tend to ensure a qualitative improvement of strategic assessment. However, at least O/NE's chief product, NIEs, quickly made a difference.

Until that point, US experiences with producing national intelligence assessments and estimates were mixed. After the Office of Strategic Services (OSS) had been dissolved once Germany and Japan were defeated, strategic intelligence assessments were produced by INR, a former OSS unit (*Research and Analysis* [RA]) which became a permanent bureau in the DoS, by the military services, and, in more consolidated forms, by the Joint Intelligence Committee (JIC). The US JIC was founded in 1941 as a highest-level intelligence unit supporting the US Joint Chiefs of Staff. In contrast to the British Joint Intelligence Committee, however, it did not succeed in presenting analyses and estimates that a majority in the US government viewed as satisfactory.[23] When in proceedings of the committee representatives of intelligence agencies offered differing estimates, the JIC apparently tended to coordinate national estimates to the point of "becom[ing] vague and meaningless."[24] Inter alia, there was no "independent chairman" with the authority to determine which variant would go into the national estimate.[25] Later, when national estimates were produced under the auspices of the Central Intelligence Group (CIG, created in 1946) and its successor organisation, the CIA (created in 1947), the process of how national assessments were put together further reduced the gravitas of these products.[26]

The surprise of the Korean War and the sharp intensification of Cold War tensions that accompanied it led to an acute sense within the US government that it was vital to invigorate processes of strategic intelligence assessment, particularly relating to Soviet capabilities and intentions. In 1950, an urgent need was felt to offer top-level policymakers a coordinated, all-source, most authoritative and forward-looking strategic intelligence product. The product would have to distil central insights from the various analytic strands which the US IC produced in a way that made a fundamental difference as compared to previous JIC assessments and individual strands of strategic assessment within the US government.[27]

O/NE was created within the CIA in 1950. It was mandated to craft NIEs. These were conceived as lucid, coordinated estimates intended for the top levels of the US government, with a dissemination rate in most cases between 100 to 300 copies (depending especially on the classification level of the information).[28] During the Cold War, NIEs dealt with issues of fundamental strategic importance to the US government, such as Soviet military power, the evolution of the Cold War environment, Sino-Soviet relations or nuclear proliferation. NIEs were supposed to be and in many cases were the gold standard in strategic intelligence knowledge production within the US IC.[29] O/NE was supported by a Board of

70 *Andreas Lutsch*

National Estimates (BNE) under the Director of Central Intelligence (DCI) and by top analysts from US intelligence agencies who were sent to the Office for parts of their careers.

The BNE, assisted by the O/NE staff, coordinated all efforts leading to the production of NIEs. It could draw on the highest quality intelligence from across the US IC. The BNE authored and cleared drafts on the working level with participating intelligence agencies and finally "submitted those Estimates for approval to the chiefs of the respective intelligence agencies who then met together under the chairmanship of the DCI."[30] Coordinated interagency synchronisation to craft this agreed-upon high-profile analytic product was crucial. Yet, "the NIE system never demanded consensus, and the individual agencies could record dissent, and they did."[31] Thus, the attempt was made in every single NIE to consolidate views into a most authoritative, coordinated strategic intelligence product. Nevertheless, any footnote apparatus could reflect the situation that various other strands of strategic intelligence were produced by individual agencies or intelligence units in parallel to the NIE process.

Ab origine to 1967, O/NE and the BNE were chaired by influential history professors who were also OSS/RA veterans: to wit, Harvard historian William L. Langer and Yale historian Sherman Kent (1952 to 1967).[32] Hence, in the social process of coordinated strategic intelligence production during that period, historians played prominent roles. At first glance, this may also suggest a methodological importance of "the historian's approach" both to the early efforts to work towards a greater degree of consolidation of strategic analysis processes within the US IC and in shaping the production of NIEs, that is the highest quality strand of strategic intelligence knowledge.

However, this story cannot necessarily be told as a story of how historians shaped or even improved US strategic intelligence, let alone the US policymaking process, in the 1950s and 1960s. For one, as the historian Marc Trachtenberg asserts, "many officials resented mere professors exercising this sort of power, and the system in which they played a major role did not last long."[33] In the secret world of US intelligence, scepticism of intellectualism, if not anti-intellectualism, apparently remained strong not just among HUMINT operators but also among analysts, even if operators, in turn, tended to view the latter as "scholarly, ivory-towerish and impractical."[34] Spotty anecdotal evidence suggests that professorial behaviour at times tended to come across as an irritant in the collaborative effort of producing NIEs.[35] More fundamentally, it remains unclear what methodological difference it made in the process of strategic intelligence production that historians did play a seemingly prominent role in the top tier of related processes. It is important to note that Kent himself and in a generalist way referred to "the method of the social sciences," and deliberately not to a historical method, which was supposed to be applied in the process of strategic intelligence production.[36] Another prominent scholar-practitioner, Klaus Knorr, echoed this sort of understanding at the time: "as now practiced, intelligence is inconceivable without the social sciences. But except in very general ways it is hard to identify, measure, and evaluate this influence."[37]

... which never dominated strategic assessment

O/NE's function of providing coordinated strategic intelligence analysis was downgraded in the early 1970s. The pressures working against O/NE assuming a predominant role in the field of strategic assessment were plentiful and powerful. Their cumulative effect was "that the idea that the NIC – and its predecessor, the Board of National Estimates – should be the principal locus of strategic analysis was unrealistic."[38]

Intra-governmental competition apparently stood out as a principal cause. It was severe before the early 1970s, and it remained severe thereafter. Many players – the NSC, DoS, DoD, the services – sought to shape strategic planning as well as related decision-making. Necessarily, these activities involved strategic analysis, including specific intelligence inputs. The body of coordinated strategic intelligence knowledge apparently never reached the stature of being universally regarded as the ultimate analytic basis upon which strategic planning and policy could or had to be founded.[39] A deeper or systematic examination of specific causes and reasons cannot be offered here. But the chapter highlights six sources which generated pressure against a manifestation of the idea that coordinated strategic intelligence assessment might provide the ultimate analytic basis for US strategic planning and policy: predominance of policy, the difficulty of gauging intentions, competing logics in decision-making, systems analysis, politicisation and net assessment.

Predominance of policy

One general source of pressure resulted from the predominance of policy in interactions between policymakers and intelligence analysts. Intelligence analysis, including strategic intelligence analysis, never was an end but a means towards an end. A central goal was to provide informational advantage to policymakers for the purpose of enabling better policymaking. When intelligence officials and policymakers interact, two "cultures" come together and sometimes collide with each other. The "policy culture" is marked by a "fundamentally optimistic thrust" – to make progress on an issue and so forth – while "the culture of the intelligence world . . . is marked by skepticism."[40] Richard Helms, who became Director of Central Intelligence (1966–1973) under President Lyndon B. Johnson, recollected how Johnson once complained at a dinner at the White House:

> When I grew up in Texas, we had a cow named Bessie. I'd go out early and milk her. I'd get her in the stanchion, seat myself and squeeze out a pail of fresh milk. One day I'd worked hard and gotten a full pail of milk, but I wasn't paying attention, and old Bessie swung her shit-smeared tail through that bucket of milk. Now, you know, that's what these intelligence guys do. You work hard and get a good program or policy going, and they swing a shit-smeared tail through it.[41]

72   *Andreas Lutsch*

On the other hand, policymaker receptivity remained an issue from the analysts' perspective:

> Members of the IC often feel that policymakers shun complicated analysis, cannot cope with uncertainty, will not read beyond the first page, forget what they have been told, and are quick to blame intelligence when policy fails.[42]

Against this background, a notoriously difficult issue was (and is) how to evaluate the "influence" of intelligence on national security decision-making, that is, of intelligence in general and of strategic intelligence in particular.[43]

By the early 1970s, charges against the O/NE-system had piled up. Among these were criticisms that analysts shunned the necessary level of interaction with the policymaking world, that the strategic intelligence knowledge they produced was too far away from the policymakers' needs and that analyses were not generally of a quality that would always warrant the label "most authoritative." A culmination point was reached when the National Security Council under Nixon's National Security Advisor Henry A. Kissinger bypassed the O/NE-system in terms of strategic assessment. O/NE was even abolished in 1973 and, after a transient period of experimentation with a looser system, succeeded by the NIC in 1979.[44] These upheavals apparently shattered the idea that intelligence analysts from a single, premier strategic intelligence unit in government and with a professional ethos of speaking truth to power would closely interact with, provide an ultimate type of assessment to and at the same time remain largely unimpeachable by the policy community.[45]

The difficulty of gauging intentions

Another source of pressure working against a predominating role of O/NE (and later of the NIC) in strategic assessment was that, when it came to the crucial issue of assessing adversary intentions – like the intentions of Soviet leaders during the Cold War – US decision-making was most of the time not crucially inspired, let alone predominantly shaped, by coordinated strategic intelligence. According to one explanation, policymakers and intelligence officials infer long-term political intentions of adversary states based on different indicators. Leaders tend to focus more on "vivid information" like their – often emotionally swayed – memory of face-to-face meetings and conversations with foreign leaders. Intelligence analysts tend to "prioritize information in which it has the most expertise, which in most cases will pertain to the adversary's military capabilities."[46]

Former intelligence practitioners concur: "the best intelligence available to both sides [during the Cold War] was about military matters."[47] "Intelligence's contribution [to understanding Soviet intentions] did not count for so much," "diplomatic and military advice was more important," and understanding Soviet intentions was "more important" than the surveillance of military capabilities.[48] This being said, strategic intelligence made an enormous difference, on the basis of modern IMINT and SIGINT capacities, in providing "reassurance" against fears of surprise attack or potential Soviet non-compliance with arms control obligations.[49]

In sum, gauging an adversary's intentions remained a central aspect of strategic assessment at any given time. But a predominating role of coordinated strategic intelligence did not emerge. Other players in government – leaders, diplomacy, the military – played more powerful roles. And indicators which were central from a strategic intelligence perspective (costly signals, measurable segments of military balances, etc.) were not universally acknowledged as the best ones to produce knowledge about and estimates of adversary intentions.

Competing logics in decision-making

The competition of logics in the process of national security decision-making also eroded the idea of a predominating role of the knowledge produced by strategic intelligence, including coordinated analyses produced by a single strategic intelligence analysis unit like the O/NE or NIC: even if strategic intelligence succeeded in injecting its knowledge – say, threat assessments – into the mindsets of policymakers, these policymakers could still opt for policies which were less than optimal in light of what intelligence might have suggested, because other logics had a greater impact on decision-making. The logic of alliance politics is an example.[50]

Consider one example. In the early Kennedy period, the assessment gained currency within the US government that the estimated threat of the peacetime Soviet army, consisting of 175 divisions, did not mean that this impressive force had a combat-ready strength of 175 fully equipped and fully manned divisions. This was one important detail in the broader message: The Soviet conventional threat was less severe than commonly assumed. From a policy perspective, this intelligence assessment could easily be referred to when formulating preferences suggesting that there was room to profoundly adapt Western strategy without weakening deterrence, to delay the use of nuclear weapons should a war occur and so on.[51] The intelligence estimate was coldly received by the West-German government at the time, including the BND and its chief, Reinhard Gehlen, who was not convinced.[52] From the perspective of US policymakers who also sought to inhibit both a German nuclear force and a rapprochement between the Soviet Union and West Germany, there were hence limits as to how far German leaders could be pushed in terms of reforming NATO strategy as long as German strategic threat assessments differed substantially from US ones. Thus, at least two logics competed in terms of their relative impact on the formulation and implementation of US policy: a logic of "rationalizing" NATO strategy in line with national strategic threat assessments and a logic of alliance politics, including nuclear non-proliferation. In this case, whatever US strategic intelligence stated about the real degree of the Soviet conventional threat, the idea of seeking Germany's assent to modifying the existing strategy, which relied on the threat of using nuclear weapons should deterrence fail, did appear to be too politically costly. Yet, continuity in NATO strategy, in turn, hardly elevated the political impact of strategic intelligence estimates within the US government.

On the other hand, even the limited steps that were indeed taken in the 1960s to reduce the reliance on nuclear weapons in NATO strategy were enough to provoke

74 *Andreas Lutsch*

criticism that, instead of objectively informing US policymakers, US strategic intelligence estimates were either intelligence to please or, if realistic, ignored by policymakers. Consider an example from late 1966 when former West German Minister of Defense Franz Josef Strauß complained to John J. McCloy, who at that point served as President Johnson's appointee for Anglo-American-German consultations on military strategy. Strauß said that the strategy of "flexible response" was

> based on an entirely new estimate of Russian capabilities. There was the most rapid build-up and build-down of Russian divisions all on the desks of the Pentagon. Intelligence was always advanced "to fit the strategy of the political scientists" . . . all the new strategy was an attempt to minimize the risk for the homeland of the United States as the Soviet nuclear power grew.[53]

It was not clear who Strauß meant when he referred to "political scientists."[54] He might have been alluding to the implementation of "Systems Analysis" in the US Department of Defense under Kennedy's Secretary of Defense, Robert S. McNamara.

Systems Analysis

Systems Analysis represented yet another source of pressure against the idea of O/NE assuming a predominant role in strategic assessment. This economic problem-solving approach was introduced within the US Department of Defense in the McNamara years which were crucial particularly with regard to US strategic forces policy, planning and acquisition. It represented a major innovation in the way procurement processes for strategic nuclear forces were conducted. It imposed a rationalising cost-effectiveness perspective on the procurement process, which thus far had been dominated by the services. Hence, Systems Analysis in some sense also appeared as scientification of US strategic assessment. It was also connected to estimative projections of Soviet nuclear force development in the medium and long run.

In theory, this was yet another avenue through which the analysis of intelligence could exert a measure of influence on US policymaking. In practice, Systems Analysis was conceptualised and carried out largely independently from all-source, coordinated strategic intelligence assessment which ran in parallel, while the vehemence of its underlying estimative assumptions posed a challenge to the latter. A central estimative assumption informing the application of Systems Analysis was that a well-managed US nuclear force build-up could give the Soviet Union sufficient incentive to reciprocate US restraint: the Soviets would have an incentive not to build forces which the United States regarded as destabilising (e.g., heavy and MIRVed ICBMs or ABM) in the context of an emerging relationship called Mutual Assured Destruction.[55]

But by the mid-1970s, it had become clear that this estimative assumption had not turned out to be a correct anticipation of Soviet behaviour:

In short, the Soviet political-military leadership appears to have rejected the "mutual assured destruction" reasoning advanced by Robert McNamara and his followers as the desirable foundation of strategic stability, including "crisis stability" and "arms race stability". . . . Soviet behavior in the 1970s gave many American observers the impression that the USSR was seeking superiority.[56]

It remains to be examined to what extent US strategic intelligence assessment was affected by this separate thread of estimative assumptions which had informed the application of Systems Analysis and hence US strategic nuclear force policy during the 1960s. In any case, the strategic nuclear threat represented the very core of "the Soviet military threat" throughout the Cold War. And the application of Systems Analysis in US strategic force policy – with its estimative assumptions about Soviet behaviour – cushioned the relative impact of strategic intelligence assessments and estimates on Soviet strategic force policy, planning and procurement.

Politicisation

The issue of politicisation is not so much about whether government activities in strategic planning or policy usurp intelligence functions but, rather, whether and how each sphere – intelligence and policymaking – impinges upon the other.[57] Politicisation represented yet another pressure point against the idea that coordinated strategic intelligence might be acknowledged as the ultimate body of knowledge pertaining to the most important threats to US national security.

One episode from the interim period when O/NE was abolished and before the NIC was established can be considered as a prominent example. In 1976, the political détente process decelerated, SALT II negotiations created heated debate, and a new bipartisan "Committee on the Present Danger" (CPD) was formed to rally against détente policy when the Ford Presidency came to an end. Estimating current and future Soviet military capabilities and intentions became a contentious issue. DCI George Bush came to raise questions about whether the latest NIEs on Soviet strategic nuclear forces and related Soviet intentions adequately assessed what the Soviets did and what their intentions were in this field. In June 1976, Bush requested that a "competitive analysis" of those NIEs and of the material that informed the NIEs be conducted by outside experts who formed Team B.[58] As Garthoff summarised it:

> Since its purpose (and composition – it included Professor Richard E. Pipes as chairman, Paul Nitze, and retired General Daniel O. Graham) had been to develop a less optimistic view, it is not surprising it came up with more ominous findings. . . . In retrospect, it is clear that while Team B had some valid criticisms of the NIEs, fundamentally its report was far more flawed than the NIEs and merely substituted alarmist judgments on Soviet intentions for cautious ones.[59]

Team B criticised NIEs for supposedly updating a fundamentally flawed basic estimate and for passing it off as the most authoritative knowledge on the subject,

76 *Andreas Lutsch*

even though NIEs merely echoed what "mirror-imaging" suggested.[60] Team B also attacked the methodological approach, which it claimed had led analysts to underrate the Soviet threat.[61]

Team B, and hence the use of competitive analysis regarding NIEs, represented not just an increase in the competitive dynamic within the historical constellation of 1976, that is of a general dynamic which already characterised processes of intelligence analysis in the US IC. Also, it did not just challenge core aspects of the content of the established body of strategic intelligence knowledge. Rather, it let the methodological approach of coordinated strategic intelligence appear at best as deficient and at worst as "scientism," based on self-aggrandisement and "epistemological naivety."[62] Because of the overlap between the CPD and Team B and the publication of Team B's core findings, the episode was also an abuse of intelligence analysis techniques. From a methodological perspective, such techniques should serve to yield a greater degree of analytic approximation to reality outside the arena of public debate – either by letting an independent team examine the same evidence or by letting a Red Cell critique analytic findings. In sum, the

> Team B exercise was damaging . . . because it politicized the NIE process for several years to come. It also revealed that the otherwise constructive device of "competitive analysis," which every NIE chair has employed, can easily be manipulated and politicized.[63]

Net Assessment

By the time Team B was convened to review NIEs on Soviet nuclear force policy and intentions, the major agency engaged in producing the "Soviet estimate" – the CIA – had already come under fire by the emergence of an increasingly influential stakeholder in strategic assessment within the US government: the ONA.

The ONA was and still is a kind of DoD-internal think tank with direct access to the Secretary of Defense. It produced integrated strategic assessments of "Red" *and* "Blue" military strategy, based on sensitive information on "Red" (secret intelligence) and "Blue" (information on US strategy, defence policy and programmes), and with an eye to the long-term security competition with America's central competitors like the Soviet Union and China.[64] In 1969, National Security Advisor Henry Kissinger attached a net assessment unit to the White House. In 1973, ONA was established in DoD to work at the interface of strategic intelligence assessment and analysis setting the stage for US defence planning. The unit and ONA were led by Andrew W. Marshall (until 2015), a legendary figure in the US defence establishment. ONA apparently challenged some of the US IC analyses of issues like the size of the Soviet economy, the proportion of Soviet defence expenditures and related estimates of how the Soviet economy would perform:

> Perhaps the most obvious accomplishment to point to is Marshall's work on estimating the burden that Soviet military programs imposed on the USSR's

Sublimation without domination 77

economy during the 1970s and 1980s. . . . In the end, Marshall's office . . . produced more accurate estimates of the USSR's military burden for senior Pentagon leaders than did the US intelligence agencies.[65]

The impact of Net Assessment on the process of strategic assessment within the US government is not salient in many histories about the détente era and the end of the Cold War. One of the innovations that ONA induced was to enrich strategic assessment by a comparative analysis which highlighted weaknesses in the military posture, political system and economic structures of the Soviet Union and opportunities for the United States in terms of how, in which areas and by which means to best intensify the political-military competition with the Soviet Union.[66] Given its basic estimate that the Soviet Union was economically much weaker and much more burdened by its defence spending than senior analysts from the IC believed, Net Assessment apparently also contributed to a sense of optimism that there was a "possibility of winning the Cold War."[67]

Much remains to be learned about US strategic assessment in the 1970s, 1980s and at the end of the Cold War, and specifically about how this secret knowledge was produced by the established top-level strategic intelligence analysis unit, the NIC and other entities like ONA which had emerged as yet another powerful player in strategic assessment. It nevertheless seems clear that the permanence of net assessment inputs into US strategic thinking since the early 1970s also contributed to prevent a situation in which coordinated strategic intelligence products might have predominated the body of secret knowledge that would form the analytic basis for US strategic policy and planning.

Conclusion

This explorative chapter examined broad contours of the production of top-level, coordinated US strategic intelligence during the Cold War, with a focus on how processes were organisationally structured and methodologically oriented as well as on factors which inhibited a potential stature of coordinated strategic intelligence knowledge as an ultimate analytic basis for US strategic policy and planning. Only outlines of answers could be highlighted, considering the dimensions of these questions, the countless intricacies of intelligence analysis as a process as well as the breadth and depth of US experiences with strategic intelligence.

The chapter argued that, in the US case, the knowledge of strategic intelligence was produced in a complex and disaggregated intelligence system and, though the latter was distinguished since 1950 by a robust function for coordinated strategic analysis, strategic intelligence, including coordinated strategic intelligence, sublimed but never dominated strategic assessment within the US government.

After mixed experiences with a coordination unit which was rather weak in terms of its organisational standing in government, it was a fundamental change when a robust function for coordinated strategic intelligence analysis was added to the national assessment system in 1950. The O/NE, established within the CIA in that year, took on this role initially, and, from 1979 on, the NIC assumed its

78 *Andreas Lutsch*

mantle. NIEs were the signature product of both bodies. But intra-governmental competition remained too severe for strategic intelligence, including its top layer of coordinated strategic intelligence, to develop a stature which would be universally acknowledged as the ultimate strand of strategic assessment within government. The chapter highlighted specific sources of pressure which tended to limit the potential policy impact of coordinated strategic intelligence as a body of secret knowledge within the US government. Even so, this reality was never per se an appraisal of the veracity or quality of the knowledge produced by strategic intelligence, in general, and of coordinated strategic intelligence, in particular.

Notes

1 Cf., inter alia, the monograph of O/NE veteran Matthias (2001), *America's Strategic Blunders*; Dylan et al., *The CIA and the Pursuit of Security*.
2 Durbin, *The CIA*, 1–2.
3 See, among others, Fingar, *Reducing Uncertainty*, 1 and 5; George, *Intelligence*, 6.
4 Treverton, »Conclusion."
5 Kent, *Strategic Intelligence*, vii.
6 Regardless of the content, validity ("Sachgültigkeit") and veracity of knowledge, this has a dual effect. First, the selection of investigated phenomena depends on predominating self-interest conceptions in society more broadly. Second, formats within and through which knowledge is methodologically developed, produced, made available etc. vary over time and are influenced by parallel trends and conjunctures in society and its sub-systems like academia: Scheler, *Wissensformen*, 58.
7 On the centrality of this category: Mannheim, *Wissenssoziologie*, 308–324.
8 On Sarasin's point that knowledge circulation interferes with power structures in government see the introduction to this volume. Reflective of this, former O/NE and NIC practitioners cautioned that, in some prominent cases, US policymakers could well have protected themselves against flawed policy judgments, had they taken strategic intelligence more seriously and had the policy impact of US strategic intelligence thus been greater than it was. Regarding the Vietnam War: Ford, »Estimative Intelligence,« 22 f. For various examples see Matthias, *America's Strategic Blunders*.
9 Rovner, "Intelligence and National Decision Making"; Warner and Macdonald, *US Intelligence Community Reform*; Fingar, "Office of the Director."
10 Thorne and Patterson, eds., »Foreign Relations of the United States."
11 Johnson, *Analytic Culture*.
12 Colby, "Making Intelligence Smart."
13 Cradock, *Know Your Enemy*, 278.
14 Fingar, "Building a Community of Analysts."
15 Ibid.
16 Davis, *Sherman Kent*.
17 Lowenthal, "Education and Training."
18 Andrew, "American Presidents."
19 Postwar cooperation agreements had their roots in SIGINT agreements during World War II and were built upon the Anglo-American BRUSA agreement of 5 March 1946 (generally known as UKUSA Agreement): <www.nsa.gov/news-features/declassified-documents/ukusa/>. Out of this grew the 'Five Eyes' and forms of overseas bases and work sharing between Britain and the US as the British Empire contracted and the US world role increased: Walton, "Intelligence"; Benson, *US Communications Intelligence*; Ferris, *Behind the Enigma*, Chapter 8.
20 Clark, *Geospatial Intelligence*, chapters 8–12.
21 May, "Capabilities."

Sublimation without domination 79

22 Ibid., 527.
23 Valero, "American Joint Intelligence Committee."
24 Montague, "Origins."
25 Ibid.
26 Ibid., 69. At that time, agency representatives did not convene. CIG/CIA analysts drafted papers alone "and sent them to the heads of the departmental agencies for concurrence or dissent on a take it or leave it basis."
27 Hutchings, "Introduction," 6.
28 Ibid.; Ford, *Estimative Intelligence*.
29 In contrast to current intelligence, "estimates put the big judgments on the record, they represent the collective knowledge of hundreds of intelligence analysts, and they are intended to stand a test of time in most cases, two to five years": Suettinger, "Introduction (English)." On successes in estimating, e.g., of the Sino-Soviet split: Ford, *Estimative Intelligence*, 21–23.
30 Ford, "US Government's Experience." Those meetings of agency chiefs were held weekly within the *United States Intelligence Board* (USIB) which became the *National Foreign Intelligence Board* (NFIB). Out of the NFIB, in turn, grew the *National Intelligence Board* (NIB) that exists today.
31 Herman, "Intelligence in the Cold War," 59. Dissent was flagged by agency representatives before the USIB met, formally entered in (as a footnote) by the respective agency chief in the USIB session and formally agreed in the sense that all chiefs subscribed to a version of the NIE and the dissenting footnote which were clear to all: Kent, "Law and Custom," 93–98.
32 On Kent's work see ibid. and Kent, *Strategic Intelligence*.
33 Trachtenberg, *History and Policy*.
34 Hilsman, *Strategic Intelligence*, 110.
35 For an example from the early 1950s, when history professor Raymond J. Sontag, as a member of the BNE, stretched the patience of the involved heads of departmental intelligence agencies by treating these men as "his students," see Montague, *General Walter Bedell Smith*, 134.
36 Kent, *Strategic Intelligence*, 156 f. His concept of "the method of the social sciences" was exceptionally broad, since he included "the science of military strategy as a social science along with social psychology, economics, politics, sociology, geography, anthropology, history and others."
37 Knorr, *Foreign Intelligence*, 7.
38 Hutchings, "Introduction," 14.
39 For a similar point see Ford, *Estimative Intelligence*, 4: "despite the quality of NIEs and the substantial contribution they do make to decisionmakers, it cannot be said that US policy at any one time is directly based on national estimates."
40 McLaughlin, "Serving the National Policymaker," 83. He quotes Director of Central Intelligence Robert Gates who said that an intelligence analyst was somebody who "smells flowers (. . .) and then looks for the coffin."
41 Quoted in Andrew, "American Presidents," 124.
42 Jervis, "Intelligence and Policymakers," 203.
43 Regarding the US case, a skeptical understanding is that "intelligence analysis will inevitably have limited influence on policy-making because it is a duplicative step in the policy process": Marrin, "Strategic Intelligence Analysis," 727. Dahl pushed back: "perhaps we all place too much emphasis on the influence intelligence has on senior policy levels, and instead we should focus more on how intelligence can shape the way working levels of government operate": Dahl, "Strategic Intelligence Analysis."
44 Ford, *Estimative Intelligence*, 19–36. In the intermittent "National Intelligence Officer system," "some 12 senior experts in various geographical and functional specialties" (USSR, strategic forces, etc.) led the NIE-process, ibid., 25.

80 *Andreas Lutsch*

45 Notions of an ethos of speaking truth to power apparently resonated rather widely. Consider, e.g., Kent's description of strategic intelligence assessment as an exercise to achieve "a closer approximation of truth" on the basis of analytic "integrity and objectivity": Kent, *Strategic Intelligence*, 155 and 200. This sort of understanding seems to play a great role in the US IC today, at least on the declaratory level. "The Principles of Professional Ethics for the Intelligence Community," issued by the DNI in 2014, assert: "We seek the truth; speak truth to power; and obtain, analyze, and provide intelligence objectively." <www.dni.gov/index.php/who-we-are/organizations/clpt/clpt-related-menus/clpt-related-links/ic-principles-of-professional-ethics> (last accessed June 13, 2021).

46 Yarhi-Milo, "Eye of the Beholder," 18.

47 Barrass, *Great Cold War*, 392–393.

48 Herman, "Intelligence in the Cold War," 61 and ibid., 68: "On the key issue of Soviet intentions . . . intelligence's effect on Western governments was mainly to confirm other influences."

49 Herman, "What Difference."

50 Another example was the logic of not acting directly against opinions which prevailed in the US public for the time being: Cameron, *Double Game*.

51 Garthoff, "Estimating."

52 Müller, *Reinhard Gehlen*, chapters IV. 3 and 4.

53 MemCon, McCloy-Strauss, 17 Dec. 1966, Lyndon B. Johnson Library, Austin TX, Papers of Lyndon B. Johnson President, National Security File, Country File, Box 187, Germany, Memos Vol. XII, 12/66–3/67.

54 If the association here was to the work of 'strategists' outside of the US government like Bernhard Brodie, Thomas Schelling and others, the assertion about their influence was likely "overdrawn": Trachtenberg, *Social Scientists*.

55 See especially Smith and Enthoven, *How Much is Enough?*

56 Yost, *Strategic Stability in the Cold War*, 22 f.

57 Cf. Rovner, *Fixing the Facts*. Chapter 6 mentions four variants: "positive politicization" (an analyst changes his analysis to promote policy); "negative politicization" (an analyst presents intelligence peu-à-peu in the hope that a policymaker revises policy); "bottom up politicization" (an analyst presents intelligence to reinforce a policymaker's policy preference); "top-down politicization" (a policymaker expresses expectations about results of analyses).

58 Team B and the leading circle of the new *Committee on the Present Danger* overlapped, including Paul H. Nitze and the chairman of Team B, Richard Pipes.

59 Garthoff, *Détente and Confrontation*, 607 f.; Cahn, *Killing Détente*.

60 NIE judgments were ill-founded, Team B asserted, due to a "conceptual flaw" called "mirror-imaging, i.e., the attribution to Soviet decision-makers of such forms of behavior as might be expected from their US counterparts under analogous circumstances." *Intelligence Community Experiment in Competitive Analysis: Soviet Strategic Objectives. An Alternative View. Report of Team 'B'*, December 1976, 1, CIA Electronic Reading Room [online].

61 NIEs had "misperceived the motivations behind Soviet strategic programs" and this was "due in considerable measure to concentration on the so-called hard data, that is data collected by technical means, and the resultant tendency to interpret these data in a manner reflecting basic US concepts while slighting or misinterpreting the large body of 'soft' data concerning Soviet strategic concepts": ibid.

62 Jones and Silberzahn, *Constructing Cassandra*, 40–44.

63 Hutchings, "Introduction," 12f.

64 Mahnken and Marshall, eds., *Net Assessment*.

65 Krepinevich and Watts, *The Last Warrior*, 261 "Marshall's growing suspicions about the economic problems lurking beneath the surface of the Soviet behemoth were neither widely shared by the US intelligence community or the military. (. . .) In the end,

however, Marshall's long-term competition framework would lead the Defense Department to adopt what he called competitive strategies, which placed greater priority on imposing disproportionately larger costs on the USSR's military efforts," ibid., 154f. The latest historical research questions the hypothesis of grand failure on the part of the CIA and NIC when it comes to the economic dimension of the 'Soviet estimate': Trachtenberg, "Assessing."

66 Apparently, Net Assessment analyzed issues with an eye to long-term trends in the Cold War competition: military balances, weapon systems and capability comparisons, economic capacities, historical evaluations, and technological trends affecting great power competition. In contrast to Systems Analysis, Net Assessment was a "form of descriptive analysis, in contrast to cost-effectiveness analysis, which is largely normative or prescriptive": Pickett et al. "Net Assessment."

67 Krepinevich and Watts, *The Last Warrior*, 151.

Bibliography

Andrew, C. 2009. "American Presidents and their Intelligence Communities." In *Secret Intelligence: A Reader*, ed. C. Andrew, R. J. Aldrich, and W. K. Wark, 116–128. London and New York: Routledge.

Barrass, G. 2009. *The Great Cold War: A Journey Through the Hall of Mirrors*. Stanford, CA: Stanford University Press.

Benson, R. L. 1997. *A History of US Communications Intelligence during World War II: Policy and Administration*. National Security Agency, Center for Cryptologic History.

Cahn, A. H. 1998. *Killing Detente: The Right Attacks the CIA*. University Park, PA: Pennsylvania State University Press.

Cameron, J. 2018. *The Double Game: The Demise of America's First Missile Defense System and the Rise of Strategic Arms Limitation*. New York: Oxford University Press.

Clark, R. M. 2020. *Geospatial Intelligence. Origins and Evolution*. Washington DC: Georgetown University Press.

Colby, E. A. 2007. "Making Intelligence Smart." *Policy Review*, August & September. www.hoover.org/research/making-intelligence-smart (accessed June 13, 2021).

Cradock, P. 2002. *Know Your Enemy. How the Joint Intelligence Committee Saw the World*. London: John Murray.

Dahl, E. J. 2018. "Review of Marrin, 'Why Strategic Intelligence Analysis Has Limited Influence [. . .]'." *H-Diplo* No. 783. http://tiny.cc/AR783 (accessed June 13, 2021).

Davis, J. 2002. "Sherman Kent and the Profession of Intelligence Analysis." *Kent Center Occasional Papers* 1, no. 5.

Director of National Intelligence. 2014. "The Principles of Professional Ethics for the Intelligence Community." www.dni.gov/index.php/who-we-are/organizations/clpt/clpt-related-menus/clpt-related-links/ic-principles-of-professional-ethics (accessed June 13, 2021).

Durbin, B. 2017. *The CIA and the Politics of US Intelligence Reform*. Cambridge: Cambridge University Press.

Dylan, H., Gioe, D., and Goodman, M. S. 2020. *The CIA and the Pursuit of Security: History, Documents and Contexts*. Edinburgh: Edinburgh University Press.

Ferris, J. 2020. *Behind the Enigma: The Authorized History of GCHQ, Britain's Secret Cyber-Intelligence Agency*. London: Bloomsbury Publishing.

Fingar, Th. 2011. *Reducing Uncertainty: Intelligence Analysis and National Security*. Stanford, CA: Stanford University Press.

Fingar, Th. 2014. "Building a Community of Analysts." In *Analyzing Intelligence: National Security Practitioners' Perspectives*, 2nd edition, ed. R. Z. George and J. B. Bruce, 287–302. Washington DC: Georgetown University Press.

Fingar, Th. 2017. "Office of the Director of National Intelligence: From Pariah to Piñata to Managing Partner." In *The National Security Enterprise: Navigating the Labyrinth*, 2nd edition, ed. R. Z. George and H. Rishikof, 185–203. Washington, DC: Georgetown University Press.

Ford, H. P. 1993. *Estimative Intelligence*. McLean, VA: The Association of Former Intelligence Officers.

Ford, H. P. 1995. "The US Government's Experience with Intelligence Analysis: Pluses and Minuses." *Intelligence and National Security* 10, no. 4: 34–53.

Garthoff, R. L. 1990. "Estimating Soviet Military Force Levels." *International Security* 14, no. 4: 93–116.

Garthoff, R. L. 1994. *Détente and Confrontation: American-Soviet Relations from Nixon to Reagan, Revised Edition*. Washington, DC: The Brookings Institution.

George, R. Z. 2020. *Intelligence in the National Security Enterprise: An Introduction*. Washington, DC: Georgetown University Press.

Herman, M. 2013. "Intelligence in the Cold War: Did It Matter?" In *Geheimdienste, Diplomatie, Krieg. Das Räderwerk der internationalen Beziehungen. Zum 65. Geburtstag von Wolfgang Krieger*, ed. C. Collado Seidel, 55–70. Berlin: LIT Verlag.

Herman, M. 2013. "What Difference Did It Make?" In *Intelligence in the Cold War: What Difference Did it Make?*, ed. M. Herman and G. Hughes, 132–147. London and New York: Routledge.

Hilsman, R. 1956. *Strategic Intelligence and National Decisions*. Glencoe, IL: The Free Press.

Hutchings, R. 2019. "Introduction." In *Truth to Power: A History of the US National Intelligence Council*, ed. R. Hutchings and G. F. Fingar, 1–22. New York: Oxford University Press.

Jervis, R. 2010. "Why Intelligence and Policymakers Clash." *Political Science Quarterly* 125, no. 2: 185–204.

Johnson, R. 2005. *Analytic Culture in the US Intelligence Community: An Ethnographic Study*. Washington, DC: Center for the Study of Intelligence.

Jones, M., and Silberzahn, Ph. 2013. *Constructing Cassandra: Reframing Intelligence Failure at the CIA, 1947–2001*. Stanford, CA: Stanford University Press.

Kent, Sh. 1949. *Strategic Intelligence for American World Policy*. Princeton: Princeton University Press.

Kent, Sh. 1994. "The Law and Custom of the National Intelligence Estimate [1965/1974]." In *Sherman Kent and the Board of National Estimates*, ed. D. P. Steury, 93–98. Washington, DC: Center for the Study of Intelligence.

Knorr, K. 1964. *Foreign Intelligence and the Social Sciences*. Princeton, NJ: Center of International Studies.

Krepinevich, A., and Watts, B. D. 2015. *The Last Warrior: Andrew Marshall and the Shaping of Modern American Defense Strategy: Foreword by Robert M. Gates*. New York: Basic Books.

Lowenthal, M. M. 2014. "The Education and Training of Intelligence Analysts." In *Analyzing Intelligence: National Security Practitioners' Perspectives, Second Edition*, ed. R. Z. George and J. B. Bruce, 303–318. Washington, DC: Georgetown University Press.

Lowenthal, M. M. 2017. *Intelligence: From Secrets to Policy*, 7th edition. Thousand Oaks, CA: SAGE.

Mahnken, T. G., and Marshall, A. W., eds. 2020. *Net Assessment and Military Strategy: Retrospective and Prospective Essays*. Amherst: Cambria Press.

Mannheim, K. 1964. *Wissenssoziologie*. Berlin and Neuwied: Luchterhand.

Marrin, S. 2017. "Why Strategic Intelligence Analysis Has Limited Influence on American Foreign Policy." *Intelligence and National Security* 32, no. 6: 725–742.

Matthias, W. C. 2001. *America's Strategic Blunders: Intelligence Analysis and National Security Policy, 1936–1991*. University Park, PA: Pennsylvania State University Press.

May, E. R. 1985. "Capabilities and Proclivities." In *Knowing One's Enemies: Intelligence Assessment before the Two World War*, ed. E. R. May, 503–542. Princeton: Princeton University Press.

McLaughlin, J. 2014. "Serving the National Policymaker." In *Analyzing Intelligence: National Security Practitioners' Perspectives, Second Edition*, ed. R. Z. George and J. B. Bruce, 81–92. Washington, DC: Georgetown University Press.

Montague, L. L. 1972. "The Origins of National Intelligence Estimating." *Studies in Intelligence* 16, no. 2: 63–70.

Montague, L. L. 1992. *General Walter Bedell Smith as Director of Central Intelligence*. University Park, PA: The Pennsylvania State University Press.

Müller, R.-D. 2017. *Reinhard Gehlen. Geheimdienstchef im Hintergrund der Bonner Republik. Die Biografie. Bd. 2: 1950–1979*. Berlin: Ch. Links.

Pickett, G. E., Roche, J. G., and Watts, B. D. 1991. "Net Assessment: A Historical Review." In *On Not Confusing Ourselves: Essays on National Security Strategy in Honor of Albert and Roberta Wohlstetter*, ed. A. W. Marshall, J. J. Martin and H. S. Rowen, 158–185. Boulder, CO: Westview Press.

Rovner, J. 2011. *Fixing the Facts: National Security and the Politics of Intelligence*. Ithaca, NY: Cornell University Press.

Rovner, J. 2018. "Intelligence and National Decision Making." In *The Oxford Handbook of US National Security*, ed. D. S. Reveron, N. K. Gvosdev, and J. A. Cloud, 136–141. New York: Oxford University Press.

Scheler, M. 1980 [[1]1924]. *Die Wissensformen und die Gesellschaft*. Dritte, durchgesehene Auflage. Bern and Munich: Francke Verlag.

Smith, K. W., and Enthoven, A. 1971. *How Much is Enough? Shaping the Defense Program 1961–1969*. Santa Monica, CA: RAND.

Suettinger, R. L. 2004. "Introduction (English)." In *Tracking the Dragon: National Intelligence Estimates on China during the Era of Mao, 1948–1976*. Washington, DC: NIC 2004–05.

Thorne, C. T. Jr., and Patterson, D. S., eds. 1996. *Foreign Relations of the United States 1945–1950: Emergence of the Intelligence Establishment*. Washington, DC: Government Printing Office.

Trachtenberg, M. 2010. "Social Scientists and National Security Policymaking." *Discussion Paper*. www.sscnet.ucla.edu/polisci/faculty/trachtenberg/cv/cv.html (accessed June 13, 2021).

Trachtenberg, M. 2011. "History and Policy." *Discussion Paper*. www.sscnet.ucla.edu/polisci/faculty/trachtenberg/cv/cv.html (accessed June 13, 2021).

Trachtenberg, M. 2018. "Assessing Soviet Economic Performance During the Cold War: A Failure of Intelligence?" *Texas National Security Review* 1, no. 2: 76–101.

Treverton, G. F. 2019. "Conclusion." In *Truth to Power: A History of the US National Intelligence Council*, ed. R. Hutchings and G. F. Treverton, 198–208. New York: Oxford University Press.

Valero, L. A. 2000. "The American Joint Intelligence Committee and Estimates of the Soviet Union, 1945–1947." *Studies in Intelligence* 44, no. 3.

Walton, C. 2019. "Intelligence, US Foreign Relations, and Historical Amnesia." *Passport: The SHAFR Review* 50, no. 1: 33–39.

Warner, M., and Macdonald, J. K. 2005. *US Intelligence Community Reform Studies Since 1947*. Washington, DC: Center for the Study of Intelligence.

Yarhi-Milo, K. 2013. "In the Eye of the Beholder: How Leaders and Intelligence Communities Assess the Intentions of Adversaries." *International Security* 38, no. 1: 7–51.

Yost, D. S. 2011. "Strategic Stability in the Cold War: Lessons for Continuing." *Challenges, Proliferation Papers*, no. 36.

Zegart, A. B. 1999. *Flawed by Design: The Evolution of the CIA, JCS, and NSC*. Stanford, CA: Stanford University Press.

4 American security databases and the production of space, 1967–1974

Enhancing or obscuring patterns?

Jens Wegener

Introduction

Several years ago, in the wake of the Edward Snowden revelations, the German news magazine *Der Spiegel* trained an infrared camera on the US Embassy complex in Berlin and discovered curious heat signatures emanating from a windowless structure on the building's roof. The mysterious annex, *Der Spiegel* concluded, was part of the National Security Agency's global surveillance infrastructure detailed in the Snowden materials and thus served to spy on one of America's closest allies.[1] This preoccupation with the physical evidence of electronic surveillance echoed events surrounding similar revelations in the 1980s and 1990s, which had sent journalists and hobbyists alike searching for installations connected to the ECHELON intelligence networks run by the Five Eyes SIGINT alliance between the United States, Canada, Great Britain, Australia and New Zealand. Obviously, embassies and other diplomatic or military posts in foreign countries have been used as bases for intelligence operations for millennia. Yet, while the occasional exposure of a spy operating out of these missions tends to elicit at least as much bemusement about fake moustaches and would-be-James-Bond theatrics as genuine outrage, there appears to be an elevated level of concern attached to the quiet, invisible application of electronic surveillance methods.

This discrepancy points to the extent to which innovations in information processing and knowledge production on the part of intelligence agencies reverberated in the public sphere, even shaping people's perception of their environment. It is no accident that reactions to these more recent disclosures share certain features with events from the early 1970s, especially a little-remembered intelligence scandal involving the intelligence arm of the US Army. While the Watergate Scandal and President Richard M. Nixon's attempt to enrol the CIA in his campaigns against political rivals often looms large in discussions of government secrecy, it tends to be forgotten that the Watergate revelations resonated powerfully at the time because they intersected with a public debate on surveillance and democratic norms that was well underway by the time Nixon's transgressions became public. In January 1970, or two and a half years before the term "Watergate" began to make front-page headlines, Christopher H. Pyle, a former Army intelligence officer, published a detailed account in the *Washington Monthly*, alleging the existence

DOI: 10.4324/9781003147329-5

86 *Jens Wegener*

of a vast domestic spying operation run by the US Army's Intelligence Command (USAINTC). Allegedly, the Army utilised both old-fashioned spies and informants as well as cutting-edge technology such as a computer database to track the political activities of anti-war protestors and civil rights activists in an effort to control political unrest in the country. According to Pyle, the operation was slated to be expanded significantly in the immediate future, with dire implications for civil liberties:

> If the Army's fascination with the collection of domestic intelligence continues to grow as it has in the recent past, the Intelligence Command could use military funds to develop one of the largest domestic intelligence operations outside of the communist world.[2]

The ensuing scandal inspired a debate about governmental "data banks" that would set the template for intelligence scandals and inspire critical approaches to government surveillance not only in the United States but in democratic societies around the world.

The extent of the government's powers to surveil its own population in the name of national security is a subject of perennial debate in democratic societies, touching on conceptions of national identity as well as necessitating politically challenging trade-offs between individual liberty and collective security. In a general sense, when the US Army's military intelligence components rather haphazardly inserted novel technology, in this case through the process of digitisation, into this equation, the result was a case study of the possible unintended consequences that attended the scientisation of knowledge production in the national security field. More specifically, the episode offers a contained example of the circulation of knowledge systems between academic, state institutions and the public.

In opting to computerise production of their intelligence threat assessments, the US Army essentially modified the way it constructed the world for senior military and civilian leaders.[3] Once publicly revealed, however, the notion of an ever-present yet largely invisible government computer gazing upon its citizenry was widely perceived as a fundamental challenge to liberal constructions of space, especially of the so-called public square. In his *Production of Space*, Henri Lefebvre argued that one of the strongest mechanisms concealing the social constructedness of space was what he called the "illusion of transparency" in Western societies: according to the Enlightenment tradition, space was viewed as "innocent, as free of traps or secret places."[4] Security databases for counterintelligence purposes challenged this paradigm by promising to uncover what was hidden while themselves remaining in the shadows of the national security apparatus.

The most jarring element of the scandal can thus be conceptualised as a clash between the representational space of the public square, permeated with liberal values of accessibility and transparency, and the securitised, technocratic space – "conceived space" in Lefebvrian terminology[5] – of the intelligence bureaucracy. Insofar as quantitative social science methods employing computer technology were closely linked to the larger modernist project of social science, this conflict could not but reverberate back into political discourse, popular culture, and, ultimately, the academic institutions that had originally produced these modernist knowledge systems. Although modernisation theory was already controversial by the end of the decade,[6] incidents such as the USAINTC scandal served to further discredit the entire intellectual project of expert-guided social change and opened the door to post-modern critiques. For instance, public reactions to computerised intelligence systems contributed to an emerging critical master narrative of governmental surveillance centred on the imagery of the "panopticon" that has proved markedly resilient. As David Lyon has argued in a survey of the theoretical assumptions underlying the field of surveillance studies, the field's continuing preoccupation with the panopticon appears outdated and is indicative of the lasting legacy of the "Enlightenment privileging of vision as a means to order and control."[7] Yet, the proliferation of computing technology in intelligence work also challenged the idea of a singular centre of surveillance, be it Langley or the Lubyanka, with a more diffuse notion of the government's watchful eye. Ultimately, the USAINTC databases were early examples of the type of digital surveillance infrastructures for intelligence and policing purposes that Mike Davis has identified as partially responsible for turning American cities into "post-liberal" spaces in the 1970s and 1980s.[8]

This chapter is based on declassified government records, archival materials from the American Civil Liberties Union, as well as reports detailing the US Congress's investigations into the matter in the early-to-mid 1970s.[9] The aim is to use the US Army surveillance scandal to probe the utility of examining counterintelligence databases as a technology shaping knowledge of space in two ways: firstly, by allowing intelligence services to surveil social spaces that appeared difficult to reach by other means, and, secondly, by affecting the public's knowledge, or lack thereof, of its government's national security architecture.

Security databases as a spatial technology

Computerised databases produced knowledge for the purpose of enhancing the government's control over its sovereign territory and its wider sphere of influence. By linking spatial to individual biographical information, security databases stood in the tradition of technologies of human geography that had been devised over the centuries, from the cartographical works of the Renaissance to aerial reconnaissance during the two world wars. For all their variations across organisational and subject contexts, early counterintelligence databases in the late 1960s and early 1970s followed a very similar blueprint that was largely dictated by the off-the-shelf hardware solutions they employed: they were static lists, usually divided into biographical, events, and/or organisational files, and often connected through a set of IDs for cross-referencing. Data usage was minimised and opportunities for employing statistical methods maximised by utilising alpha-numerical codes instead of plain text wherever possible. The time savings achieved by this computerisation in the course of the day-to-day investigative work of intelligence agencies should not be overestimated. What these systems did represent was a new way of

88   *Jens Wegener*

modelling the social geography of societies with a view to detecting imminent threats. They can be seen as a further step in the "process of progressive elevation of the gaze, which by extending human vision beyond the immediate horizon . . . allowed humans to master distance and project power beyond the limits of the human body."[10]

Such a perspective does not necessarily need to adopt a monolithic perspective on power and space. Indeed, contest rather than hegemony over spaces was an integral part of the conflicts of the 1960s. For instance, early Black Panther Party activism would challenge police brutality in Black neighbourhoods by sending African-American patrols, armed with guns and notepads, onto the streets both as a deterrent and to document police misconduct.[11] For both protestors and security agencies of the state, carving out and maintaining spaces of exclusive control – be they secret government installations or occupied college campuses – was a key goal.[12]

The early debate over intelligence databases also casts a light on the interrelationship between digital technology, the nation and the global. In the 1960s and 1970s, protest movements were increasingly embedded in transnational contacts and discourses in ways that challenged the idea of a self-contained, national politics. Such global connections could broaden activists' mental maps, leading them to view themselves as part of global struggles against injustice.[13] Viewed against the backdrop of the Cold War, such contacts could also easily raise the spectre of possible subversion in the eyes of Western (and Eastern) security services, leading these agencies to diagnose a knowledge gap in the transnational space, to be filled with new technological capabilities. Part of the story of the surveillance scandals of the 1960s and 1970s is thus that the very means which had allowed global ideological communities to thrive – for example international postal agreements, electronic communications networks, computerised airline booking systems – were now being employed by states as collection methods to reconstruct the social web of transnational politics. Public exposure of such intelligence operations tended, in turn, to undermine public confidence in the state.[14] This constellation casts the computer as an ambiguous symbol of the spatial reordering between the national and the global, construed as either an instrument of state power in a tale of panoptic surveillance or a facilitator of globalisation, in which the computerised database "keeps the globals in the sieve and washes out the locals."[15] The security database may thus serve as an example of what Saskia Sassen has characterised as the "disassembling of the national," in which the tools and capabilities of the nation-state evolved, over time, into constitutive parts of global systems.[16]

The Army's computerised surveillance infrastructure

From the moment computers entered the national security bureaucracy of the United States in the context of the early Cold War, optimising control over space had been a key theme in the way the new technology was applied. The combination of nuclear weapons with long-range bombers and, later, ballistic missile technology created a genuinely novel threat environment in which defending the territorial integrity of the United States was dependent on continual surveillance of air space and on real-time calculations of aircraft trajectories and possible interception vectors that exceeded human capabilities. The Development of the Semi-Automatic Ground Environment (SAGE) in the 1950s was a response to this new threat. It also was the starting point of government funding for computer research and served as a major boost for the nascent American computing industry, which soon decisively outpaced its European competitors. SAGE has been aptly characterised by Paul Edwards as part of a "closed world" discourse, "a dome of global technological oversight" in which every event was enrolled, whether rhetorically or through real-time calculation, into the global Cold War.[17]

A major extension of the use of electronic data processing (EDP) came in the 1960s and is closely associated with the figure of Secretary of Defense Robert McNamara, under whose leadership the Pentagon became famously keen to employ modern management concepts, including statistical techniques. The Vietnam War became a proving ground for this vision of marrying the art of war with the science of rational administration. A McNamarian project that can be seen as, if not an immediate precursor, at least a close cousin of the domestic civil disturbance infrastructure was the Hamlet Evaluation System (HES). It was initiated in late 1966 by CIA officer George W. Allen in response to the Secretary of Defense's dissatisfaction with the government's inability to objectively measure the "pacification" process in South Vietnam. Instead of relying on impressionistic bird's-eye assessments from senior commanders or intelligence officers, HES would build a picture from the ground up, starting with the lowest level of South Vietnamese administrative organisation – the country's roughly 12,000 hamlets. District Advisors would periodically visit each hamlet in their region and assign scores on a number of criteria seen as indicative of stability. These were then fed into a computer at US Military Assistance Command to produce a range of quantitative measurements for stability over time, such as charts, trend lines or color-coded maps.[18]

The validity of HES's output was soon called into question for a number of methodological and political reasons, but to the extent that the programme failed it was certainly not for a lack of effort. A contemporary CIA history emphasises the novel challenges presented by the programme, noting that HES posed "formidable problems in data processing."[19] Consulting on the project were some of the finest minds of American social science through such contractors as the RAND Corporation and ARPA. The programme was a major step forward in the military's production of cartographical, or conceived, space by combining social science and cartography in virtual real-time. Up-to-date intelligence on socio-economic conditions could be fed into the computer, manipulated with an array of statistical techniques, overlaid onto graphic representations of the "battle-space" and then collectively inform operational decisions. Above all, as a joint military-civilian project, HES attested to the Army's, but also the larger intelligence community's, faith in technology's ability to transform a murky situation based on complex social relations into "legible, systemic narratives."[20]

90 *Jens Wegener*

This project must have been fresh in the minds of Pentagon leaders when in the summer of 1967 violent protests erupted in a series of American cities, most notably in Detroit and Newark. The sudden outburst of violence surprised policy-makers, and the Lyndon B. Johnson Administration reacted by tasking federal agencies with uncovering the sources of social unrest. For military leaders, mean-while, the events threw into stark relief how unprepared the US Army was to fulfil its legal obligation to quell domestic uprisings and restore order at a time when most of its resources were committed to an overseas conflict. While troops in Viet-nam could rely on the latest advances in aerial and satellite reconnaissance to guide their operations, their comrades deployed to restore public order in Detroit "had little more than Esso road maps to guide them," according to a newspaper report.[21]

In the weeks following the initial violence, the Pentagon strove to rapidly improve its response to what became known as the "civil disturbance" problem, with Brigadier General John J. Hennessy placed in charge of a special study group. As a result, a new Directorate for Civil Disturbance Planning and Operations (DCDPO) was created under the authority of the Chief of Staff of the Army. The task group also endorsed the idea of a "statistical data base" to track outbreaks of violence across the country. While the explicit database reference in the Hen-nessy Report would seem to suggest that the computerisation of Army intelligence was a conscious decision to aim for a scientisation of intelligence knowledge, the uncoordinated and improvised implementation of the idea tells a different story. At least at three separate Army facilities around the country, officers appear to have launched computerisation efforts in response to pressure from military com-manders for quicker and more comprehensive information. USAINTC commander William H. Blakefield was known to remind subordinates that he wanted them to "beat the Associated Press" in terms of reporting speed.[22] Thus, the Army's scat-tershot approach provides a clear example of political pressures, in conjunction with contemporary modernisation discourses circulating at the highest levels of the Pentagon and the Johnson administration, driving computerisation, rather than any thought-out program of "scientisation."

Located in the Pentagon's basement and stretching over several dozen offices, conference and service rooms, the DCDPO was a textbook example of a Latou-rian centre of calculation in which data, expertise and physical resources were enrolled into a single project. There were areas devoted to mapping, media moni-toring, communications, as well as a dedicated computer centre.[23] The purpose was to bring the resources of the United States military and cooperating federal, state and local agencies such as the Department of Justice and municipal police departments to bear on the "civil disturbance" issue. The databases were mainly fed by so-called "spot reports" from army intelligence units, but Federal Bureau of Investigations (FBI) reports and newspaper clippings also formed the basis for computer entries. Robert E. Jordan, the Army's General Counsel at the time, later explained the largely additive and indiscriminate collection effort as inherent in the professional identity of the officers: "The difficulty is that intelligence people . . . are 'pack rats.' There is a strong tendency to keep, organize and manipulate what-ever information happens to come into the system."[24] Congressional investigators would later discover that one set of databases had been operated by the Continental Army Command (CONARC), while another system launched by the Fourth Army was still in its very early stages. The largest and most controversial of the databases was operated by USAINTC's own headquarters.

Due to its mission of screening army personnel for security clearances, USAINTC already held millions of personal files by the mid-1960s, including special files on "subversives" seen as a direct threat to military security.[25] In the weeks after the Detroit and Newark riots, a new "incident file" for keeping track of protests, outbursts of political violence, internal army security incidents and so forth was begun that utilised an automated punched card index for quick access. In the summer of 1968, this index was then transferred to an old IBM 1401 computer, which had been used as a back-up system by the base's Data Handling Center. Having been upgraded with additional memory capacity, the computer's database grew from 100,000 to 280,000 entries on 47 reels of magnetic tape between November 1968 and February 1970.[26] The incident file was complemented by a "biographical data file" that would eventually contain about 4,000 entries and gave additional personal information and coded membership in any of 770 groups, from the Communist Party of China to the NAACP.

The Army's attempts to employ technology as a tool for clarifying the social structure of American dissent were by no means unique. By the second half of the 1960s, everywhere in the American intelligence community, particularly in counterintelligence, computers were beginning to be utilised for extending the view of the government into spaces not easily illuminated by other means, such as human informants. Taking inspiration from projects such as HES, in the fall of 1967 the Research Analysis Corporation, an Army-affiliated think tank, proposed that the Army's counterintelligence branch should develop a complex computer system that would produce forecasts on how many troops would be needed to contain uprisings in specific American cities.[27] The suggestion was rejected; however, the idea that computers offered a technological solution to the government's tenuous grip on the security situation in the country, specifically its college campuses and urban centres, would inspire a host of EDP initiative – in both military and intelligence units. The data architecture of USAINTC's Incident Database is particularly instructive in this regard: in addition to a narrative description of the protest or similar occurrence, all entries contained numerical codes associated with persons and organisations that had been observed in connection with the event. This, a congressional report noted, allowed analysts to search the entire database "to produce lists of members of particular organizations and lists of organizations to which specified persons belonged."[28] The system therefore became a powerful cross-referencing tool that could be used to track a person's presence at events over time and space, essentially providing a visual representation of their movement around the United States.

The original purpose of this data architecture was to lay the empirical groundwork for advanced statistical computer analyses, which, army intelligence officials hoped, would enable them to effectively predict imminent violence, giving military units precious time for planning and deployment purposes. Colonel James D.

92 *Jens Wegener*

Akins, CONARC's chief intelligence officer, even contemplated coding socio-logical data on major urban areas into the computer, including "income dispar-ity between minority and majority groups, . . . segregation, lack of jobs, lack of recreation facilities, police brutality." Combined with the travel patterns of known "agitators," he hoped this data would point to areas where violence was likely to occur.[29] Backing for the concept of employing computers as predictive tools came from the top levels of the Pentagon, including senior generals and Army Chief of Staff Harold K. Johnson, for whom the databases apparently became something of a "pet project."[30]

There was, nevertheless, a striking gap between the scale of the Army's designs and the relatively minor investments in infrastructure and intellectual firepower. Paul Jordan, the head of USAINTC's computer centre later admitted that, in fact, "no attempt was made to analyze the information."[31] This was partly due to a lack of expertise. Congressional investigators later openly mocked the intelligence offi-cers who had overseen the design of these databases for dabbling in social science without seeing the need to consult any trained social scientists. During one inter-view they suggested, without much pushback, that the officers had taken their cues on possible indicators of incipient violence from *Newsweek* articles or "just kind of seat of the pants feeling."[32] On the one hand, this overconfidence on the part of Army intelligence points to the extent to which the language of social science had become such a common trope in intelligence circles that even practices derived from quantitative sociology were seen as part of the inherent skill set of trained intelligence professional, not specialist techniques requiring external expertise. The lack of contractor support as well as a general under-investment in technical infrastructure may also have been caused by senior officials at the Pentagon who were less convinced of the entire scheme than either the top generals or the officers on the ground.[33]

The main obstacle to the grander design of the civil disturbance databases, how-ever, was that political and policy support began to wane after only a few months. In April 1968 the assassination of Martin Luther King Jr. led to a wave of violent uprisings in dozens of American cities, affecting all regions of the United States. The wide geographic distribution and socio-economic variety of areas affected convinced military and civilian leaders that the military's ability to predict the locations of future disturbances was "extremely limited" and likely not technically feasible.[34] Indeed, the longer the unrest lasted, the more the search for root causes moved away from domestic, sociological paradigms and towards national security concerns grounded in Cold War narratives. This included lobbying by influential members of Congress, who pressed the intelligence services for evidence that the unrest gripping the country was part of a communist plot directed from Moscow or Beijing to undermine public order in the United States.[35]

Military intelligence participated in the search for external instigators, but with-out much success. A CONUS Intelligence study dated June 28, 1968, was char-acteristic of the vague prose that proliferated in intelligence evaluations across the US government at the time: "No definite intelligence exists to substantiate foreign control, direction, or significant financial support to civil rights or anti-war elements," the document declared. However, it then caveated this statement, noting "continuing grave concern" on the subject and listing a number of loose ends that merited further investigation, such as the clear desire of communist regimes to foment dissent within the United States, the high potential that disaffected American youths would become intelligence targets for communist agencies and the generally leftist politics of foreign anti-war groups.[36] These questions found their institutional expression in a series of guidance letters and collection plans issued between 1967 and 1969, in which various elements of the Department of Defense instructed Army intelligence units on the ground to pay special attention to evidence of ties between American protestors and foreign actors. A USAINTC collection plan listed "foreign element participation" as one of 11 reporting categories. Agents were encouraged to look for foreign nationals seeking to steer or disrupt meetings or conferences. They were also ordered to report on foreign travel by "American activists in civil rights organizations who have attempted to obtain support for these organizations in foreign countries."[37]

Public scrutiny and post-modern space

The Army's foray into the digital "civil disturbance" space ended even quicker than it had begun. Within days of the system becoming public knowledge in January 1970, orders went out to all commands to halt the development of all counterintelligence databases and to begin destroying all tapes and paper records associated with them.[38] Soon publicly recognised as a cover-up, the Pentagon's reaction to unwanted publicity only served to further underscore the apparent gulf between public expectations of the nation's military as an accountable and, ultimately, observable institution and the new allegations of the military operating a vast, secret surveillance infrastructure. Over the previous decades, military installations in the continental United States such as Army forts, Navy bases and coastal gun batteries had served as symbols of the nation's defence of its shores as well as its growing ability to project military force around the world. In the 1970s, this narrative was challenged by a critique that cast government and especially national security installations as *loci* of threats to liberty and democracy. The veil of security and secrecy that surrounded them served to obscure their true danger. The USAINTC scandal's contribution to this new view of the relationship between government, technology and space can be schematically sketched in the following five steps.

The first step was the publication of Christopher Pyle's allegations in the *Washington Monthly*, suggesting that the government had constructed a technological surveillance infrastructure that quite consciously subverted established aesthetics of democratic accountability. The famous March on the Pentagon in October 1967, in which tens of thousands of anti-war protestors had used a planned rally at the Lincoln Memorial to cross the Potomac for a tense stand-off at the gates of the Pentagon, had demonstrated the extent to which the seat of American military power had itself become a target of dissent. That the headquarters of the Department of Defense would emerge as a contested symbol of America's

94 *Jens Wegener*

military involvement in Southeast Asia and, more broadly, the country's Cold War posture, was part and parcel of a tradition of democratic accountability. After all, Washington, DC, was a planned city whose vast avenues and open lawns reflected the values of its Enlightenment authors with their preference for sweeping vistas and physical manifestations of the public square. While the Pentagon's grounds were off-limits to all but a relatively small circle of authorised personnel, its striking layout and highly accessible location near several main thoroughfares of the Greater Washington, DC, area placed it in the tradition of the nation's public architecture.

The very fact that the Army's novel technological intelligence infrastructure had remained hidden from public view for almost two years, at a time when interest in the protest movement and in the government's response to it was high, suggested that avoiding scrutiny was part of the technology's appeal to the Pentagon. For one, the public could only guess as to the extent of the Army's intelligence operations directed from the facility, shielded from external scrutiny in the basement of a secure government building. In the summer of 1968, a journalist described the DCDPO as a "gaping hole the size of a drydock in the Pentagon's basement," as army officials could not agree on a final layout due to disputes over money and priorities.[39] Furthermore, there was the question to what extent the Pentagon was even at the heart of the Army's surveillance apparatus. While the DCDPO bundled military intelligence analysis, the same was not necessarily true for intelligence collection, and there is no doubt that at least when it came to computerised data collection, the centre of gravity lay neither in Arlington, VA, nor in Washington, DC. The computer operating USAINTC's incident database was housed, far away from the public-facing architecture of the nation's capital, in an inconspicuous "wire-mesh 'cage' located inside a gray metal warehouse" at Fort Holabird in Southeast Baltimore. CONARC ran its databases from its headquarters at Fort Monroe in Virginia and the Fourth Army's incipient computer program was based at Fort Hood in Texas.

A second step was a legal counterattack by civil society groups against what they saw as an illegal intrusion of the Army on the constitutional rights of Americans. Within weeks of the *Washington Monthly* article, the ACLU filed a lawsuit against the Department of Defense on behalf of Arlo Tatum, an activist working with conscientious objectors, who had been explicitly named in Pyle's expose. *Laird v. Tatum* would eventually reach the Supreme Court and to this day ranks as a landmark case – a "philosophical origin point"[40] – in American jurisprudence delineating the surveillance powers of the federal government. It also sharpened competing claims regarding control over the public sphere. To the ACLU, the Army's maintenance of the intelligence databases, along with other unlawful behaviour, was unconstitutional because their very presence was intended to "harass and intimidate" political dissenters.[41]

In particular, the Army's databases presented an implicit assault on cherished norms seen as central to the nation's self-image as a land of unbounded opportunity. Americans believed that law-abiding citizens did not owe the government a running tally of their activities and their whereabouts. By the late 1960s, the fact that large-scale computerised databases had the potential to more effectively transmit information across the vast territorial expanse of the United States had become a topic of public discussion. While in the past, simply moving to another state might have helped evade the memory of past financial transgressions, automated credit bureau files now meant that such records were readily available around the country. In 1967, the FBI had inaugurated its National Crime Information Center, a central computer system at FBI headquarters that allowed law enforcement officers anywhere in the United States to check personal and license plate information against a national database within minutes of making a stop. While many Americans welcomed these changes as symbols of modernity, others worried that the inefficiencies addressed by these computer systems had been integral to some of the freedoms Americans had enjoyed.

In a third step, the government countered these claims by seeking legal rulings that explicitly exempted intelligence computer databases from the sphere of democratic accountability. In its legal filings in response to *Laird v. Tatum* and in other similar cases, the government did not so much seek to make a positive case for the controversial programmes but disputed the public's right to know about them in the first place, including, in the specific case, the ACLU's right to compel testimony or documentation from the Army. In seeking to delineate an exclusionary zone the eye of the public could not be permitted to reach, the district court judge, siding with the government, repeatedly likened the Army's computer systems to "the morgues of the newspapers in this country." It was an analogy that on the one hand refused to draw a distinction between the right of private organisations to collect information in pursuit of constitutionally protected projects of public accountability and the government's effort to collect data on its citizens. Furthermore, the word "morgue," with its connotations of mortality, also invoked for the country's national security infrastructure the type of special protections against trespassing usually reserved for sacred or taboo spaces.[42]

The fourth step took the matter out of the secluded spheres of social activism and legal proceedings and into the broader arena of public debate, ensuring that the Army's conduct would serve as a point of reference in discussions of surveillance, privacy and national security. Under the chairmanship of Senator Sam J. Ervin Jr. the US Senate Judiciary Committee's Subcommittee on Constitutional Rights held a series of hearings which progressively broadened from an enquiry into the military's alleged conduct into a wider investigation of the use and abuse of computing technology and personal information by federal agencies.[43] These hearings greatly increased the visibility of critiques of the Army's intelligence system as Americans read of the supposed misconduct of the government's "data bankers" and even about fears of an incipient "dossier dictatorship" in their morning newspapers.[44] Within a few years, Ervin would move on from these investigations to leading the Senate's impeachment investigations of Richard Nixon. Perhaps even more consequentially, Ervin's work on government misconduct, surveillance and privacy would set the template for the following post-Watergate investigations of the US intelligence community, which led to new restrictions on the activities of the CIA and the FBI.[45]

96   *Jens Wegener*

The fifth and final step saw critical discourses of governmental surveillance circulating nationally and transnationally, effectively serving to discredit some of the modernist social science practices that had formed the basis for the US Army's computerisation plans in the first place. The Watergate Scandal, President Nixon's resignation and subsequent investigations into CIA and FBI conduct attracted a great deal of attention and created a fruitful intellectual atmosphere for postmodern critiques of traditional sources of authority. The 1970s saw a large increase in both scholarly and popular publications dealing with the dangers of a computerised society, in which the Army scandal and subsequent cases of intelligence agencies' overreach usually served as prominent case studies.[46] While critical accounts of the impact of EDP technology on American society were certainly nothing new, moving the debate into the sphere of national security significantly heightened the stakes. Collectively, these responses to the Army scandal became a key founding moment of what David Lyon has called the "modernist frame" of critical surveillance studies, a first school of the incipient discipline that placed the nation-state and its agencies at the centre of a panoptic surveillance infrastructure.[47] Consider that Henri Lefebvre's *The Production of Space* was published in 1974. A year later, Michel Foucault published *Discipline and Punish*, whose impact on ideas on panoptic surveillance can hardly be overstated. Even earlier, Gary T. Marx's *Civil Disorder and the Agents of Social Control* (1970), an early point of reference for the field of surveillance studies, was itself the result of Marx's immersion into the field of civil rights protests.

Conclusion

In today's historical memory, the Army surveillance scandal ranks as a second- or third-tier scandal, overshadowed by the subsequent Watergate scandal and associated disclosures of FBI and CIA misconduct. Yet in many ways the events of 1968 to 1971 set the template for a post-modernisation of space that lastingly undermined liberal ideals of the government as a custodian of the public square. It thereby exemplifies the pitfalls of the ever-closer relationship between intelligence work and the social sciences that had developed in the 1960s. The Army's initial conceptual framework in creating its databases had centred on finding riot "indicators" and posited that the civil disturbance problematic was entangled in broader issues of crime and social justice in urban areas. This would have enabled the Johnson Administration to enrol the fight against rioting into the anti-crime and anti-poverty fight of President Johnson's Great Society program. This approach proved ultimately ineffective, not least because at the subordinate command levels where these projects were implemented, "social science" remained more of an aspiration and a slogan than a practice.

The disclosure of these operations in Christopher Pyle's article than proved a jarring experience as the logic of Army Intelligence's conceived space, with its underlying assumptions as to where the locus of domestic threats lay in the United States, collided with the everyday experiences of the public. The military then responded to the scandal by at least reaffirming, if not significantly broadening its claim to an arcane sphere outside the bounds of public scrutiny. In a filing in response to a lawsuit brought by the ACLU the Army's lawyers almost taunted the opposing side with its inability to substantiate any claims of adverse impact in the absence of greater openness by the government: "plaintiffs allege that the Army has breached its duty because they, the plaintiffs, are afraid – afraid of the unknown."[48] By thus calling attention to the public's inability to even perceive the potential traps set by its surveillance systems, the government effectively drew back the curtain on the "illusion of transparency" that had been foundational to the liberal project.

In the process, the idea of social change directed by bureaucrats wielding the tool of social science lost a great deal of appeal once it was viewed as wedded to the state's coercive power and directed quite indiscriminately at the public. As the fallout from the Army intelligence scandal, as well as similar revelations about the FBI and the CIA that came to light in the post-Watergate era, resonated with the American and foreign publics, post-modern – in the strict sense of the term – critiques of the liberal state, including of liberal-capitalist spatial organisation, began to proliferate. In the process, the events of the early 1970s became so intertwined with the historical development of the conceptual toolkit of surveillance studies that there is a risk of reproducing the very discourses that were themselves contingent outcomes of the events being examined. Careful study of the historical context of these events, including the utilisation of biographical approaches is thus needed to avoid circular reasoning and to gain a fuller picture of the intelligence/surveillance conundrum.

A direct outcome of the controversy surrounding the Army's surveillance practices and a somewhat curious artefact is a stipulation of the Privacy Act of 1974 which mandates to this day that American federal agencies file public notices documenting all of their computer systems processing personal information. Unlike many other disclosure and transparency requirements, not even classified systems such as those run by the CIA are completely exempt, even if descriptions are sometimes enigmatic and code names are withheld for security reasons. For instance, an entry for a system which presumably is a late and distant relative to the Army's security databases of the 1970s, the Defense Intelligence Agency's Department of Defense Insider Threat Management and Analysis Center, offers few details about its scope or operational details, but the record is nevertheless highly specific on a particular point: the primary location of the database is at 27130 Telegraph Road in Quantico, Virginia.[49]

Notes

1 "Das Spionagenest am Brandenburger Tor," *Spiegel Online*, 28 October 2013. <www.spiegel.de/politik/ausland/waermebilder-von-mutmasslichen-us-spionagenest-in-berliner-botschaft-a-930327.html> (last accessed July 15, 2021).
2 Pyle, "CONUS Intelligence," 6.
3 Cf. Introduction, 3.
4 Lefebvre, *Production of Space*, 28.
5 Ibid., 38–39.

98　*Jens Wegener*

6　Cf. Latham, *Modernity as Ideology*.
7　Lyon, "The Search for Surveillance Theories," 4.
8　Cf. Davis, *City of Quartz*, 223 and 253.
9　See especially "Reports and Other Records Relating to the United States Army Intelligence Command," Entry UD 1073, RG 319 Records of the Army Staff, NARA II RG 319; and "Background Papers for 'The Role of Federal Forces in Civil Disturbances, 1945–1971', Entry 145-V, RG 319 Records of the Army Staff, NARA II RG 319; Subgroup 2, ACLU Records, Princeton Mudd Library.
10　Muscara, "Maps," 377.
11　Cf. Bloom and Martin, *Black Against Empire*, 59.
12　On Black nationalist conceptions of space, see Tyner, "Defend the Ghetto," 105–118.
13　Cf. Malloy, *Out of Oakland*; Lucks, *Selma to Saigon*; Klimke, *Other Alliance*.
14　Cf. Wegener, "Order and Chaos"; Kirchberg and Schmeer, "Traube Affair"; Bergien, "'Big Data' als Vision"; Vries, "Central Intelligence Agency Scandal."
15　Bauman, *Globalization*, 51.
16　Cf. Sassen, *Territory, Authority, Rights*, 21.
17　Edwards, *Closed World*, 1.
18　Cf. Young, "Computing War Narratives," 9–10.
19　"A History of the Hamlet Evaluation System (HEC)," ca. 1973, CIA CREST <https://www.cia.gov/readingroom/docs/CIA-RDP80R01720R000200120009-4.pdf>
20　Young, "Computing War Narratives," 1.
21　"Army Fed Names of 18,000 U.S. Civilians into it Computers in 2-Year Operation," *New York Times*, 18 January 1971.
22　Ibid.
23　See blueprints in Folder "103–05 Civil Disturbance: Army Operations Center, 1968," in "Background Papers for 'The Role of Federal Forces in Civil Disturbances, 1945–1971'," RG 319, Entry 145-V, Box 1, NARA II.
24　*Military Surveillance: Hearings Before the Subcommittee on Constitutional Rights of the Committee on the Judiciary. United States Senate. Ninety-Third Congress, Second Session* (Washington: GPO, 1974), 18.
25　*Military Surveillance of Civilian Politics: A Report of the Subcommittee on Constitutional Rights. Committee on the Judiciary. United States Senate* (Washington, DC: GPO, 1973), 61.
26　Cf. Jordan, "Memorandum for Colonel McCartney; Subject: Conus Intelligence Incident File," 3 February 1971, doc. 39, Folder "Feb 1971: 27–88a," Entry UD 1073, RG 319 Records of the Army Staff, NARA II.
27　*Military Surveillance of Civilian Politics: A Report*, 77.
28　Ibid., 62.
29　Memo by J.A. McChristian, "House Investigation of Army Surveillance," 11 February 1971, doc. 59, Folder "Feb 1971: 27–88a," Entry UD 1073, RG 319 Records of the Army Staff, NARA II. *Military Surveillance of Civilian Politics: A Report*, 62.
30　*Military Surveillance: Hearings before the Subcommittee on Constitutional Rights of the Committee on the Judiciary*, 300.
31　Jordan, "Memorandum for Colonel McCartney."
32　Memo by J.A. McChristian, "House Investigation of Army Surveillance," 11 February 1971.
33　Milton B. Hyman of the Defense Department's Office of the General Counsel testified that the Office of the Assistant Chief of Staff for Intelligence went along with the database project but "never really seemed enthusiastic about it" as they doubted its promised predictive capabilities; cf. "Military Surveillance Hearings," 300.
34　David E. McGiffert, Under Secretary of the Army, to Gen. Bruce Palmer, Vice Chief of Staff, 5 February 1969, Folder "103–05 Civil Disturbance: Intelligence Activities, 1970," in "Background Papers for 'The Role of Federal Forces in Civil Disturbances,

1945–1971'," RG 319, Entry 145-V, Box 9, NARA II; "Army Fed Names of 18,000 U.S. Civilians into it Computers in 2-Year Operation," *New York Times*, 18 January 1971.

35 Cf. Wegener, "Order and Chaos."

36 OACSI, "Counterintelligence Research Project: Civil Disturbances – CONUS – 1968," 28 June 1968, in "Background Papers for 'The Role of Federal Forces in Civil Disturbances, 1945–1971'," RG 319, Entry 145-V, Box 1, NARA II.

37 USAINTC Collection Plan, 23 April 1969, reproduced in "Military Surveillance of Civilian Politics. A Report," p. 126.

38 Cf. Memo by Stanley R. Resor, "Restrictions on Intelligence Operations Involving Civilian Activities," 6 March 1970, Box 1489, Folder "Laird v. Tatum, 1968–1971," ACLU Records, Princeton Mudd Library.

39 Maffre, "Army Riot Unit Marks Time."

40 Vagle, *Being Watched*, 15.

41 Initial Filing in Tatum v. Laird, Box 1490, ACLU Records, Princeton Mudd Library.

42 Oral arguments, District Court, 22 April 1970, Box 1490, ACLU Records.

43 See *Federal Data Banks, Computers and the Bill of Rights: Hearings Before the Subcommittee on Constitutional Rights of the Committee on the Judiciary, United States Senate, Ninety-second Congress, First Session* (Washington, DC: GPO, 1971); U.S. Senate Subcommittee on Constitutional Rights, *Federal Data Banks and Constitutional Rights: A Study of Data Systems on Individuals Maintained by Agencies of the United States Government* (Washington, DC: GPO, 1974).

44 "Checking on the Government's Data Bankers," *Washington Star*, 14 March 1973; "Senators Hear of the Threat of a 'Dossier Dictatorship'," *New York Times*, 23 February 1971.

45 On the Church Committee's intelligence investigations see Johnson, *Season of Inquiry*.

46 See Miller, *Assault and Privacy*, 40–41; Halperin, *The Lawless State*, 156–159; Burnham, *Rise of the Computer State*, 36–38; more generally, see Stone and Warner, *Data Bank Society*; Neier, *Dossier*.

47 Lyon, "Search for Surveillance Theories," 10.

48 Brief of Appellee. Tatum v. Laird. US Court of Appeals for the District of Columbia, Box 1728, Folder "Tatum v Laird, 1965–1971," ACLU Records, Princeton Mudd Library.

49 <www.federalregister.gov/documents/2019/03/22/2019-05540/privacy-act-of-1974-system-of-records>.

Bibliography

Bauman, Z. 1998. *Globalization: The Human Consequences*. New York: Columbia University Press.

Bergien, R. 2017."'Big Data' als Vision: Computereinführung und Organisationswandel in BKA und Staatssicherheit (1967–1989)." *Zeithistorische Forschungen/Studies in Contemporary History* 14, no. 2: 258–285. www.zeithistorische-forschungen.de/2-2017/id=5488.

Bloom, J., and Martin, W. E. 2012. *Black Against Empire: The History and Politics of the Black Panther Party*. Berkeley: University of California Press.

Burnham, D. 1980. *The Rise of the Computer State*. New York: Random House.

Davis, M. 2006. *City of Quartz: Excavating the Future of Los Angeles*. Verso: London.

Edwards, P. N. 1997. *The Closed World: Computers and the Politics of Discourse in Cold War America*. Cambridge, MA: MIT Press.

Federal Data Banks, Computers and the Bill of Rights: Hearings Before the Subcommittee on Constitutional Rights of the Committee on the Judiciary, United States Senate, Ninety-second Congress, First Session (Washington, DC: GPO, 1971).

100 *Jens Wegener*

Halperin, M. 1933. *The Lawless State: The Crimes of the U.S. Intelligence Agencies*. New York: Penguin Books.

Johnson, L. K. 2015. *A Season of Inquiry: The Senate Intelligence Investigation*. Lexington, KY: University of Kentucky Press.

Kirchberg, C., and Schmeer, M. 2019. "The 'Traube Affair': Transparency as a Legitimation and Action Strategy Between Security, Surveillance and Privacy." In *Contested Transparencies, Social Movements and the Public Sphere*, ed. S. Berger and D. Owetschkin, 173–196. Basingstoke: Palgrave Macmillan.

Klimke, M. 2011. *The Other Alliance: Student Protest in West Germany and the United States in the Global Sixties*. Princeton: Princeton University Press.

Latham, M. 2000. *Modernization as Ideology: American Social Science and 'Nation Building' in the Kennedy Era*. Chapel Hill, NC: University of North Carolina Press.

Lefebvre, H. 1991. *The Production of Space*. Malden: Blackwell Publishing.

Lucks, D. 2014. *Selma to Saigon: The Civil Rights Movement and the Vietnam War*. Lexington, KY: University Press of Kentucky.

Lyon, D. 2006. "The Search for Surveillance Theories." In *Theorizing Surveillance: The panopticon and Beyond*, ed. D. Lyon, 3–20. Devon: Willan Publishing.

Malloy, S. 2018. *Out of Oakland: Black Panther Party Internationalism During the Cold War*. Ithaca: Cornell University Press.

Military Surveillance of Civilian Politics: A Report of the Subcommittee on Constitutional Rights. Committee on the Judiciary. United States Senate (Washington, DC: GPO, 1973).

Military Surveillance: Hearings Before the Subcommittee on Constitutional Rights of the Committee on the Judiciary. United States Senate. Ninety-Third Congress, Second Session (Washington, DC: GPO, 1974).

Miller, A. 1971. *The Assault and Privacy: Computers, Data Banks and Dossiers*. Ann Arbor, MI: University of Michigan Press.

Muscara, L. 2018. "Maps, Complexity, and the Uncertainty of Power." In *Handbook On the Geographies of Power*, ed. M. C. Coleman and J. A. Agnew, 362–379. Cheltenham: Edward Elgar Publishing.

Neier, A. 1975. *Dossier: The Secret Files They Keep on You*. New York: Stein and Day.

Pyle, C. 1970. "CONUS Intelligence: The Army Watches Civilian Politics." *Washington Monthly* (January 1970): 4–16.

Sassen, S. 2008. *Territory, Authority, Rights: From Medieval to Global Assemblages*. Princeton, NJ: Princeton University Press.

Stone, M., and Warner, M. 1970. *The Data Bank Society: Organizations, Computers and Social Freedom*. London: Allen & Unwin.

Tyner, J. A. 2006. "'Defend the Ghetto': Space and the Urban Politics of the Black Panther Party." *Annals of the Association of American Geographers* 96, no. 1: 105–118.

U.S. Senate Subcommittee on Constitutional Rights. 1974. *Federal Data Banks and Constitutional Rights: A Study of Data Systems on Individuals Maintained by Agencies of the United States Government*. Washington, DC: GPO.

Vagle, J. 2017. *Being Watched: Legal Challenges to Government Surveillance*. New York: NYU Press.

Vries, Tity de. 2012. "The 1967 Central Intelligence Agency Scandal: Catalyst in a Transforming Relationship between State and People." *Journal of American History* 98, no. 4: 1075–1092.

Wegener, J. 2020. "Order and Chaos: The CIA's HYDRA Database and the Dawn of the Information Age." *Journal of Intelligence History* 19, no. 1: 77–91.

Young, D. 2017. "Computing War Narratives: The Hamlet Evaluation System in Vietnam." *APRJA* 6, no. 1: 1–15.

5 Knowledge transfer and technopolitics

The CIA, the West German intelligence service and the digitisation of information processing in the 1960s

Rüdiger Bergien

Introduction

It is hard to dispute claims made in recent research that the West German Federal Intelligence Service (BND) had reached a low point in its development in the 1960s.[1] It was demoralised by the unmasking of the head of BND counterespionage, Heinz Felfe, as a Soviet Committee for State Security (Komitet gosudarstvennoi bezopasnosti, KGB) spy in 1961. It was also disorganised to the point of paralysis as its president Reinhard Gehlen, a former Wehrmacht general, had established a kind of personal rule that contained elements of nepotism as well as the embezzlement of funds. Gehlen had seemingly resisted any demands to modernise the Pullach-based service both from within and by politicians in Bonn. In the late 1960s, the real condition of his service flew in the face of his public claim that the BND had to be "a kind of 'scientific institute' that could make statements about the most diverse areas of the state and the economy of foreign countries."[2]

However, there were also actions that stand out from the general status quo within the Pullach "Augean stables" that Gehlen's successors had to muck out after he left in 1968.[3] Technical reconnaissance might appear to be one of these,[4] and the BND approach to computerisation another. Indeed, the two IBM 360 computers that were delivered to the Pullach BND headquarters in the summer of 1966 were among the very first of this revolutionary model that were ever used in an intelligence service.[5] Moreover, there is evidence that the arch conservative BND director Gehlen had recognised the strategic importance of computerisation and declared it a priority on several occasions;[6] in September 1966 even the Chief of the CIA Munich liaison station pointed out that "automation of data handling in Catide is one of 'Utility's' special interests."[7] This strong interest, the CIA man continued, was indeed behind Gehlen's repeated attempts to get a briefing for some BND employees on electronic data processing (EDP) matters at the CIA headquarters, which had even started to get on Gehlen's CIA contacts' nerves.[8] Can we therefore conclude that the ageing BND director, despite his overall failure to modernise his service, had seen which way the wind was blowing, at least in this area? Could this even be grounds to tone down harsh judgements of backwardness against the BND in these years?

DOI: 10.4324/9781003147329-6

102 *Rüdiger Bergien*

A further sentence from the CIA report quoted here sheds a slightly different light on Gehlen's interest in computerisation. "He" – Gehlen – the CIA man continues, wants computerisation "done right," which means that he "wants it to be compatible with American military and intelligence systems."[9] At a time when many different EDP systems were or were not "compatible" with each other was far from being common knowledge, these words indeed seem salient. They allow the interpretation that it was not, or at least not primarily, technological far-sightedness that made Gehlen embrace computerisation. Rather, he might have realised that EDP compatibility could create a link between his service and the CIA that was more than desired given the existential dimension this partnership had for the smaller partner. In Gehlen's view, computerisation obviously had a political dimension, and it seems reasonable to assume that the CIA was very aware of the opportunities its technologically advanced position offered in the realm of partner service relations.

There is much evidence now that computer knowledge did indeed gain a strategic quality in the Cold War struggle. In addition to nuclear and missile technologies, EDP was among the "Cold War's most significant technological systems."[10] Moreover, at least in the 1950s and 1960s, "computer nationalism" was a dominant pattern, not only in the field of national security.[11] Therefore, in contrast to influential metanarratives about an unstoppable, free-floating "computer revolution" at the dawn of the digital age, computer knowledge did not come without a price and was shaped by power relations. Therefore, this contribution aims not only to explore the scope and forms of US EDP support to the BND; it also tackles the question of whether this support relates to a US Cold War hegemony over smaller Western allies. Gabrielle Hecht and Paul Edwards introduced the term "technopolitics" to address a "strategic practice of designing or using technology to enact political goals."[12] Did the introduction of computer technology by the BND follow a similar pattern? Is it therefore misleading to interpret the delivery of IBM 360 mainframes to Pullach as evidence of internal modernisation efforts? Does this delivery instead illustrate the continuing BND dependence on its former "parent service"?

Recent research indicates that US intelligence services might have been proficient at conducting technopolitics. John Ferris has shown that the National Security Agency (NSA) enabled its British sister service Government Communications Headquarters (GCHQ)[13] to acquire up-to-date computer hardware, thereby becoming not only "the largest and most sophisticated EDP user outside the United States" but also dependent on further access to US technology.[14] Likewise, US services provided the BND with the technology necessary to conduct electronic reconnaissance (ELINT), yet on the condition that the West German service delivered all the data that was collected directly to its US partners.[15] However, beyond specifying such examples, neither intelligence historians nor specialists in the history of computing have yet systematically addressed the transfer of technical knowledge between clandestine Cold War services. This is not only due to source problems – Richard Aldrichs' GCHQ monograph has proven that a lot can be done without privileged source access.[16] Rather, this lack of attention reflects the fact that the significance of the history of digitisation has not been widely recognised by the history of the intelligence community.

Computers, for example, are barely mentioned in Christopher Andrews' magnificent MI5 history.[17] John Ferris dedicated just ten of its 800-page GCHQ official history to computerisation, even though GCHQ (or, to avoid repetition: "this service") was largely shaped by digital technologies as early as the 1950s.[18] Although first approaches to early CIA computer use have been made,[19] a comprehensive investigation of CIA computerisation is still a desideratum,[20] and the early use of EDP in the BND is a *tabula rasa*. Neither Jon Agar's appeal to question the "place of the secret state in the history of computing"[21] nor Michael Warner's claim that we need a deeper "understanding of how technology affects intelligence 'systems'" – as he considers these effects fundamental to an intelligence history of the second half of the twentieth century[22] – has met much positive response up to now.

The following analysis of CIA–BND relations in the field of early computer use is based upon declassified CIA files that are available through the CIA's digital reading room, as well as BND documents that have been declassified for the first time for this study. I focus first on the CIA's activities in the field of the automation of information processing in the 1950s and early 1960s to gain insights into why the CIA developed an interest in data handling by its partner services and to clarify the experiences that constituted its frame of reference in how they perceived the BND and other partner's activities. I then review the state of information processing within the BND in the 1950s and its attempts, beginning in 1958/59, to get its "information chaos" under control through technical means. In a third step, I examine whether, and to what extent, the CIA and the BND interacted in relation to the computerisation of information processing in the 1960s.

CIA data processing in the 1950s

The roots of what we may label CIA technopolitics in the field of information processing lay in the 1950s and relate to the activities of two CIA departments: the "Office for Central Reference" (OCR) and the "Record Integration Division" (RID). The first, OCR, was part of the Directorate for Intelligence (DD/I), which acted as the CIA's analytics branch and was responsible for providing CIA analysts with all the documents, records, photographs, academic literature, statistics and so on that they needed for their day-to-day work.[23] The second department, RID, was OCR's equivalent within the Deputy Department of Plans (DD/P), which was, its innocent title notwithstanding, responsible for information acquisition – the practice of spying – as well as for covert operations. Consequently, RID focused rather on the registering, storing, indexing and so on of *incoming* information; it was collection-orientated and less concerned with the needs of analysts. However, the overlap between the tasks and practices of the OCR and the RID was significant, and differences stemmed rather from a different socio-biographic profile; many OCR employees were educated, trained library professionals and favoured an approach to information management that was based on elaborate classification systems, indexes and subject catalogues. In contrast, the RID's organisational

104   *Rüdiger Bergien*

subculture may have been shaped less by an academic frame of reference and more by the agency's practical needs.[24]

The OCR and the RID experienced rapid augmentation during the 1950s. Even though CIA historians redacted all staff figures during their declassification of relevant documents, we can reconstruct that the OCR's predecessor unit started with a few dozen employees in 1947 and counted several hundred by the mid-1950s.[25] This growth reflected broader socio-technical transformations – particularly a sharp increase in technically mediated communication – as well as the perceived need to collect any available information about the Soviet Bloc. The result was a flood of incoming information, a "data explosion," as the CIA's written material frequently states.[26] File registries were bursting at the seams.[27] The RID's "Main Index," which was to centrally record all of the "Agency's" file units, grew from 500 thousand to 14 million index cards between 1947 and 1959.[28] Similarly, the number of "name traces" multiplied from a few hundred searches per day at the beginning to approximately 1,000 per day towards the end of the 1950s. In the early 1960s, internal documents increasingly mention an "analysis gap" – a sharp discrepancy between the amount of incoming information and DD/I's ability to make use of it. In the words of OCR employee Joe Becker, a brilliant expert and rising star in the emerging field of information sciences:[29]

> While the information explosion has inundated the intelligence community with printed information it is incapable of processing, the means we use for treading through the collected maze of recorded information are the same as we used in the days of Mata Hari.[30]

However, with hindsight this reproach must be interpreted as rhetoric rather than an accurate description of the CIA's use of information technology up to this point. From the late 1940s, the OCR and RID had sought to counter the flood of information with the previously unprecedented mechanisation of information processing. As early as 1947/48, the Office for Document Control (ODC),[31] the predecessor of the OCR, had introduced the Intellofax system, considered to be the first fully automated information system in the world.[32] In the 1950s, both the OCR and the RID carried out dozens of projects in the field of microfilming, automatic indexing and even automated translation, in close cooperation with leading technical enterprises such as IBM and Eastman Kodak, and sometimes made use of the research capacities of the Massachusetts Institute of Technology (MIT).[33] In 1959, the DD/P Systems Group, which operated "Walnut," an oversized microfilm reader-printer system, had even received the service's first non-SIGINT[34] computer, an IBM 650, to make "Walnut" retrieval system operational.[35] The OCR however only started using its computers in January 1963 when two IBM 1401/1410 systems were developed for the programming of OCR's CHIVE project, which was designed as a general information system for the entire CIA.[36] This was late for a department that perceived itself as the agency's central information service provider; Becker was possibly addressing this particular shortcoming with his "Mata Hari" reference.

Knowledge transfer and technopolitics   105

"Walnut" as well as "CHIVE" exemplify some overarching patterns of CIA information processing technicisation interwoven with political aspects. The first pattern that can be recognised is the involvement of private companies such as IBM and Eastman Kodak, and it showed these vendors' great influence on the CIA's technicisation line. "CHIVE," for example, as a million-dollar computer-based information system, was initiated because of an IBM staff evaluation recommendation.[37] Moreover, contract personnel were crucial to hardware maintenance and programming in the 1960s and beyond. Large parts of programming work were done by contractors – mostly from IBM – through in-house projects. For the CHIVE project, for example, between 15 and 20 IBM programmers were permanently on the spot,[38] while in August 1969 the CIA director of computer services described the potential loss of the eight IBM system engineers (who were providing support on a permanent basis in case of software problems) as "critical" to some of the agency's computer components such as RID.[39] These close ties, however, have a political dimension as they express a political will to make vendors such as IBM part of a national security complex – the tendency of CIA protagonists to declare such involvements as matter-of-fact necessities notwithstanding.

Even more clearly, a technopolitical dimension of early CIA EDP use becomes visible through a second pattern, the strive for intelligence data "interagency compatibility." It is this endeavour that helps explain the importance that the OCR and RID laid on a standardisation of information storage and processing. One of their central aims was to make keyword catalogues, the "intelligence subject code" (ISC) or a "biographic data questionnaire" obligatory – not only for CIA departments but also for the US intelligence community as a whole.[40] Institutionally, standardisation was to be promoted by the increasingly important "Committee on Documentation of the US Intelligence Board" (CODIB). In the early 1960s led by the OCR's department head Paul Borel, CODIB used "task forces," "working groups" and sub-panels to develop standardised procedures that were to be recommended to all US intelligence organisations. More often than not, the work of these task forces seems to have been painstaking and lengthy; the "Working Group on Remote Systems Input," for example, ended up empty-handed after four years, as the contracted enterprise – General Dynamics/Electronics – had failed to develop an electronic typewriter for the remote input of classified information that met the acoustic standards as well as the agreed size and weight of the device.[41] However, it becomes quite obvious that CODIB searched for technical solutions for a political aim: "to unify all intelligence processing."[42]

This leads to a third pattern, which can be summarised as a tendency to "think big" and to move information processing from a service task to a core activity of the CIA, potentially catalysing a process that, in retrospect, appears to be a transformation from "espionage to intelligence."[43] One large-scale idea promoted by DD/P Counterintelligence staff as early as 1962 was the development of an "interagency biographic information network" – the integration of CIA, FBI, the Secret Service, et al's biographic files into a network of retrievable electronic databases;[44] another idea was the aforementioned "CHIVE" information system: "CHIVE" was intended to be no less than the central information system for the

106   *Rüdiger Bergien*

whole agency, an "all-source retrieval system" that would cover "every type of printed document, including maps and photos, at whatever classification level."[45] At that time, this seems to have been a somewhat utopian vision whose realisation, however, would have significantly increased the OCR's importance for the whole CIA analysis process. At the dawn of the digital age, large EDP systems as well as access to large data resources were equated with institutional power. We need to keep this perception in mind when moving now to the CIA's attempts to gain influence on its West German partner services' information processing.

First steps were made in 1958, when employees of the BND's record-keeping department were invited to visit the CIA agency headquarters in Washington where they were briefed about CIA plans to automate its central biographic registers. In March 1959, a "Mr. Jessel" – most probably a senior staffer of the CIA's DD/P Systems Group – gave a lecture on CIA information processing at the US Embassy in Bonn-Bad Godesberg before representatives of the BND and its domestic sister service, the BfV.[46] Officially, lectures like Jessel's in Bonn-Bad Godesberg were declared as some kind of development aid for the West German services in terms of digitisation. However, the underlying intentions clearly went beyond that. Jessel's lecture, his visit to the BfV record-keeping branch in Cologne and several computer briefings for the BND in the following years served to present the hardware and software used by the CIA as exemplary models to emulate.

In internal CIA correspondence talk was much more open and the technopolitics approach was barely covered up. High-ranking CIA representatives expressed their goal of expanding US influence on West German services via EDP ("to establish and prove our machine hegemony");[47] in the mid-1960s, CIA representatives declared to the President of the BND, the BfV and the Federal Criminal Police Office (BKA) "that we desire as much as it were possible to have mechanical records systems employed by German agencies to be compatible with our own."[48] The fact that BKA President Paulinus Dickopf, who was listed on the CIA payroll, endorsed this plan ("he fully appreciated this and endorsed the idea")[49] is just as unsurprising as the approval of BND President Reinhard Gehlen and BfV President Hubert Schruebbers. However, the information processing service units of the BND were themselves far from won over by the CIA's approach to digitisation.

Data processing in the Gehlen Organization

Compared to the CIA, the state of information processing within the BND in the late 1950s can only be described as backward. As the service's leadership saw itself as primarily responsible for looking for indicators of a Soviet attack, without much need for medium-to-long-term information storage, the technical means of information processing were largely missing up to 1956. Punch card technology, in use at the CIA since 1947, did not exist, nor did the microfilming of documents or even standardised indexing procedures. Instead of central card indexes, the BND of the 1960s still used hundreds of small and micro card indexes, which were created largely without keyword catalogues or classification systems and often contained duplicate and triplicate information. This often made

Knowledge transfer and technopolitics 107

information retrieval a Sisyphean task; in the words of Hans Dieckmann, director of the BND organisation department in the late 1950s, it was a "waste of time" with "random results."[50] In hindsight, Ebrulf Zuber, who later became the first director of the BND data centre, described the early Gehlen service's information processing principle as one of "uncoordinated desktop data storage" – each person stored incoming information "with their personal tools . . . according to their own invented logic."[51]

However, the BND was not ignorant of its weaknesses in information processing, and things began to change when the CIA-funded Gehlen service became a federal authority in April 1956. By March 1, 1957, president Gehlen had ordered the establishment of an archive unit within the BND organisation department (referred to internally under the cipher "666" and from 1962 onwards as "777") and charged this unit with the task of making the flow of incoming information retrievable. It was assigned "666" to build "a central document archive with accompanying mechanized documentation" – the term "mechanized" indicates here that a punch card system was to be implemented.[52] In practice, this meant that in the years to follow, the 70 or so employees of "666" added signatures to each incoming document and then recorded the signatures on a punch card, together with keywords taken from the document's content.[53] Using the keywords – as well as the names of people, organisations and so on – "666" staffers could answer incoming information requests much faster than before as they were spared the task of going through hundreds of paper index cards manually.

However, that was how it should have worked in theory. In practice, the limitations of punch card technology for processing data en masse quickly became apparent; in particular, the punch card's limited capacity for data storage functioned as a bottleneck. As early as 1959 – obviously inspired by "Mr. Jessel's" briefings – the "666" staff began to consider the question of how to convert the service's factual documentation – already under the care of "666" – as well as the central biographic database – at that time still located in the counterintelligence subdivision – to EDP.[54] Initially, the BND solicited offers from a range of manufacturers, from Bull to Zuse KG. As it was considered to be "unfortunate" to be "wholly dependent upon a foreign brand," clear efforts were made to secure a West German manufacturer.[55] Surprisingly, Nixdorf was the vendor of choice for some time,[56] a 1950s "start-up" enterprise that specialised in the building of relatively small electronic calculators.[57] However, because of their technical limitations when it came to magnetic tape technology, the Paderborn-based company had little to offer compared to IBM's rapid technical advances, and ultimately, the CIA's EDP briefings suggested a reorientation. It was probably not by coincidence then that at the end of 1962 Franz von Kaufmann (code name "Kreuzburg") took over as head of "777" (as "666" was now called). Von Kaufmann had worked for IBM Germany for seven years, and we may assume that this previous occupation was the reason that the BND personnel management initiated his recruitment.[58] In the summer of 1964, IBM Germany not only received an order for an IBM 360/40 computer but was further tasked with developing a concept for digitising the service's biographic files as well.

108 *Rüdiger Bergien*

The decision in favour of IBM was probably received with satisfaction by the CIA, which closely observed the considerations and actions of "666." One premise of the CIA's goal of "machine hegemony" over the BND – hardware compatibility – was thus fulfilled. Even more important, however, was the question of how the BND would organise its databases, how it intended to structure its data records and who should be given access to digitised information. These questions, referring to the "software" dimension of computerisation,[59] were more closely connected to topics such as control and influence than the hardware dimension. However, in the view of the CIA, the BND approach to software problems went wrong from the very beginning.

Retrospective reports from the CIA claim that they had patiently tried to introduce their own approach to the BND from the 1960s: indexing and cataloguing documents and biographic data before transferring it to new storage formats.[60] The men in Pullach had to be reminded several times that the BND must centralise its card indexes before even thinking about buying a computer; CIA employees had offered BND experts the "machine language" – that is the data record formats – of a counterintelligence file from their own biographic records as a model at least once.[61] In the early 1960s, these attempts by the agency to pass on computer knowledge to the BND were not to be taken for granted; in the wake of the unmasking of BND employee Heinz Felfe as a KGB spy in 1961, the CIA had sealed itself off more tightly from the BND; internally, the CIA issued the directive that in future "the depth of operational cooperation . . . which largely characterized our earlier relations [with the BND] is to be avoided."[62]

Employees of "666" and "777" did not necessarily however appreciate this generosity, at least not according to the CIA; they were reluctant to accept what CIA employees like "Mr. Jessel" tried to convey to them. The head of "777," Franz von Kaufmann, was particularly sceptical about the amount of work the CIA OCR did to index and catalogue factual and biographic documents. In March of 1964 von Kaufmann offered his impression of the planned CIA biographic register with the observation that it would be "almost impossible" to submit "cross-sectional queries" – that is queries based on a combination of search terms, such as age and nationality – to this database "unless strict notations are prescribed that are practically equivalent to encryption."[63] In the BND, such a "coding" of places, nationalities, activities and so on would hardly be possible. Therefore, "777 strived for mechanical data 'retrieval' of material that was as unsorted as possible."[64] For example, von Kaufmann wanted to make documents accessible by keywords taken directly from the respective document (and not from a classification system such as the 'Intelligence Subject Code'). This procedure, at that time called "term system," had also been considered within the CIA but was rejected by the "librarians" in the OCR: "To library professionals," according to Colin Burke in his history of CIA information processing, "that" (the term system) "was an insult, heresy."[65]

Thus, it is no surprise that the CIA experts perceived the BND's preparations for EDP as amateurish, even more so because "777" staff in Pullach intended to manage the introduction of their EDP largely without external contractors, who were so important for CIA computerisation (and which might have made BND information processing more transparent to CIA eyes as von Kaufmann was quite reserved in giving his American partners insights). IBM Germany had indeed been asked by the BND to write a concept for the digitisation of its central biographic search registry. Yet a high-ranking CIA officer noticed with bewilderment that this concept was written by IBM "without IBM having had the opportunity to enter BND premises, and without having any exposure to BND file problems."[66] Whether he was bewildered by the BND's lack of professionalism or out of fear that von Kaufmann's closed-shop mentality could mess up CIA's technopolitics approach to exchange computer knowledge for BND intelligence data, the reaction of "Mr. Dykes" – Mr. Jessel's successor in the role of CIA EDP advisor in Pullach – on the BND digitisation was outspoken. He declared it as "unworkable."[67]

In the spring of 1965, everything suggested that in information processing matters there had been a breakdown in CIA–BND communication. The CIA side may have expected the establishment of "machine hegemony" over BND "777" to run as smoothly as it did with BND electronic reconnaissance. In this case, faced with the alternative of dropping out of the information exchange with Anglo-American services, the BND ELINT division had procured an IBM 360/30 system in early 1965[68] and received coding procedures from the partner services, in return for which it made its own collected ELINT data available to its partners.[69] In contrast, from the CIA point of view, the BND "777" archive branch did not listen to advice and refused to do its homework. Internally, CIA officers called department head von Kaufmann a "fool and a menace to the project."[70] With no payoff for their own digitisation-developmental aid and therewith a failure of their technopolitics in sight, the Chief of the CIA Eastern European Division even questioned whether further "ADP Briefings" for the BND were useful at all. The BND, the CIA man argued, was still occupied with fundamental "document, index and information retrieval problems." If this was the case, a visit from BND employees to CIA headquarters – something Director Gehlen had personally explicitly requested – "would be a sterile and probably counterproductive exercise."[71]

A fresh start

In the spring of 1965, it seemed that the transfer of computer knowledge from the CIA to the BND had come to a standstill before it had even really begun. Up to this point, von Kaufmann's behaviour seems to have been in line with critical interpretations of the BND as a service incapable of modernising itself, as he obviously refused to accept high-tech knowledge even if it was served on a silver platter. But things were not quite that simple.

Admittedly, CIA assessments of BND computerisation were justified at least insofar that von Kaufmann took the second step before the first, that is ordering a high-end mainframe without having a detailed plan about how to use it. On the other hand, von Kaufmann's scepticism about the CIA's information systems was not unfounded either – even if he most probably didn't know about it. In the mid-1960s CIA's most advanced information management project – the aforementioned project "CHIVE" – developed into a perfect example of early computerisation

110   *Rüdiger Bergien*

mismanagement as it increasingly became considered overcomplex, lacking clear goals and having been shaped by "language barriers" between the "computer people" (IBM contractor personal) and "everybody else."[72] Moreover, there was a certain discrepancy between the self-confident goal to establish "machine hegemony" over a partner service with a very different cultural and historical background and the fact that the CIA had little to offer in addressing these differences beyond declaring its own experiences as a guideline into digitisation. It might have been a certain awareness of the limits of their technopolitics approach that made CIA liaison officers ready to accept a BND attempt for a fresh start of EDP-cooperation in the spring of 1965.

This restart was closely linked with the appointment of Ebrulf Zuber (codename "Ackermann") as head of the documentary and information branch.[73] This appointment was in itself a clear statement by BND President Gehlen to make digitisation a priority. Even though he embodied the "shadows of the past" that weighed heavy on the service – he was a former member of the Waffen SS and was delegated to the SS main office (SS-Hauptamt) during the war[74] – he was also one of the BND hopes for the future. In the 1950s, he had earned merit in GDR reconnaissance; as unsuccessful as the BND's efforts at GDR espionage had been as a whole, the groups led by Zuber stood out again and again as "exemplary units."[75] In the early 1960s, Gehlen had given Zuber responsibility for the BND's "operational security" division; after the aforementioned unmasking of BND counterintelligence officer Heinz Felfe as a KGB agent, this was just about the most sensitive position the service had to offer. With responsibility for IT implementation, Zuber was now given another "hard nut to crack" – whereby his good contacts with the CIA, as well as his many years of operational experience, were qualities that set him apart from his predecessor von Kaufmann.

Zuber quickly understood that introducing comprehensive EDP to the BND would require a change in organisational structures. The 45-year-old saw this as an opportunity to make the BND a more effective service. As a first step, at the end of 1964, he had already managed to merge the factual documentation – the "777" division – and the Central Biographic Index – until then part of the counterintelligence subdivision – into a new organisational unit – the "Central Office for Personal Information, Documentation and Automation" (CDA), which was now subordinate to him.[76] This was an important step towards the centralisation of information processing, and, accordingly, CIA liaison officers perceived it as crucial to the introduction of computers. Zuber's mid-range goals, however, went beyond this. His aim was to establish a "BND Information Center" that would have been strikingly similar to the structure of the CIA's OCR. Like OCR, the BND information centre would have encompassed all the service areas related to knowledge production: the subject files and biographic information system as well as the language service, the central library and the entire EDP area.[77] That OCR served as a blueprint for the Zuber's information centre is at least a likely supposition.

Be it his readiness to learn from his US partners or because of his more friendly manner, the CIA, for its part, was enthusiastic about Zuber. They were pleased to see that Zuber had put an end to the compartmentalisation that had always hindered the exchange of information on IT issues until that point; during an EDP workshop in Pullach in June 1965, Zuber gave the CIA representatives detailed information about the BND files, which Kaufmann had previously withheld ("as a result of our demand for a description of the CATIDE[78] indexing and file system, we received details never before reported").[79] In addition, CIA staff were impressed by Zuber's personality; his "total grasp of the [EDP] principles and problems at all levels is truly remarkable." On later occasions, Zuber's CIA contacts continued to praise his "unending thirst for knowledge," characterising him as "exceptionally well-read and well-informed,"[80] and repeatedly placed emphasis on his background as a "professional intelligence officer" and someone who had led undercover agents and who himself had obtained secret information. In the view of members of DD/P, the CIA's procurement division, which in the 1960s still considered itself a "service within a service," it was likely that Zuber's background created mutual understanding that qualified him as a mediator of knowledge transfer between the two services.

Although the status quo of BND information processing proved to be even worse than the CIA had assumed – Zuber's credible efforts to end von Kaufmann's policy of sealing off BND information processing from CIA eyes caused the transfer of "computer knowledge" to pick up speed again. During the aforementioned workshop in Pullach in June 1965, one of the DD/P Systems Group employees had offered Zuber the opportunity to have CIA specialists analyse the linguistic structure of the BND's biographic file records ("to give CATIDE the benefit of the linguistic endeavours in name groupings which had taken place over the last several years in the United States").[81] In addition, the Agency offered to provide classification systems, such as a world locations gazetteer "especially for USSR and Eastern Bloc countries," a "name group index for surnames and given names," a "working occupations key," the CIA Intelligence Subject Code and more.[82]

When Zuber visited CIA headquarters in the fall of 1966 – such visits always represented an honour of distinction for the partner services' representatives[83] – he received further detailed information about tracing techniques and the phonetic system used by DD/P SG.[84] At his request, other CDA employees also received IT training in the United States in the following years, including his deputy Friedrich Sturz, who spent three weeks travelling the United States in 1969 as a guest of the CIA.[85] Perhaps these meetings on an equal basis contributed to the fact that under Zuber, the CDA also adopted procedures from OCR and the DD/P Systems Group that had been rejected outright only a few years previously. In any case, from about 1968 onwards, the BND also awarded IT development contracts to outside companies – for example, the programming of the "automatic information system for messages" (AUTIMEL) to automatically index incoming messages; four IBM experts are said to have worked on this project simultaneously.[86] In return, the CDA's work under Zuber's direction increasingly earned the praise of CIA EDP specialists. "CATUSK[87] has made excellent progress" in the development of their biographic register, according to a report from July 1969;[88] "they are proceeding step wise in an orderly fashion and clearly are learning as they move on," reads a further report from July 1970.[89]

112 *Rüdiger Bergien*

Taken together, these reports reflect an image of the BND which, after a phase of partial "refusal to learn" in the first half of the decade, had now, under Zuber's leadership, grown into the role of the quick-to-learn pupil that the CIA had intended for it from the outset. Finally, one should ask to what extent the CIA benefited from its involvement in BND computerisation. The goal was "to obtain better quality name traces and CI (Counterintelligence) information from that service." Did this occur? Did the CIA take advantage from the fact that Zuber, in charge of the BND's EDP, planned to model his "BND Information Center" after the CIA's set-up?

The end of big plans

There are at least two CIA EDP projects the agency explicitly and repeatedly requested the BND to contribute the data it had itself collected. The first appears in archival records under the name "Joint Soviet Travel Program." It was intended to record all legal foreign travels of Soviet citizens in a machine-readable database to get starting points for counterintelligence measures.[90] Confronted with American demands, Zuber repeatedly managed to evade a clear commitment by, for example, expressing "interest in the Soviet program but even more [interest] in satellite travel"[91] – that is the travels of GDR, Czechoslovakian and Polish citizens. In the case of a second database, the counterintelligence database "EGIS" (East German Intelligence Service), the BND only delivered analogue information (i.e. in paper form) and blocked all CIA plans that went beyond this.

Indeed, from about 1967, the CIA had expected the West German services to adopt the EGIS machine language and to record personal information on Stasi employees directly in the EGIS format. The CIA could then have stored these data records directly in the EGIS database, which ran on an IBM computer at CIA headquarters.[92] This arrangement was rejected by the West German services. "In principle," Ebrulf Zuber explained to a CIA representative during a meeting in Pullach in March 1969, "it would hardly be sustainable in the long run if the EGIS system could be run solely on a machine located in Washington and not also on a machine located in Germany." Zuber also openly rejected the idea that BND employees could collect data for a database used primarily by the CIA.[93] His suggestion was that the EGIS system including the complete data repository, would have to be made available to a German service. Since the BfV did not have a mainframe computer at that time, "the transfer should take place as soon as possible [*sic*] to the BND."[94]

Here, at the latest, the debate about the best way to process intelligence data in a transatlantic context proves to be political powerplay. Surprisingly, the West German services, as the weaker side, managed not only to evade the status of CIA data collection point but also got something the CIA initially hadn't wanted to them to receive. After several years in which the use and location of this "joint intelligence database" was disputed, the CIA decided that its idea of a hierarchically structured joint intelligence database – receiving all data and controlling information output itself – wasn't enforceable. Instead, around 1975 it provided the BfV and the BND with the complete EGIS dataset. Without any compensation, the "agency," whose

Knowledge transfer and technopolitics 113

representatives had still dreamed of "machine hegemony" a decade earlier, had given away development work and a data repository whose significance as intelligence in the BND was to be judged as extremely high, as late as 1979.[95]

Moreover, Zuber's approach to developing BND information processing organisational structures following the OCR example was never to be realised in the form originally planned. The goal of centralising the service's information processing had aroused the suspicion of the BND's division and subdivision heads from the very beginning. The units responsible for intelligence analysis felt particularly threatened in their core competencies; any attempt by the EDP units to standardise messages, reports and personal information triggered an allergic reaction among the staff.[96] In mid-1969, a CIA employee, almost regretfully, reported to Washington that Zuber's attempts to modernise the BND by means of EDP were increasingly meeting with internal resistance. In particular, Zuber's idea to use ADP for

> [m]onitoring the effectiveness of any Division, Branch, Station, Base, Desk Officer, and individual agent or operation . . . has apparently frightened a number of people who now fear that the computer is their enemy, and they refuse to cooperate.[97]

The new BND President Gerhard Wessel, however, did not seem prepared to back Zuber, nor to support the establishment of the information centre. Wessel must have seen that this would have brought even more unrest to a BND which, after Reinhard Gehlen's departure and under a federal government led for the first time by the Social Democrats, he, Wessel, would be expected to undergo a large number of reforms anyway. Obviously, Zuber and his EDP modernisation course were sacrificed in favour of Wessel's reform programme. Against his will, and to his great disappointment, Zuber was transferred to a higher management position in the BND collection division in the summer of 1970.[98] "He felt," his contact at the CIA meant, "that he was being eased out too soon and replaced by someone so greatly different from himself and that the job might seriously suffer from this change."[99]

Zuber's successor as the leading BND EDP manager, Otto Leiberich, was indeed a very different personality. Leiberich was highly competent regarding the technical aspects of his task. He had earned a doctorate in mathematics and served in the quasi-scientific BND Central Bureau for Encryption and Decryption (Zentralstelle für das Chiffrierwesen, ZfCH) for several years. Yet he had no experience in intelligence.[100] Leiberich abandoned the idea of reinventing the BND by means of EDP and steered the computer centre to a service function – "provision of service became the slogan," as Zuber-loyalist Friedrich Sturz wrote in an angry retrospective.[101] Leiberich might have given the BND its first functioning central biographic information system with "PEDOK"[102] (which Zuber, despite CIA praise, had failed to achieve). Nevertheless, the years in which the principle of "thinking big" as applied to the computerisation of the BND were over. As in many other organisations, the euphoria of the new era was followed by a period of IT-related conflicts and disputes over resources and goals, which would not end

114 *Rüdiger Bergien*

until one or two decades later with the horizontal networking of IT systems and the triumph of personal computers.

Conclusion

According to master narratives in the history of technology, from the 1950s, computerisation occurred as a "digital flood,"[103] as a force of nature, a technical revolution that companies, public authorities, universities and so on could not escape. Coupled with this pattern of interpretation is the idea that computer knowledge already circulated relatively freely at this time. Certainly, this knowledge was bound to the expertise of manufacturers such as IBM. But in these narratives, computer knowledge appeared easy to adapt and disseminate.

Recent research has shown that, in contrast to these narratives, computer knowledge was indeed a much desired and contested resource in enterprises as well as in the civil service and especially in the national security sector.[104] Here, computer knowledge was not only a much sought after but also a restricted form of knowledge because it was closely related to the way in which a intelligence service worked and produced its product: secret state knowledge. Consequently, CIA EDP support for its partners was not of an altruistic nature. It followed a technopolitical rationality as it had conditions attached. These conditions were, inter alia, a payback in the form of better and faster access to the intelligence information available within the BND. This expectation stood behind the term "machine hegemony."

In the field of technical reconnaissance, this calculation apparently worked out, as a sidelong glance at the ELINT division of the BND has shown. In the area of personal information, biographic intelligence, and acquisition management, however, things were different, at least in the 1960s and the early 1970s. This form of information processing in the CIA as well as in the BND proved to be strongly coupled to the respective organisational structures and routines. Therefore, a linear transfer of the CIA approach – which was based on comprehensive classification systems, centralisation and the integration of computer manufacturers – to the BND would not have been possible even if the archive units "666" or "777" had been wholly receptive from the beginning. In addition, even though Zuber, after taking over in 1965, was very willing to cooperate, there was never a unilateral transfer of digital data from Pullach to its larger partner service.

With all caution due to the fragmentary archival basis, one might use the BND–CIA interaction regarding computerisation as an example that technopolitics – the design of technologies to fulfil particular political purposes – requires not only a technological imbalance between a more and a less developed state, enterprise or secret service. It required the less developed side's perception that getting the technologies in prospect was not only desirable but also an existential question. That was the case in the BND ELINT division that could have stopped its work without access to its partner services collection techniques. However, it wasn't the case with the BND archival and information section. Thus, the "expert advice" provided by Mr. Jessel and Co. may have been conceived as such in the late 1950s and the early 1960s but resulted in one-sided "development aid" from which the US service profited indirectly at best.

However, the CIA did not end this episode empty-handed. What was probably more important than direct benefit in the form of the transfer of digitised data was that in the course of the 1960s, the CIA and in particular IBM became central points of reference for every form of EDP planning activity undertaken by the West German security authorities. Even in the 1970s, visits to IBM laboratories and CIA (not to mention the NSA) computer centres were places of West German tech pilgrimage where domestic and criminal intelligence officers – and most probably also Zuber's and Leiberich's successors – aimed to find a blueprint for the next stage of EDP development.[105] Perhaps this created deeper and long-lasting dependencies than any transfer of counterintelligence data could ever have done.

Notes

1 Dülffer, *Geheimdienst in der Krise*; Wolf, *Die Entstehung des BND*.
2 Ibid., 390.
3 Ibid., 642.
4 Müller, *Wellenkrieg*.
5 The CIA received its first IBM 360 models at about the same time while BND's domestic 'sister service', the "Office for the Protection of the Constitution" (BfV) only received an IBM 360 in 1971. See the contribution from Christopher Kirchberg in this volume.
6 He did so, for example, in an interview given on the occasion of his leaving, Dönhoff, "Der Mann ohne Gesicht."
7 "Catide" = CIA cryptonym for the BND, "utility" = CIA cryptonym for Reinhard Gehlen.
8 Chief Munich Liaison Basis to Chief Eur. Catide Zroarlock Ujdraco ADP Briefings (9 September 1966). CIA CREST Database, Doc. ID: special collection, nwcda7/187, Zuber, Ebrulf, Vol. 1_0042.
9 Ibid.
10 Hecht and Edwards, "The Technopolitics of Cold War."
11 Ibid., 296.
12 The concept of "technopolitics" is elaborated by ibid, 274.
13 GCHQ = Government Communications Headquarters.
14 Ferris, *Behind the Enigma*.
15 Müller, *Wellenkrieg*, 328–338.
16 Aldrich, *GCHQ*.
17 Andrew, *The Defence of the Realm*.
18 Ferris, *Behind the Enigma*. It is worth mentioning that Aldrich's, *GCHQ*, was more receptive towards GCHQ's use of EDP despite, and in contrast to Ferris, being restricted to using only declassified material.
19 Burke, *America's Information Wars*; Wegener, "Order and Chaos."
20 The state of research is somewhat better on the early use of computers in the field of intelligence cryptoanalysis and "Signals Intelligence," see Burke, "It Wasn't All Magic."
21 Agar, "Putting the Spooks Back In?," 102–124, here 124.
22 Warner, "Reflections on Technology and Intelligence Systems," 133–153, here 135.
23 Burke, *America's Information Wars*, 178–179.
24 While OCR's inner workings, and to some degree its socio-biographic profile, is the subject of Burke's *America's Information Wars*, not much is known about RID despite

116   *Rüdiger Bergien*

the fact that the Whistleblower Philipp Agee started his agency career in this department. Agee, *Inside the Company*, p. 29.

25 Burke, *America's Information Wars*, 175.
26 It remains questionable, however, to what extent this information flood can be considered unique to 1950s/60s. Proponents in the field of information history argue that complaints about information overload date back to the eighteenth century. Rosenberg, "Early Modern Information Overload," 1–9; see also Eppler and Mengis, "The Concept of Information Overload," 325–344.
27 Chief DD/P Systems Group to CIA Records Administration Officer: Disposition of DD/P Files in Records Center, 15.6.1962. CIA CREST Database, Doc. ID. CIA-RDP70–00211R000800300021-6.
28 CIA General Services Office, Records Management and Distribution Staff: Records Management Program, Survey Report of the Records Integration Staff and Western Hemisphere Division, July 1953. CIA CREST Database, Doc. ID. CIA-RDP70-00211R000900180001-1.
29 Hayes, "Joseph Becker."
30 Joseph Becker (OCR): Ideas on Processing Information, 11.7.1961. CIA CREST Database, Doc. ID. CIA-RDP80B01139A000200080004-0, 3.
31 ODC = Office for Document Control.
32 Burke, *America's Information Wars*, 103.
33 Ibid., 280, 317–318.
34 SIGINT = Signals Intelligence.
35 The first ever computer owned by the CIA was an ALWAC III, used for scientific calculations. It was installed in September 1957 in the CIA's "National Photographic Intelligence Center" (NPIC) to process the photographic data collected by the U2 reconnaissance planes.
36 History of Project CHIVE, 12.9.1967, CIA CREST Database, Doc. ID. CIA-RDP80B01139A000600160003-8, 10.
37 Ibid., 67–68.
38 In the mid-1960s, 16 of the 91 members of the "CHIVE Task Force" were IBM employees. History of Project CHIVE, 12.9.1967, CIA CREST Database, Doc. ID. CIA-RDP80B01139A000600160003-8, 24–25.
39 Acting Director of Computer Services and Chief Information Processing Staff, O/PPB: Impact of New IBM Policy on Systems Engineering Support, 22.08.1969. CIA CREST Database, Doc. ID. CIA-RDP80–01794R000100210011–6.
40 Accordingly, OCR presented the approval of the ISC "as the basis for the subject and area indexing of intelligence reports" by all US intelligence services in September 1956 as an important success. Draft OCD/OCR Chronology 1952–1966, 27.02.1969. CIA CREST Database, Doc. ID. CIA-RDP84-00951R000200200001-9.
41 United States Intelligence Board, Committee on Documentation, General Dynamics Machine Language Typewriter: Report and Findings, 3.1.1966, CIA CREST Database, Doc. ID CIA-RDP80B01139A000200110024-4.
42 Burke, *America's Information Wars*, 203.
43 Warner, *The Rise and Fall of Intelligence*.
44 Proposal for a Biographic Information Network, with a covering letter from Richard Helms, CIA DDP, to Robert I. Bouck, Secret Service, 3.10.1964, 10.01.1962. CIA CREST Database, Doc. ID CIA-RDP80B01139A000300040020-5.
45 Borel, "Automation for Information Control," 25–32, here 27.
46 Hans-Joachim Postel, betr. Neuordnung des Karteiwesens, here: Vortrag von Mr. Jessel (CIA) über die Erfahrungen bei der Anwendung des Hollerithverfahrens [. . .], 28.3.1959, BArch Koblenz, B 443, 2817, o.Bl. (p. 7).
47 Bonn Element, Frankfurt to Chief Munich Liaison Basis: CART/CATHINK/CATIDE – Visit of @Feller, 23.3.1965. CIA CREST Database, Doc. ID: special collection, nwcda ZUBER, EBRULF VOL. 1_0017.

Knowledge transfer and technopolitics   117

48 Contact Report, 30.7.1965, CIA CREST Database, Doc. ID. Special Collection, nwcda 7/187, Dickopf, Paul, Vol. 2_0019.
49 Ibid.
50 Wolf, *Die Entstehung des BND*, 387.
51 CDA an 106 D pers., betr. Vortrag CDA in Abt.Ltr.-Konferenz am 24.7.1968 mit Anlage (Vortragsmanuskript), 05.08.1968, BNDA, 1714_OT, Bl. 1–32, here Bl. 7.
52 This information is listed in 777, Nr. 89/64 geh. Az.: 170, Dokumentation und Archivwesen, 29.12.1964 (Vortragsfolge von 777 im Januar 1965), BNDA 4047, o.Bl. (p. 2)
53 Ibid.
54 666, Nr. 208/59, Aktennotiz betr. Planung von CIA für die maschinelle Aufbereitung von umfangreichen Personenkarteien, 6.4.1959, BNDA 6002, o.Bl.
55 Ibid.
56 666 an 261 über 16, betr.: Mechanisierung der Zentralen Personensuchkartei, 15.12.1960, BNDA 6002, o.Bl.
57 Leimbach, *Die Geschichte der Softwarebranche*, 73–74.
58 "Kreuzburg" was an IBM employee from 1947 to 1954. In 1954 he moved to Siemens & Halske. BNDA, VASI 30574, Bl. 12.
59 For the encompassing use of the term "software" by the 1960s contemporaries see Schmitt, *Die Digitalisierung der Kreditwirtschaft*, 67–69.
60 "It has been reiterated to the BND that according to Agency experience it would be folly to seriously consider ADP without first having defined and concentrated on their own document, index and information retrieval problems; that management must take charge, define objectives and limitations realistically." CIA Acting Chief Eastern Europe Division an CIA Assistant Deputy Director for Plans: Automatic Data Processing, 24.05.1965. CIA CREST, Special Collection, nwcda7/187, Zuber, Ebrulf, Vol. 1_0024.
61 Bonn Element, Frankfurt to Chief Munich Liaison Basis: CART/CATHINK/CATIDE – Visit of @Feller, 23.03.1965. CIA CREST Database, Doc. ID: Special Collection, nwcda ZUBER, EBRULF VOL. 1_0017.
62 Cited in Krieger, *Partnerdienste*, 244, on the crisis in relations between the CIA and the BND after the Felfe unmasking, see ibid, 242–248.
63 777, betr.: Mechanisierung der Zentralen Suchkartei, 18.3.1964, BNDA 4047, o.Bl.
64 Ibid.
65 Burke, *America's Information Wars*, 140.
66 CIA Acting Chief Eastern Europe Division to CIA Assistant Deputy Director for Plans: Automatic Data Processing, 24.05.1965. CIA CREST, Special Collection, nwcda7/187, Zuber, Ebrulf, Vol. 1_0024.
67 Ibid.
68 PFH, Notiz zur Besprechung mit [. . .], Betr.: Änderung in den ELINT-Codierungsverfahren, 21.12.1964, BNDA 4047, o.Bl.
69 Müller, *Wellenkrieg*, 328–339.
70 Memorandum for the Record: Discussions with CATIDE on Index Mechanization, Joint Soviet Travel, 7–10 June 1965, 23.6.1965. CIA CREST Database, Doc. ID. Special Collection, nwcda7/187, Zuber, Ebrulf, Vol. 1_0025.
71 CIA Acting Chief Eastern Europe Division to CIA Assistant Deputy Director for Plans: Automatic Data Processing, 24.05.1965. CIA CREST, Special Collection, nwcda7/187, Zuber, Ebrulf, Vol. 1_0024.
72 In 1967 CHIVE project staff became dissolved. History of Project CHIVE, 12.9.1967, CIA CREST Database, Doc. ID. CIA-RDP80B01139A000600160003–8, 27–8.
73 49 an 48 f. CDA, betr. Zentralstelle für Personenauskunftswesen, Dokumentation und Automatisierung des BND, 19.10.1964, BNDA 4047, o.Bl.
74 Born in the then Czech *Sudetenland* in 1920, Zuber joined the Waffen-SS in 1939, and was assigned to the SS-*Hauptamt* in 1942. He returned to the front in 1944 as a

118   *Rüdiger Bergien*

company commander in an armored infantry regiment. In 1947 he joined the Gehlen service with the help of his friend Friedrich Sturz, an SS comrade who also hailed from the Sudetenland. (Rass, "Leben und Legende," 26; Sälter, "Kameraden," 45–47).

75 Heidenreich, *Die DDR-Spionage*, 263.

76 This was probably all the easier for Zuber, as he was still in charge of the service's organizational safety-unit, including counterintelligence.

77 BND, CDA an BND, 106 D pers., betr. Vortrag CDA in Abt.Ltr.-Konferenz am 24.7.1968 mit Anlage (Vortragsmanuskript), 05.08.1968, BNDA, 1714_OT, Bl. 1–32, here Bl. 29.

78 CATIDE = cryptonym for "BND."

79 Memorandum for the Record: Discussions with CATIDE on Index Mechanization, Joint Soviet Travel, 7–10 June 1965, 23.6.1965. CIA CREST Database, Doc. ID. Special Collection, nwcda7/187, Zuber, Ebrulf, Vol. 1_0025.

80 [. . .] to CIA Chief Europe, Subject: RYBAT CATUSK UVJENTURE; @Ackermann graphological Assessment, 11.4.1968, CIA CREST Database, Doc. ID. Special Collection, nwcda7/187, Zuber, Ebrulf, Vol 1_0092.

81 Memorandum for the Record: Discussions with CATIDE on Index Mechanization, Joint Soviet Travel, 7–10 June 1965, 23.06.1965. CIA CREST Database, Doc. ID. Special Collection, nwcda7/187, Zuber, Ebrulf, Vol. 1_0025.

82 Nr. 37/65 VS-vertr., 9.7.1965: "Document Storage and Retrieval and General System of Biographic Indexing" (Protokoll über die Vortragsveranstaltung vom 7.6.–10.6.1965), BNDA 4047, o.Bl.

83 See Krieger, *Partnerdienste*, 203–217.

84 Upon his return to Pullach, Zuber "portrayed his visit in the most glowing terms to all who would listen," according to the Chief CIA Munich Liaison Base. Zuber frequently emphasized "the great value of the trip to him personally as well as to the entire ADP project at CATUSK." Chief Munich Liaison Basis an CIA Chief Europe; Chief Womace Systems Group: CATUSK [. . .] UJDRACO, Zuber's Visit, 23.11.1966. CIA CREST Database, Doc. ID. GEHLEN, REINHARD VOL. 5_0066.

85 Sturz, Friedrich [DN Seipold] to Präsident BND, 1.8.1979. BNDA, 4731_OT, Bl. 23–56, here 26.

86 Ibid., 34.

87 Cryptonym for the West German Federal Intelligence Service, BND.

88 [illegible] to Chief Europe/Womace Systems Group, Subject: [illegible] Progress on Catusk ADP, 3.7.1969, CIA CREST Database, Doc. ID. Special Collection, nwcda7/187, Zuber, Ebrulf, Vol 1_0095.

89 Memorandum for the Record, Subject: Visit to CATRIBE, 21.7.1970, CIA CREST Database, Doc. ID. Special Collection, nwcda7/187, Zuber, Ebrulf, Vol 1_0099.

90 See also the contribution by Christopher Kirchberg to this volume.

91 Memorandum for the Record: Discussions with CATIDE on Index Mechanization, Joint Soviet Travel, 7–10 June 1965, 23.06.1965. CIA CREST Database, Doc. ID. special collection, nwcda7/187, Zuber, Ebrulf, Vol. 1_0025.

92 For context: Protokoll der Besprechung der EGIS-Kommission am 9.2.1968, BNDA 104441, o.Bl.; [. . .] an Chief WOMUSE: [. . .] CATHINK CASTRUP CAWHISPER EGIS MACHINE SYSTEM, 9.4.1969. CIA CREST Database, Doc. ID. Special Collection, nwcda7/187, Zuber, Ebrulf, Vol 1_0093.

93 Aktennotiz, betr.: IRCD, hier: Computerprobleme zum EGIS-Programm, 31.3.1969, BNDA 104441, o.Bl.

94 Bericht über die Besprechung am 28.3.1969 (14.00–15.30 h) in der Zentrale des BND, BNDA, 104441, o.Bl.

95 Arbeitsgruppe EDV-Bedarf Abteilung I: EDV-Konzept Abteilung I, Stand August 1979. BNDA, 3197_OT, here Bl. 36.

96 For examples of the evaluation units' harsh criticism of the planned central biographic register in: III B 3 an III B 1, betr.: Entwurf für PEDOK-Verfügung vom 1.3.1971, Bezug: Rundschreiben von III B 1 vom 20.7.1971, 22.7.1971, BArch B206/437, 276–282.

Knowledge transfer and technopolitics 119

97 Progress on CATUSK ADP, 03.07.1969. CIA CREST Database, Doc. ID: Special Collection, nwcda ZUBER, EBRULF VOL. 1_0095.
98 [. . .] to CIA Chief Europe, Subject: CATRIBE JUVENTURE, @Ackermann's Opinions on Transfers and New Appointments at CATRIBE, 16.4.1970, CIA CREST Database, Doc. ID: Special Collection, nwcda ZUBER, EBRULF VOL. 1_0097.
99 Ibid.
100 See Hange, "Nachruf," 42–43.
101 Sturz, Friedrich [DN Seipold] an Präsident BND, 1.8.1979. BNDA, 4731_OT, Bl. 23–56, here Bl. 42.
102 PEDOK = "Personendokumentation," i.e. biographic database.
103 Cortada, *The Digital Flood*.
104 For background information, see here: Edwards, *The Closed World*.
105 Further travels of BfV (domestic intelligence)-officers including himself in the USA in the 1970s mentions Postel, *So war es . . .* , 146–147.

Bibliography

Agar, J. 2016. "Putting the Spooks Back In? The UK Secret State and the History of Computing." *Information & Culture: A Journal of History* 151, no. 1: 102–124.
Agee, Ph. 1975. *Inside the Company, CIA Diary*. Harmondsworth: Penguin Books.
Aldrich, R. J. 2010. *GCHQ. The Uncensored Story of Britain's Most Secret Intelligence Agency*, London: Harper Press.
Andrew, Ch. M. 2009. *The Defence of the Realm: The Authorized History of MI5*. London: Allen Lane.
Borel, P. A. 1967. "Automation for Information Control. Review of Possibilities and Some Applications in the CIA." *Studies in Intelligence* 11, no. 1: 25–32.
Burke, C. B. 2002. "It Wasn't All Magic. The Early Struggle to Automate Cryptanalysis, 1930s–1960s." *Published by the National Security Agency (= United States Cryptologic History, Special Series, vol. 6)*. https://fas.org/irp/nsa/automate.pdf.
Burke, C. B. 2018. *America's Information Wars: The Untold Story of Information Systems in America's Conflicts and Politics from World War II to the Internet Age*. Lanham, Boulder, New York, and London: Rowman & Littlefield
Cortada, J. W. 2012. *The Digital Flood: The Diffusion of Information Technology Across the U.S., Europe, and Asia*. Oxford: Oxford University Press.
Dönhoff, M. G. 1968. "Der Mann ohne Gesicht." *Die Zeit* 17 (April 26th).
Düllfer, J. 2018. *Geheimdienst in der Krise. Der BND in den 1960er-Jahren*. Berlin: Ch. Links Verlag
Edwards, P. N. 1996. *The Closed World: Computers and the Politics of Discourse in Cold War America*. Cambridge, MA: MIT Press.
Eppler, M. J., and Mengis, J. 2004. "The Concept of Information Overload. A Review of Literature from Organization Science, Accounting, Marketing, MIS, and Related Disciplines." *The Information Society* 20: 325–344.
Ferris, J. 2020. *Behind the Enigma: The Authorised History of GCHQ, Britain's Secret Cyber-Intelligence Agency*. London: Bloomsbury Publishing, 431.
Hange, M. 2015. "Nachruf auf Dr. Otto Leiberich." *BSI Magazin*, 42–43. www.bsi.bund. de/SharedDocs/Downloads/DE/BSI/Publikationen/Magazin/BSI-Magazin_2015. pdf?__blob=publicationFile&v=2
Hayes, R. M. 1995. "Joseph Becker: A Lifetime of Service to the Profession of Library and Information Science." *Bulletin of the American Society for Information Science and Technology* 22, no. 1: 24–26.

120   *Rüdiger Bergien*

Hecht, G., and Edwards, P. N. 2008. "The Technopolitics of Cold War. Toward a Transregional Perspective." In *Essays on Global and Comparative History*, ed. M. Adas, 271–314. Philadelphia: Temple University Press.

Heidenreich, R. 2019. *Die DDR-Spionage des BND. Von den Anfängen bis zum Mauerbau.* Berlin: Ch. Links Verlag.

Krieger, W. 2021. *Partnerdienste. Die Beziehungen des BND zu den westlichen Geheimdiensten 1946–1968.* Berlin: Ch. Links Verlag.

Leimbach, T. 2010. *Die Geschichte der Softwarebranche in Deutschland.* Universitätsbibliothek, München. https://edoc.ub.uni-muenchen.de/12436/1/Leimbach_Timo.pdf

Müller, A. 2017. *Wellenkrieg. Agentenfunk und Funkaufklärung des Bundesnachrichtendienstes 1945–1968.* Berlin: Ch. Links Verlag, 328–339.

Postel, H.-J. 1999. *So war es . . . Mein Leben im 20. Jahrhundert.* Meckenheim: Warlich.

Rass, C. 2014. "Leben und Legende. Das Sozialprofil eines Geheimdienstes." In *Die Geschichte der Organisation Gehlen und des BND 1945–1968: Umrisse und Einblicke*, ed. UHK, 24–41. Marburg: UHK

Rosenberg, D. 2003. "Early Modern Information Overload." *Journal of the History of Ideas* 65: 1–9.

Sälter, G. 2014. "Kameraden. Nazi-Netzwerke und die Rekrutierung hauptamtlicher Mitarbeiter." In *Die Geschichte der Organisation Gehlen und des BND 1945–1968: Umrisse und Einblicke*, ed. UHK, 41–52. Marburg: UHK

Schmitt, M. 2021. *Die Digitalisierung der Kreditwirtschaft. Computereinsatz in den Sparkassen der Bundesrepublik und der DDR 1957–1991.* Göttingen: Wallstein Verlag.

Warner, M. 2012. "Reflections on Technology and Intelligence Systems." *Intelligence and National Security* 27, no. 1: 133–153.

Warner, M. 2014. *The Rise and Fall of Intelligence: An international Security History.* Washington, DC: Georgetown University Press.

Wegener, J. 2020. "Order and Chaos. The CIA's HYDRA Database and the Dawn of the Information Age." *Journal of Intelligence History* 19, no. 1: 77–91.

Wolf, Th. 2018. *Die Entstehung des BND. Aufbau, Finanzierung, Kontrolle.* Berlin: Ch. Links Verlag.

6 Information technology is power

The intelligence service's grab for the IT sector in Brazil

Marcelo Vianna

Introduction

In Brazil, the period between the second half of the 1970s and the beginning of the 1980s was characterised by the process of political opening under the control of the military regime. This process combined political and economic arrangements that proposed a "slow and gradual" transition to democracy under the tutelage of the civilian-military dictatorship. At the time, different social groups saw the opportunity to reorganise and claim rights. Thus, it was a period of rebirth of social movements: the new syndicalism, the student movement, and various ethnic and women's groups gained strength. Even though surveilled and repressed by the military regime, these movements were able to mobilise parts of society with themes considered vital for the restoration of democratic order and for the improvement of living conditions, such as amnesty for political prisoners and exiles, the right to strike and gender equality.

It was in this context of mobilisation that the National Informatics Policy (Política Nacional de Informática, PNI) was implemented. It was created between 1976 and 1979 and carried out by technological nationalists known as *barbudinhos* ("bearded little men"), "frustrated nationalist technologists" or "technological guerrillas,"[1] grouped in state bodies, especially in the Commission for Coordination of Electronic Processing Activities (Comissão de Coordenação das Atividades de Processamento Eletrônico, CAPRE).[2] CAPRE was linked to the Ministry of Planning and was responsible for guiding the rationalisation of Brazil's computing resources. The PNI, as a series of regulations and practices, including the control of imports, sought to enable the technological development of informatics within the country, blocking the initiatives of transnational companies led by IBM. These were the preconditions for the emergence of a national Brazilian computer and peripheral industry. By 1984, this native industry would achieve a turnover of $952 million, covering 51.2 per cent of national computer market revenues.

However, the pioneering movement of CAPRE's technological nationalists and their supporters was undermined by another movement which came to dictate the PNI's course from late 1979 until the Informatics Law in late 1984, just before José Sarney's democratic government (1985–1990). It was composed of

DOI: 10.4324/9781003147329-7

122 Marcelo Vianna

individuals, especially military officers, from the Brazilian Information Service (Serviço Nacional de Informações, SNI), and its members would lead a process of intervention culminating in the formation of the new national informatics management agency, the Special Department for Informatics (Secretaria Especial de Informática, SEI), linked to the National Security Council (Conselho de Segurança Nacional, CSN).[3] According to Ivan da Costa Marques, one of the leaders of the technological nationalists affected by the intervention, this rise of an "opportunistic group of political police agents" eliminated the "democratic ethos of PNI's origin"[4] that was practiced by technological nationalists and was considered suspect by these agents.

It is noteworthy that an intelligence agency such as the SNI – created in 1964, shortly after the civilian-military coup that ousted President João Goulart – expanded beyond its original purposes by trying to take control of areas considered strategic, such as the field of informatics.[5] This aspect has received too little attention in historiography, which remains focused on the repressive aspects of the intelligence agencies in Latin America.[6] SNI's counterparts, such as the Secretaría de Inteligencia (SIDE) in Argentina and the Dirección de Inteligencia Nacional (DINA) in Chile, were specialised in uncompromising violence against political opponents and in mobilising human and technological resources. These institutions became key players in sustaining the authoritarian regimes established in the Southern Cone in the 1970s. Their practices have been conceptualised as "state terrorism." SNI, largely committed to the surveillance and repression of Brazilian society, coordinated a similar system in Brazil and maintained an equally nationalistic and anti-communist rhetoric. However, unlike SIDE in Argentina and DINA in Chile, Brazil's SNI was also concerned with playing the role of policy maker in order to influence high state hierarchies and participate in decision-making, seeking to justify its existence in a future democratic period.

This chapter aims at exploring the process of involvement of SNI in the field of informatics throughout the 1970s, from the circulation/appropriation of knowledge to its conversion into technical and political actions that resulted in the control of this field. In this sense, "knowledge" must be perceived as a plural category,[7] as it involves different types of knowledge, disputed or not, and that were re-signified by social agents, constituting new forms of knowledge. In the context of political authoritarianism and technological transformations during the military regime, SNI used formal and informal, public and confidential knowledge, involving the agency's digitisation process, its intelligence activities (surveillance and control), its practical experience of repression and its political interests in the name of national security to gain access to the field of Brazilian informatics. In the process, SNI alienated the network of technological nationalists that had hitherto been well-established in the field of informatics and proposed its own technological agenda for the 1980s.

In turn, technical and political actions involved the orientation of political, technological and repressive knowledge to construct state policy, as Gabrielle Hecht has stated regarding the issue of nuclear energy in France.[8] This association,

Information technology is power 123

especially in a period of authoritarianism, would justify a more "technocratic" view of state problems, but without neglecting nationalist and anti-communist concerns, something incorporated into the *habitus* of SNI members. Thus, to master digital technologies was not only to use them but to configure awareness of the influence of these technologies on society, which would inspire SNI to seek to take over Brazilian informatics.

In general, this chapter will address two SNI movements in the 1970s. The first is the process of computerising its activities, involving the digitisation of procedures, including the storage and circulation of data obtained by its information collection system. The second involves an interest, born precisely from the modernisation process, which made it aspire to greater dominance over the technological field, specifically informatics. This led it not only to keep an eye on movements in the field of informatics but also to aspire to intervene directly. This process culminated in the creation of the Special Department for Informatics in late 1979, replacing the "technological guerrillas" in the formulation of Brazilian informatics policy.

The text is divided into four sections. The first analyses the relationship between national security, development and authoritarianism in Brazil. The emphasis on development and technology during the civilian-military dictatorship opened up a space for both the military and the civilian technocracy to acquire skills and make technological decisions in the field of informatics. The National Information System (Sistema Nacional de Informações, SISNI) that arose from the need to establish a "safe" environment for the country's development is also presented. The second section sketches the process of digitising SNI's activities and the system itself, with the implementation of necessary digital technologies. The third section seeks to show how this technological interest in modernising SNI activities was also accompanied by the political calculations of the military. Aiming for greater influence in areas considered strategic, SNI established monitoring of the groups that worked in the field of informatics. The final section presents SNI's direct intervention in the Brazilian informatics community, replacing the established groups to institute its command through the SEI.

The consulted sources, namely the SNI documentary collection, can be found in the Brazilian National Archive in Brasília. Among the most relevant documents are the field reports produced by the agents. These documents do not exactly stand out in terms of quality but are invaluable in assessing how much the agents were influenced by the National Security Doctrine. Through the documentation, available through the Projeto Memórias Reveladas (Revealed Memories Project), it is possible to understand how SNI produced and re-signified the information obtained in the field, including its digital processing, allowing us to generate knowledge concerning the activities of the monitoring of society. However, the reports related to SNI's intervention in the field of informatics are stored at the Ministry of Science and Technology, and their access is still restricted. The same was true for a long time for SNI's cryptographic project *Prólogo*, whose documentation hosted at the Ministry of Foreign Affairs was only released in 2011 through the "Access to Information Act."

National security, development and technology during the Brazilian civilian-military dictatorship

The military interest in the technological field was not exactly new. The development of US informatics allegedly took place in the name of the security of the country (and the Western world), based on the "closed world" discourse against the communist threat.[9] This discourse, which gathered fragments of other discourses and technologies, had the property of guiding individuals in a social space in order to create new technologies to ensure the safety of society. In Brazil, this discourse was based on the National Security Doctrine (Doutrina de Segurança Nacional, DSN), elaborated by the Superior War College (Escola Superior de Guerra, ESG) that was created in 1948 as a strategic body for the instruction of high military (and later civilian) ranks guided by nationalist and anti-communist ideas.[10]

According to the DSN, there was a strong correlation between "security," essential for "creating and maintaining political, economic and social order,"[11] and "development," a necessary condition to integrate the country into the list of developed capitalist countries, which would guarantee material means to the population and so avert the danger of communism. This correlation between security and development was viewed as important for the nation's stability and justified placing the society under the control of the military, which was seen as the only institution capable of acting on truly national interests. It is worth mentioning that these conceptions date back to the 1930s, when the Armed Forces became professional and began to act as moderators of the political field, acting in times of crisis (end of the Estado Novo in 1945, inauguration of Juscelino Kubitschek in 1955) and later claiming control of the political by unleashing the 1964 civilian-military dictatorship.

These concerns involved the technological development of the post-war country. Inspired by their moderate access to technologies, knowledge and experts from the United States and European countries, the Brazilian military sectors sought to establish technical and research training spaces, such as the Technological Institute of Aeronautics (ITA) in 1949 and the Technical School of the Army/Military Institute of the Army (ETE/IME) in 1959. With regard to informatics, IBM's "uncomfortable" dominance[12] of the Brazilian market, the incipient electronic components industry in Brazil and the key role of technology for the national security of the country motivated the military to undertake early analyses of national resources and computer projects, starting with the Working Group for Computer Applications in 1958.[13] In the same period, the first prototypes were conceived at military institutions, although these were still only for didactic purposes: the "Zezinho" (ITA) and "Lourinha" computers at ETE/IME, the latter under the guidance of Helmut Schreyer.[14] However, the best-known initiative is the agreement signed between the Brazilian Navy and the Brazilian Development Bank (Banco Nacional de Desenvolvimento Econômico, BNDE) in 1971: the development of a minicomputer prototype in order to overcome the technological dependence on the English manufacturer Ferranti, which equipped the Brazilian frigates.[15]

The evolution of the work transformed the field of informatics in the country, leading to the emergence of the national computer company COBRA (Computadores Brasileiros) and the development of the G-10 minicomputer by the University of São Paulo (USP) and the Catholic University of Rio de Janeiro (PUCRIO) in the 1970s.

Although the military was relegated to a more discreet role throughout the 1970s due to the ascendancy of civilian technocracy in state policy planning, it did not leave the field of informatics. While some military members worked with Brazilian IT companies, such as COBRA, Digibrás and Federal Data Processing Service (Serviço Federal de Processamento de Dados, SERPRO), others offered their expertise in electronics or telecommunications on the private market.[16] Although dispersed, the circulation of technical knowledge guided by the concept of national security informed the military's view of the role that technologies should play, which would influence those who would act within SNI.

Conceived in June 1964, SNI had the purpose of "supervising and coordinating, throughout the national territory, information and counter-information activities, particularly those pertaining to national security."[17] Thus, it integrated the repressive tripod (surveillance, censorship and repression) encouraged by the military regime. According to Suzeley Mathias, the service developed a "culture of secrecy" among its members, characterised by a strong level of secrecy about and intricacy in its activities, proper to authoritarian regimes.[18] SNI established itself as a very professional source of information,[19] even though the institution was heavily influenced by the state's tradition of violence and suspicion towards certain social groups dating back to the colonial period.

SNI became the coordinator of the SISNI, established by the military regime in 1970. At first, the Central Agency of SNI in Brasilia coordinated the integrated system, collecting the information produced by its 12 regional agencies, by the Security and Information Divisions (DSI) in the ministries and by the Security and Information Assessments (ASI) produced in state-owned companies, in local government agencies and in universities, as well as in information centres of agencies such as the Federal Police Department and the Ministry of Foreign Affairs (CIEx). SNI also collaborated with the dreaded Military Information Centres (CIE, CENIMAR, CISA), directly involved in the repression and torture of regime dissidents, and several state security agencies, which provided for the lack of regional SNI agencies in some parts of the huge country. On the characteristics of the system, Carlos Fico observed:

> SISNI was not, of course, a structure simply focused on collecting information capable of supporting the decision-making of the Brazilian authorities. It was, above all, a system of espionage and indictment, which was based on the assumption that no one was totally immune to communism, subversion or corruption.[20]

This authoritarian model had an influence on SISNI's information production method. The system brought together medical records, field and analysis reports,

126 *Marcelo Vianna*

and newspaper and magazine clippings, all assembled under the name of an individual, a social group (such as a political party), a company or a theme, forming the so-called Chronological Archives of Entry (Arquivos Cronológicos de Entrada, ACE). Each ACE document, as it was elaborated, could have deleterious effects on public trajectories, for instance those of officials identified as subversives in "concept records" (the official name was Biographical Data Survey, LDB)[21] and whose careers were thus interrupted.

Technological knowledge through digitisation

Formally, SISNI's operations could reach all sectors of Brazilian society. In reality, its effectiveness was more limited: in addition to the lack of control over the repressive apparatus, rivalries between the intelligence agencies of the Armed Forces and the poor quality of information, it depended on an efficient technological infrastructure. There is evidence that the CIA had been contributing training and technical resources to Brazilian intelligence agencies since the 1950s. However, the extent of the transfer of technology and knowledge has not yet been studied thoroughly. J. Patrice McSherry, for example, pointed out that Operation Condor's (1975) technology infrastructure involved CIA-supplied computers for intelligence agencies in the participating countries (including Brazil), operating a database similar to the Phoenix Program that was applied in Vietnam in the late 1960s for the identification and elimination of insurgents.[22]

The question of what computational technologies were applied, and how they were applied, by SNI to obtain "better" or "faster" data processing is addressed in Debora Gerstenberger's contribution to this volume. Suffice it to note here that the Central Agency of SNI already incorporated an IBM computer, supported by SERPRO, in 1969, during SISNI deployment. Considering that SERPRO was the country's agency with the largest database expertise, gained from the registration of taxpayers in 1967 with the help of USAID technicians, this seemed a logical approach. However, little is known about this exchange, which led to the registration of 1,200,000 information-holding punch cards by 1978.

What is certain is that technological activities were boosted by the rise of Octavio Aguiar de Medeiros,[23] when he was invited by the then chief of the agency (and his close friend), João Baptista Figueiredo, to lead the newly created National School of Information (Escola Nacional de Informações, EsNI) in 1975. Medeiros reinforced the performance of the school as a permanent centre of thought and action in addition to the theoretical teaching of ESG, focused on "concrete" problems related to the formation of agents at different levels.[24] According to an SNI member, Octavio Medeiros was "electronically and technologically oriented,"[25] which explains the concentration of the agency's expertise in the technological area (electronics) and its attempt to modernise the intelligence activities of SNI through the use of computers. This process of digitisation, although confidential, evinced the participation of IBM do Brasil in the alienation of computer resources and the co-optation of specialists such as Navy officer Antonio de Loyola Reis[26] and mathematician Octavio Gennari Neto.[27]

As a result, in 1978, an IT department was created at EsNI, incorporating IBM 3231 and FACOM m360 computers into the Central Agency, along with consultation terminals, microfilm readers and printers, which enhanced the work of the SNI analysts.[28] One of the databases available to SNI analysts was the Information Document Archiving and Retrieval System (Sistema de Arquivamento e Recuperação de Documentos para Informação, SARDI). Implemented in December 1978 through IBM's STAIRS software, the system would concentrate the ACE documents produced by the regional SNI departments, as well as LDB documents, medical records and other records considered relevant. In general terms, the SARDI database sought to concentrate summaries of ACE documents produced by the analysts, enabling subsequent consultations in the microfilm collection (see Figure 6.1).[29]

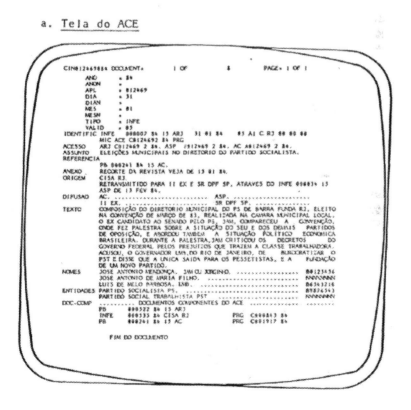

Figure 6.1 ACE documents subsystem screen, as illustrated in a 1984 SARDI user's manual.

Source: BR DFANBSB V.8.TXT, AGR.DNF.38. SNI Collection. National Archive.

128 *Marcelo Vianna*

In addition to SARDI, the most relevant innovation was the integration of the so-called external systems: SNI had full access to Federal Police systems (such as SINPI – National System of Wanted and Prohibited People, and STI – International Traffic System), the public data network Aruanda, the Polvo project (land vehicle database, created by SERPRO) and other databases.[30] In sum, there was an undeniable predisposition by the information community to expand the registry to "the greatest number of people, if not all, who had their names conveyed by SNI."[31] This required eliminating redundancy and creating indexes in order to rationalise the control of information, guiding more effective actions. In practical terms, this only partially materialised: while there was an undeniable expansion of state surveillance capacities, the quality of the processed information was not improved. Given the logic of indictment adopted by SISNI, typical of repressive knowledge, the agents used circular reports, frequently based on unreliable sources such as torture or denunciations, to identify "subversive people." This led to the description of SNI as a "hollow-headed monster" by regime critics in the 1980s.

Despite the contradictions, SNI was involved in technological projects considered of interest, such as RENAPE and Prólogo,[32] which would reinforce the interest in controlling the field of Brazilian informatics, going beyond the digitisation of its activities. The first technological project, officially titled "National Registry of Natural People" (Registro Nacional de Pessoas Naturais, RENAPE), was an ambitious project initiated by SERPRO in the late 1960s to create a large computerised database capable of concentrating basic information about each Brazilian citizen. As part of the Interministerial Commission of RENAPE throughout the 1970s, SNI wanted to access this formidable database to enhance its surveillance and repression activities.

The Prólogo project was born from the Brazilian government's need to respond to the economic crisis caused by the Oil Shock of 1973. The crisis caused the government to seek to attract new trade and technological partners as alternatives to the United States in a policy of "responsible pragmatism" practised by Minister of Foreign Affairs Azeredo da Silveira. Both the Ministry of Foreign Affairs (Itamaraty)[33] and SNI were aware of the fragility of the communication system with the Brazilian embassies, which was susceptible to blockages[34] and interceptions that put at risk the policy established by the regime. This shared perception of both agencies regarding information secrecy[35] brought their specialists closer. In 1977, they joined forces in a project to construct a cryptographic communication system of their own. Army officer Edson Dytz from SNI[36] would lead the process, promoting the reverse-engineering of Crypto AG cryptographic equipment in order to establish a national system (see Figure 6.2) – but, to the disappointment of those involved, it had a high ratio of foreign components, revealing an uncomfortable state of technological dependency.

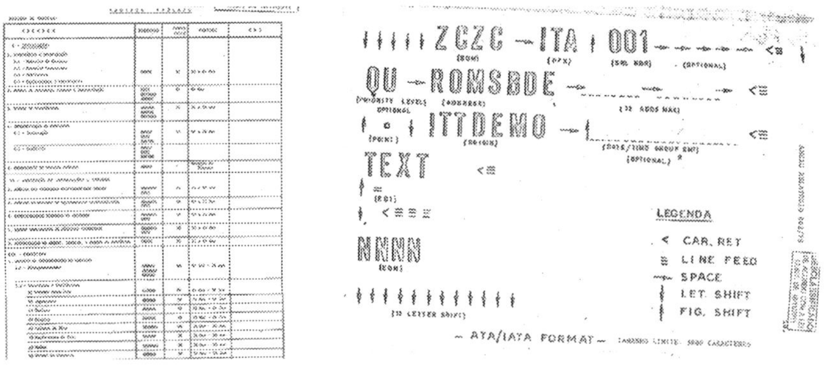

Figure 6.2 Report and sample of cryptography of the Prólogo project (1978–1979).

Source: Image taken from the Archive of the Ministry of Foreign Affairs. Access to Information Act. Request number 09200.000121/2014–83, date 05/02/2014. Documents from Archive of the Ministry of Foreign Affairs (Itamaraty).

Reaching out for the field of informatics

The digitisation process was one of the facets of SNI's new technological horizons, and it reflected a strategy to maintain the agency's power. The political opening process of the Ernesto Geisel administration (1974–1979) and the extermination of much of the armed resistance to the regime raised questions about the need for such a huge apparatus, which now had to be justified. This may explain why SNI progressively displayed an interest in occupying areas considered of national interest, with the military officers taking the leading role in the process.[37] In addition, gathering information on various strategic topics helped the SNI military officers see themselves as capable. This brought SNI closer to the CSN during the Figueiredo government (1979–1985), when, under the leadership of General Danilo Venturini, it sought to concentrate in the agency the capacity to support governmental decisions on strategic issues such as "nuclear energy" or "amnesty" (see Figure 6.3). According to René Dreifuss, for SNI, which would act as an executive arm of CSN, this was about establishing itself as a "crucial center of influence"[38] to guide state policies, representing a true institutionalisation of the authoritarian regime.

As SNI increasingly realised the importance of digital technologies for the country's security and development, the agency began to collect data on individuals or social groups working in the field of informatics, mapping existing interests. In this respect, it should be noted that the dynamics of the organisation of the field of Brazilian informatics in the 1970s were distinctly marked by SNI's modus operandi.

130 *Marcelo Vianna*

Figure 6.3 Caricature by Hilde Weber published in the daily newspaper *O Estado de S. Paulo* in January 1980 on CSN's ambitions to control strategic areas.

Source: Political cartoon by Hilde Weber, *O Estado de São Paulo*, January 6, 1980, 7.

CAPRE was initially established in 1972 to implement measures to rationalise computational resources, considering the period of expansion that the Brazilian market experienced during Brazil's economic "miracle" (1968–1973).[39] Relatively "fragile" in the state structure, CAPRE established programmes and practices that progressively attracted the technical-scientific community, such as the National Computer Training Programme (1974) and the CAPRE Information Bulletin (1973). This circulation and exchange of knowledge between the community and CAPRE, duly enhanced by the actions of the technological nationalists, bore fruit in the so-called SECOMU (Seminar on Computing at the University). Organised by CAPRE, the SECOMU events allowed the academic community to discuss not only technical aspects, such as the installation of data processing centres, but

Information technology is power   131

the very direction of the computerisation of Brazilian society as well. Assuming a nationalist political position, universities generated the first computational technologies and envisioned the possibility of making them viable in the national market, with due support from the Brazilian Informatics Policy.

The deterioration of the country's balance of payments in 1975 provided CAPRE with the means to implement its policy of technological autonomy: import controls. From 1976, CAPRE began to regulate imports of data processing equipment, establishing priority quotas for items it deemed indispensable. And from 1977 onwards it removed foreign competition to national companies manufacturing minicomputers by restricting multinationals' access to the market and seeking to encourage the production of relatively simple peripherals, such as modems and terminals. Ambitiously, CAPRE encouraged the formation of associations – such as the Brazilian Computer Society, the Association of Data Processing Professionals and the Brazilian Computer Industry Association – that provided a broader public debate on technologies, dialoguing with the very process of re-democratisation experienced by the country in the late 1970s.

This search for technological autonomy, inspired by the CEPAL-led projects[40] of the 1950s, was relatively in line with the authoritarian nationalist discourse, which allowed CAPRE's practices to be tolerated throughout the Geisel administration (1974–1979). The main difference was in the conduct of autonomy: while technological nationalists saw it as a way of legitimising CAPRE's decisions, SNI and military sectors guided by the concept of national security were reluctant to cede the conduct of autonomy to an "unstable" public debate over which they would not have effective control. Not surprisingly, the public debates promoted by CAPRE in the late 1970s were seen as inadequate by SNI[41] and generated monitoring of its activities.

One of those monitored by SNI was the Rio de Janeiro Association of Data Processing Professionals (APPD/RJ) (see Figure 6.4). Founded in 1977, it was staffed by CAPRE officials and quickly came to represent the technical-scientific community working in private and public data centres in the state of Rio de Janeiro. APPD/RJ actively participated in congresses in the area, antagonising the military officers and fighting for the rights of IT professionals.

The report obtained from an infiltrated agent underlined that APPD/RJ and similar entities from other states of the federation, such as Rio Grande do Sul and São Paulo, was characterised by a rapid growth in the number of members and "by the aggressiveness in the pursuit of its goals."[42] In SNI's view, APPD – especially the Rio de Janeiro section – managed to occupy spaces of public debate, held discussions with important parliamentary leaders who were considered "communists" and was preparing to form a national union. This risk was accentuated by the belief that subversive elements were part of APPD/RJ's staff and could thus paralyse computerised systems in the country through a strike.[43] APPD/RJ leaders who fell under suspicion included Ezequiel Pinto Dias and Gílcio Martins. Former students of the Technological Institute of Aeronautics, expelled during the civilian-military coup in 1964, were system analysts who "survived" the regime's persecutions in the bureaucratic structure of SERPRO in the 1970s and were strongly identified

132 *Marcelo Vianna*

Figure 6.4 CISA/SNI's reports from December 26, 1977, about APPD activities.
Source: ACE 7600/77, BR DFNANBSB V.8.MIC, GNC.CCC.77007600 – Dossier. SNI Collection. National Archive.

with the technological nationalists of CAPRE. The SNI reports demonstrate an effective surveillance of their activities, with the concept records mentioning their education and training, their "subversive" relationships and the events they participated in. As already observed by Carlos Fico, the repetition of information in subsequent reports in the 1980s only seemed to reinforce SNI's conviction that APPDs were ideological institutions aimed at destabilising the state and were very dangerous due to their access to such technological resources.

CAPRE itself became the subject of a complaint to SNI in 1978 when it was accused by a modem manufacturer of making decisions specifically to harm it. A year earlier, CAPRE had sought to organise the modem market in the country, considering that modems were essential technological devices, especially for processing networks of minicomputers distributed across the country. Given the low technological complexity, CAPRE encouraged universities to create modem projects and make them viable for national companies.

The company ICC/Coencisa, encouraged by more liberal sectors of the government, sought to invest in modem production through a joint venture with a US company. CAPRE realised that the venture would frustrate local development and began restricting imports from ICC/Coencisa. In response, the joint venture partner protested to the authorities, denouncing the attempt to destroy its company.[44] SNI

Information technology is power   133

received the complaint and proceeded to explore the usual indictment method: gathering concept records from the Executive Secretary and his technical advisor, as well as minutes from CAPRE and other technical documents. Since no irregularities were found, SNI came to the conclusion that CAPRE could be replaced as the governing agency of informatics.

Explicit control: the creation of the special department for informatics

SNI's entry into the fight for control of Brazilian informatics was evident in the transition from the Ernesto Geisel to the João Baptista Figueiredo administration in 1978. The fact that Figueiredo was the former head of SNI and had friendly ties with Octavio Medeiros, now head of SNI's Central Agency, provided the political opportunity to intervene in the field of informatics. For Joubert Brízida, then a colonel and adviser to SNI, it was a "fantastic opportunity" to see if "the path chosen by CAPRE was achievable, feasible, convenient."[45] The issue was about the military regaining the leading role in a sensitive area that was led by the technological nationalists, who were greatly distrusted by the military for their actions, considered "subversive."

Two major investigative devices were proposed through which SNI could exercise its technological and repressive knowledge. The first one was known as the Cotrim Commission,[46] conceived in the agreement signed between CNPq, the Foreign Ministry and SNI on December 22, 1978, for "information exchange" and "mutual provision of technical assistance." Upon completion of the Cotrim Commission's mission, the Information Technology/Special Working Group (GTE/I) was formed on October 5, 1979, as a second device, involving SNI, CSN, the Foreign Ministry, the Department of Planning and the Armed Forces General Staff.[47] Together, they recommended a restructuring of the agencies involved and sought to define a global policy regarding IT technologies in the name of national security and development.

The investigations, conducted by SNI agents, used roundtables with specialists in the field of informatics and public authorities, technical studies, visits to factories, government agencies and universities throughout the country, and questionnaires, in addition to the information gathered by SNI through its main activities. Their activities took place within the "culture of silence," without revealing the objective of the interviews. The investigative activities produced rich material – the GTE/I reports alone consisted of 787 pages – covering everything from the survey of raw materials available in the country for the production of microelectronic components, to the situation of the computer industry, to research and training sites in informatics in the country.

The network of technological nationalists criticised SNI's actions through public events and the press, and brought together portions of the technical-scientific community, businessmen and even the military to denounce the demobilisation of CAPRE.[48] But this did little to affect the opinions of the information community: the activities highlighted CAPRE's "fragility," pointing out not only the political limits of its ability to control PNI – such as the absence of clear policies for

134 *Marcelo Vianna*

microelectronics or software – but the agency's own susceptibility to pressures from the groups working in the field of informatics. This pressure came not just from the attempts at interference by foreign corporations, such as IBM and Burroughs, but also from more extreme nationalist technological groups.

It is important to highlight that SNI possessed enough knowledge to elaborate a technical and political action to reach its objective, the control of PNI. The SNI experts who participated in the intervention process, such as the military officers Joubert Brízida, Edison Dytz and Loyola Reis, represented a tremendous concentration of technical knowledge. Originating from the staff of the electronics specialists of the Armed Forces,[49] they had rendered services to SNI. Although leadership may have been authoritarian, the reports show that they were aware of the contemporary specialised technical and sociological literature. This allowed them to contrast the information from different technological nationalists in the interviews and to produce reports without much reliance on external technical assistance, reinforcing SNI's own "culture of secrecy." The culture of secrecy also seemed to contribute to the subsequent removal of its former allies, such as the representatives of the Ministry of Foreign Affairs, and to reinforce the conviction in its decision-making capacity in leading PNI.

But SNI also possessed practical knowledge, based on manipulation and co-optation. SNI explored the differences between technological nationalists regarding the model of technological autonomy. A more pragmatic group within CAPRE advocated the acquisition of foreign technology packages as a way to skip developmental stages, a model proposed by the competition for domestic minicomputer manufacturing in 1977. Another group, better represented in the technical-scientific community (including APPD/RJ), understood that it was necessary to complete this stage, betting on the production of technologies generated in the research centres.[50]

SNI was able to exploit this division in the scientific community, presenting its concern about the technological issue to appeal to a portion of the dissatisfied. Although there was no ideological identification with SNI, there was convergence with a group of São Paulo scientists attracted by the common cause of technological autonomy and the recognition of their expertise in the computational field.[51] Some of them, after being summoned to testify during the investigative phase, realised that the new power represented an opportunity to execute their technological projects.[52] After being passed through the ideological filter, those who were approved came to occupy positions in the SEI and/or worked with the Technological Centre for Informatics (Centro Tecnológico para Informática, CTI), created in 1982 by the SEI to be a technological pole of the area, giving them a place to implement their ideas.[53]

Conclusion

SNI's process of intervention in the field of informatics was successful. The agency's technological awakening in the 1970s led it to the digitisation process, which would bring greater capacity for data processing. The information gathered through fieldwork, such as by infiltrated agents or informants, reports from the SISNI member agencies and complaints, were microfilmed and entered in the

Information technology is power 135

SNI computer systems, which in the 1980s would allow more agile access by the agents. However, the knowledge generated by SNI, coloured by the DSN, made no distinction between sources if they indicated the target's guilt. In general, the digitisation process expanded the capacity for surveillance and data accumulation, without being able to overcome analytical poverty, caused by the assumption of a permanent conspiracy of corrupt or communist subversives against the state.

Even so, SNI's knowledge has been re-signified to the point of transposing the very field of digital technologies. The concern with the "fragility" and "subversion" of members of APPD/RJ, CAPRE and other members of the technical-scientific community encouraged SNI to extend its dominance over informatics policy. SNI agents had the necessary technical knowledge to hold public debates, as well as control over the background (based on the agency's information) that enabled SNI to remove or co-opt factions between the technical-scientific community and technocracy. In summary, the combination of knowledge of different types (*habitus*, ideological, technical knowledge) created the conditions for SNI to position itself as the group with the greatest power in the field of Brazilian informatics.

SNI's efforts led to the creation of the SEI on August 10, 1979. It was directly linked to the Presidency of the Republic and to CSN and, in short, was to advise and run PNI. The SEI accumulated a large number of tasks, ranging from the "promotion and protection" of software, service, equipment and system companies to "national empowerment in the production of electronic and electromechanical components and basic inputs for these components," exercising a market restriction through import controls. Representatives of SNI were contemplated to fill real positions of command in the new agency, such as the Executive Bureau and the Department for Strategic Affairs.[54]

However, the process took a heavy toll: while it managed to combine knowledge to propose its technical and political actions, demobilising the nationalist technological network and imposing control through a centralised body, it was insular and averse to the participation of different actors and institutions in the field of informatics in decision spheres.[55] The SEI would remain known as an instrument of the "dictatorship of SNI colonels,"[56] feeding a social imaginary that blamed them for the technological backwardness of the country.

Notes

1 Adler, *Power of Ideology*; Evans, *Embedded Autonomy*; Dantas, *Guerrilha Tecnológica*.
2 CAPRE was created by Decree No. 70.370 on April 5, 1972, and restructured by Decree No. 77.118 on February 9, 1976.
3 Created by Decree No. 84.067 on October 8, 1979.
4 Marques, "Brazil's Computer Market Reserve."
5 In our research, we interpret the field of informatics in Brazil as a space of struggles and forces in which its agents are constantly in dispute over its primacy, applying its available resources (expertise, powers, networking) in order to institute their technical and political actions, Bourdieu, *Raisons pratiques*; Hecht, *Radiance of France*.

136 *Marcelo Vianna*

6 Research on the conception and functioning of Operation Condor has not yet explored the technological dimensions, in terms of the computerized systems employed, which were fundamental to its actions.

7 Burke, *What Is the History of Knowledge*; Lässig, "History of Knowledge."

8 Hecht, *Radiance of France*.

9 Edwards, *Closed World*.

10 Oliveira, "Doutrina de Segurança Nacional."

11 Escola Superior de Guerra, *Manual Básico*, 26.

12 IBM's "uncomfortable dominance" referred to how technological nationalists felt about the power that the US company had over computer technologies installed in the country. IBM had cornered between 70 and 80 per cent of the national markets of Latin America. In Brazil it held 73 per cent of the computer market in the country in 1971, and this was considered by the nationalist sectors as an obstacle to development, given the company's low technological openness and high interference in digitization methods.

13 Langer, "Generations"; Vianna, *Burocratas e especialistas*.

14 Helmut Schreyer was a pioneer of informatics and designed the Z3 computer with Konrad Zuse in 1941.

15 Special Working Group – FUNTEC 111 (GTE-111). Decree No. 68,267 issued on February 2, 1971. The origins go back to the initial study contracted at the Federal University of Brasilia in 1968, which found a strong technological dependence in the field of Brazilian informatics.

16 Mathias, *Militarização da burocracia*.

17 Article 2, Law 434, issued on June 13, 1964.

18 Mathias, *Militarização da burocracia*.

19 Fico, *Como eles agiam*.

20 Idem, 100.

21 "LDB – Data on persons, as detailed as possible, with the primary purpose of preserving the interests of National Security and efficiency of Public order. It will cover the topics: ideological position, attitude towards the March 31 Revolution, Subversive Activities, administrative probity, functional or professional efficiency, and civil conduct." Slides on SNI systems. BR DFANBSB V.8.TXT, AGR.EVE.14 – Dossier. SNI Collection. National Archive.

22 McSherry, *Predatory States*.

23 General Octavio Medeiros (1922–2005) was director of EsNI between 1975 and 1978 and head of SNI between 1978 and 1985. It is acknowledged that during his tenure, SNI achieved formidable power, although parts of its activities were also made public through scandals such as the Riocentro attack and the Baumgarten case. D'Araújo et al., *Volta aos quartéis*; Antunes, *SNI & ABIN*.

24 Antunes, *SNI & ABIN*.

25 Interview with Joubert Brízida on May 28, 2013. Technological insight grew out of the general's experiences during his time as a military attaché in Israel, where he followed the Yom Kippur War in 1973 and was in close contact with Mossad and Shin Bet, Israel's intelligence agencies. The Yom Kippur War demonstrated the importance of intelligence and technology activities, prompting Israelis to reinforce existing services (Unit 8200) as a way to address these technical needs – concerns that may have influenced Medeiros.

26 Reis served in the Military Office of the Presidency of the Republic. He was considered an electronics specialist, with a master's degree in computer science.

27 At the time of the consultation, he was president of the Data Processing Company of São Paulo (PRODESP) and had extensive experience in implementing data centres, including the Federal Senate Data Centre (PRODASEN) and ample access to both political and military authorities of the period.

Information technology is power   137

28 In the regional agencies, there was at least one video terminal and four microfilm readers. The Central Agency had 18 terminals and 35 microfiche readers, demonstrating the concentration of information in the federal capital.

29 By 1984, the system had processed 555,267 documents, of which 149,232 were ACE documents and 100,796 were records (LDB).

30 In addition to the Condornet system, which gathered data from all those considered targets for Operation Condor.

31 SARDI – Proposals Concerning the Philosophy of the System. Document from 1983. BR DFANBSB V.8.TXT, AGR.DNF.20. SNI Collection. National Archive.

32 Vianna, *Burocratas e especialistas.*

33 Due to the wide range of diplomatic contacts, Minister Azeredo da Silveira was interested in incorporating telecommunications and computer technology into the Foreign Ministry's work. Office of the Minister of Foreign Affairs to the President of the Republic on 06/04/1974. Access to Information Act. Request number 09200.000121/2014–83, date 05/02/2014. Documents from Archive of the Ministry of Foreign Affairs (Itamaraty).

34 In January 1973, the Federal Communications Commission (FCC) notified the Brazilian embassy in Washington, demanding that it stop the radio station broadcasts of the Brazilian Aeronautical Commission present in the representation. Office of the Chief Minister of the Military Cabinet to the President of the Republic on 01/27/1975. Access to Information Act. Request number 09200.000121/2014–83, date 05/02/2014. Documents from Archive of the Ministry of Foreign Affairs (Itamaraty).

35 Interestingly, there did not seem to be any suspicions about the technological reliability of the Crypto AG systems adopted by Brazilian state agencies, to the point that SNI's technical service proposed manufacturing national versions of these systems (the agency had 15 Crypto BCX-52 in 1977). The article by Brustolin, Oliveira and Peron (2020) demonstrated that the CIA, when it assumed effective corporate control of Crypto AG in the 1970s, had full access to the cryptographic codes of the Crypto AG systems implemented in different state agencies worldwide. In the Brazilian case, the issue is even more sensitive because the country, in addition to being the largest user of Crypto AG equipment in South America, became a supplier of these systems to the countries involved in Operation Condor (2020, p. 22). It is, therefore, still a topic to be elucidated by future research.

36 During his time at ETE/IME, Dytz acted under the tutelage of Helmut Schreyer in the group that developed the "Lourinha" computer. He also graduated as a military engineer and worked in the telecommunications department of the Presidency of the Republic before being invited to work in the Prólogo project, under ESNI's tutelage. Interview with Edison Dytz on March 7, 2013.

37 In the big picture, it cannot be denied that two of SNI's three heads became Presidents of the Republic (STEPAN 1983) and one of them became Chief of Staff, Stepan, *O que estão pensando os militares.* As Eliézer de Oliveira (1987) noted, based on an authoritarian paradigm whose origins were in Oliveira Vianna and Alberto Torres, the military assumed the role of leaders of the ruling elite of the country, committing it to the search for self-determination and development; in practice, in the areas that seemed vital to them, such as informatics, it seemed that SNI itself intended to assume this leading role.

38 Dreifuss and Dulci, *As forças armadas,* 168.

39 The "Brazilian miracle" can be understood as the period of strong expansion of the Brazilian economy between 1968 and 1973. Part of this process emerged as an attempt by the military governments of the period to promote a policy of accelerating development, with incentives for exports, consumer credit, investment in major infrastructure works and attraction of foreign investments. Successful in numbers, with average annual GDP growth rates of 11.2 per cent and industrial expansion of 13.3 per cent, the model accentuated the process of concentration of income in the country and deepened the country's dependence on raw materials (oil) and technologies.

138 *Marcelo Vianna*

40 A United Nations agency created in 1948, the Economic Commission for Latin America and the Caribbean (Comissão Econômica para a América Latina e o Caribe, CEPAL) had as its main objective to promote the region's economic development and coopera-tion. CEPAL was a space for developmental intellectuals like Raúl Prebisch and Celso Furtado, constituting theses and policies that aimed to overcome the economic depen-dence of Latin American countries through substitutive industrialization of imports. Among the CEPAL concerns were the issue of technological development, necessary to enable the industrialization of the member countries.
41 Marques, "Brazil's Computer Market Reserve."
42 ACE 3278/80. BR DFANBSB V.8.MIC, GNC.CCC.80003278. SNI Collection. National Archive.
43 Information 724/79/DSI/MF. Infiltration of Executive, Judicial and Legislative Powers. 10/29/1979 – ACE 12232/80. BR DFANBSB V.8MIC, GNC.AAA.80012232 – Dossier. SNI Collection. National Archive.
44 "Brief report on the difficulties encountered in implementing ICC/Coencisa in Brazil," undated. It is part of the set of complaints brought to SNI. Infão 03/09/1978. ACE 112475/78. BR DFANBSB V.8.MIC, GNC.AAA.78112475 – Dossier. SNI Collection. National Archive.
45 Interview of Joubert Brízida with the author on May 28, 2013.
46 The commission's name was derived from the formal coordination by ambassador Paulo Cotrim, a representative of Itamaraty, who was involved in the relations of this agency with SNI and was a strong defender of the intervention in the field of informatics.
47 Decree no. 83.444 created the GTE/I, whose work lasted officially from May 17, 1979, to September 14,1979.
48 An example was the motion approved in the VI Software/Hardware Seminar against operations conducted "primarily by agencies responsible for state security" that left "civil society unprotected against the threats that may represent to it the improper and inadequate use of informatics." *DataNews*, RJ, 08/15/1979.
49 As Suzeley Mathias observed, there was a military specialization in the area of com-munications, evidenced by the rise of military personnel at Embratel, Telebrás and other related state-owned companies, Mathias, *Militarização da burocracia*.
50 Vianna, *Burocratas e especialistas*.
51 One example was the Laboratory of Digital Systems of USP, which had built the first national computer with integrated circuits, nicknamed "Ugly Duckling," in 1972.
52 In fact, the power of SNI was a factor of imbalance in the field of informatics, quickly perceived by other agents not only for its repressive dimension.
53 One example is José Rubens Dória Porto, who was linked to the University of São Paulo (USP) and one of the designers of PADE, a medium-sized computer developed by the university. Dória Porto was invited to take on the coordination of microcomputers in SEI in 1980 and the direction of CTI in 1982. During the Sarney administration, he held the highest position at SEI between 1985 and 1986.
54 Occupied respectively by Joubert Brízida and Edison Dytz. Joubert Brízida would become Special Secretary of Informatics between 1982 and 1984 and, with his depar-ture, Edison Dytz took over and would remain in that post until 1985.
55 Tapia, *Trajetória*.
56 Title of the series of reports of the newspaper O Estado de S. Paulo between 08/26/1984 and 09/01/1984. Information 113/19/AC/84 from 09/12/1984. BR DFANBSB V.8.MIC, GNC.AAA.84044665 – Dossier. SNI Collection. National Archive.

Bibliography

Adler, E. 1987. *The Power of Ideology: The Quest for Technological Autonomy in Argen-tina and Brazil*. Berkeley: University of California Press.

Information technology is power 139

Antunes, P. C. B. 2002. *SNI & ABIN. Uma leitura da atuação dos serviços secretos brasileiros ao longo do século XX*. Rio de Janeiro: FGV.

Bourdieu, P. 1994. *Raisons pratiques: sur la théorie de l'action*. Paris: Seuil.

Brustolin, V., Oliveira, D., and Peron, A. E. R. (2020). "Exploring the Relationship between Crypto AG and the CIA in the Use of Rigged Encryption Machines for Espionage in Brazil." *Cambridge Review of International Affairs*: 1–34. https://doi.org/10.1080/0955 7571.2020.1842328.

Burke, P. 2016. *What is the History of Knowledge?* Cambridge: Polity Press.

D'Araújo, M. C., Soares, G. A. D., and Castro, C. 1995. *A volta aos quartéis: a memória militar sobre a abertura*. Rio de Janeiro: Relume-Dumará.

Dantas, V. 1988. *Guerrilha Tecnológica: A verdadeira História da Política Nacional de Informática*. Rio de Janeiro: LTC.

Dreifuss, R., and Dulci, O. 2008. "As Forças Armadas e a Política." In *Sociedade e Política no Brasil pós-1964*, ed. B. Sorj and M. H. Almeida. Rio de Janeiro: Centro Edelstein de Pesquisas Sociais.

Edwards, P. E. 1996. *The Closed World: Computers and the Politics of Discourse in Cold War America*. Cambridge, MA: MIT Press.

Escola Superior da Guerra. 1975. *Manual Básico*. Rio de Janeiro: ESG.

Evans, P. B. 1995. *Embedded Autonomy: States and Industrial Transformation*. Princeton: Princeton University Press.

Fico, C. 2001. *Como eles agiam. Os subterrâneos da ditadura militar; espionagem e polícia política*. Rio de Janeiro: Editora Record.

Hecht, G. 2009. *The Radiance of France: Nuclear Power and National Identity after World War II*. Cambridge: MIT.

Lagôa, A. 1983. *SNI: como nasceu, como funciona*. São Paulo: Brasiliense.

Langer, E. D. 1989. "Generations of Scientists and Engineers – Origins of the Computer Industry in Brazil." *Latin American Research Review* 24, no. 2: 95–111.

Lässig, S. 2016. "The History of Knowledge and the Expansion of the Historical Research Agenda." *Bulletin of the GHI* 59: 29–58.

Marques, I. 2015. "Brazil's Computer Market Reserve: Democracy, Authoritarianism and Ruptures." *IEEE Annals of the History of Computing* 23 no. 4: 64–75.

Mathias, S. K. 2004. *A militarização da burocracia: a participação militar na administração das Comunicações e da Educação, 1963–1990*. São Paulo: Unesp.

Mathias, S. K., and Andrade, F. 2012. "O Serviço de Informações e a cultura do segredo." *Varia Historia. Belo Horizonte* 28/48: 537–554.

McSherry, P. J. 2005. *Predatory States: Operation Condor and Covert War in Latin America*. Lanham, MD: Rowman & Littlefield Publishers.

Oliveira, E. R. 1987. "Doutrina de Segurança Nacional: Pensamento Político e Projeto Estratégico." In *Militares, pensamento e ação política*, ed. E. H. Oliveira, 53–86. Campinas: Papirus.

Stepan, A. 1983. "O que estão pensando os militares." *Novos Estudos CEBRAP* 2, no. 2: 2–7.

Tapia, J. R. P. 1995. *A Trajetória da Política de Informática Brasileira*. Campinas: Papirus.

Vianna, M. 2016. *Entre burocratas e especialistas: a formação e o controle do campo da Informática no Brasil (1958–1979)*. Porto Alegre: PUCRS.

7 The computer as document shredder

Video terminals and the dawn of a new era of knowledge production in Brazil's Serviço Nacional de Informações

Debora Gerstenberger

Introduction

On December 4, 1978, digital computers were introduced into the Brazilian National Intelligence Service, the Serviço Nacional de Informações (SNI). These were display terminals of the IBM 3270 type which were most commonly used in corporations. According to a contemporary IBM advertising brochure, the 3270 Information Display System could improve information flows and "effect significant reductions in total system costs."[1] In retrospect, IBM is more critical of its "display screen with a keyboard attached." According to the online IBM corporate archives site, a 3270 terminal was "a non-programmable (sometimes called 'dumb') workstation." The text-based terminal had "only rudimentary communications capabilities." It did not have its own hard disk but depended on the cable connection to its control unit. One of the earliest models consisted of 12 rows and 80 columns of text characters, "no more and no less."[2]

The SNI leadership, however, celebrated the terminals as a novelty. From 1979 on, annual reports by the Central Agency of SNI in Brasília proudly referred to the digital technology:

> On 4 December 1979, we completed one year of the implementation of informatics at the Central Agency; the difficulties with the pairing of the service's peculiar necessities with the limitations of the systems were absorbed, considered and resolved to our satisfaction.[3]

If problems (which were said to have been overcome) were mentioned in the first annual report, assessments were more positive in the following years:

> On 4 December 1980, we completed two years of the implementation of Informatics at SNI. The experience gained in these years has enabled the establishment of routines and procedures that very much contributed to the better performance of the service.[4]

DOI: 10.4324/9781003147329-8

The computer as document shredder 141

Figure 7.1 Illustration of IBM 3270 display terminals taken from an advertising brochure.
Source: Courtesy of International Business Machines Corporation, © (1977) International Business Machines Corporation.

142   *Debora Gerstenberger*

The same statement was repeated each year with almost identical wording.[5]

If SNI's authorities constantly reiterated the successful implementation of computer technology like a mantra, they *constructed* it as a watershed moment and loaded it with a positive meaning. Simultaneously, they created a new age through the division into a "pre-computerized era" and a "computerized era." Apparently, the IBM terminals served as a starting point for a new era that placed digital technology at the heart of the intelligence service.

Common sense holds that digitisation goes hand in hand with an *increase* in data. However, at SNI the opposite was true: one of the most important tasks involved in the implementation of the new digital technology was the *elimination of information*. In fact, the intelligence service destroyed 95 per cent of its data stock in the course of digitisation. How is it that SNI used the computer as a metaphorical document shredder? What can we learn from the radical transformations in the production of intelligence knowledge? How is this process of elimination of intelligence data linked to the state's governmentality?

This chapter starts from the following assumptions: When SNI installed IBM video terminals in December 1978, the production of intelligence – as well as the institution itself – was in a period transformation. The result was new intelligence knowledge – and eventually, a new intelligence knowledge producer.

The Brazilian National Intelligence Service was created in 1964, shortly after the coup d'état that established a long-lived authoritarian regime. The service combined the tasks of domestic and foreign intelligence, that is these two areas were not institutionally separated. SNI was an important political instrument and even a "kingmaker," as evidenced by the fact that two former chiefs of SNI went on to become presidents of Brazil: Emílio Médici (1969–1974) and João Figueiredo (1979–1985).

Compared to other military dictatorships in Latin America, the Brazilian one seems to have been more benign. Many thousands of deaths due to state terror in Chile and Argentina contrast with some hundreds in Brazil. However, there *was* systematic state terror. Estimates put the number of people that had the traumatic experience of passing through the "basements" of Brazilian institutions of state security at 50,000. Of these, 20,000 were subjected to the violence of torture.[6]

Even though the role of the secret service as the scaffolding of a "killing machine"[7] and one of the most important pillars of the Brazilian authoritarian regime has frequently been emphasised, surprisingly little research has been carried out into its internal processes. Until the early 2000s, research about SNI as an institution was almost non-existent.[8] Since Carlos Fico's pioneering work,[9] only a few monographic studies have analytically examined SNI, its functioning, its networks, its information system and its "intelligence community."[10] The involvement of SNI in IT politics and industry has recently come under scrutiny (see Marcelo Vianna's contribution in this volume).[11] However, as is true for most intelligence services in Latin America and worldwide, SNI's core business, the *production of intelligence*, as well as its *precise linkages to the governmentality of the state*, remain largely unexplored.[12]

The computer as document shredder   143

What actually *is* intelligence? Michael Herman once established a definition of intelligence knowledge which in fact is helpful for the writing of the history of data processing by intelligence services: "Intelligence in government is based on the particular set of organizations with that name: the 'intelligence services' or 'intelligence community'. Intelligence activity is what they do, and intelligence knowledge, what they produce."[13] In other words, intelligence knowledge depends on and is the result of the practices of a specific intelligence community. This definition makes sense, for it contains not an essentialist but a relational notion conditioned by the social group. It is flexible enough to entail all sorts of intelligence knowledge production through time and space.

However, just like all other communities,[14] intelligence communities do not consist of humans alone. The production of intelligence knowledge is the result of an interplay of heterogeneous, human (informants, analysts, captives, ordinary people, etc.) and non-human (paper files, pens, typewriters, bugging devices, computers, etc.) elements. Although – or rather *because* – the succession of different information technologies certainly does not fit into a simple narrative of evermore efficient data processing, technologies should be prominently considered. Current history of technology teaches us that humans should be analysed in the context of their machines and machines should be analysed in the context of humans.[15] Science and technology studies have taught us that it is not possible to simply "introduce" a new technological artefact into an existing institution or group; whenever a new element is inserted, the whole collective changes.[16] History of knowledge, for its part, insists that the materiality of media does not just *influence* (bureaucratic) knowledge. Rather, the properties of documents (in their different forms) "matter in all kinds of far-reaching ways." They are epistemic objects.[17]

The aim of this chapter is to explore the new "computerised era" that started in 1978 from the internal perspective of the Brazilian intelligence service. The goal is to find out how it changed the processing of intelligence knowledge and how the changes are linked to the state's governmentality. Choosing an inductive perspective means not assuming a priori that there was an all-powerful process called "digitisation" in which the Brazilian intelligence service eventually took part. Rather, this analysis endeavours to listen to and follow the actors in order to find out how and why they thought that digital computers decisively transformed their practices and institution. Instead of explaining the movements of the actors through time and dates, or through the development of certain machines that were produced in industrialised centres, the aim is to explain "the construction of time itself on the basis of the agents' own actions and translations."[18]

The analysis covers the first five years of computer terminals (1978–1983) at SNI. The primary sources used in this analysis consist mainly of reports and instructions written by Section 06 "Research and Archive" (Pesquisa e Arquivo) of the Central Agency (Agência Central, AC) in Brasília, which was the section most involved in the process of digitisation. In a close reading of these documents, the most important transformations in the core business of an information service – the gathering, storing and administration of intelligence knowledge – will be singled out.

144 *Debora Gerstenberger*

In the first section, I will sketch the position of the SNI at the end of the 1970s. In the second section, I will focus on the expectations formulated by SNI authorities and the frustrations they suffered after the implementation. In the third to fifth sections, the production and processing of data with the help of the new digital tools will be more closely scrutinised, before the results of the analysis are summarised in the final section.

The SNI after the "leaden years"

When SNI introduced computer technology in 1978, Brazil – like most of the other Latin American states – was still under authoritarian military rule. However, the so-called leaden years (*anos de chumbo*), the period of harshest repression (1968–1974), had already passed. From 1974 on, President General Ernesto Geisel propagated "political détente" (*distenção política*). This caused great concern within the Brazilian security communities. Their opposition to this project was one of the factors that decisively influenced Geisel's project of a "slow, gradual and safe" liberalisation of the regime.[19]

President João Figueiredo (1979–1985) subsequently promised to "make Brazil a democracy." During his administration, the Brazilian security apparatus became less "bloodthirsty." It is recognised that the Brazilian military regime (and prominently, its intelligence and security apparatuses) systematically used executions and disappearances as an instrument for the annihilation of political opposition. The final report of the National Truth Commission published in 2014 lists 171 dead and disappeared due to state terror for the years between 1964 and 1979, and nine between 1980 and 1985.[20] Even if the official numbers surely do not reflect the full picture of repression and persecution (and the estimates are higher), they do indicate a trend.

However, what happened during the political détente was the opposite of what some hardliners had feared: rather than losing resources, SNI obtained even more. What seems paradoxical at first sight should not come as a surprise if one considers the background. Firstly, as mentioned earlier, João Figueiredo had been director of SNI from 1974 to 1978, and he loved the secret services.[21] Secondly, at a time in which violence and torture had fallen into disrepute, it was easier for the military government to legitimise a strong information service (which also existed in liberal Western states) than a huge security apparatus. In fact, SNI became a refuge for hard-line military personnel that had to "disappear" due to their actions during the "leaden years." The accommodation of military personnel from other institutions was even given a name: "luxury funeral."[22]

During the Figueiredo administration, SNI counted 5,000 employees, 400 of whom worked in the Central Agency in Brasília. The second-largest of the 12 regional agencies was that of São Paulo with about 200 employees. The other regional agencies had less *servidores*, but none fewer than 60. Lucas Figueiredo summarised this development as follows:

> Despite the functional decadence that the institution suffered, it reached its peak of gigantism during the Figueiredo administration. The more diminished

its reason for being was, the more the "monster" grew. Under the auspices of its former director, the secret service wallowed in money.[23]

The area occupied by SNI – the *cerrado* ("closed area") – was huge: with 200,000 square metres, it was "half as big as the Vatican" and resembled, in its organisational and spatial structures, some First World secret services headquarters. Located in the south of the southern wing of Brasília's *plano piloto*, in the police sector, it included its own hospital, a TV studio and a special operations troop formed of paratroopers. Representatives of foreign partner services that visited SNI found its facilities and equipment "jaw-dropping."[24]

The following sections deal with the question of how the computerisation of SNI's data stocks at the end of the 1970s took place, and how this fit in a phase of "political détente" and a change of direction towards democracy.

Expectations and frustrations: digital technology and its discontents

Even though the actual date of the physical arrival of the video terminals at SNI was so heavily emphasised, digitisation did not exactly begin with the reception of the new technological artefacts. Rather, it was envisioned and planned beforehand. In September 1978, the Central Agency's head of cabinet, Jecy Serôa Motta, wrote a "Study about the implantation of the systematics of data processing at SNI" in which the hopes and expectations vested in computer use become apparent. The explicit goal was to transfer the data, most of which existed on paper documents hosted by the General Archive (Arquivo Geral, ARGE), into the new digital database (*banco de dados*).[25]

The benefits of digitising the ARGE directory were listed in five points, from "a" to "e."[26] The first advantage was seen in the "speed of recovery of knowledge within SNI," and the second in the "ability to concentrate all knowledge in a single database." The author emphasises that the Central Agency was to have "access to all segments of the databases of the regional agencies (AR)," which would facilitate consultation and increase the speed. "C" addresses the "marked decrease in the flow of documents" between the agencies. "D" reads: "Decrease of the physical space of the ARGE by 98 per cent, resulting in greater ease of handling as well as less personnel and material." Last, but certainly not least, a "greater security" of the documentation is mentioned, "mainly against fires."

In sum, the main goals of computerisation were the centralisation of the archive, faster availability of information, better communication between the Central Agency in Brasília and the 12 regional agencies located in bigger cities of different Brazilian states, and security of the data (especially protection from fire). All in all, it was hoped that the introduction of new technology would increase the *efficiency* of intelligence production. With its efforts to digitise the archive, SNI cannot be considered as a latecomer; intelligence services of many European "First World" states established their first digital databases in the (late) 1970s or 1980s.[27]

146 *Debora Gerstenberger*

Were hopes and expectations associated with the digital system fulfilled? In 1982, a strategic report (*relatório estratégico*) was issued on the basis of an opinion poll among the users of the computer system about its "almost four years" of functioning. The users at SNI and at its intelligence training centre EsNI had been asked "totally open questions," with the "aim not to direct the answers in any way." The report aimed to reveal "the most significant shortcomings, the most expected benefits, as well as what the system users think about the contents of the Information Database."[28]

Of the 786 persons in SNI and EsNI who dealt more closely with the new digital tools, 430 were surveyed, including 232 "heads and analysts," 137 "auxiliaries" and 61 "others." According to the analysis of the responses, the most important problems were the "entry of unimportant documents," "difficulty to retrieve information via terminal," "problems related to microfiche," "delay in terminal response time," "lack of terminals and readers," difficulties in "sharing [data] between agencies," "terminal offline," "delay in the entry of documents," "faulty registers" and "inability of the user to use the system." From the existing sources it is not clear exactly how the questionnaire was designed. However, it is quite striking that the analysis brings forth no positive assertions.

The problems revealed by the answers were partly related to hardware (computer terminals and microfiche) and partly to human practices or (lack of) knowledge or skills. Some problems were certainly home-made and were results of management decisions. For example, granting full access to the regional offices to data held at the head office, and the free exchange of data between the regional offices, was not really desired. In any case, it is quite telling that in the eyes of many users it was indeed quite difficult to produce intelligence by using the new digital system, since it resulted in many "unimportant" or faulty documents and in difficulties in retrieving information via the terminals. The reasons given by the users for this included the "lack of a definition concerning the adequate type of information for the different areas" and the "lack of a manual for the users of the system."

SNI's management actually understood the result of the poll as a fundamental critique, "[c]onsidering that certain items of failures and suggestions (including all those related to the content of the Information Database) are related to the philosophy and structure of the system." In the conclusions, it was noted that, "basically," a "detailed revision of the entire system" was needed, "from its most general definitions, its objectives and functions, to the more operational elements."[29] The aim was now to "expand the use of the system."[30] To do so, it was "imperative to define a management for the system, with exclusive dedication," "[d]efine a policy for the contents of the database" and "[i]mprove the filing and entry system." These statements in fact sound like a thorough disillusionment and the need for a new beginning.

However, the management (probably the head of the "research and archive" section) tried to make the best of the results.

We are sure that with this survey we have reached the main objective of its application: to obtain from the users of the system an evaluation of its

The computer as document shredder 147

performance, as well as suggestions for its improvement. The participation rate and the quality of the answers given allow us to affirm that the current system has the support of its users and that it has a favourable field for its development.[31]

Interestingly, the motto under which the report was written and which was placed in capital letters at the head of the first page phrased the existing problems and difficulties – as well as adaptations and corrections – as something natural from the outset: "THE REAL DEVELOPMENT OF A SYSTEM STARTS AFTER ITS IMPLEMENTATION."[32]

This certainly clashed somewhat with the statements made in the annual reports, which had only reported successes. From today's point of view, however, this sentence is astonishingly compatible with approaches and theories from science and technology studies and the history of technology: whenever a new (technical) element enters the scene, many transformations take place and the entire collective changes. The consequences are rarely entirely calculable at the beginning, and unintended effects are frequent.[33]

One major problem was certainly the regional disparities. The Central Agency in Brasília had more resources, more equipment, more material (the heads of Section 06 usually stated that they had "sufficient" resources to achieve the objectives), as well as more and better trained personnel, than the agencies in the peripheries. At headquarters, attention was paid to further training of the staff. The analysts of the Central Agency received, before December 4, 1978, "preparation and training" for "the new system" given by the staff of the IT department of SNI's National Intelligence School (EsNI).[34] In 1979, two terminal operators received evening classes in "system analysis" for eight months at the Empresa Técnica de Consultoria e Projetos of Brasilia's Catholic university Pontifícia Universidade Católica. They were chosen by the head of Section 06 and provided with a scholarship by the Department of Informatics of EsNI.[35]

The situation was quite different in the peripheries, as one can deduce from the responses in the survey. Here, the departments had fewer computer terminals and fewer staff, who were also less well trained. From the beginning, the head office of the Central Agency accepted that the regional offices "would not be integrated into the system in the short term" but would only have access to the digital database later.[36] Also, it was sometimes explicitly stated that there was no plan for the "general liberalization of the database of the system." For instance, headquarters reacted rather irritably to the regional offices' request to have a telephone contact person at headquarters who could, for example, provide information about a suspicious person who was a resident of another state. They feared that these telephone enquiries would generate too much work.[37] Apparently, communication between the peripheries was not considered overly important.

Another major problem was the acceptance of the computer terminals by the staff. Headquarters always feared that "the system" would be rejected by the users. In a 1983 report, the head of "Documentation, Telecommunications and Information Technology Division (D/7)," which was the successor of Section 06, stated

148   *Debora Gerstenberger*

that one of the main efforts of the year had been "to try to make the analyst believe in the terminal and in what he himself had ordered to be implemented." The "maximum" effort was made "so that there would be greater intimacy of man with the machine." He continued:

> Something has been achieved and much is still to be achieved; however, the need has arisen to create the researcher's internship so that on each terminal there is a specialist in retrieving the documents from our vast and complex database.[38]

Even in 1985, there were still frequent appeals in the documents for SNI staff to encourage the "progressive use of the resources offered by Information Technology." The desire was for the user to turn into a "highly participative element of the process," which indicates that they were not exactly that.[39] Apparently, the "intimacy of man with machine" and the "belief" in the video terminal left much to be desired. Most of the staff simply did not like working with the computer terminals, and the heads of section had trouble motivating them.

What we can see here is that computers were not logical machines that spread within the intelligence community automatically. Computers did not prevail because they were convincing. Rather, they were convincing because they were enforced by SNI authorities who obliged the employees to put them into practice.[40] In the top echelons of SNI, there was an unconditional *will for computerisation.*

The sources indicate that the heads of the individual sections as well as the SNI directorate had very precise ideas about what the database of intelligence activities should look like in the future and how it should be organised. What they had in mind was a completely different form of data processing than before – which also served a different political goal than before. Yet the problems and frustrations of the staff may point to the fact that the "big picture" and the future direction of SNI as well as the meaning and importance of the digital database in the overall fabric of national security were not communicated down to all levels.

Elimination of data: the computer as document shredder

As mentioned in the introduction, SNI *destroyed* most of the existing datasets in the course of digitisation. These datasets were intelligence documents (*Infão, Infe e, and Apreciação*) and entailed information on persons, institutions or events. In general, those records that contained biographical information on alleged suspects were the most important and thus the most numerous. The research and queries of the analysts in the paper archive and later on the digital terminals mostly referred to persons, less often to institutions or events.

At their creation, all records produced by SNI were provided with an expiration date that ranged between two and five years. Apparently, however, some data volumes had accumulated in the 14 years of the archive's existence. The digitisation project was thus an opportunity to separate the wheat from the chaff.

Using the reference date of 4 December 1978 (the date of the introduction of computer terminals), the entire data inventory was divided into two parts and

The computer as document shredder   149

labelled accordingly. All data files that had been compiled before that date were affixed with a "D–," and all data files that had been compiled after that date were given a "D+."[41] Thus, the introduction of computer technology brought about a decisive quality feature for the records: the new datasets were *positive*, the old datasets were *negative* by their labelling. The explicit goal was to review all "D–" datasets, delete parts of them and convert the rest into "D+" by digitising them. Eventually, the stock of "D–" data was to be completely eliminated.

At the beginning of the digitisation process, the General Archive (ARGE) at the Central Agency possessed 115,854 archive units called ACE (Arquivo Cronológico de Entrada) of the "old" stock ("D–"). Approximately one year after the implementation of the terminals, a total of 73,500 of these had been re-evaluated: 30,679 had been "implemented in" (so entered into) the database (about 42 per cent), and 42,821 (about 58 per cent) had been destroyed.[42]

The head of Section 06 drew a positive balance from this elimination process in an annual report for 1979:

> The implementation of IT in the Central Agency brought, as a main consequence, a significant reduction in the quantity of documents stored in the memory of the Central Agency. This reduction is compensated by the increase in the quality of these documents, with a view to the final activity, which was obtained through the judicious and objective work of the analysts of the Central Agency.[43]

In the following years, the "massive and systematic elimination of ACEs" deemed unserviceable was frequently praised as a measure that would make research "more functional and objective."[44] In proposals concerning the "philosophy of the system" (*propostas relativas à filosofia do sistema*) that circulated probably from 1982 on, the authorities emphasised that the digital system would give "more importance to the saving of knowledge and not documents (redundancy)."[45]

In some of the regional agencies, the destruction of "old" data in the course of digitisation was almost total: the regional agency of Rio de Janeiro possessed an archive of 396,789 documents when the digitisation process started. By the end of 1981, the agency had destroyed 216,159 documents out of 218,242 that had been "re-evaluated" so far – a full 99 per cent. Only 660 documents had been implemented into the digital database. The regional agency of São Paulo had destroyed about 95 per cent of the datasets under re-evaluation and implemented 3,617 out of 156,478 documents. In some agencies of the poorer northern and north-eastern regions (Fortaleza, Belém, Manaus), up to 99.3 per cent of the data stock was eliminated, whereas none of the documents had been digitised by December 1981 (here, regional disparities become apparent again). All in all, 95 per cent of SNI's total datasets had been destroyed by the end of 1981, whereas only 1.2 per cent had been digitised and microfilmed (see Figure 7.2).[46]

The evaluation of the datasets was described as a very complex and "time-consuming" work which required "meticulous analysis," searches on the terminal

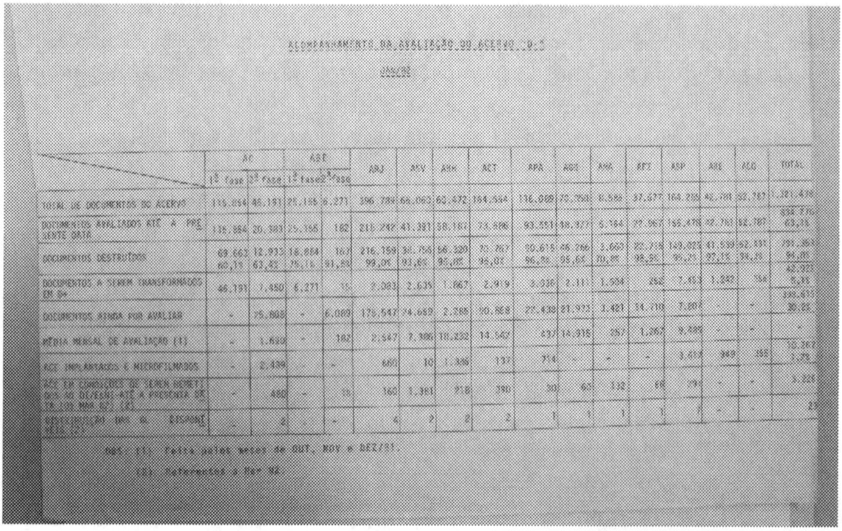

150 *Debora Gerstenberger*

Figure 7.2 List of destroyed and digitised documents.

Source: Photograph of archival document by the author. Anonymous, "Relatório de atividades da seção Pesquisa e Arquivo (SE-06) de 04 dez 78 a 28 fev 83" (n. d.). ANBSB. SNI. Administração Geral. Relatórios de atividades. Caixa 01, Camisa 21, without pagination.

and on microfiche.[47] In the Central Agency and in the regional agencies, the work of re-evaluation lasted until February 1983 or even longer.[48]

However, not long after the establishment of computer terminals, the Central Agency proudly announced:

> On 21 July [1980], when the last ACE archive 'D menos' [of the first phase of re-evaluation] was sent to the DI/EsNI in order to be microfilmed, the era of the paper archive in the Central Agency ended. Consequently, the activities of this subsection ceased.[49]

The actual digitisation, that is the entry of the data of a record, took place at the Departamento de Informática of the Escola Nacional de Informações (DI/EsNI), also located in the *cerrado*, to which the AC and the regional agencies sent the prepared documents. The reasons for EsNI playing such an eminent role in the digitisation process was that it was a relatively new institution (founded in 1971), possessing the newest equipment and strong ties to the United States (see also the contribution by Samantha Viz Quadrat in this volume). The younger personnel were probably also more inclined to computer technology.[50]

The elimination of paper documents was clearly something the SNI authorities dearly wanted. However, it was not easy for the analysts to put it into practice, as

The computer as document shredder 151

the controversies about "related documents" (*documentos relacionados*) show: in one month (June/July 1979), 2,047 related documents were retrieved from the ARGE in order to digitise them. Of these, 424 (21 per cent) were prepared for digitisation and microfilming, 635 (31 per cent) destroyed and 988 (48 per cent) left in their paper form as *documentos relacionados*. But the head of Section 06 did not like the handling of the *documentos relacionados*, of which he claims to have "inherited" 12,000. He argued that the documents in question were known only to one analyst, or at most to one chief of section; they were not "accessible" in the system. They represented a paper archive already accounting for 16 drawers but were "very rarely" consulted. All in all, the chief of Section 06 judged the "related documents" to be "a very easy solution for an analyst who is undecided between destroying a document and implementing it in the AC's database." For this reason, he had used the visits of the staff to his section to make them aware of the inconvenience of producing this type of document.[51]

The work of persuasion was crowned with success: in the following months, there was a progressive increase in the percentage of digitised ACE and destroyed documents. In July/August 1979, a total of 1,875 documents were retrieved from the ARGE. Of these, 33.6 per cent were digitised, 50.4 per cent were destroyed and 16 per cent were left in paper form as *documentos relacionados*. In the following month, after several more appeals, 38.5 per cent of the documents were digitised and 57.5 per cent destroyed. Only 4 per cent remained as *documentos relacionados*.[52] The reduction in the number of "related documents" was explicitly praised by the head of Section 06; he expressed his "sincere thanks to the AC staff for their complete acceptance of our appeal."[53]

This example shows that it was difficult for the agents "on the ground" to let go of the paper documents. They struggled to unequivocally assign the documents and to decide whether and for which purposes they were still useful. SNI authorities, on the contrary, perceived ambiguous (paper) documents as a burden, not a treasure. In case of doubt, the destruction of a document was preferred.

Actors use technological artefacts as instruments because they want to enforce their interests, cement their positions and strengthen and expand their power and influence.[54] Yet, once new tools are acquired, the procurers are no longer the ones who determine all processes; the machines have a say too. In many sources produced by SNI it becomes clear that the computer had its own settings. In June 1982, for instance, it was stated that documents from the old "D–" stock that did "not satisfy the rationale of the computer" (*não satizfazem a crítica do computador*) had to be treated separately and that there "had to be a solution."[55] Interestingly, the documents had to adapt to the computer system, not the computer system to the paper documents. There was also frequent talk about the computer "rejecting" data. The "documents rejected by the computer" (*documentos rejeitados pelo computador*) had to be sent back to Section 06 for "correction or completion" and submitted again at DI/EsNI.[56]

It is not clear from the documents of Section 06 "Research and Archive" exactly which reasons were behind the massive destruction of data. The three main criteria for selection found in the sources – unimportant, unreadable, does not meet the

152   *Debora Gerstenberger*

criteria of the computer – are not explained in more detail. However, the selection mechanisms can partly be reconstructed from SNI's internal communications.

Some documents were generally not suitable for digitisation, or rather were "documents that do not meet the requirements for implementation in the database." This was the case with attachments (*anexos*) whose physical shape caused problems, like newspaper clippings, original photographs, audio cassettes, books or samples of toxic substances. These things were previously archived in physical file folders together with the dataset. Now, they were "unreadable," that is they could not be digitised or microfilmed. The respective originating department had to archive these items separately and note their existence in the record, however.[57]

Other documents caused problems by their content, for instance if it was too "unreliable." All intelligence documents were classified from "A-1" to "F-3" according to their "trustworthiness," that of the informant and that of the likelihood of the content revealed by the informant, "A-1" being the "most reliable" and "most probable" information. Documents down to "B-3" were implemented in the digital database. Yet, due to software design and user interface, documents below this confidence level (e.g. "C-1") were rejected and stored as paper documents for "up to a year" in the respective section. After that period they were destroyed if the information was not validated, in order to prevent "parallel archiving" on paper.[58]

Usually, higher classifications of sources referred to information provided by SNI staff themselves, whereas other informants would receive classifications below B-3. Agents of the D, E and F type were mostly casual informants (paid or unpaid), or spontaneous informants: people who had a certain complicity with the regime and who voluntarily agreed to cooperate. Informants of the "C" type, who constituted the majority, were usually lower-ranking members of the Armed Forces, typically sergeants who had received training at EsNI.[59]

How are we to interpret that the greater part of the information provided by informants with the labels C to F was now *systematically* and *technically* excluded from the database because the computer software did not allow the entry of information "below B-3"? One could cautiously conclude here that, on the one hand, an *amateurish view* of the population (even if provided by military personnel) became less important and, on the other hand, that *practices of denunciation* by civilians were also devalued. Conversely, the informants from within the ranks (i.e. SNI staff), who could be civilians as well as military personnel, experienced an upgrade. Their observations and compilations of information now almost exclusively formed the basis of all intelligence knowledge, since only their products were included in the digital database.

Yet what does it actually mean that most of the documents were now characterised as "unimportant"? Carlos Fico described the data production technique of SNI and the entire intelligence community from 1964 onwards as a technique of *accumulating data*. At times, information documents classified as "confidential" contained no more than the content of a newspaper note or widely known facts.[60] Personal files were characterised by the constant addition of new details, along the lines of "it is stated that xy is/has done. . . ." According to Fico, "reiteration was the

The computer as document shredder 153

main technique of inculpation of the community of information."[61] It is probable that all these files lost their importance when political opening was sought, and thus the prosecution of "subversive" persons became less relevant.

It is also probable that the SNI leadership wanted to rid itself of incriminating material with a view to re-democratisation. In 2012, one of Brazil's most important national dailies, the *Folha de São Paulo*, devoted several articles to the destruction of "more than 19,000 secret documents" from 1981 onwards. According to one article, Reserve General Newton Cruz, who headed the central agency of SNI between 1978 and 1983, said in a telephone interview that he did not remember the details of the destruction of the papers but that it had all been "according to the law of the time." According to the article, the then 87-year-old Newton Cruz stated: "SNI existed to advise the President of the Republic on government policy. It is an organ of information, and information was born from doctrinally resolved processing. It fulfilled its role and ended there." The general also stated that documents were destroyed primarily to protect persons who had been SNI informants and who had reported on a certain problem "under the guarantee of professional secrecy."[62]

It was not only the observers who were protected but also some of the observed. Some documents were likely to cause discomfort to the military, such as a report on "trafficking" that referred to a relative of former president Emílio Garrastazu Médici (1969–1974). Other destroyed documents described alleged "foreign bank accounts" of the former governor of São Paulo, Adhemar de Barros. Some of the eliminated documents also dealt with people who had died before 1981. The analysis of the records suggests that SNI sought to get rid of all data on dead people, perhaps because it considered that they were no longer of importance to the dictatorship's surveillance activities.[63]

Osmany Meneses de Carvalho, the former head of Section 06, was also interviewed by *Folha de São Paulo*. The then 75-year-old described the destruction as "part of the routine." "Periodically, we would review the archive. What was no longer worthwhile was discarded, it was not even evaluated by me." He described the destroyed documents as "things from the past."[64]

To sum up, different political, ideological and practical questions and strategies seem to have been important in the decision to eliminate 95 per cent of the existing intelligence information in 1978. However, it is noteworthy that the technical requirements of the computer were decisive, since they played well into the hands of the SNI decision-makers. If the leaders of SNI intended to leave the old data behind anyway (and with it the old practices of information-gathering and processing), the computer acted as a catalyst: only at the moment when the individual documents were prepared for digitisation could they be sorted out "massively and systematically." The argument of the computer "rejecting" the document was a convincing reason for destruction. Thus, with the introduction of computer terminals, SNI was able to free itself from the ballast of old data and address the new political goals and the new way of governing technically. The computer did not stand for more efficiency of the old system. It stood for a change in the governmentality of the state.

154   *Debora Gerstenberger*

Condensation of data: the importance of writing a summary

Digitisation was accompanied not only by a massive quantitative change in the number of datasets but also by a qualitative change which went along with the *condensation* of the contents of the remaining records. From the very outset, SNI's authorities did not intend to transform all information of an archival unit into digital data. Rather, a hybrid form was envisaged. The aforementioned digitisation "plan" written in 1978 already prescribed that all intelligence documents would be archived in the database in a *tabular form*, which would also have a part reserved for a summary (*resumo*). The idea was that the analyst at the computer terminal would select the subject (*assunto*) on the basis of this summary and would then access the microfilms containing the full texts *only if necessary*.[65]

Thus, the most important, most time-consuming and most complicated part of the preparation of the dataset was precisely the compilation of an "auxiliary sheet" containing the basic data and the summary in a maximum of ten typed lines (see Figure 7.3). It was crucial that this one-page *Folha Auxiliar* be filled in "properly" (this is underlined in the original instructions) and attached to every record, as it represented its entry ticket into the digital database.[66] In the following months and years, the compilation of the *Folha Auxiliar* caused frequent problems.

Even if "normative instructions" concerning the *Folha Auxiliar* were issued frequently,[67] standardisation left much to be desired. Often, records had to be returned to their originating sections because they had "compilation errors." These processes of sending back and forth the faulty records for the ACE took up more and more of the volume of correspondence of Section 06. Gradually, the proportion increased from 20 per cent in June 1979 to 40 per cent in December 1979. The head of the IT subsection of Section 06 complained that "elementary errors" in filling out the summary or "inadequate indexing" on the *Folha Auxiliar* impaired research at the terminals. He feared that this could be a factor for "discrediting of the system" and one of the reasons for the emergence of "parallel archives" in the various sections.[68]

In 1981, another "normative instruction" emphasised the compilation of the *Folha Auxiliar* as an "extremely relevant activity," since "clarity, accuracy and security of the knowledge that will be recorded for the benefit of the entire system" depended on it.[69] The preparation of the summary was explained in more detail. The objectives were to highlight the "core idea" and the "basic data" of the ACE in order to "enable greater speed and objectivity to future research and recovery work."[70] In the case that an ACE consisted of "several documents," the analyst must choose one, "preferably the one with the highest hierarchy," to "itemise it on the auxiliary sheet and prepare the summary to cover the significant facts of all the documents in the file."[71]

The problems with the creation of the auxiliary sheet can already be deduced from the instructions: compressing an entire dataset, which could include not only several documents but also appendices such as cassettes, photos and journal articles, into ten typed lines, was indeed a daunting task. It can be assumed that the summary of a dataset depended on the interpretations of the respective analyst, as there was a great degree of leeway in compiling the *Folha Auxiliar*.

Since the analysts were forced to use the computer terminals first during the search, and since the results of the search initially showed the summaries of the

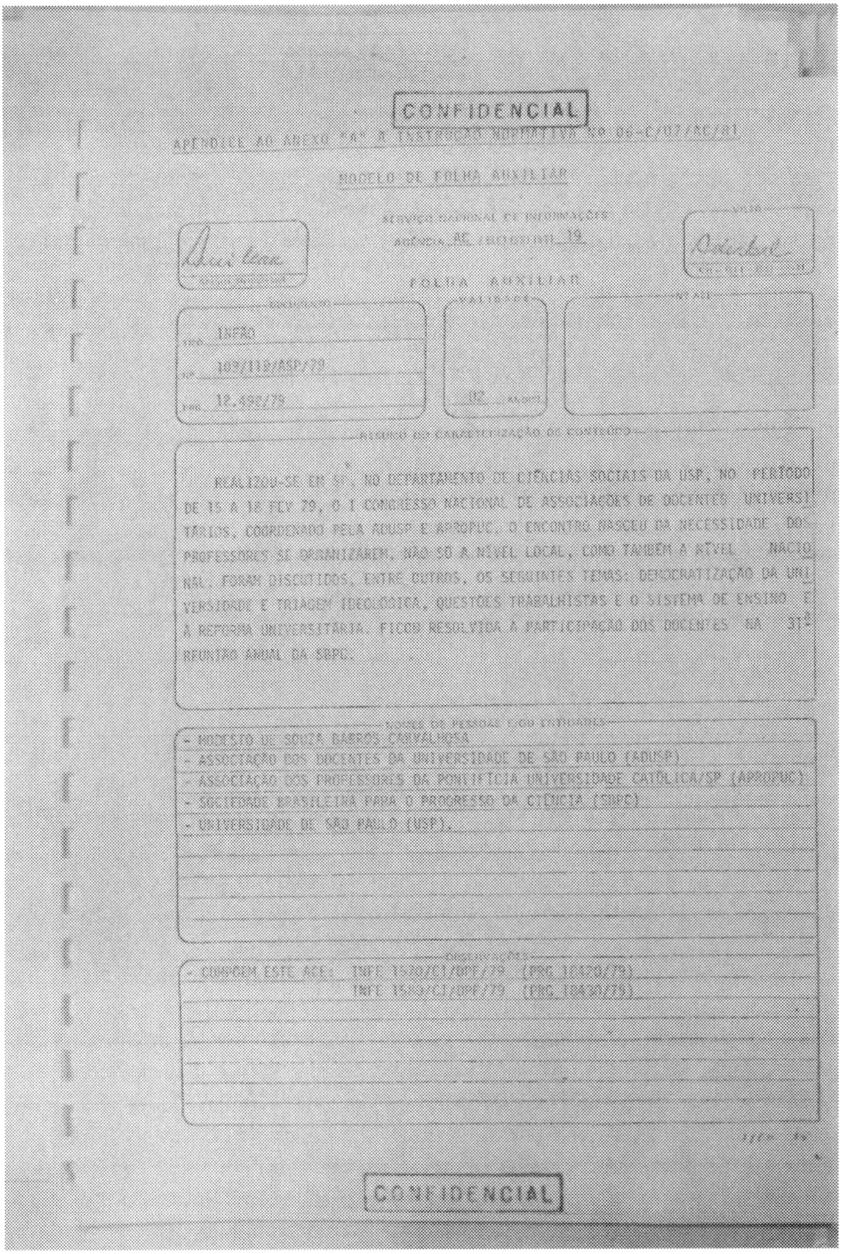

CONFIDENCIAL

APÊNDICE AO ANEXO "A" À INSTRUÇÃO NORMATIVA Nº 06-C/07/AC/81

MODELO DE FOLHA AUXILIAR

SERVIÇO NACIONAL DE INFORMAÇÕES

FOLHA AUXILIAR

INFÃO

109/119/ASP/79

12.490/79

02

REALIZOU-SE EM SP, NO DEPARTAMENTO DE CIÊNCIAS SOCIAIS DA USP, NO PERÍODO DE 15 A 18 FEV 79, O I CONGRESSO NACIONAL DE ASSOCIAÇÕES DE DOCENTES UNIVERSITÁRIOS, COORDENADO PELA ADUSP E APROPUC. O ENCONTRO NASCEU DA NECESSIDADE DOS PROFESSORES SE ORGANIZAREM, NÃO SÓ A NÍVEL LOCAL, COMO TAMBÉM A NÍVEL NACIONAL. FORAM DISCUTIDOS, ENTRE OUTROS, OS SEGUINTES TEMAS: DEMOCRATIZAÇÃO DA UNIVERSIDADE E TRIAGEM IDEOLÓGICA, QUESTÕES TRABALHISTAS E O SISTEMA DE ENSINO E A REFORMA UNIVERSITÁRIA. FICOU RESOLVIDA A PARTICIPAÇÃO DOS DOCENTES NA 31ª REUNIÃO ANUAL DA SBPC.

- MODESTO DE SOUZA BARROS CARVALHOSA
- ASSOCIAÇÃO DOS DOCENTES DA UNIVERSIDADE DE SÃO PAULO (ADUSP)
- ASSOCIAÇÃO DOS PROFESSORES DA PONTIFÍCIA UNIVERSIDADE CATÓLICA/SP (APROPUC)
- SOCIEDADE BRASILEIRA PARA O PROGRESSO DA CIÊNCIA (SBPC)
- UNIVERSIDADE DE SÃO PAULO (USP).

- COMPOEM ESTE ACE: INFE 1530/CI/DPF/79 (PRG 10420/79)
  INFE 1533/CI/DPF/79 (PRG 10430/79)

CONFIDENCIAL

Figure 7.3 Model of a *Folha Auxiliar* containing the data that would be digitised.

Source: Newton Araújo de Oliveira e Cruz (head of Central Agency), "Anexo 'A': Instruções para o preenchimento da Folha Auxiliar," em: "Normas para a remessa de documentos ao Departamento de Informática" (Instrução normativa 06-C/07/AC/81) (21 December 1981). ANBSB. SNI. Administração Geral. Documentação, Caixa 08, Camisa 33, p. 1.

156 Debora Gerstenberger

datasets, it can be assumed that the results of an enquiry differed significantly from those in the paper archive (whose datasets did not have any summary). After all, the results depended more heavily on the work previously done by the analyst who had composed the summary. The raw material was not only "cooked"[72] but was moreover strongly flavoured and only offered in small bites. Technically, the *Folha Auxiliar* that was *attached* to each dataset meant an *increase* in information for a record. Practically, in a first step, it meant a drastic *reduction* in and *bias* of information for the individual who was searching for a subject at the computer terminal.

Increasing connectivity: the striving for external databases

Even though the entire digitisation process may have been plagued by problems from the user's point of view, the management was adamant about the new digital database. What is more, not long after the introduction of the IBM computer terminals, attempts were made to significantly expand the pool of digital data. That state security institutions (in Latin America and elsewhere) were not the first bodies to buy and use computer technology is well known. Scientific institutions, private sector institutions and also other institutions of public administration were generally more progressive in this regard.[73] Probably not coincidentally, about the same time as the digitisation of SNI's own data holdings, the plan was now to gain access to external databases held by such institutions on a large scale (see also Marcelo Vianna's contribution in this volume).

As early as 1979, a computer terminal of *Projeto POLVO* ("Project Octopus") of the Road Traffic Department had successfully been established and integrated in SNI. Project Octopus included a database of all vehicle registration data in Brazil.[74] According to the annual report by Section 06, this allowed for "quick access to important data about vehicles registered in the national territory – owner, address, characteristics of the vehicle, etc."[75] The Serviço Federal de Processamento de Dados (Serpro) that provided the know-how for the vehicle database described *Projeto Polvo* as the very first "on-line" system in the whole of Latin America.[76]

Since the beginning of the military dictatorship, there had been efforts by the governments to engage in informatics. Serpro, founded in 1964, played a particularly important role in the informatisation of Brazil's state institutions and beyond.[77] The databases provided by Serpro were now particularly interesting for the Brazilian secret service. SNI planned the establishment of a connection to Serpro's database ARUANDA (an archiving and distribution service for socioeconomic, financial and technical-scientific information)[78] in 1979.

But the "octopus" and other databases provided by Serpro were not enough. Rather, SNI wanted even more tentacles: the Subseção de Informática (SSI) subsection of Section 06 proposed the integration of a terminal linking the AC to the database of the Federal Police (Departamento de Polícia Federal) which was, according to a hand-written notice, "already resolved!" (*já resolvido!*) in 1979.[79] Furthermore, the installation of a "PRODASEN terminal" (a congressional information system of the Federal Senate of Brazil established in 1972)[80] was considered "opportune," for it was "particularly important for research on legislation."[81] The installation of a terminal connecting SNI to the databases of the Instituto Brasileiro de Geografia e Estatística (IBGE) was also desired.[82]

The computer as document shredder 157

Perhaps due to its large territorial dimensions, Brazil stands out among Latin American states for its particularly strong tradition and history of (geographical) institutions providing the state with statistical data Otero, "Socio-History of Statistics." In the context of digitisation, these data riches seem to have become all the more attractive to the secret service. All these proposals were visualised, planned and concretised according to a "work plan" of the IT department of EsNI in 1981. The idea was to establish a switching device that would connect the individual SNI dependencies with the databases of the aforementioned institutions via a terminal (see Figure 7.4).

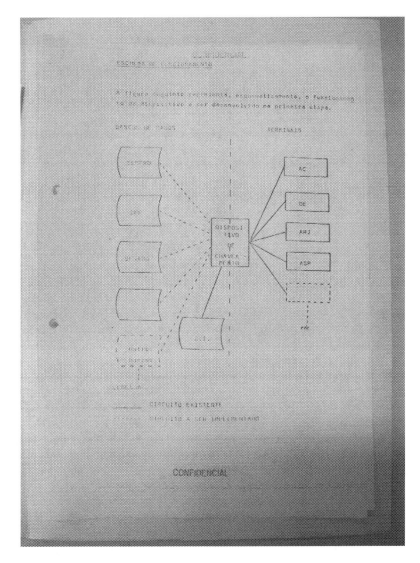

Figure 7.4 Network of different databases at SNI, as envisioned in 1981.
Source: Photograph of an archival document by the author. Leal (head of IT department at EsNI) "Relatório de Acompanhamento das atividades/necessidades da AC/SNI" (see note 81).

158   *Debora Gerstenberger*

The establishment of the external databases at SNI and the processing of the data obtained from these databases cannot be analysed in detail here. Suffice it to say that the process of digitising its own archives (and destroying the largest part of the paper files) went along with efforts to obtain more general, more extensive (statistical) data about Brazilian society from external sources. If SNI's authorities were averse to their own "old" paper archives, they were all the more enthusiastic about different external digital databases – and about a greater connectivity between them.

Conclusion

The introduction of new digital technology in December 1978 did not immediately make SNI's data processing activities more effective. In fact, SNI's computerisation was slow, difficult and fraught with troubles. The constant repetition in the annual reports that the digital computers had made the work "more efficient" from the very first day on must be viewed as bureaucratic "whitewashing." There is evidence that SNI analysts were considerably more "blind" compared to pre-digital times at least until 1983. The responses to the 1982 survey show that there were massive problems with the new digital database. The employees complained about the lack of equipment, lack of training, restricted access, incoherent policy concerning the contents of the database, offline terminals and so on. Furthermore, the fact that only a summary of a dataset was provided digitally reduced and coloured the "cooked" raw material considerably.

Nevertheless, SNI authorities propagated and enforced the new technology and devalued older technologies. This becomes exceedingly clear in the division of the records into "D–" and "D+" units, the closure of the paper archive at headquarters only one and a half years after the introduction of the first video terminal and, above all, the destruction of 95 per cent of SNI's "old" analogue intelligence documents.

A narrative in which new (digital) techniques bring about a *greater quantity of data* and emerge for the purpose of *greater repression* by the security institutions in an authoritarian regime would completely miss the mark in the Brazilian case. All in all, it can be stated that the slogans "quality instead of quantity" and "knowledge instead of documents" used to define SNI's digitisation project led to a glaring shortage of data. Due to the new computer technology, entire groups of documents fell by the wayside. Where there was doubt about how to classify them, single documents or even entire bundles of documents were simply eliminated. Apparently, the loss of a large portion of the intelligence information was acceptable and even desirable if it meant catapulting oneself from the analogue to the digital era. In sum, there was a strong *will to digitise* against all obstacles and a *desire to enter a new era of intelligence knowledge production*.

If it is true that ignorance is not the "opposite" but an important and integral part of the state's (and also intelligence's) knowledge,[83] in the case of SNI one can actually speak of a *self-inflicted partial amnesia*. Most probably, the institution was willing to "forget" most of the details concerning individuals because these

The computer as document shredder   159

details and/or individuals no longer mattered as much. Relevant representatives of the intelligence community (heads of section and chiefs of staff) were convinced that now, in the "computerised era," they were on their way to obtaining the "right knowledge." It is certainly no coincidence that the digitisation of SNI's own databases and the extreme shortage of self-produced intelligence knowledge happened almost simultaneously with the linking to external databases. The "right knowledge" contained *fewer details* on specific (subversive) persons and *more encompassing (statistical) data* on the whole population; it was also *more interconnected*.

The introduction of digital computer terminals was certainly a welcomed project in this phase of political "détente," of a change of direction towards democracy and of a forced reinvention of the Brazilian intelligence service. It is quite likely that SNI's authorities did not simply want to enter a new (digital) era as an end in itself. The technical caesura, as has been shown, was also a political caesura: on the basis of a new system of data processing and new "raw material," the Brazilian secret service strove for a *new form of governmentality*.

The study of the introduction of computer technology into SNI not least brings to light the material aspects of the intelligence service's data production, more precisely the importance of technological artefacts. The quantitative and qualitative changes in the intelligence knowledge were not simply *incentivised* by the new technology when the digitisation process started. Rather, the very "rationale" of the computer had a decisive influence on the processes of elimination and condensation of data. After all, it was the computer that "rejected" or "accepted" documents. The digital computer played a key role in the establishment of a new era of intelligence knowledge.

Notes

1 IBM International Business Machines Corporation, Data Processing Division (n.d.), *IBM 3270 Information Display System*. New York: IBM. I want to thank Joël Glasman, Rüdiger Bergien and Constantin Goschler for comments on earlier versions of this article.
2 <www.ibm.com/support/knowledgecenter/zosbasics/com.ibm.zos.znetwork/znetwork_261.htm> (last accessed May 31, 2021).
3 Osmany Meneses de Carvalho (head of Section 06), "Relatório da SE-06 referente ao ano de 1979" (7 January 1980). ANBSB. SNI. Administração Geral. Relatórios de Atividades. Caixa 01, Camisa 12, 4.
4 Osmany Meneses de Carvalho (head of Section 06) "Relatório da seção de pesquisa e arquivo (SE-06), referente ao ano de 1980" (14 January 1981). ANBSB. SNI. Administração Geral. Relatórios de Atividades. Caixa 01, Camisa 13, p. 6.
5 Itamar Soares Mendes (head of Section 06), "Relatório da seção de pesquisa e arquivo (SE-06) referente ao ano de 1982" (14 January 1983). ANBSB. SNI. Administração Geral. Relatórios de Atividades. Caixa 01, Camisa 18, 7.
6 Gorender, "Prefácio."
7 Schwarcz and Starling, *Brasil*, 459.
8 Antunes, *SNI & Abin*, 22.
9 Fico, *Como eles agiam.*
10 Antunes, *SNI & Abin*; Quadrat, *Poder e informação*; Figueiredo, *Ministério do silêncio.*
11 See also Vianna, "Segurança nacional."

160   *Debora Gerstenberger*

12 Carlos Fico has dedicated a five-page long chapter to the production of information, Fico, *Como eles agiam*, 95–100.
13 Herman, *Intelligence Power*, 2.
14 Latour, *Reassembling the Social*.
15 Heßler, "Menschen – Maschinen."
16 Latour, *Reassembling the Social*.
17 Gitelman, *Paper Knowledge*; Felten and Oertzen, "Bureaucracy as Knowledge."
18 Latour, *Pasteurization of France*, 51.
19 Fico, *Como eles agiam*, 211f.
20 Brasil. Commissão Nacional da Verdade, *Relatório*, 439.
21 Figueiredo, *Ministério do silêncio*, 290.
22 Ibid., 272 and 295.
23 Ibid., 295 and 300.
24 Ibid., 297.
25 Jecy Serôa Motta (head of SNI cabinet) "Estudo sobre implantação da sistemática de processamento de dados no SNI" (15 September 1978). ANBSB. SNI. Administração Geral. Documentação. Caixa 08, Camisa 25.
26 Ibid., 1–2.
27 The FBI had established a "National Crime Information Center" in 1967. The Western German *Bundeskriminalamt* startet digitization efforts in 1972. The *National Police Computer* of the British Metropolitan Police started working in 1975; corresponding facilities in France or Italy were not operational until the 1980s, Bergien, *Big Data als Vision*, 262f.
28 Anonymous, "Relatório estratégico baseado em pesquisa de opinião sobre o Sistema de informação" (n.d.). ANBSB. SNI. Administração Geral. Documentação. Camisa 15, Caixa 11.
29 "Análise final," ibid., unpag.
30 "Análise," ibid., unpag.
31 "Introdução," ibid., unpag.
32 Ibid.
33 Latour, *Reassembling the Social*, 63–86.
34 Anonymous, "Relatório de atividades da seção Pesquisa e Arquivo (SE-06) de 04 dez 78 a 28 fev 83" (n.d.). ANBSB. SNI. Administração Geral. Relatórios de atividades. Caixa 01, Camisa 21, without pagination.
35 Carvalho (head of Section 06), "Relatório" (see note 3), 4.
36 Motta (head of cabinet), "Estudo" (see note 25), 3.
37 Anonymous, "Relatório dos assuntos tratados durante a visita à Agência de Curitiba (ACT) nos Dias 01 e 02 de Jun 82" (1982). ANBSB. SNI. Administração Geral. Relatórios de atividades. Caixa 01, Camisa 16, 4.
38 Jecy Serôa da Motta (head of D/7), "Relatório anual da Divisão de Documentação, Telecomunicações e Informática (D/7), referente ao ano de 1983" (16 January 1984). ANBSB. SNI. Administração Geral. Relatórios de atividades. Caixa 01, Camisa 23, p. 4.
39 Zey Bezerra de Mello (head of Section 0621), "Plano de ação para o desenvolvimento das atividades da GERIN" (n. d.) [1985]. ANBSB. SNI. Administração Geral. Planejamento de Atividades. Caixa 01, Camisa 01, p. 2.
40 Latour, *Pasteurization of France*, 54.
41 Motta (head of cabinet), "Estudo" (see note 36).
42 Carvalho (head of Section 06), "Relatório" (see note 3), 3.
43 Ibid., 1.
44 Mendes (head of Section 06) "Relatório" (see note 5), 5.
45 "Estudo sobre Implantação Sistema de Arquivamento e Recuperação de documentos para informação (SARDI)," chapter "Propostas relativas à filosofia do sistema" (n.d. [c.1982]). ANBSB. SNI. Administração Geral. Documentação. Caixa 08, Camisa 25, p. 1.

The computer as document shredder 161

46 Anonymous, "Relatório de atividades da seção Pesquisa e Arquivo (SE-06) de 04 dez 78 a 28 fev 83" (n. d.). ANBSB. SNI. Administração Geral. Relatórios de atividades. Caixa 01, Camisa 21, without pagination.

47 Itamar Soares Mendes (head of Section 06), "Relatório da seção de pesquisa e arquivo (SE-06) referente ao ano de 1982" (14 January 1983). ANBSB. SNI. Administração Geral. Relatórios de Atividades. Caixa 01, Camisa 18, 6.

48 Anonymous, "Relatório de atividades da seção Pesquisa e Arquivo (SE-06) de 04 dez 78 a 28 fev 83" (n. d.). ANBSB. SNI. Administração Geral. Relatórios de atividades, Caixa 01, Camisa 21, without pagination.

49 Carvalho (head of Section 06), "Relatório" (see note 4). 4.

50 About the EsNI see Andrade, "Estrutura do Serviço Secreto"; Andrade, *Escola Nacional de Informações*; Quadrat, *Poder e informação*; Quadrat, "Preparação dos agentes."

51 Osmany Meneses de Carvalho (head of Section 06) to head of SNI cabinet, Memo 037/06/AC/79 "Situação de Documentos relacionados" (19 September 1979), ANBSB, SNI. Administração Geral. Relatório de Atividades camisa 10, Caixa 01, p. 1.

52 Ibid., p. 3.

53 Ibid., p. 2.

54 Gugerli, *Wie die Welt*, 84.

55 "Relatório dos assuntos tratados durante a visita à APA nos dias 02 e 03 de Jun 82." 1982. ANBSB. SNI. Administração Geral. Relatórios de Atividades. Caixa 01, Camisa 15, p. 1; "Relatório dos assuntos tratados durante a visita à Agência de Curitiba (ACT) nos Dias 01 e 02 de Jun 82" (n.d.). ANBSB. SNI. Administração Geral. Relatórios de atividades. Caixa 01, Camisa 16, p. 1.

56 Osmany Meneses de Carvalho (head of Section 06) "Reavaliação da massa 'D menos' 2a Fase" (19 September 1980). ANBSB. SNI. Administração Geral. Documentação. Caixa 08, Camisa 30, p. 3.

57 Newton Araújo de Oliveira e Cruz (head of Central Agency), "Normas para remessa de documentos ao Departamento de informática (Instrução normativa No. 06-C/07/AC/81)" (1981), ANBSB. SNI. Administração Geral. Documentação. Caixa 08, Camisa 33, p. 10.

58 Newton Araújo de Oliveira e Cruz (head of Central Agency) "Normas para remessa de documentos ao Departamento de informática (Instrução normativa No. 06-C/07/AC/81)" (21 December 1981), ANBSB. SNI. Administração Geral. Documentação. Caixa 08, Camisa 33, p. 9. For the classification of informants see also Fico, *Como eles agiam*, 95.

59 Magalhães, "Lógica da suspeição."

60 Fico, *Como eles agiam*, 99.

61 Ibid., 101.

62 Anonymous, "'Foi tudo de acordo com a lei', diz general que chefiava extinto SNI," *Folha de São Paulo*, 2 July 2012. <www1.folha.uol.com.br/poder/2012/07/1113591-foi-tudo-de-acordo-com-a-lei-diz-general-que-chefiava-extinto-sni.shtml> (last accessed June 3, 2021); Valente, R. "Ditadura destruiu mais de 19 mil documentos secretos," *Folha de São Paulo*, 2 July 2012. <www1.folha.uol.com.br/poder/2012/07/1113575-ditadura-destruiu-mais-de-19-mil-documentos-secretos.shtml> (last accessed June 3, 2021).

63 Valente, R. "Ditadura destruiu mais de 19 mil documentos secretos," *Folha de São Paulo*, 2 July 2012. <www1.folha.uol.com.br/poder/2012/07/1113575-ditadura-destruiu-mais-de-19-mil-documentos-secretos.shtml> (last accessed June 3, 2021).

64 Anonymous, "'Foi tudo de acordo com a lei', diz general que chefiava extinto SNI," *Folha de São Paulo*, 2 July 2012. <www1.folha.uol.com.br/poder/2012/07/1113591-foi-tudo-de-acordo-com-a-lei-diz-general-que-chefiava-extinto-sni.shtml> (last accessed June 3, 2021).

65 Motta (head of cabinet) "Estudo" (see note 25), 1.

66 Newton Araújo de Oliveira e Cruz (head of Central Agency) "Remessa de documentos ao ARGE (Instrução interna no. 024/07/AC/79" (17 January 1979). ANBSB. SNI. Administração Geral. Documentação. Caixa 08, Camisa 29, p. 2.

162 *Debora Gerstenberger*

67 Newton Araújo de Oliveira e Cruz (head of Central Agency), "Instrução interna No. 024/07/AC/79" (17 January 1979). ANBSB. SNI. Administração Geral. Caixa 08, Camisa 29, p. 2.
68 Ibid.
69 Oliveira e Cruz (head of Central Agency), "Anexo 'A': Instruções para o preenchimento da Folha Auxiliar" (see note 68), 1.
70 Newton Araújo de Oliveira e Cruz (head of Central Agency) "Normas para a remessa de documentos ao Departamento de Informática" (Instruçãõ normativa 06-C/07/AC/81) (21 December 1981) ANBSB. SNI. Administração Geral. Documentação. Caixa 08, Camisa 33.
71 Ibid., 2–3.
72 Räsänen and Nyce, "The Raw is Cooked."
73 Gerstenberger, "Martial Masculinity."
74 Carvalho, *Trajetória da internet*.
75 Carvalho (head of Section 06), "Relatório" (see note 3), 2.
76 Carvalho, *Trajetória da internet*, 63.
77 Pereira, "Pré-história da informática"; Vianna, "Visão tecnopolítica," 3.
78 Oliveira, "Serviço ARUANDA."
79 Antonio José B. de C. Mendes Leal (head of IT department at EsNI), "Relatório de Acompanhamento das atividades/necessidades da AC/SNI" (22 September 1981). ANBSB. SNI. Administração Geral. Relatório de atividades. Caixa (s/n), Camisa 14, unpag.
80 Baaklini, "Prodasen."
81 Carvalho (head of Section 06), "Relatório" (see note 3), 5.
82 Mendes (head of Section 06) "Relatório" (see note 5), 7.
83 Rappert and Balmer, "Ignorance is Strength."

Bibliography

Andrade, de Oliveira F. 2014. "A estrutura do Serviço Secreto na ditadura militar: a formação dos agentes secretos na Escola Nacional de Informações." *Em tempo de Histórias* 24: 120–138.

Andrade, de Oliveira F. 2014. *A Escola Nacional de Informações: a formação dos agentes para a inteligência brasileira durante o regime military*. MA dissertation, University Estadual Paulista.

Antunes, P. 2002. *SNI & Abin: uma leitura da atuação dos serviços secretos brasileiros ao longo do século XX*. Rio de Janeiro: Fundação Getúlio Vargas.

Baaklini, A. I. 1994. "Prodasen: The Congressional Information System of the Federal Senate of Braszil." *Government Information Quarterly* 11, no. 2: 171–190.

Bergien, R. 2017. "'Big Data' als Vision. Computereinführung und Organisationswandel in BKA und Staatssicherheit (1967–1989)." *Zeithistorische Forschungen/Studies in Contemporary History* 14, no. 2: 258–285.

Brasil. Comissão Nacional da Verdade. 2014. *Relatório Volume I* (Recurso eletrônico). Brasília: CNV.

Carvalho, M. S. 2006. *A trajetória da internet no Brasil: do surgimento das redes de computadores à instituição dos mecanismos de governança*. MA dissertation, Universidade Federal do Rio de Janeiro.

Felten, S., and Oertzen, Chr. v. 2020. "Bureaucracy as Knowledge." *Journal for the History of Knowledge* 1, no. 8: 1–16.

Fico, C. 2001. *Como eles agiam. Os subterrâneos da ditadura militar: espionagem e polícia política*. Rio de Janeiro: Ed. Record.

The computer as document shredder 163

Fico, C. 2012. "História do Tempo Presente, eventos traumáticos e documentos sensíveis. O caso brasileiro." *Varia História* 28, no. 47: 43–59.

Figueiredo, L. 2005. *Ministério do silêncio. A história do serviço secreto brasileiro de Washington Luís a Lula (1927–2005).* Rio de Janeiro: Ed. Record.

Gerstenberger, D. 2019. "Challenging Martial Masculinity. The Intrusion of Digital Computers into the Argentinian Armed Forces in the 1960s." *History of Technology* 34: 165–186.

Gitelman, L. 2014. *Paper Knowledge: Toward a Media History of Documents.* Durham and London: Duke University Press.

Gorender, J. 2001. "Prefácio." In *Como eles agiam. Os subterrâneos da ditadura militar: espionagem e polícia política,* ed. C. Fico, 9–14. Rio de Janeiro: Ed. Record.

Gugerli, D. 2018. *Wie die Welt in den Computer kam. Zur Entstehung digitaler Wirklichkeit.* Frankfurt am Main: S. Fischer.

Herman, M. 1996. *Intelligence Power in Peace and War.* Cambridge: Cambridge University Press.

Heßler, M. 2019. "Menschen – Maschinen – MenschMaschinen in Zeit und Raum. Perspektiven einer Historischen Technikanthropologie." In *Provokationen der Technikgeschichte,* ed. M. Heßler, 35–68. Paderborn: Ferdinand Schöningh.

Latour, B. 1993. *The Pasteurization of France.* Cambridge, MA: Harvard University Press.

Latour, B. 2005. *Reassembling the Social: An Introduction to Actor-Network-Theory.* New York: Oxford University Press.

Magalhães, Dias Prepohl M. 1997. "A lógica da suspeição. Sobre os aparelhos repressivos à época da ditadura militar no Brasil." *Revista Brasileira de História* (São Paulo) 34, no. 17.

Oliveira, Ferreira de B. 1984. "Serviço ARUANDA: uma introdução ao sistema." *Serviços e Sistemas Ciência da Informação* 13, no. 1: 73–79.

Otero, H. 2018. "Socio-History of Statistics on Latin America." *Histoire & Mesure* 33, no. 2: 13–32.

Pereira, L. de Almeida. 2017. "Por uma pré-história da informática no Brasil: os anos de formação (1958–1974)." In *Dimensões da história e da memória da informatica no Brasil,* ed. L. de Almeida Pereira and M. Vianna, 11–34. Jundiaí: Paco Editorial.

Quadrat, S. V. 2000. *Poder e informação: O sistema de inteligência e o regime militar no Brasil.* MA dissertation, UFRJ.

Quadrat, S. V. 2012. "A preparação dos agentes de informação e a ditadura civil-militar no Brasil." *Varia História* v. 28: 19–41.

Rappert, B., and Balmer, B. 2015. "Ignorance is Strength? Intelligence, Security and National Secrets." In *Routledge International Handbook of Ignorance Studies,* ed. M. Gross and L. McGoey, 328–337. London: Routledge.

Räsänen, M., and Nyce, J. M. "The Raw Is Cooked: Data in Intelligence Practice." *Science, Technology, & Human Values* 38, no. 5 (September 2013): 655–677.

Rodrigues, V. A. Câmara. 2017. *Documentos (in)visíveis: arquivos da ditadura militar e acesso à informação em tempos de justiça de transição no Brasil.* Aracajun: EDISE.

Schwarcz, L. M., and Starling, L. M. 2015. *Brasil: uma biografia.* São Paulo: Companhia das Letras.

Vianna, M. 2013. "Uma visão da tecnopolítica em Informática na sociedade brasileira – um olhar sobre a revista Dados e Ideias (1975–1979)." In *9° Encontro Nacional de História da Mídia. Caderno de Resumos v. 1,* 1–13. Ouro Preto: Alear.

Vianna, M. 2015. "Segurança Nacional e Autonomia Tecnológica o avanço do Serviço Nacional de Informações sobre o campo da Informática brasileira (1978–1980)." In *Anais do XXVIII Simpósio Nacional de História,* 1–16. Florianópolis: ANPUH.

8 Turkish intelligence, surveillance and the secrets of the Cold War

Blocked modernisation?

Egemen Bezci

Introduction

> As I understand it, there are only 12 officers employed in the intelligence section of the General Directorate of Security in Istanbul. Six of them are responsible for the administrative work in the back office, and the other six spend all their time in coffee houses by eavesdropping on the gabbles of the rudimentary elements of this threat. These officers possess neither the adequate brain power nor the culture to detect subversive cells and the radio communications between them.[1]

The aforementioned relates the appraisal of a ruling Democratic Party (*Demokrat Parti*) MP in the Turkish parliament in February 1951 in response to the minister of the interior highlighting the lack of technical capabilities within the Turkish intelligence community. Turkey was on the door to becoming a North Atlantic Treaty Organization (NATO) member in 1952 after transforming its government into a multi-party democracy. A lack of technical intelligence capabilities within the Turkish intelligence was one of the serious issues under discussion as the country was being integrated into the Western alliance. Both the foreign threat from the Soviet Union and domestic subversion during this transformation period were important agenda items for Ankara to monitor.

Due to the administrative organisation of the police force, its responsibility was confined only to urban areas and the military-controlled gendarmerie forces were responsible for the law enforcement in the rural part of the country. Only 25 per cent of the population resided in urban areas, while 75 per cent still lived in rural parts of the country. This demographic ratio changed rapidly over the course of the Cold War, with internal immigration, rising levels of education and industrialisation being localised in major cities such as Istanbul and Ankara.[2] Changing demographics, people's mode of life, new threat structure and the emerging spread of new radical left and right ideas during the Cold War forced the Turkish intelligence apparatus to adopt new tools and methods to enhance its capabilities. It was imperative to ensure a smooth intelligence sharing framework between these organisations and to analytically evaluate this information in a timely way for the decision-makers.

These transformation efforts coincided with the rise of computational power to be used in the intelligence methodologies. The Turkish intelligence organisations,

DOI: 10.4324/9781003147329-9

Blocked modernisation? 165

however, faced challenges adapting to these new technologies for intelligence analysis, let alone creating home-grown technological capabilities. Turkey's alliance with the Western security umbrella during the Cold War enabled Ankara to acquire partial professionalisation and procure technical advancements to alleviate the flaws in its home-grown capabilities to produce intelligence knowledge. The subsequent governments tried to empower an over-arching civilian intelligence agency immersed in technological developments and professionalisation to inform them on matters related to national security. What obstacles stood in the way of trying to move the Turkish intelligence community in this direction? Did the repeated successful (1960, 1971 and 1980) and unsuccessful (1962 and 1963) military coups challenge the efforts to create an efficient channel of communication between the intelligence community and the decision-makers? These questions remain largely unanswered in the literature and will be addressed in this chapter. The chapter will exploit primary archival sources from Turkey, the United States and the Eastern Bloc to demonstrate that the binary nature of the Cold War rivalry and Turkey's geostrategic position in the soft under-belly of the Soviet Union resulted in Western countries providing Ankara with sophisticated intelligence tools and some degree of scientisation of its intelligence community. The domestic political turmoil, bureaucratic rivalry, pejorative perception of the intelligence among the politics and the frequent coups, however, hampered efforts to move the national intelligence agency beyond secret police for incumbent governments.

Scientific production of military and strategic intelligence on foreign adversaries has gained attention for professionalising the analytical research as the highest possible deliverable for the decision-makers.[3] However, this chapter shows that even a NATO member's intelligence service can lack from scientisation of its intelligence collection and analysis methods due to the peculiarities of the domestic conditions. This chapter also shows that the role of computation in battlefield intelligence and the signal intelligence (SIGNIT) could alter the intelligence collection methodologies in a limited way due to the difference in organisational culture and requirements of the intelligence agencies.

This chapter is organised into three sections presenting the complex domestic and international factors behind the problem of the technological and scientific transformation of Turkish intelligence. The first section outlines intelligence in the Turkish context and the raison d'état behind the Turkish intelligence organisation as a government apparatus. It shows that the Turkish intelligence organisation in the government bureaucracy was entangled with the concept of intelligence as a political power, while the young Turkish republic established its foundations in society. The second section examines the government efforts to reform the intelligence apparatus to professionalise the analysis and collection. The findings propose that the decades-long violent political clashes, deep-rooted economic problems and the military's dominance over the strategic intelligence prevented the professionalisation of the national intelligence. The third section delves deeper into final efforts to overhaul national intelligence following the 1980 coups and highlights the efforts to procure further computational technology, acquire qualified human capital and enhance the legal capabilities against bureaucratic stagnation.

Politics of Turkish intelligence

The Turkish intelligence community during the Cold War was not a monolithic bureaucratic organisation but, rather, a combination of several departmental and strategic intelligence branches of the government, running their own operations without much oversight and coordination. The Turkish National Intelligence Organization, the Gendarmerie Intelligence Command, the Turkish General Staff Intelligence Branch, the Turkish National Police Intelligence Bureau and the Foreign Ministry all had their own intelligence collection and analysis agenda and frequently overstepped each other's boundaries.[4] The organised and official civilian intelligence agency National Intelligence Organization (MIT) was not officially formed until 1965. Before the creation of MIT, the intelligence activities were conducted through loosely connected networks and personnel seconded from the military, police and the foreign ministry. The information sharing among the different members of the intelligence community was not possible due to the lack of a legal framework, which only became possible with a new law in 1983. The Turkish General Staff's Intelligence Division had an exclusive monopoly over the analysis of the strategic intelligence informing the country's foreign policy imperatives. This ambiguity did not only stem from a lack of clarity regarding the bureaucratic division of labour but also from a reflection of different agencies and their vision on the intelligence apparatus and its role for shaping Turkish national security. This was reinforced by another peculiarity: generally there is an organisational division of labour between domestic and foreign intelligence services, such as that between the CIA and the FBI or the BND and the BfV. In the Turkish case, however, the competing intelligence organisations in the bureaucracy were tasked with both domestic and foreign intelligence, through different tactics, technology and the relationship with the decision-makers.

It is not rare for intelligence agencies to be utilised in tasks out of their core functions of intelligence gathering. There are various peripheral functions of the intelligence agencies changing according to the political leader and state characteristics. The overarching theme of these functions across different nations [sic]"have something to do with protecting or expanding the center of gravity of the state and its power."[5] Turkey's state apparatus, especially its security organs, did not have a consensus about what should be the main tasks of intelligence, and which organisational and legal tasks should define its power and role. The frequent coups and the coup attempts are the prominent examples of these contentious politics within the Turkish state during the Cold War. Institutional and intra-personal rivalry between the civilian and military intelligence agencies played a crucial role in the development of the Turkish intelligence community.[6]

As the United States National Security Council accurately evaluated in October 1960, "Turkey's political problem has been one of tyranny by an unchecked majority, and what the Turkish political system requires is an appropriate set of institutional checks and balances on pure majority rule."[7] Besides the lack of institutional frameworks enabling the Turkish intelligence community, the country's military showed strong praetorian tendencies and held a tight grip on the security apparatus dominating several organisations within the government such as the intelligence organisation, national security council and even the higher education council.[8] The Turkish military, especially after the 1960 military intervention conducted by the lower echelons, experienced a tug of war between the rival groups, ranging from ultra-nationalists to the left-wing revolutionaries, necessitating the successful putschists to employ the National Intelligence Organization to constantly spy on the military itself to prevent further coup attempts.[9]

The problematisation of what intelligence knowledge should do, thus, can be conceptualised among the web of complex international and domestic political considerations. The intelligence knowledge is derived from secret and difficult to obtain information. As practitioner-turned-scholar Stephen Marrin accurately describes, the intelligence knowledge provides "the ability to change another's behavior to do something they otherwise would have not done."[10] The power exercised through the intelligence knowledge requires the government and its intelligence service to possess ultimate knowledge about people and society.[11] Intelligence gathering during the early Cold War meant that Turkey depended heavily on human intelligence (HUMINT) sources rather than SIGINT or ELINT (electronic intelligence) tools. HUMINT is a low-tech tool that lacks the clarity and real-time potential of technology-heavy methods.[12] HUMINT, in a Foucauldian sense, can also be seen "as a set of material elements and techniques that service as weapons, relays, communication routes and support for the power and knowledge relations that invest human bodies and subjugate them by turning them into objects of knowledge."[13] The emerging analytical and technological applications enable governments to exercise the power stemming from the intelligence knowledge "by making the power applied greater; by making the speed of power application faster; by enabling the collection and analysis of greater volumes of information; and by enabling the information or knowledge to be provided to decision makers faster."[14] The problem of which organisation should have access to the knowledge, the elected decision-makers or the military, and what should be done with that information are the questions that hampered the effectiveness of intelligence knowledge to guide the national security politics in Turkey.

A characteristic conflict developed when the centre-right Democratic Party (*Demokrat Parti*) took over the government from the Republican People's Party after the 1950 national elections. This marked a turning point in Turkish politics since it was the country's first experience of a successful multi-party democracy and transition of power since the founding of the republic in 1923. The Democratic Party took the control of the national intelligence upon their electoral triumph. The irony is that it was the same intelligence apparatus that once had tormented the Democratic Party under the single-party regime until 1950. During the defence planning meetings in the parliament, the newly elected Democratic Party wanted to increase the budget for the national security service. The Democratic Party visioned that a more potent intelligence agency, with increased budget and personnel would align itself more with the NATO standards for intelligence analysis and collection. However, a member of the commission from the same party, also

168   Egemen Bezci

a Turkish war hero, Ali İhsan Sabis recalled a remarkable story to raise opposition to this request:

> Dear friends, there is no doubt that an intelligence office is needed for the security. But it has been proven that this office has been abused. As a matter of fact, the commission showed the records, since 1946, indicating where its budget was spent. There is also my name in these records. My dear friends: For 27 years, I was being surveilled by the National Security Service, day and night; one night, they even broke into the shoe shop opposite my house to spy on me. We came face to face with the intelligence officers several times, I spit in their faces. This money was being spent for them.[15]

Even the country's war hero, who had fought in the war of liberation between 1918 and 1922, had a pejorative view of the intelligence service. Sabis' reservations had some truth since the previous president, also a renowned war hero, İsmet İnönü, had used the intelligence service to harass Sabis due to their personal rivalry. The newly elected Democratic Party acknowledged the misconduct and violations of the intelligence service under previous governments, yet they failed to turn the tide. Instead of creating a more civilian and professional intelligence service, the military continued their dominance over the security establishment. Finally, the Democratic Party was ousted by a military coup in 1960, and its leading politicians including the Prime Minister, Foreign Minister and the Minister of Finance were executed by the putschists. The intelligence agency could not – more accurately did not – inform the civilian politicians of the coming coup, but sided with the military allowing them to topple the government. Following the coup, the putschists purged a large number of personnel who were loyal to the civilian government and working closely with NATO to professionalise the intelligence community. The CIA reported to President Eisenhower that the purge "impedes . . . joint activities with [Turkey], since many key contact men have been retired."[16] The frequent coups and the subsequent purges in Turkey during the Cold War were major obstacles due to losing human capital, and organisational knowledge for the modernisation of the intelligence.

The efforts to turn the tide to confine the intelligence service to a more effective intelligence-gathering position formalised with the establishment of National Intelligence Organization (MIT) in 1965. The formation of the MIT was timely in a way that Turkey was transitioning to a more democratic framework with Westernisation efforts of its national security structure. Ironically, however, these Westernisation efforts such as the establishment of the National Security Council (MGK) mimicking its American counterpart, where civilian and military decision-makers form the country's foreign and security policy, did not curb the military's predominant position in the security policies – on the contrary, it acted as a mechanism of military's control over the civilian policies.[17] The problem of delivering timely and accurate intelligence to the prime minister, and accelerating the intelligence cooperation among different departments persisted despite various urgent policy requirements.

Blocked modernisation? 169

The national intelligence organisation was founded with a bipartisan consensus to modernise the state intelligence mechanism to professionalise the process. The spokesperson from the government defending the draft of the national intelligence law during the parliamentary discussions in 1965 was hopeful about this new organisation.

> We, as a party, are in favor of this new organization, which fills an important gap. This organization been working illegally until now . . . there was no organization in which can gather all of the intelligence from other ministries to provide evaluated intelligence to the Prime Minister. . . . The Chief of Staff's intelligence unit was busy with strategic intelligence. This new law gives life to this new organization [MIT] with a more comprehensive legal basis.[18]

Although MIT was founded as the primary intelligence agency to guide the national security policies, there were several political, economic and social obstacles. Soon after the MIT was formed, the country experienced wide-scale domestic turbulence due to the militant revolutionary movements and the foreign policy crises due to the Cyprus dispute. The Cyprus problem required new intelligence sources independent of the NATO to inform Ankara's foreign and security policies, further moving MIT away from NATO standards. Moreover, the military engaged another coup d'état to oust the civilian government in 1971. All of the MIT's spymasters until November 1992 were military generals seconded from the Turkish General Staff. The spymasters' direct loyalty stayed with the Turkish General Staff rather than their civilian superiors. Süleyman Demirel, who was the ousted prime minister in 1971, would later complain in a witty way about the intelligence agency:

> For example, if two tribes clashed in Angola with each other, [MIT] briefs me about this stuff every morning this many tribe members died during the clashes; but they never inform me if there is an intrigue in Ankara to overthrow the government.[19]

MIT, indeed, did not become an organisation to help the civilian leaders to conduct the country's national security policies. The military dominance of the organisation continued well beyond the Cold War. These hampered both the relationship between the MIT and the decision-makers, and the relationship between MIT in regard to the other organisations in the bureaucracy. This was particularly apparent during the 1970s when the country experienced large-scale domestic turmoil due to the terrorism, and the MIT fell short to cooperate with the national police to thwart these events despite its recently acquired technical capabilities for surveillance.

Modernisation, intelligence and unrest

Turkey's geostrategic location adjacent to the Soviet Union made it a prime location for hosting ultra-secret SIGINT bases to spy on the Soviet Union. The legal framework for these bases was the Status of Forces Agreement between Turkey

170   *Egemen Bezci*

and the United States signed in 1954. Some of them are still operational today with amendments in July 1969 and December 1986 respectively giving more overall control and involvement of the Turkish personnel in these bases.[20] These bases were not only ad hoc intelligence bases but also acted as regional communication centres for the relay of SIGINT from other stations back to the National Security Agency (NSA) headquarters at Fort Meade.[21] The American bases were exclusively staffed by American personnel who were trained and deployed for the specific purpose of SIGINT collection. It was estimated that three-quarters of Western intelligence on Soviet strategic weapons came from these bases.[22]

SIGNIT capacity of these bases was not transferred to Turkey; therefore, it did not require Turkish intelligence to establish databases to process the information acquired from them. Under the US Mutual Security Assistance Program, the parties entered a lend-lease agreement. Turkish authorities possessed limited knowledge regarding the exact nature of these SIGINT capabilities. Intelligence collected from these highly technical and secretive bases were randomly passed to the Turkish authorities on a need-to-know basis.[23] The SIGINT cooperation was not a manifestation of technopolitics by "using technology to enact political goals."[24] The US strategic dependence to these bases, on the contrary, enabled Turkey to amplify its influence in the transatlantic relations while giving the Turkish military intelligence some degree of know-how transfer in SIGINT matters.[25]

The Turkish military established a parallel and more comprehensive relation with the US military and intelligence authorities through the office of the Joint United States Military Mission for Aid to Turkey in Ankara, which included training and knowledge transfer in fields such as intermediate-range ballistic missiles and highly secretive operations such as the U-2 spy plane. The National Security Council policy on Turkey noted in 1960 that "The United States furnishes the Turkish Armed Forces included in Military assistance program objectives with virtually all of the military supplies and equipment which are not domestically produced."[26] Most of the technology transfer negotiations were conducted without consultation with the Turkish foreign ministry.[27] As a result, the Turkish Armed Forces and its intelligence branch became the pioneering government institution to receive and adopt technical know-how on the rise of computational systems in the Cold War.

Technology transfer mostly occurred through training and procurement for the Turkish military as part of the effort to modernise the Turkish Armed Forces. The major Turkish SIGINT capabilities remained under the control of the Turkish military's Turkish General Staff Electronic Systems Command (Genelkurmay Elektronik Sistemler Komutanlığı, GES). GES was founded concurrently with the Turkey–United States lend-lease agreement in 1954, and it existed under the control of the General Staff until it was incorporated into the MIT in 2012.[28] Subsequently, through the GES, the military units acquired Automatic Information Technology Units (OBI) for military intelligence purposes. The limited know-how transfer in terms of SIGINT matters enabled the Turkish military intelligence to launch its own military operation, such as the 1974 Turkish military intervention to Cyprus outside of the NATO command structure. The SIGINT, however, was limited to matters of military intelligence such as C3I (Command, Communication, Control and Intelligence) purposes for effective battle theatre operations. MIT, in cooperation with the GES, used this procured technology for the reconnaissance of the Greek and Cypriot military positions ahead of the Turkish military intervention of Cyprus in 1974.[29] Although this information was useful for the tactical aspects of the covert operation, it created a mental block for a peaceful solution on the island. The intelligence analysis is not solely an issue of throwing all the collection capabilities on the target but also about overcoming one's bias to understand the adversary's mindset and capabilities in the relevant context (Figure 8.1).[30]

The development of the computer technology industry was a fundamental part of the Cold War grand strategy.[31] This fundamental aspect of the Cold War enabled the intelligence relationship between Turkey and the United States to develop into a distinct pattern in a quasi-independent realm outside of the ups and downs of bilateral diplomatic and political relationships. The US dependence on the SIGINT bases on Turkish soil and the necessity to modernise the Turkish Armed Forces to ensure efficient technical cooperation became immune to the dips in the relationships, such as the US arms embargo on Turkey following the Turkish military intervention into Cyprus in 1974. The embargo lasted between 1975 and 1978; however, SIGINT cooperation continued without much impact.[32] In accordance with the binary nature of Cold War rivalry, technological development in the United States and technological diffusion to allies followed US military objectives and shaped the development of information technology in both the United States and Turkey.[33] This technology transfer, however, did not support a shift towards a professional intelligence knowledge production for the civilian intelligence as envisioned in the intelligence law in 1965.

The US Mutual Security Assistance Program to Turkey accelerated Turkey's social and political transformation in terms of urbanisation and the free-market

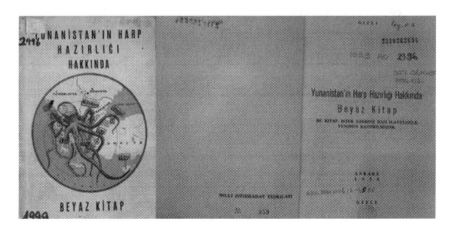

Figure 8.1 White Book on Greece's War Preparedness

Source: National Library of Turkey: 1999AD2996: Yunanistan Harp Hazırlığı Hakkında Beyaz Kitap (Secret) [The White Book about the Preparation of Greece for War], National Intelligence Organization (MIT), 1970.

172 *Egemen Bezci*

economy, in addition to modernising its military. However, this social and political transformation was not flawless. The American ambassador, George McGhee, who was also one of the architects of the US aid to Turkey, envisioned that the flow of American enterprises such as General Electric would turn Turkey into a success story and transform Turkey's Mediterranean coastal cities, such as Adana, into an urban hub of technology and commerce in the region.[34] According to this plan, Turkey would soon reach its potential to create its own qualified human capital, and have its own technology producing industry. This vision, however, did not come to fruition. On the contrary, the increasing American presence in the country, multiplied along with rapid urbanisation, social inequalities and existing ethno-religious fault lines, resulted in instability that would haunt the country for more than two decades, including military coups in 1960, 1971 and 1980.

The US Mutual Assistance Program to Turkey was not only aimed at modernising the Turkish military and infrastructure; it was also aimed at creating an urban class that was commerce savvy with a free-enterprise attitude that would eventually transform Turkey into a well-functioning capitalist democracy. The consensus, including the CIA's assessment of Turkey, was that socialism had little appeal among Turks.[35] This was, however, not an accurate picture of the evolving social dynamics in Turkey. The social and economic crisis spanning the country over the decades between 1945 and 1980 demonstrated that the emerging urban youth and the Kurdish nationalist movement had an aptitude for socialist ideas as a way of curbing the rising American influence in the country.[36] Moreover, the rising public sentiment among the new political class was that socialist ideas might be more of a solution to the country's chronic problems than the Western alignment and capitalist democracy could provide.[37] The SIGINT cooperation between the Western alliance and Turkey was symbolised by the existence of the US military bases in Turkey.[38] Although the exact nature of these bases was not known to the public, the large antennas and high dishes located in the heavily guarded remote locations attracted attention and exposed these secret bases as possible targets for militant leftist activists. These bases symbolised cooperation and Western support, and as symbols of the CIA's existence in the country, they supported the Turkish government in suppressing the leftist dissidence at home.[39] The public mistrust of the intelligence agencies are expected in a democracy since the intelligence organisations cannot service the public desire for transparency due to the nature of their clandestine work.[40] This mistrust, however, also spread to the civilian politicians who were, at least according to the law, the final consumers of the intelligence knowledge.

One incident is worth noting here. On March 26, 1972, the Turkish leftist militant group the Turkish People's Liberation Front, led by Mahir Çayan, raided a British ultra-secret Government Communications Headquarters (GCHQ) base in the remote Black Sea village of Kızıldere and kidnapped and executed three full-time GCHQ officers. The militants, except one who later became a leftist politician and member of the parliament in Turkey, were killed in an operation by the Turkish security service's attempts to rescue the GCHQ officers. The ironic part of this incident is that neither the Turkish public nor the militants themselves knew

Blocked modernisation? 173

the exact nature of that base or whether the officers were even from the GCHQ. The militants believed that the foreigners were foreign technicians working in a foreign military base. This symbolic incident shows the climax of the contention between the rising radicalisation of politics within Turkey against the country's Western alignment. The armed left-wing attacks on the foreign intelligence bases did not end the scope or depth of SIGINT cooperation between Turkey and the West. Even after the Kızıldere incident, Turkey and Britain engaged in further cooperation between the GCHQ and the GES in February 1974 and maintained the bases on Turkish soil.[41] The available archives neither in Turkey nor in the United Kingdom indicate if these bases ceased to exist after the Cold War.

MIT, however, did not enjoy the benefits of the technical capabilities that the GES and the Turkish General Staff posed for the SIGINT capabilities. Yet there was high bipartisan consensus in the organisation's inception. This positive consensus was apparent in MP İhsan Ataöv's remarks in parliament during the discussions that initiated the national intelligence law in 1965:

> My dear friends, our national security is one of the issues we will focus on today. Apart from political beliefs, it is one of our most important duties to save the country from being the tool of some ill-intentioned people as the basis of our work, which will ensure the development of the country and ensure peace in the country. As I have mentioned here a few times, in this country, there may be people and groups who want to lead the society towards their bad intentions by hiding behind some national issues, which the citizens are sensitive about, and exploiting them. I hope that the National Intelligence Organization will be very sensitive against them within the framework of the new law and will not give life to these ideas.[42]

The armed political movements during the late 1960s and the early 1970s influenced the subsequent ethnic and political movements by establishing a tradition of political violence in the country. In an intelligence assessment by the CIA in September 1984, the agency argued:

> Turkish terrorism has its roots in the sweeping demographic, economic, and sociological changes that have occurred over the last three decades. Until significant improvements can be achieved in dealing with the resulting problems – unemployment, inequitable land and income distribution, overtaxed urban facilities, and festering religious and ethnic tensions – terrorism will remain a threat.[43]

These unanswered crises further fuelled political violence, which pushed the country into a situation short of a civil war between the left- and right-wing militant groups claiming the lives of more than 5,000 people.[44] It was apparent from the daily attacks and the high-level political assassinations that MIT did not have the capacity for countering terrorism on a large scale. The intelligence knowledge gained through the electronic databases works at best when the environments are

174   *Egemen Bezci*

predictable enabling intelligence agencies to process large amount of data coming from various sources for more efficient dissemination.[45] The environment that the MIT operated to counter the terrorism in 1970s was highly unpredictable with rapid movements of the terrorists between the rural and urban areas, even sometimes crossing borders to neighbouring countries or to Europe. MIT's capacity was limited to make meaningful analysis of the ever-changing targets with various motives operating in different areas and sometimes cross-border. These flaws are not unique to MIT since it is often difficult to find patterns among many false leads for ever-changing terrorist attacks before they happen.[46] MIT requested an amendment to its law to enhance its counterterrorism intelligence capacity in 1978, but that draft stalled in the parliament for two years until the parliament was abolished by the military coup. MIT's lack of access to the databases of other departments, that is police or gendarmerie, for synthesising the intelligence coming from various urban and rural sources hampered its effective use for the limited scope of the SIGINT surveillance capacity that it had.

During the dark decade of the Turkish history of the 1970s, intelligence was perceived by the public and the politicians alike as a symbol of the various factions within the security bureaucracy to support the groups akin to their ideologies. The parliamentary discussions during that time reveal that the intention of the professionalisation of the intelligence apparatus through the establishment of MIT succumbed to the domestic turmoil. The prominent Turkish politician Deniz Baykal from the centre-left Republican People's Party (CHP), who was the minister of energy and natural resources in the previous government, made a candid statement:

> We have heard from the Deputy Prime Minister here that this Government is in cooperation and close contact with some non-governmental organizations that are not part of the official state structure. . . . We have witnessed in the Assembly that the [paramilitary nationalist] commandos were declared as subsidiary organizations to the state. It is now understood that the reports of the National Intelligence Organization are given not only to the commando organizations, but also to the leaders of the political parties who waged jihad [against us].[47]

The turbulence in the domestic politics and the militant polarisation clogged the efforts to reform the national security apparatus by further cementing the public perception that the reason behind the armed violence was the country's own intelligence agency arming the right-wing nationalist groups against the left-wing groups and parties. The MIT, thus, suffered from a pejorative connotation to its public and political perception.

Less than two decades after MIT's foundation, however, the civilian politics failed. Turkey's efforts to establish a consolidated democracy with an effective civilian intelligence was defeated. Indeed, just six months before the 1980 military coup, Bayram Turan Çetin, a member of parliament from the centre-left CHP even confessed: "Dear friends, since we entered the multi-party political life, we, who have been keeping the word 'democracy' on our tongues, no matter which

Blocked modernisation? 175

party is in power, cannot organise our political life without the help of our Armed Forces."[48]

Soon after these remarks the military staged a coup followed by massive purges, detentions and limitation of most of the civil and political liberties. The political parties were banned and politicians were imprisoned, followed by several executions of the political prisoners. Besides causing a landscape change in the Turkish political life with a new constitution introduced by the military rule, a new intelligence law with extended powers was legalised as well. Following the coup, the required intelligence on the domestic political movements within the society, including key actors and their movements, needed to be extracted and coded in a searchable database to decipher patterns against which to deploy surveillance as social sorting.[49] The mass surveillance on society required computation, digital storage and collection capabilities. The civilian governments after the 1980 coup took steps to curb the military's dominance over the intelligence strengthening the National Police forces as opposed to the MIT.

Coding and digitisation

Eavesdropping on the ordinary conversations of citizens and reporting on these citizens was perceived as an intelligence and surveillance activity in the Turkish context. Until as late as 1957, it was not rare for the prime minister to receive Turkish intelligence reports on citizen discussions among themselves during their daily ferry commutes crossing the Istanbul straits.[50] The HUMINT activities perceived any common material, such as a common conversation on a daily commuter ferry, as data for intelligence purposes. This network of human agents spying on its citizens and even reporting simple conversations as intelligence created a deluge of data – large volumes of information written exclusively on paper records. The increasing threat of terrorism during the 1970s required new technologies to step up the speed of information processing. The computation technology used, in terms of both the collection of intelligence and storing it in a searchable database, alleviated the work of Turkish intelligence regarding the processing of surveillance tasks.

A detailed Soviet intelligence report on Turkey indicates that the Turkish intelligence started to use modern technical listening devices with high sensitivity and reliability, which were procured from Western countries. The progressive miniaturisation allowed these devices to be installed in the walls of residential houses and foreign consulates as well as in portable objects of everyday use, such as ashtrays, flower vases and even coffee cups. The listening devices were installed not only in the apartments and business premises of occupants targeted by Turkish intelligence but also in hotels, restaurants, clubs and other public places frequented by foreigners.[51]

Since Turkey could not produce the technology itself, it was imperative for Ankara to acquire the necessary capacity through foreign grants or procurement. For instance, in September 1973, the Turkish government signed an agreement with Motorola Cooperation to supply radio telecommunication devices and other

176 *Egemen Bezci*

additional equipment worth USD 519,615.44 (approx. 3 million USD in today's prices).[52] There was, however, a skill shortage to initiate an automated information management system within MIT. The most tech-savvy personnel were employed in the military intelligence and GES for SIGINT purposes. Therefore, MIT approached Hans-Joachim Postel, the architect of Nachrichtendienstliches Informationssystem (Intelligence Agency Information System, NADIS). Postel visited Ankara in the summer of 1975 to set up the database, which was known as OBIUM (Automated Information Processing Center). In the fall of the same year, MIT's new recruits for the information technology visited Cologne to attend a two-week training on how to use this new system,[53] which worked but was only limited to the intelligence gathered by the MIT. As opposed to the NADIS' intelligence sharing abilities across the departments, OBIUM could not integrate the intelligence produced by the other departments.

Turkish intelligence, however, continued to procure computer parts, particularly 4341 LI processors from IBM in 1980 to enhance the computational power of the data centre within the intelligence organisation.[54] FORTAN H was used as a fast complier with the IBM processors to process data from the various registries in MIT, including remote sensors, or the digitisation of previously hand-coded records. The timing of the procurement of these computer materials coincided with a massive Turkish current account deficit, as the incumbent governments struggled to find resources to service their foreign debts.[55] Intelligence requirements triumphed over economic concerns regarding the importation of these items. The technology itself, however, was not the sole requirement for an effective intelligence analysis. The government bureaucracy, divided into competing factions, did not cooperate with MIT enabling the intelligence organisation to access the basic data such as the population census. Burhanettin Bigalı, the spymaster of MIT, was explicitly raising this concern during the discussions after the 1980 military coup about reforming and establishing the MIT as a state-wide intelligence organisation to guide the national security policy:

> Dear Chief of General Staff, we established [a data centre] within our own structure. This is our information processing center called OBIUM. We do not have access to the State Institute of Statistics Information Processing Center, the Information Processing Center established by the Ministry of Interior, and the Ministry of Justice. If we can connect our Data Processing Center with the data processing centers of other institutions, then we can press a button and get [necessary] information from there. We can do this without going to other ministries. Some of them do not give us this information, they do not show it, they work as a separate unit, a separate section. As such, we are enacting a new law to provide the State's central intelligence agency [MIT] State-wide intelligence; I think that this authority should be given to us.[56]

The intra-agency rivalry was a serious obstacle before establishing an effective data processing structure for the Turkish intelligence community. As Bigali mentioned during the discussions in the National Security Council, the competing

Blocked modernisation? 177

members of the Turkish intelligence community were reluctant to share their data with each other, even when it could prevent a serious terrorist attack, or inform the decision-makers on a critical matter. The civilian leaders had a major distrust for MIT for its past record on not informing them about the military coups. Therefore, after the 1980 military coup, the national police force's intelligence unit had the support of the civilian leaders believing that the police, which was subordinate to the ministry of interior, was more loyal to the civilian leadership. Therefore, the civilian government increased funding and capacity for the police unit during the 1980s to establish its own data centres through the country.[57] In accordance with the civilian endeavours to increase the technical capacities of the ministry of interior, they were also increasing technical cooperation between the Turkish national police and the *Bundeskriminalamt*.[58] Shifting towards a central database management for the intelligence services can create a backlash from the public for privacy considerations and also from other organisations on the basis that a central system would not address specific needs of the local agencies.[59] In the Turkish case, the intra-agency rivalry and the personal feuds were in such high levels that all the efforts on standardisation could be wiped off once the officers who created that database were appointed to another post. Musa Tüzüner, an intelligence officer at the national police forces during the 1980 and 1990s, reflects the scope of the rivalry through his own experience:

> [I] built up an intelligence aquarium, in which I included the bibliographic intelligence data of all terrorist group members within my jurisdiction. I periodically updated the intelligence aquarium not only with verified intelligence but also with raw and unverified intelligence, and shared these data with the unit members in my region as well as with other intelligence agencies' units in the intelligence community. As a result, intelligence community members working together against terrorist threats were able to carry out many successful operations. Ironically, after I had left that jurisdiction for a new post, my former subordinates accused me of having sold the bibliographic intelligence dataset to other intelligence agencies in the Turkish intelligence community and then proceeded to erase the database. For me, such accusations were the price of sharing intelligence. Fears of such outcomes along with a variety of other factors all may play a role in deterring intelligence officials from sharing intelligence.[60]

Intelligence sharing is a necessary part of maintaining an effective electronic database and also processing the intelligence to acquire a comprehensive picture of intelligence per given data. The electronic system created in various national, police and the military agencies further compartmentalised the intelligence limited to their specific units. The intelligence requirements of the end of the Cold War to reveal illicit terrorist and criminal networks included "formal information sharing procedures, and information itself made as 'shareable' as possible."[61] In the Turkish case, however, each intelligence organisation saw the other members of the intelligence community as a rival rather than a partner organisation. The

178 Egemen Bezci

distinct organisational cultures across MIT, police and the military intelligence raised informal barriers before the standardisation and centralisation of the data for intelligence purposes.[62]

The bureaucratic barriers were not the only problem before making the state-wide intelligence knowledge production to guide the national security policies. The turbulent decade prior to the 1980 coup and the MIT's pejorative perception made it difficult for the organisation to recruit the qualified civilian talent who were trained in the information technology. Bigali acknowledged this by asking to increase the monetary and social condition of MIT employees:

> A head of department at TRT [State owned TV and Radio broadcasting agency] receives 82,700 liras, ours receives 79 thousand liras, less than a head of department at TRT. We can't find highly educated staff who can speak a foreign language, some of them out of fear, some of them say "Is it possible to risk my life for 'that amount of money?'"[63]

The lack of human capital to staff the MIT was a deeper problem than monetary compensation. The professionalisation and scientific of the foreign intelligence services such as the CIA depended on a cross-fertilisation of knowledge production between the academia and the intelligence services during the Cold War.[64] The rising number of departments focusing on Russian and Soviet studies in the American universities during the Cold War did not only help CIA to recruit the graduates of these programmes but also opened new channels between the intelligence community and the academy. The Agency even established an academic coordinator position in 1966 to further tap into the scientific knowledge produced in the universities.[65]

This was not the case in the Turkish example. During the Cold War, there was only one department focusing on Russian language and culture which was located at the Ankara University. There was one institution in Istanbul, the Institute for Research on Turkish Culture (Türk Kültürünü Araştırma Enstitüsü, TKAE) that studied the Turkic nations behind the Iron Curtain. Several researchers and professors from this institute cooperated with the MIT.[66] Moreover, some researchers from this institute were sent to the Federal Republic of Germany for training on their employment in the Turkish intelligence organisation. For instance, Enver Altaylı, who was also a research assistant at TKAE, recalls that after he was recruited to the MIT, the organisation sent him to the Federal Republic for a year-long training course in 1967 at the Institut für Ostrecht at the University of Cologne to study under Professor Boris Meissner.[67] The relationship between the TKAE and the intelligence services remains an open question and requires further research. There are, however, indications in the archives that both CIA and MIT might have been collaborating with several figures associated with the institute to engage covert operations in the Turkic nations behind the Iron Curtain.[68]

The technological developments for intelligence collection and process are important factors in creating intelligence knowledge. The Turkish experience shows that the technological developments only cannot make an intelligence organisation effective to undertake its tasks, yet alone establish a nation-wide intelligence knowledge framework. The relationship between the decision-makers and the intelligence agencies, the intra-agency cooperation, status of the human capital and the organisational are all necessary pillars to complementing each other.

Conclusion

Turkish efforts to employ technological developments for the intelligence community demonstrate that intelligence knowledge is not a process by and of itself. The Cold War enabled the Turkish intelligence community to acquire novel computational and communication technology developments from Western allies prior to others within the bureaucracy. These technological developments, however, did not manifest themselves as a professionalisation or scientisation of the Turkish intelligence community. The Turkish experience during the Cold War shows that the regime type, nature of the security threats, civil-military relations and domestic socio-economic conditions are also important factors to consider when analysing how technological development could affect intelligence communities.

At the dawn of the Cold War, Turkey had a HUMINT intensive intelligence organisation that was highly politised and its powers were abused by the incumbent government to suppress their rivals. MIT had a pejorative perception among the civilian leaders and the public alike. The Turkish military had increasing control over the MIT due to its overwhelmingly military dominated organisational structure. The civilian leaders sought to establish MIT as a central and professional civilian intelligence agency, yet this aim was not successful. This tug of war between civilian and military leaders over the MIT hampered the organisation's status to be the centralised intelligence agency accessing the intelligence from various sources.

Apart from the organisational culture, the Turkish intelligence community lacked the home-grown capabilities to produce technological developments for data processing. Thanks to Turkey's NATO membership several of these technological developments were procured from its Western Allies, such as the United States, the United Kingdom and the Federal Republic of Germany. The United States provided the Turkish Army with the SIGINT capacity that was aimed for strategic intelligence collection on the Soviet Union. This advanced capacity, however, was not transferred for the civilian intelligence agency. The SIGINT capacity stayed with the Turkish General Staff even long after the Cold War ended. The Turkish General Staff, due to its internal education system, was able to train its own officers for the SIGINT mission, and some occasions could second them to MIT. MIT, however, lacked the necessary human capital without a strong connection with the Turkish academia. MIT's selected new recruits received training from the Federal Republic of Germany on the data processing methods, but the number of recruits was not adequate to dramatically increase MIT's capacity. MIT, thus, depended on the military's support to fill its human capital gap. The frequent coups and the subsequent purges damaged the organisational culture to establish a permanent scientific intelligence knowledge base. To limit the military's influence

180   *Egemen Bezci*

in the civilian politics over MIT, the subsequent civilian governments during the 1980s empowered the national police in the domestic scene. MIT remained as an organisation that is exclusively associated with intrigues and covert operations, while the police intelligence gradually outpaced the MIT's electronic database capabilities. This, however, further fuelled the rivalry within the bureaucracy and hampered the success of the intelligence community, lowering its public image. Further research is necessary to highlight the extent of the intelligence knowledge applications in the Turkish intelligence community during the Cold War. However, as this chapter has shown, there are important domestic aspects to consider when analysing intelligence knowledge where the technology does not necessary create professionally efficient intelligence communities.

Notes

1 TBMM Tutanakları (Turkish Parliament Minutes, hereafter referred as TBMM): Şevket Mocan, MP Tekirdağ, B:50 O:1, 24 February 1951, 670.
2 Turkish National Statistics Organization, Şehir-Köy Nüfus Oranı, 05 Mart 2021, data. tuik.gov.tr.
3 See Scoblic, "Beacon and Warning"; Best, *National Intelligence Council*.
4 Turkish intelligence studies are in the embryonic stage, with limited independent academic research. There is, however, a slowly growing historiography on this issue. For a detailed description of the Turkish intelligence community during the Cold War, see Bezci, *Turkish Intelligence*, 46–51.
5 Stout and Warner, "Intelligence is as Intelligence Does," 520.
6 Gingeras, *Heroin, Organized Crime, and the Making of Modern Turkey*; Bezci, *Turkish Intelligence and Cold War*.
7 Eisenhower Presidential Library and Archives: White House, Office of the Special Assistant for National Security Affairs: Records, 1952–61: NSC Series Policy Paper Subseries: Box 29: "US Policy on Turkey," 5 October 1960.
8 Esen, "Praetorian Army in Action"; Sarigil, "Civil-Military Relations."
9 Esen, "Praetorian Army in Action," 215.
10 Marrin, "Intelligence Analysis Theory," 828.
11 Herman, *Intelligence Power*, 11.
12 Wark, "Learning to Live with Intelligence," 629.
13 Foucault, *Discipline and Punish*, 29.
14 Marrin, "Intelligence Analysis Theory," 828.
15 TBMM, Ali İhsan Sabis, MP Afyon Karahisar, B:50 O:1, 24 February 1951, 667.
16 Bezci, *Turkish Intelligence and Cold War*, 255.
17 Bezci and Öztan, "Anatomy of the Turkish Emergency State."
18 TBMM, Hilmi Aydınçer, MP Aydın, B:79 O:3, 23 March 1965, 540.
19 Birand, Dündar and Çaplı, *12 Mart: ihtilalin pençesinde demokrasi*.
20 Bezci, *Turkish Intelligence and Cold War*, 157
21 Aldrich, *GCHQ*, 301.
22 Ibid.
23 Bezci, *Turkish Intelligence and Cold War*, 157–158, 164.
24 Hecht, "Introduction," 3.
25 Gerald R. Ford Presidential Library: National Security Council Institutional Files: NSSM 227 – U.S. Security Policy toward Turkey, " September 1975, p. 3
26 Eisenhower Archives, National Security Council Series, Policy Series, Box 29: "NSC 6515/01: Note by the Executive Secretary to the National Security Council on US Policy Toward Turkey, 5 October 1960."

Blocked modernisation? 181

27 Bezci, *Turkish Intelligence and the Cold War*, 158.
28 <www.mit.gov.tr/2937.html>.
29 Kadıoğlu and Bezci, "The Mystery of Intra-Alliance Intelligence," 11.
30 Aldrich, "Strategic Culture as a Constraint."
31 Edwards, *The Closed World*, 2.
32 Gunter, "United States-Turkish Intelligence Liaison Since World War II."
33 Edwards, *The Closed World*, 44.
34 Truman Archives, George McGhee Files Box 1, Memorandum of Conversation between Ambassador McGhee and Foreign Minister Koprulu on 1 February 1952.
35 Bezci, *Turkish Intelligence and the Cold War*, ch. 5.
36 Samim, "The Tragedy of the Turkish Left."
37 Hashimoto and Bezci, "Do the Kurds Have 'No Friends but the Mountains'."
38 Holmes, *Social Unrest and American Military Bases*.
39 Aldrich, *GCHQ*, 302.
40 Goschler, "Intelligence, Mistrust and Transparency."
41 BCA: 311–8–19: "Prolonging the Electronic Intelligence Cooperation between Turkey and the United Kingdom in Turkey," 18 February 1974.
42 TBMM, İhsan Ataöv, MP Antalya, B:79 O:3, 23 March 1965, 544.
43 CIA-RDP85S00316R000200160005–8: Turkey: Threat of Resurgent Terrorism, An Intelligence Assessment, September 1984.
44 Sayari, "Political Violence and Terrorism in Turkey"; decade spanning 1975 and 1984 also witnessed the ASALA attacks on Turkish targets, including the assasinations of Turkish diplomats abroad. Concurrently with these attacks MIT engaged in covert operations against ASALA (Armenian Secret Army for the Liberation of Armenia) terrorism, see: Bezci, "Turkish Diplomatic Security."
45 Puyvelde, Coulthart and Hossain, "Beyond the Buzzword."
46 Byman, "The Intelligence War on Terrorism," 849.
47 TBMM, Deniz Baykan, MP Antalya, B:99 O:2, 3 July 1975, 496.
48 TBMM, Bayram Turan Cetin, MP Bolu, B:50 O:1, 22 February 1980, 560 .
49 Lyon, ed., *Surveillance as Social Sorting: Privacy, Risk, and Digital Discrimination*.
50 BCA: 68.429.15: Başbakanlık Özel Kalem Müdürlüğü, İstihbarat Raporu, 29 May 1957.
51 Archiwum Instytutu Pamięci Narodowej, Warsaw, AIPN: 02386/130: Files on Turkish Intelligence Service: 66: Intelligence situation in Turkey: 1973–1984.
52 BCA: 312–18–19, "Electronic Devices to be Imported for the National Intelligence Agency," 9 April 1974.
53 Postel, *So war es*, 145. Author would like to thank Professor Rüdiger Bergien for sharing this information.
54 BCA: 389–47–1, "Import Tax Waiver for the Turkish National Intelligence Agency to Procure Necessary Airplane Parts, and Computer Equipment," 28 February 1980.
55 Barkey, "Crises of the Turkish Political Economy," 47–63.
56 TBMM:M. G. Konseyi B: 177 O: 1, 24 October 1983.
57 Archiwum Instytutu Pamięci Narodowej, Warsaw, AIPN: 02386/130: Files on Turkish Intelligence Service: 66: Intelligence situation in Turkey: 1973–1984.
58 BCA: 30–18–1–2, "The delegation headed by Saffet Arıkan Beduk was sent to the Federal Germany, representing the Government of the Republic of Turkey, between 27 June and 3 July 1985, to discuss the cooperation between the Turkish-German Police Organization," 26 June 1985
59 Bergien, "»Big Data« als Vision," 269.
60 Tüzüner, "Insights of Intelligence Insiders," 53.
61 Jones, "Intelligence Reform," 385.
62 Tüzüner, "Insights of Intelligence Insiders," 55.
63 TBMM:M. G. Konseyi B: 177 O: 1, 24 October 1983
64 See Engerman, *Know your Enemy*; Price, *Cold War Anthropology*.
65 Hulnick, "CIA's Relations with Academia."

182 *Egemen Bezci*

66 Aytürk, "The Flagship Institution of Cold War Turcology."
67 Interview with Enver Altaylı by Turkish journalists in 1999. Between minutes 10 and 12, he talks about his training with Professor Boris Meissner in the Federal Republic, <www.youtube.com/watch?v=BX_Z34WaUrQ>
68 Library of Congress: Archibald Roosevelt Paper (CIA Station chief in Istanbul), Box1: Personal Diary: Note on Zeki Velidi Togan, circa. 1952.

Bibliography

Aldrich, R. 2010. *GCHQ: The Uncensored Story of Britain's Most Secret Intelligence Agency*. HarperCollins: London.

Aldrich, R. 2017. "Strategic Culture as a Constraint: Intelligence Analysis, Memory and Organizational Learning in the Social Sciences and History." *Intelligence and National Security* 32, no. 5: 625–635.

Aytürk, İ. 2017. "The Flagship Institution of Cold War Turcology. Türk Kültürünü Araştırma Enstitüsü, 1961–1980." *European Journal of Turkish Studies. Social Sciences on Contemporary Turkey* 24: 1–20.

Barkey, H. 1984. "Crises of the Turkish Political Economy: 1960–1980." In *Modern Turkey: Continuity and Change*, ed. A. Evin, 47–63. Wiesbaden: Verlag für Sozialwissenschaften.

Bergien, R. 2017. "'Big Data' als Vision. Computereinführung und Organisationswandel in BKA und Staatssicherheit (1967–1989)." *Zeithistorische Forschungen* 14, no. 2: 258–285.

Best, R. A. 2009. *National Intelligence Council: Issues and Options for Congress*. Washington, DC: Congressional Research Service.

Bezci, E. 2019. "Turkish Diplomatic Security." In *Diplomatic Security: A Comparative Analysis*, ed. E. Cusumano and C. Kinsey, 164–179. Stanford, CA: Stanford University Press.

Bezci, E. 2019. *Turkish Intelligence and the Cold War: The Turkish Secret Service, the US and the UK*. London: Bloomsbury Publishing.

Bezci, E. B., and Öztan, G. G. 2016. "Anatomy of the Turkish Emergency State: A Continuous Reflection of Turkish Raison d'état between 1980 and 2002." *Middle East Critique* 25, no. 2: 163–179.

Birand, M. A., Dündar, C., and Çaplı, B. 2008. *12 Mart: ihtilalin pençesinde demokrasi*. Ankara: İmge Kitabevi.

Byman, D. 2014. "The Intelligence War on Terrorism." *Intelligence and National Security* 29, no. 6: 837–863.

Edwards, P. N. 1996. *The Closed World: Computers and the Politics of Discourse in Cold War America*. Boston: MIT Press.

Engerman, D. C. 2009. *Know Your Enemy: The Rise and Fall of America's Soviet Experts*. Oxford: Oxford University Press.

Esen, B. 2021. "Praetorian Army in Action: A Critical Assessment of Civil–Military Relations in Turkey." *Armed Forces & Society* 47, no. 1: 201–222.

Foucault, M. 1978. *Discipline and Punish: The Birth of the Prison*. New York: Vintage House.

Gingeras, R. 2014. *Heroin, Organized Crime, and the Making of Modern Turkey*. Oxford: Oxford University Press, 2014.

Goschler, C. 2019. "Intelligence, Mistrust and Transparency: A Case Study of the German Office for the Protection of the Constitution." In *Contested Transparencies, Social*

Movements and the Public Sphere, ed. D. Owetschkin and S. Berger, 153–171. London: Palgrave Macmillan.

Gunter, M. 2003. "United States-Turkish Intelligence Liaison Since World War II." *Journal of Intelligence History* 3, no. 1: 33–46.

Hashimoto, C., and Bezci, E. 2016. "Do the Kurds Have 'No Friends but the Mountains'? Turkey's Secret War against Communists, Soviets and the Kurds." *Middle Eastern Studies* 52, no. 4: 640–655.

Hecht, G. 2011. "Introduction." In *Entangled Geographies: Empire and Technopolitics in the Global Cold War*, ed. G. Hecht, 1–12. Cambridge and London: MIT Press.

Herman, M. 1996. *Intelligence Power in Peace and War*. Cambridge: Cambridge University Press.

Holmes, A. A. 2014. *Social Unrest and American Military Bases in Turkey and Germany Since 1945*. Cambridge: Cambridge University Press.

Hulnick, A. S. 1986. "CIA's Relations with Academia: Symbiosis Not Psychosis." *International Journal of Intelligence and Counter Intelligence* 1, no. 4: 41–50.

Jones, C. 2007. "Intelligence Reform: The Logic of Information Sharing." *Intelligence and National Security* 22, no. 3: 384–401.

Kadıoğlu, A. I., and Bezci, E. 2020. "The Mystery of Intra-alliance Intelligence: Turkey's Covert Operations in the Cyprus Conflict." *Middle Eastern Studies* 56, no. 4: 638–652.

Lyon, D., ed. 2003. *Surveillance as Social Sorting: Privacy, Risk, and Digital Discrimination*. London: Routledge.

Marrin, S. 2007. "Intelligence Analysis Theory: Explaining and Predicting Analytic Responsibilities." *Intelligence and National Security* 22, no. 6: 828.

Postel, H. 1999. *So war es . . . Informationstechnologie im Verfassungsschutz 1955–1980*. Meckenheim: Warlich.

Price, D. H. 2016. *Cold War Anthropology: The CIA, the Pentagon, and the Growth of Dual Use Anthropology*. Durham: Duke University Press.

Samim, A. 1981. "The Tragedy of the Turkish Left." *New Left Review* 126, no. 1: 60–85.

Sarigil, Z. 2011. "Civil-Military Relations Beyond Dichotomy: With Special Reference to Turkey." *Turkish Studies* 12, no. 2: 265–278.

Sayari, S. 2010. "Political Violence and Terrorism in Turkey, 1976–80: A Retrospective Analysis." *Terrorism and Political Violence* 22, no. 2: 198–215.

Scoblic, J. P. 2018. "Beacon and Warning: Sherman Kent, Scientific Hubris, and the CIA's Office of National Estimates (August 2018)." *Texas National Security Review*: 99–117.

Stout, M., and Warner, M. 2018. "Intelligence is as Intelligence Does." *Intelligence and National Security* 33, no. 4: 517–526.

Tüzüner, M. 2014. "Insights of Intelligence Insiders on (Non-) Sharing Intelligence Behaviors." *All Azimuth: A Journal of Foreign Policy and Peace* 3, no. 2: 51–66.

Ülman, A. H., and Tachau, F. 1965. "Turkish Politics: The Attempt to Reconcile Rapid Modernization with Democracy." *The Middle East Journal*: 153–168.

Van den Berg, M. A. 2014. *The Intelligence Regime in South Africa (1994–2014): An Analytical Perspective*. Unpublished thesis. Potchefstroom: North-West University.

Van Puyvelde, D., Coulthart, S., and Hossain, M. S. 2017. "Beyond the Buzzword: Big Data and National Security Decision-Making." *International Affairs* 93, no. 6: 1397–1416.

Warhola, J. W., and Bezci, E. B. 2010. "Religion and State in Contemporary Turkey: Recent Developments in Laiklik." *Journal of Church and State* 52, no. 3: 427–453.

Wark, W. 2019. "Learning to Live with Intelligence." In *Secret Intelligence: A Reader*, 2nd edition, ed. C. Andrew, R. J. Aldrich, and W. K. Wark. New York: Routledge.

9 Solid modernity

Data storage and information circuits in the communist security police in Poland

Franciszek Dąbrowski

Introduction

Communist secret police forces faced a specific dilemma in their role as information processors and knowledge producers. On the one hand, their access to all forms of potentially relevant information was virtually unlimited and the flow of information received on a daily basis was almost endless. On the other hand, their efforts to actually make use of and analyse the incoming data were impeded by their over-centralisation, a lack of analytic capacities and a certain preference for actively fighting their perceived enemy, resulting in the subordination of bureaucratic systems to the needs of field work. Accordingly, some scholars perceive communist secret police organisations as "blind data hydra."[1] But does this image correspond to the secret police's information processing practices? Were the Eastern services indeed fundamentally ineffective in their information processing – or did they succeed in catching up with the development of Western services, to some extent? Is it possible to identify a particular path of communist secret police forces into the information age, even though this path was cut short by the collapse of the state Socialist regimes in 1989–91?

The history of information processing by the Polish communist security police (Służba Bezpieczeństwa, SB) provides an opportunity to approach answers to these questions. The SB was established in the fall of 1956 within the Ministry of Internal Affairs (Ministerstwo Spraw Wewnętrznych, MSW), as the successor organisation to the notorious Security Department (Urząd Bezpieczeństwa, UB, recte: Ministerstwo Bezpieczeństwa Publicznego, MBP 1945–1954, and Komitet do spraw Bezpieczeństwa Publicznego, KdsBP, 1954–1956).[2] The SB was, in a sense, a state security service "hidden" within the MSW. Until 1990, the SB was responsible for foreign intelligence and counterintelligence, as well as combating and prosecuting anti-communist and "anti-state" activities, and for monitoring state and society, with a staff of nearly 25,000 full-time employees and approximately 90,000 informants at the height of its activities in the 1980s.[3] In order to fulfil these tasks, the SB had to process large quantities of information on a daily basis. The means it developed to succeed in this field are quite telling not only for secret police historiography in particular but also for a history of secret knowledge production in general.

DOI: 10.4324/9781003147329-10

Solid modernity 185

The following chapter sketches out general information concerning the systems and databases launched by the MSW and its subordinate units. Furthermore, it points to the aims of such modernisation and the terms of its advancement. The aim is to describe the general features and tools of the system of information storage as well as the information circuit system in the SB between the 1950s and 1980s. Moreover, the chapter analyses the role and function of the systems of the communist dictatorship within the security police that emerged from the visible tension between the general properties of data management and special secrecy requirements. In addition, it analyses the development of electronic systems of data storage and indexing as well as information circuits and evaluation as an outcome of the modernisation of methods used, and measures taken by the security police.

Traditionally, communist secret police organisations appear mostly as organs of repression and safeguarding of power and were in charge of conducting "total surveillance" and perpetrating violence. Yet their role as information processors and knowledge producers has only recently come into focus in historiography.[4] Until now, only basic research has been undertaken with regard to information processing by the Polish communist secret police in the form of organisational histories as well as through collecting and publishing relevant source materials.[5] Comparative perspectives between communist secret police organisations regarding the archiving and evaluation of data are of increasing importance to historiography. In the case of SB information proceedings, the comparison with both the East German state security service[6] and with the Czechoslovak communist secret police[7] appears especially promising.

In this chapter, first the structures and practices of the Polish secret police's information processing will be described as they emerged in the second half of the 1940s and partly continued to guide their actions until 1989/90. Second, this chapter will sketch the content and functioning of the SB's electronic information systems, which began to emerge in the late 1960s. In a last step, discussion will concern the extent to which digitisation brought efficiency gains to the Polish secret police, possibly transforming it into an even more effective surveillance organ, and also where the limits of these efficiency gains lay.

Card indexes and registries inside and outside Bureau "C" of the Ministry of Internal Affairs

The registration, evaluation and storage of information as well as measures to keep information secret were core activities of communist Poland's security police. Particularly, the main registry and archive branch, *Biuro "C" MSW* (Bureau "C"),[8] can be considered to be the SB's inner circuit of information. It must be distinguished from the information evaluation units that were part of the operative branches and acted independently from the registry and archival system. The evaluation of the information gathered during so-called operative cases, which was the jargon commonly used in Soviet-style intelligence agencies[9] to describe ongoing investigations against "undesirable" persons or those under suspicion, was long considered

186   *Franciszek Dąbrowski*

a mere part of the reporting procedure in a chain of command. This means that, in contrast to contemporary Western intelligence standards, the procurement and evaluation of information was not separated. Only with the launch of the electronic evaluation systems (and the need to organise and handle the tools and work structure in the units) in the second half of the 1970s did changes occur in this respect. However, even then, those evaluation systems were handled in the staff sub-units of the security police.

The reporting system itself was based on a specified scheme. This included "situation information" (sometimes also "[public] moods information" – especially that drawn from randomly and clandestinely opened letters), and information concerning the operative branches' ongoing investigations and activities. Several regulations about the exchange of data formed a system of inner control as well as a hierarchy of data circulation and operative cases. The reporting system, which served to determine the efficiency of particular operations, was an important factor in the activity of the security service not only at its lowest level but also of the security service as a whole. It contributed to the construction of a vast system of social control over Polish society.

The Bureau "C" MSW system also contained the central address registry – except for the registries of operative cases – and was interconnected with local personal identity card registries. Personal identity cards were compulsory as were the registration of permanent and temporary addresses.[10] Considering that all Polish citizens' employee records were also accessible to the security service (although not as easily because the resources were run by the MSW and its local branches), the range of data available about large parts of the population was significant and contributed to the totalitarian character of the system.

The general registration proceedings included data concerning people, objects or facts relevant to ongoing operative processes. The main card indexes on both operative cases and archived records were the subject of contrasting rationalities. On the one hand, the card indexes were designed to also keep the registered data secret internally. On the other hand, they should offer quick access to the data, even if only for authorised parties. The contradiction between both aims should be overcome by setting a hierarchy of access to the data through a so-called "coordination" procedure. The operative unit was a "registration host" that decided on the disclosure of information to the other units. The coordination procedures were also designed to exclude possible double registration of persons of interest by different units of the security apparatus.[11] However, routine as well as the most advanced operative cases required a number of cross-checks in several resources.[12] The application of the inner secrecy rule as well as the coordination procedure trod a very difficult path in the first decades of the Communist security police in Poland. The initial separation of the card indexes between local and central, and the apparent poor exchange of data led, for example, to situations whereby several units registered and ran case files concerning the same person (see below).

The organisational culture of the communist secret police was based – among other features – on pedantic reporting and registering of the data collected. In the Polish communist secret police apparatus, several local or specialised card

Solid modernity 187

indexes and registries had been established as early as in the 1940s. Names which "came through" (meaning "were mentioned in," to use secret service jargon) in the minutes of interrogations were meticulously indexed and registered in a special card index of names.[13] The official compulsion to register as much data as possible resulted in further overloading of the card indexes. The consequence of this compulsion to record everything was remembered by a functionary of the foreign intelligence branch of the MBP (Ministerstwo Bezpieczeństwa Publicznego, Ministry of Public Security)[14] in the 1950s:

> [A]lmost everything that looked suitable was indexed, and literally everything was written in capital letters. Just so that no name was omitted. . . . The card indexes then (it was not only the ignorance about the matter in hand, but frequently also ignorance of the language) indexed such names as Winston Spencer Churchill, Josip Broz Tito, Harry Truman, Charles Andre de Gaulle, and even *Klavier-spiel* [*sic:* German for "piano playing"], because, the person indexing could not imagine that there are languages where every noun is written with a capital letter. . . . Every one of those cryptonyms and pseudonyms [mentioned in operative reports] were to be decoded and put into the card index . . . [that] swelled to the enormous size, and instead of being helpful, it became a bane for the work.[15]

In addition to this self-inflicted information overload, the culture of inner secrecy also burdened the activities, not least in combination with a relatively poor administrative and legal culture in the 1940s and 1950s[16] as well as the separation of data registered in local and central registries (established by instructions issued in 1948):[17] contemporaries[18] observed duplicate operative cases and information chaos from the start. The organisational answer was an increasing simplification and centralisation of data handling procedures, as seen in the sequence of changes in the normative acts concerning registration of operative processes, relevant case files and data in the period from 1948 to 1962.

The most important changes were introduced in 1955 and from 1960 to 1962. The need to improve the systemic faults of the system set up in 1948 – especially the separation of data registered in local and central card indexes – was at the heart of the concepts of system changes that emerged in 1954/1955. Initially, these changes were proposed as part of a reform of the whole Ministry of Public Security (MBP), whose functions after its dissolution were ultimately partly taken over by the MSW. The then acting director of Department II of the MBP, Michał Taboryski, was a member of the committee that drew up the plan.[19] Taboryski had already presented a blueprint for the reorganisation of his branch in June 1954 (prepared by his close associate, Antonina Taube).[20] Characteristically, the expertise of the Soviet adviser in Department II, Colonel Zakharov, impacted the next blueprints made in 1954/1955 to a significant extent.[21] A series of instructions for operative processes,[22] registration and archiving[23] introduced a more centralised (however internally divided) system. However, it soon became obvious that the card indexes were not only growing enormously in size but that they were also overloaded

188   *Franciszek Dąbrowski*

with "unconfirmed" data (i.e. entered without links to documentation), redundant, "operationally outdated" and so on. That was the reason for updating the card indexes (in fact, withdrawal of whole categories of entries from the card index) ordered in June 1955 and conducted further in 1956.[24]

Yet, the need to enhance information processing efficiency endured. The next step in centralising the archive and registration system was made by a series of instructions and guidelines for the registry issued from June to October 1960.[25] They resulted in an uniform central operative card index and registration tools, and a separate centralised card index of informants, agents and other people who were cooperating. Another change occurred in 1962, when the card indexes of informants were merged into a central card index. Simultaneously, a separation of data between the statistical card indexes and operative information card indexes was introduced.[26] The system of separating operative and personal data in centralised card indexes (following the GDR pattern) was abandoned in 1972, when the next general reform of the registration system in the MSW occurred.[27] What is worth noting is that the registry reform of 1972 followed the logic of the inner secrecy of the operative work and aimed to secure the secrecy of data in paper card indexes. The new challenges posed by electronic registries and databases were not addressed by this reform.[28]

The general structure of Bureau "C" registry from the 1960s contained several main card indexes: the so-called statistics card index contained information about active operative procedures; the "general information card index" (*kartoteka ogól-noinformacyjna*, KOI) contained entries with personal data of persons of interest in active or archived case files; the so-called thematic card index indexed several "thematic" categories in the archived case files, and a number of auxiliary card indexes, for example, Catholic priests and parishes. The general population address card index and those of the criminal police, also governed by Bureau "C," complemented the system.

The traditional paper-based card indexes were unsuitable as a multi-search tool. To access the required information, it was necessary to arrange the number of so-called thematic auxiliary card indexes according to address, occupation, known foreign languages and so on. The separation of the structures responsible for operative activities and registry resources (specific card indexes, and archived collections of the specific categories of case files, for example) meant that every new operative process was accompanied by the establishment of a new indexing tool. This took place, for example, when the system for the surveillance of priests was launched in 1963[29] and when the duty to register "hostile acts" was introduced in the same year.[30] Likewise, the establishment of the SOUD system in 1977, that is the joint data repository of Communist foreign intelligence services in Moscow, reflected new joint efforts by the Eastern Bloc secret police agencies in fighting their "external enemies."[31]

The Bureau "C" registries played a central role in the circuit of information concerning operative processes in the Ministry of Internal Affairs. However, there were a number of separate card indexes in the other MSW units that met the specific needs of their activities, ultimately producing a data maze. The passport card indexes and PNG (*persona non grata*) index, as well as the passport files repository were run by the passport control office. The "W" branch, that is postal censorship (also a unit of the security service), ran its own indexes including addresses of people under surveillance (domestic and abroad), seized letters, commissioned or self-performed checks and "W documents" (i.e. seized or copied letters) passed to the operative units of the SB.[32] The "B" branch, that is surveillance unit, ran three card indexes: of people, addresses and cars of operative interest.[33] The technical-operative branch ("T") also kept some records of activities.[34] The operative registry and archive of the Ministry of Internal Affairs foreign intelligence (*Departament I MSW*) were separated from the general operative registry and archive in Bureau "C," mainly because of the security measures: the sources and operations abroad, means of contact and so on were to be kept in strict secrecy.

The connection between the Bureau "C" registries and the parallel resources of MSW Department I was established by the procedure of registering ("securing") the people affected in the general information operative card index of Bureau "C."[35] Department I's registry was smaller than Bureau "C's" and comprised of a general personal operative card index (with no indications of the character of the operative interest connected to the person affected), an object card index, a registry log, an archival log, an operative archive (of closed case files), and a personal accounts card index (listing the active case files assigned to the case officers). The Department I information analysis unit ran its own system to separate the information processed. The operative information was arranged according to countries of origin and matters involved in a so-called parole order (Polish: *hasłownik*), which enabled quick sorting and extraction of the information needed.[36] The scheme of information processing was then – together with the registry resources – transferred into and merged with the EPIW electronic system and added to several software devices to enhance the analysis of the "operative situation."

The whole system, combined with the powers of the security police (formal, as well as informal), made a powerful tool with which to control society. The communist dictatorship was not a Benthamian "panopticon" because for practical reasons the system could not observe all its citizens (and the generally high level of social discontent and distrust did not enable "citizen's habits of self-control" to be built). However, state data-harvesting was very wide, and state control of social movement was very high. This state of affairs built tension between citizens, who had limited possibilities for career progression without state and party approval, and the state apparatus, with its oppressive daily routine and special units that were able to focus on selected individuals and groups. Of course, there were some internal obstacles to the "transparency" of society for the state apparatus; some caused by systemic deficiencies (such as the lack of personal indexes of land and mortgage registers that therefore did not allow the tracking of all the property of people under surveillance, for example), or poor professional practice, and data overflow. As an anecdotal reference, the passage from the memoirs of Marek Kazimierz Barański (the renowned medievalist and opposition activist) could be mentioned here:

A year after release from internment [in 1982], and more than ten years after our wedding, at least we have obtained our own flat. . . . We registered the

190   *Franciszek Dąbrowski*

change of address according to the law, but in Mostowskis' Palace [Warsaw's SB headquarters] it was somehow overlooked. The summons to the Palace were still sent to the old address. . . . It lasted for almost two years. Finally, they realised that I had moved, and the summons was sent to the proper address. This time I had to go. I met the same UB functionary as always and congratulated him on the efficiency of the SB activity, since after two years they had noticed that I had changed addresses. The UB man lost countenance a bit but said: "we know everything about you. You are going to Switzerland, and we do not have anything against it. You already have the passport." I replied that I was surprised because I had not applied for any passport. This time the UB-man was surprised. . . . This meeting convinced me that our omniscient UB was tragically uninformed, since they could not find me for so long, although I was not hiding.[37]

The SB unit responsible for the invigilation of Barański apparently did not notice his change of address immediately and eventually checked the address data after a significant (almost two year) delay; they also did not notice his withdrawal of his passport application. The poor professional practice may also be seen here as a lack of the integration of data resources: the case officer did not regularly check the data of the person under surveillance in the address card index, and changes to addresses and passport applications were not reported to the relevant operative unit.

Introducing electronic information systems

The structural history of units that dealt with EDP in the Ministry of Internal Affairs offers a specific insight into the character and usage of secret police data resources and systems. In 1969, a separate unit in the MSW, the Centre of Electronic Data Processing (Ośrodek Elektronicznego Przetwarzania Informacji, OEPI) was established and tasked with the introduction of digital technologies. The OEPI was associated with the ministry's technical-operative devices construction centre Special Technology Works (Zakład Techniki Specjalnej, ZTS). The aims and use of devices and systems developed in OEPI and ZTS were chosen by interested parties, that is the ministry's relevant units. OEPI became independent from the technical-operative devices branch Informatics Centre of Ministry (Ośrodek Informatyki MSW, OI MSW) in 1971 and was integrated into the Information Technology Bureau (Biuro Informatyki) department of the MSW in 1973. In 1980, it was finally merged with SB's Bureau "C" MSW (operative registry and archives).[38] The IT office, the *Biuro Informatyki*, also became a part of the SB, as well as three sections that governed the electronic registry system ZSKO (Zintegrowany System Kartotek Operacyjnych, Integrated System of the Operative Card Indexes) and information evaluation systems.[39] Hence, there was a general tendency to transfer formerly separate research and technical units within the MSW to the ministry's secret police branch, the SB.

The first computers used were domestically produced ZAM-41 and AMC-1 models. By 1989, a remarkable range of hardware systems had been added, some

Solid modernity 191

procured from the West and some from the Soviet Bloc. From the late 1960s onwards, Bureau "C" saw the emergence of the electronic data systems as an opportunity to improve its work even more as the number of the card registration records (mainly concerning the active operational proceedings and recently archived files) to be entered into the system exceeded two million. In the course of the 1970s, a plan for the general electronic index of the operative registrations emerged. The ZSKO, which was created for that purpose, was intended to mirror the general information card index (Kartoteka Ogólnoinformacyjna, KOI).

The structure of the ZSKO and its range of functions evolved continuously. The initial 1970 blueprint contained a two-tier structure that consisted of the personal index and an operative database (the latter appears to have been abandoned in the 1970s). The next step was a plan to build a cluster comprising several elements: the database of personal information and information concerning registered operative processes (Centralny Rejestr Osób i Spraw, CROS) which was reactivated in 1979; the module for reporting to the ministry's leadership (System Informacji Kierownictwa)[40] – conceived of as a search engine and analysis device as well as an electronic channel for command and reporting; and several thematic subsystems (i.e. systems and databases indexing specialised operative information).[41] However, only the database mirroring the general operative card index (KOI) was actually launched.[42] The end of the 1980s saw another new development concept for the ZSKO – this time supposedly in response to practical experiences. The planned update would have been a cluster of the systems, integrating the operative registry, thematic information systems of operative and technical-operative units, and a registry recognition system for the analysis of registered data.[43] However, the transition to democracy caused the system to be scrapped in 1989/90, and only some remains of its database were salvaged. The blueprint never appears to have been implemented.

The plans for the development of the ZSKO aimed to be a high-profile tool for MSW activities: The intended reporting module for the ministry's leadership and the proposed integration with the computerised evaluation of information from operative units of SB and with the "B" (surveillance) unit registry would have formed powerful machinery. It would have enabled the security police to check and examine almost every piece of information gathered on an unprecedented range. However, these ambitious plans for creating a reporting module and interconnecting the ZSKO with other systems were never achieved. Similarly, the ZSKO never managed to contain every record from general operative card indexes. Only the most important data concerning active operative processes and persons of interest were entered into the system.[44]

In the end, the ZSKO, despite all the planned stages of expansion, was nothing more than an electronic index. It stood in clear continuity with paper indexes of the 1940s, 1950s and 1960s. In comparison, the foreign intelligence branch of the Ministry of Internal Affairs, Department I, developed a significantly more elaborate electronic system of data circulation and evaluation.[45] The EPI (or EPIW) (Elektroniczne Przetwarzanie Informacji [Wywiadowczej], Electronic [Intelligence] Data Processing) system was in fact a cluster of several systems, databases and

192 *Franciszek Dąbrowski*

programmes, which had been continuously improved upon and expanded since 1978.[46] The EPIW was a functional equivalent of the East German SIRA system;[47] the former's general scheme of processing and information channelling was outlined by Władysław Bułhak.[48] However, description of the system architecture still awaits detailed study.

EPIW comprised the registries of persons and operational procedures as well as information gathered. It included information evaluation and circulation tools, as well as many other subsystems and minor databases. The operative information evaluation and circulation subsystem mirrored the existing manual system (that was already quite efficient). The integrated approach to the registration of the operative processes, persons, files, information and other data enabled the multilevel evaluation of data, its sources, the efficiency of its own structures and possible disinformation attempts. Due to the integrated approach, the EPIW system could be used in some respect as a system for the whole Ministry of Internal Affairs – at least according to a declaration that was presumably made by Colonel Stefan Paluch. He was the head of the crew preparing the EPIW system, and in 1977 he became the deputy head of the XVIII division in the *Departament I* MSW, which governed the operative registry and archive of the department as well as managing its electronic system. Paluch was an engineer rather than a manager, and it can be presumed that he concerned himself with the system launch in terms of its efficiency and achievable functions while neglecting the importance of organisational culture; the prevailing culture of "inner secrecy."[49] The latter would have ruled out the possibility of using a system designed for foreign intelligence information to be used for domestic surveillance and operative practice.[50]

While EPIW was programmed to evaluate secret information gained from abroad, domestic operative information evaluation systems were also developed. In the second half of the 1970s, the ESFAZA system (Elektroniczny System Ewidencji Faktów-Zagrożeń – used in Department III MSW from 1974 to 1985),[51] ESEZO (Elektroniczny System Ewidencji Zainteresowań Operacyjnych; introduced in Departments III, IV, V, and VI MSW gradually from 1981),[52] EZOP (Automatyczny System Ewidencjonowania Zainteresowań Operacyjnych), used as a pilot system in Department IV MSW in 1970s), ESPIN (used in Department II MSW) and the information system of the surveillance branch (*Biuro "B"* MSW, Bureau "B")[53] were launched successively.[54] The general working feature of those systems was registering every single piece of operative information (from informants' reports, postal surveillance, etc.) and marking the people and events mentioned in them with codes, which were entered into the system, and where the data registered could be analysed as a whole in the range of the operative line. However, the ESFAZA system followed the logic of registration and reporting of categorised "facts and threats." It was therefore not adapted to the general logic of the operative cases that affected people or objects – as it quickly appeared to be only partially efficient.[55] Consequently, the ESFAZA system and the pilot EZOP-IV system were replaced by clones of the ESEZO system – simpler and better adapted to the operative praxis. ESEZO system clones worked separately in the operative departments of the ministry, gathering information from its units

Solid modernity 193

and territorial branches ("pillars"). The integration of the operative information evaluation systems (as planned in the EZOP and ESEZO systems) with ZSKO (i.e. with MSW general registry) was planned, but apparently never achieved.[56]

In addition to information evaluation and analysis, two other information systems that emerged in the 1970s were aimed primarily at the surveillance of the movements of the Polish people: SERP (System Ewidencji Ruchu Paszportowego, the Registration System of Border Movement) and EZOP, the electronic registration system of travel bans for Polish citizens. Both were based on the large data resources run by the MSW passport control branch that together with its cooperating institutions and border guard troops (Wojska Ochrony Pogranicza, WOP) was one of the major tools of communist security and social policy, as Dariusz Stola showed in his study.[57] The passport branch's data collection consisted of citizens' passport applications, a vast passport card index, the PNG index and even a card index of Polish citizens who were barred from returning to Poland.

The comprehensive use of both systems thus points to the central importance that control over identity and travel documents had for communist regimes. The electronic recording of passport and identity card data in particular and of biographical data in general was considered an effective means of combating Western espionage, as well as subversive activities and escape attempts. Therefore, in the 1970s the Polish People's Republic developed its own general population database, which was known under the acronym PESEL. It combined data from address card indexes and registration offices. PESEL, running on West German Siemens mainframes (that were delivered despite the COCOM embargo), secured control over the data of the whole Polish population and provided a unique identification number for every individual in the country. However, the PESEL system was not only the general population database. It was planned that it should contain several subsystems to store data concerning university graduates (MAGISTER), people who had been decorated by the state (SEOP), medical personnel (SEKAMED) and anyone who had been arrested and/or sentenced (SESTA).[58] The additional launch of SERP (System Ewidencji Ruchu Paszportowego, the system of the border movement registration integrated with PESEL) was intended to improve control over border movement. The planned interconnection of PESEL and ZSKO was to provide the PESEL identification numbers to the MSW electronic operative registry.[59]

It is worth stating that in all the aforementioned systems the shift from the "manual" card indexes to the electronic systems did not take place immediately. The transfer of data was never completed in the case of ZSKO (and apparently in other cases too), and the maintenance of the card index system was upheld in parallel to the electronic one. The planned operative information evaluation systems were not burdened with the entry of "historical" data. Their aim was to deal with the current flow of information to be processed (though on an enormous scale); that resulted in the relatively swift launch of those systems such as the flawed ESFAZA, and then the ESEZO. However, it must be stressed that information evaluation systems still enabled the processing of the operative data on an unpreceded scale. They constituted remarkable progress in the matter of data processing, incomparable to previous reporting systems.

194   *Franciszek Dąbrowski*

The limitations of EDP use by the Polish communist security police (SB)

Up to this point, the digitisation of data resources in Polish security policy from the late 1960s onwards can be structured into four parallel processes. An early focus of activity was the digitisation of registration resources, namely in the shape of the ZSKO, a process intended to enhance the speed and efficiency of internal communication. Secondly, advanced reporting and information evaluation systems were developed – EPIW, ESFAZA and ESEZO – which were, thirdly, intended to become integrated with the ZSKO registration system. Finally, the security police started to use large population data resources – most prominently, the PESEL system – that had become digitised in the context of general administrative/political aims; these resources were integrated with the SB operative information systems to some extent.

The implementation of the electronic devices and systems was intended to enable the quick and comprehensive evaluation of the data gathered. As difficult as it is to judge in retrospect how effective these technical systems were, we can assume that these goals were achieved to a certain extent. The operative registry and archive tools were already structured to provide a statistical preview of security police activities. The electronic databases enabled speedy and efficient cross-checks (which were very troublesome using traditional paper card indexes). Moreover, progress was made in operative information gathering and evaluation; the systems developed in operative units enabled the security police to evaluate and analyse data and statistics it had not had access to prior to computerisation. While the simple digitisation of registries had already enhanced SB activities, the planned integration of systems would have meant a significant leap in the efficiency of data processing.

However, the history of digitisation of the communist security police in Poland is far from a success story. The systems were built up over a very prolonged period and their concepts continuously changed. The example of the changing designs of ZSKO system, as summarised above, is of significant weight here.[60] The main operative and technical-operative units of the MSW used separate electronic systems of operative data evaluation (and apparently with little chance of being interoperative); the ESFAZA system was used despite its known deficiencies, and so on and so forth.[61] One of the reasons for the use of separate operative data processing systems (and thus separation of operative data resources) was the prevailing culture of inner secrecy. This culture demanded that the information acquired was reported upwards along the chain of command. The functional division of units in the security police meant that the differences in practices of documenting their activities could have been substantial, and the systems were developed or functioned separately. In particular, the EDP systems in the division IV of SB (that dealt with surveillance of the Church) had significantly different operative report form and coding sheets.

The separation of resources and systems was not damaging in every case. The peculiar example of the EPI (EPIW) foreign intelligence system shows that

Solid modernity   195

good design and compatibility with an existing information circuit made for an efficient system. However, even though the EPI (EPIW) was declared to have been designed as the "system for the entire interior ministry," it contained elements typical of the information processing circuit in foreign intelligence. In this context, a particular form of departmental egoism on the part of the MSW becomes apparent; while the central EDP service units endeavoured to integrate systems and offer overarching technical solutions, the operative units tended to stubbornly cling to the separateness of their own systems. We may presume that this reluctance to integrate one's own system with other systems indicates not only a kind of socio-technical conservatism but also an unwillingness to share one's "own" – an unwillingness that was rooted in the service's culture of "inner secrecy."[62]

One of the substantial problems of the system's inability to function was that of data input. The problem was particularly visible in the system's governing of the mass data circuit. The difference between the number of passports issued and the number of entries in the SERP passport control system in 1981–1982 was in the range of more than several tens of thousands. Moreover, the unit responsible for passport control, *Biuro Paszportowe MSW*, recalculated a new the number of Polish citizens who stayed abroad in 1983.[63] The liberalisation of passport issue and travel abroad in 1988 resulted in another crisis. The amount of data to be entered into the system increased significantly, the control cards that were issued with passports (that were to be given to the border control on departure) were in many cases illegible and not fit for processing. In 1989, of the 9.5 million passports issued, only two million were registered in the system as being used to travel abroad. Due to the data input crisis, the number of cards awaiting processing numbered 1.3 million in November 1989 – as a result, data input to the SERP system was halted in December 1989, and the system was practically closed.[64]

Another instance is the substantial time-lapse of data input into the ZSKO system.[65] The ZSKO did not cover the entire general operative index of Bureau "C" MSW – only the most important and current data were entered. As previously mentioned, "historical" data was only of secondary interest to the security police. Even though SB cherished its "long memory," the latter was not assessed as particularly useful in current operative work.

Computer hardware was the other matter to be dealt with. The relative technical backwardness of the Soviet Bloc industry significantly impaired the use of electronic systems and led to an amazing diversity of hardware in use. The communist security police in Poland used American systems (Honeywell-Bull H-6030 and H-6040) as core hardware for MSW systems, particularly the ZSKO system. IBM PC XT/AT were used for the general software processing, West German Siemens mainframes (models 4004/45, 7755, 7748, 7760) were used for the PESEL system as well as for the SERP border movement control system.[66] Hungarian computers (Riad R-11B) were used to handle the criminal police's electronic register of "lost property," the aforementioned Polish systems (AMC-1, ZAM-41) were pioneering devices and used in the very first information systems launched in MSW. In

196   *Franciszek Dąbrowski*

addition, the Polish Mera 9150 and Riad R-32 were used as subsidiaries to the H-6030 and H-6040, K-202 by EPIW – the foreign intelligence system, whereas the Mera 100B and Mera 660 were used for the border control data systems. Hardware from France was also used: a Honeywell Bull G-118 computer was generally used for the data exchange with teletypes as well as for the EPIW foreign intelligence system. Finally, a Danish system (Regnecentralen RC8000) was used by the border control unit at Warsaw airport.[67] All in all, the efficiency of devices (and data transfer) varied. The use of multiple models certainly tied up a considerable amount of technicians' resources and even common RIAD standards were not enough to guarantee the interconnection between devices.

The diversity of devices in use was caused by several factors; in the beginning, when the pioneering domestic constructions were used (AMC-1, ZAM-1, K-202), the requirements of working with significant data volume pushed MSW to acquire efficient Western devices, some officially – as in Siemens for PESEL system. The COCOM restrictions however, as well as economic and financial austerity, led to the use of devices belonging to the Warsaw Pact ESEVM platform (Russian. *Единая система электронных вычислительных машин*, Polish: *Jednolity System Maszyn Cyfrowych RIAD*, the Unified System of Electronic Machines)[68] and domestically produced Mera devices.

Ever since the 1960s the introduction of computers was connected with the idea of networking databases and massively accelerating the horizontal transfer of data between different organisations – government agencies, the military and the intelligence services.[69] However, there is no definite evidence to suggest that the introduction of electronic systems contributed to the information exchange between the Polish security police and other Soviet Bloc services. The only well-researched instance of cooperation – the SOUD system – shows something quite the contrary; the data to be reported to SOUD was registered by the relevant structure (*Wydział V Biura "C" MSW*, V. Division of Bureau "C") in traditional card index and registry logs and the SOUD operator in MSW did not have access to the system's terminal.[70] In the remaining sources there is no significant trace of plans for the integration of domestic systems nor with Soviet or Soviet Bloc information systems.

The systemic arrangement of the massive inflow of data was apparently the most desired effect of using electronic systems. However, the most important questions concerning the quality of information were to be asked and answered before it was entered into the system. These included: Is the source reliable? Is the information reliable? Does the information show signs or traces of disinformation? And so on. As a matter of fact the preliminary evaluation of the information was completely independent from its eventual further use – and belonged to the basic elements of work with informants and the use of information gathered in operative processes, that is "in the field."[71] In fact, such initial evaluation of the singular information was one of the points in the forms used as input documents for the electronic systems. It might be presumed that mass evaluation of the information gathered could enable extraction discrepancies, singularities as well as cross-checking of the data and the source's reliability.

Conclusion

It seems that the eventual development of the electronic data harvesting, storage, and evaluation systems in the communist security service might have led to the emergence of a juggernaut of combined deep information insight and enhanced operative capabilities (that were already of totalitarian character and practice). The highlighting of such an approach is evident in the history of the PESEL system. PESEL was invented and generally designed by the security service, however it developed as "civilian" (interconnecting the MSW, civil census offices and local administration across the country). PESEL was incorporated into the security police, "re-securitised" once it was already tested and functioning.[72] As is characteristic of communist security police, there were neither restraints nor hesitation concerning citizens' or privacy rights in the planned developments of electronic data systems (in the same way as when the traditional card indexes were constructed). On the contrary, the data gathering and juxtaposing capabilities of the new tools were seen as of key importance, and it was generally considered more important to keep the resources obtained secret. Competition with the West was a significant motivating factor because Western governments, by digitising their citizens' data, were able to impede attempts to send agents to their countries with forged identities and documents. Information and data protection rights were not an issue then – for instance, the 1983 act concerning the office of the minister of internal affairs did not include any stipulations concerning data gathering.[73] There were no institutional restraints (e.g. judicial control) at that time, nor any kind of internal code of conduct limiting the capture and use of people's even most fragile data – on the contrary, it would rather be an advantage.

Seemingly, the electronic data evaluation systems could be seen by service's management as some kind of magic box, providing them with immediate access to all the data they needed. However, the construction of some of the elements of the intelligence data evaluation system cluster EPI (EPIW) shows that only the retrieval of specific types of analyses were intended in the design of specific subsystems. Following the previously developed information practices in electronic form also secured receipt of the results of the data processing. The retrieval of general statistics from systems was also embedded in the previous reporting practices of the registry unit (and the operation with big general figures was also well-understood by the service's management). However, unanswered questions remain: Whether the security service's management was able to point to the new directions in the future developments of the electronic systems and its usage? Or were they rather defining their expectations towards the new tools on offer based on their own previous experiences in spy-mastering?

Notes

1 For further information on this view, see Booß, *Vom Scheitern der kybernetischen Utopie*, 12.
2 For an overview of the history of UB and SB and some of its general features, see: Szwagrzyk, ed., *Aparat bezpieczeństwa w Polsce*, vol. 1; Piotrowski, ed., *Aparat*

198 Franciszek Dąbrowski

bezpieczeństwa w Polsce, vol. 2; Terlecki, *Miecz i tarcza komunizmu*; Piotrowski 2008, ed., *Aparat bezpieczeństwa w Polsce*, vol. 3; Jusupović and Leśkiewicz, eds., *Historyczno-prawna analiza struktur*; Bagieński, *Wywiad cywilny Polski Ludowej*; Kozłowski, *Koniec imperium MSW*.

3 See Ruzikowski, ed., *Instrukcje pracy operacyjnej*, 13–16.

4 Pioneering work in these fields has primarily been done by institutions in charge of keeping and reviewing the paper archives of Communist secret police forces such as the Polish Institute for National Remembrance (IPN) or the German *Stasi-Unterlagenbehörde* (BStU).

5 See especially Komaniecka-Łyp, ed., *Ewidencja operacyjna*, passim; Komaniecka, ed., *Instrukcje pracy pionów*, passim; see also Komaniecka, "Struktura i normatywy pionu"; Komaniecka, "Informatyzacja Biura"; Komaniecka-Łyp, ed., *Ewidencja operacyjna*, 34–44; Komaniecka, ed., *Instrukcje pracy pionów*, 21–25, 35–38, 50–54; Hermański, Jusupović and Wróblewski, "Cywilne organy bezpieczeństwa państwa," 114–115, 113–114, 118, 120–121, 122, and Piotrowski, ed., *Aparat bezpieczeństwa w Polsce*, 14–16, 20–21; Piotrowski 2008, 32–36; Dziurok, ed., *Metody pracy operacyjnej aparatu*, doc. no. 70, July 6, 1963, 336–345, doc. no. 73, 23 December 1963, 352–355; Bagieński, *Wywiad cywilny owej*, vol. 1, 563–595; Bagieński, ed., *Instrukcje i przepisy wywiadu*; Zieliński, "Przykłady dokumentacji wytworzonej"; Zając, "Ślad pozostaje w aktach"; see also Komaniecka-Łyp, ed., *Ewidencja operacyjna*, 67–68. Unfortunately, the dictionary of archival and operative registry terms concerning Communist security police and military security units in Poland, prepared by the team consisting of Franciszek Dąbrowski PhD, Robert Nowicki, Katarzyna Pawlak-Weiss PhD and Wojciech Sawicki, was published only in abridged and simplified form as a supplement to the online archival inventory of the Institute of National Remembrance (see entries in *Dictionary*).

6 See especially Jedlitschka and Springer, ed., *Das Gedächtnis der Staatssicherheit*; Lucht, ed., *Das Archiv der Stasi*; Engelmann and Joestel, *Die Zentrale Auswertungs- und Informationsgruppe*; Booß, *Vom Scheitern der kybernetischen Utopie*.

7 Schovánek and Žáček, "Lustrace v evidencích bezpečnostních složek."

8 The predecessors of Bureau "C" were: *Biuro* Ewidencji Operacyjnej, BEO [Bureau of the Operative Registry] MSW 1956–1962, Centralne Archiwum [Central Archives] MSW 1956–1962, Departament X KdsBP 1954–1956 [Department X of the Committee of the Public Security], and Departament II MBP 1945–1954 [Department II of the Ministry of Public Security).

9 See the definition of "operative process" with respect to the East German State Security: <www.bstu.de/mfs-lexikon/detail/operativer-vorgang-ov/> (last accessed May 15, 2021).

10 Compulsory issue of identity cards as well as address register were policing means introduced in 1939–1942 by German and Soviet occupation administrations, and – with some cosmetic changes – essentially upheld by the Communist dictatorship in the peacetime.

11 For details concerning "coordination" procedures see Zieliński, "Przykłady dokumentacji wytworzonej," 153–155; Zając, "Ślad pozostaje w aktach," 26–27; cf. Komaniecka-Łyp, ed., *Ewidencja operacyjna*, 67–68.

12 See Zieliński, "Przykłady dokumentacji wytworzonej," passim.

13 In the 1950s, interrogations were led in most important cases by the *Biuro Specjalne/Departament X MBP* ("Special Bureau," then Department X of the Ministry of Public Security, special unit charged with "containing the provocation within Party." See Rokicki, ed., *Departament X MBP*, passim. On the general features of the investigative proceedings led by MBP units, see papers in volume published by Magdalena Dźwigał and Paweł Skubisz, Dźwigał and Skubisz, eds., *Piony śledcze aparatu bezpieczeństwa publicznego*.

14 The MBP became dissolved in late 1954 and was replaced by the Committee of Public Security. See *Decree 1954: Dekret z dnia 7 grudnia 1954*.

Solid modernity 199

15 Memoir of Ryszard Kaczorowski as cited by Bagieński, *Wywiad cywilny Polski Ludowej*, vol. 2, 250–251.
16 Cf. i.a. Komaniecka-Łyp, ed., *Ewidencja operacyjna*, 34–47, 52–56.
17 See Komaniecka-Łyp, ed., *Ewidencja operacyjna*, 52–54.
18 Ibid., 55–56.
19 See Zieliński, "Utworzenie Departamentu X Komitetu," 158.
20 Ibid., 158–159.
21 Ibid., 160–161, 164.
22 Instruction no. 03/55 and 04/55 of 11 March 1955, published by Ruzikowski, ed., *Instrukcje pracy operacyjnej*, 47–92.
23 Instruction no. 017/55, 018/55 of 9 April 1955, published by Komaniecka-Łyp, ed., *Ewidencja operacyjna* 2017, doc. no. 38, 39, 314–338.
24 See Komaniecka-Łyp, ed., *Ewidencja operacyjna*, doc. no 41, 344–349, doc. no. 42, 350–351, doc. no. 45, 366–370, doc. no. 47, 372–373.
25 See Komaniecka-Łyp, ed., *Ewidencja operacyjna*, doc. no. 50, 51, 52, 386–415. The issuing of these instructions was parallel to the issue of the new instruction for operative cases no. 03/60 of 2 July 1960, published by Ruzikowski, ed., *Instrukcje pracy operacyjnej*, 94–120.
26 Komaniecka-Łyp, ed., *Ewidencja operacyjna*, doc. no. 55, 56, 426–454. This step followed the pattern of the East German Stasi F16 and F22 card indexes, that became introduced in 1962.
27 See instruction no. 079/72 of 2 August 1972, and guidelines of 18 November 1972, Komaniecka-Łyp, ed., *Ewidencja operacyjna*, doc. 72, 533–551, doc. no. 75, 559–598. Antoni Zieliński suggested in conversation with me that the preparation of two separate index-cards with different data seemed too difficult for operative officers, and the resulting faults could lead to additional workload and blunders in the card index.
28 In fact, the first instruction concerning the registration of persons of operative interest and operative processes with accordance to the use of electronic system (apparently ZSKO) was issued only in 1984. It completed the instruction of 1972. See Komaniecka-Łyp, ed., *Ewidencja operacyjna*, doc. no. 79, 611–773.
29 By ordinance no. 0113/63 and instruction no. 002/63 of July 1963; see Dziurok, ed., *Metody pracy operacyjnej aparatu*, doc. no. 70, 336–345, doc. no. 352, 352–355; Komaniecka-Łyp, ed., *Ewidencja operacyjna*, doc. no. 60, 482–483, doc. no 61, 484–489.
30 By ordinance no. 0115/63; see Komaniecka-Łyp, ed., *Ewidencja operacyjna*, doc. no 62, 490–494.
31 Unified Registry System of Data concerning Enemy of the Warsaw Pact states = СОУД, Система объединённого учёта данных о противнике. For details on functioning of SOUD cells in the security police of GDR, Czechoslovakia, Bulgaria, and Poland see: Wegmann and Tanzscher, *SOUD*; Tomek, *Systém sjednocené evidence poznatků*; Katzounov, "Bulgaria's Participation"; Zając, "Polska w Połączonym Systemie Ewidencji Danych"; Osek and Grabowiecki, "Próba dokonania bilansu współpracy KGB"; "Połączony System Ewidencji Danych."
32 See Komaniecka, "Struktura i normatywy pionu"; Komaniecka, ed., *Instrukcje pracy pionów*, 50–63.
33 See Komaniecka, ed., *Instrukcje pracy pionów*, 21–35.
34 Ibid., 47–50.
35 For the other units of SB, the person 'secured' by the *Department I MSW* was in effect blocked for any form of operative interest, according to the "coordination" proceedings.
36 For general remarks see Bułhak, "Similar but not the same," 42ff. See also Department I inner regulations concerning information evaluation: Bagieński, ed., *Instrukcje i przepisy wywiadu*, doc. no. 79 (30 December 1971), 388–391, doc. no. 90 (30 August 1972), 440–447, doc. no. 115 (11 August 1977), 580–581, doc. no 117 (2 December 1977), 584–585, doc. no 142 (15 June 1983), 720–728, doc. no. 146 (7 November 1984), 761–764.

200 *Franciszek Dąbrowski*

37 Barański, *Wspomnienia*, 476–477.
38 See Ruzikowski, "Zarys historii Zintegrowanego," 80–81.
39 These sections were *Wydziały* IX, X, XI of the Bureau "C" MSW, and PESEL Department was enlisted as SB department. See Hermański, Jusupović and Wróblewski, "Cywilne organy bezpieczeństwa państwa," 115, 139–142.
40 The ministry's leadership reporting module was conceived of as a search engine and analysis device as well as an electronic channel for command and reporting.
41 See Ruzikowski, "Zarys historii Zintegrowanego," 81–85; cf. Komaniecka-Łyp, ed., *Ewidencja operacyjna*, 82.
42 The command module apparently did not emerge; in fact, its launching would have had heavily relied on the integration of the operative information evaluation systems of the operative units – and the latter was never achieved.
43 See Ruzikowski, "Zarys historii Zintegrowanego," 84–85.
44 For information on ZSKO system see Tadeusz Ruzikowski's extensive study as well as Mariusz Kwaśniak and Wojciech Sawicki expositions: Ruzikowski, "Zarys historii Zintegrowanego," passim; Kwaśniak, "Elektroniczne bazy danych Służby Bezpieczeństwa," 59, Sawicki, *Zintegrowany System Kartotek*.
45 Bułhak, "Similar But Not the Same," *passim*.
46 Bury, "Ochrona transmisji danych," 637–638.
47 See Konopatzky, „Möglichkeiten und Grenzen der SIRA-Datenbanken," 113–118; Konopatzky, *SIRA*, passim.
48 Bułhak, "Similar But Not the Same," 40–42.
49 See Paluch's personal file in IPN's Archive, ref. IPN BU 003175/630.
50 Even though the registry, archive, and information circuit in *Departament I MSW* was a miniature of the whole data storage and circuit if the ministry, the foreign intelligence unit operated with a notably smaller number of operative cases and data (registered informants and case files) and incoming information than any of the 'domestic' SB units. See Bułhak, "Similar but not the same," 42, footnote 71.
51 See Dąbrowski, "System informacyjny Departamentu," 556–563.
52 Ibid., 563–566.
53 See Komaniecka, "Informatyzacja Biura," *passim*.
54 Unfortunately, the relevant entries written by Robert Nowicki were not published in *Dictionary*.
55 See Dąbrowski, "System informacyjny Departamentu," 560–563; 566–567.
56 Ibid., 563–567; see also Kwaśniak, "Elektroniczne bazy danych Służby Bezpieczeństwa," *passim*.
57 Stola, *Kraj bez wyjścia?*, 23–48, 141–179, and *passim*.
58 Cf. Bury, "Ochrona transmisji danych," 638–639.
59 The aim was to secure the 100 per cent certain identification of persons of operative interest – and, due to the inclusion of the civil census data in PESEL, apparently also to enhance the usage of forged documents or false personal data by persons of interest. Ruzikowski, "Zarys historii Zintegrowanego," 82–83, 85.
60 See Ruzikowski, "Zarys historii Zintegrowanego," 81–85; cf. Komaniecka-Łyp, ed., *Ewidencja operacyjna*, 82.
61 See Dąbrowski, "System informacyjny Departamentu," 560–563.
62 However, it should be admitted that the unintegrated approach, i.e. processing of the data in the separated systems and resources would have been considerably easier (as there were less data to process).
63 Stola, *Kraj bez wyjścia?*, 313.
64 Ibid., 353.
65 See Ruzikowski, "Zarys historii Zintegrowanego," 98–101.
66 Soviet R-61 machines had been intended to run the PESEL system, yet their use was apparently postponed after failed attempts to transfer the systems used to this device, and due to the high number of damages occurring.

Solid modernity 201

67 See Bury, "Ochrona transmisji danych," 634–642; Ruzikowski, "Zarys historii Zintegrowanego," 90–96; Kwaśniak, "Elektroniczne bazy danych Służby Bezpieczeństwa," 57–59, 62–63.
68 See Maćkowiak, Myszkier and Safader, *Polskie komputery rodziły się w ELWRO*, 39–42.
69 See Rüdiger Bergien's contribution in this volume.
70 See Osek and Grabowiecki, "Próba dokonania bilansu współpracy KGB," 170; "Połączony System Ewidencji Danych," 99–100; see also Zając, "Polska w Połączonym Systemie Ewidencji Danych," 543–550.
71 See the remarks of Filip Musiał concerning operative work of Communist security police, based on the inner manuals and studies of MSW: Musiał, *Podręcznik bezpieki*, 122–147.
72 See Hermański, Jusupović and Wróblewski, "Cywilne organy bezpieczeństwa państwa," 139–142; Kwaśniak, "Elektroniczne bazy danych Służby Bezpieczeństwa," 58, 60–61.
73 See *Act 1983: Ustawa z dnia 14 lipca 1983*.

Bibliography

Act 1983: Ustawa z dnia 14 lipca 1983 r. o urzędzie Ministra Spraw Wewnętrznych i zakresie działania podległych mu organów [Act of July 14, 1983 on the Office of Minister of Internal Affairs and the Scope of Activity of the Bodies Subordinated to Him]. Dziennik Ustaw 1983, no. 38, pos. 172. http://isap.sejm.gov.pl/isap.nsf/DocDetails.xsp?id=WDU 19830380172 (accessed May 28, 2021).

Bagieński, W. 2017. *Wywiad cywilny Polski Ludowej w latach 1945–1961 [Civilian Intelligence Service of People's Poland in 1945–1961]*, Vol. 1–2. Warszawa: Instytut Pamięci Narodowej – Komisja Ścigania Zbrodni przeciwko Narodowi Polskiemu.

Bagieński, W., ed. 2020. *Instrukcje i przepisy wywiadu cywilnego PRL z lat 1953–1990 [Instructions and Regulations of Civilian Intelligence of Polish People's Republic 1953–1990]*. Warszawa: Instytut Pamięci Narodowej – Komisja Ścigania Zbrodni przeciwko Narodowi Polskiemu.

Barański, M. 2020. *Wspomnienia 1943–1989 [Memoirs 1943–1989]*. Warszawa: Państwowy Instytut Wydawniczy.

Booß, Ch. 2020. *Vom Scheitern der kybernetischen Utopie. Die Entwicklung von Überwachung und Informationsverarbeitung im MfS*. Göttingen: Vandenhoeck & Ruprecht.

Bułhak, W. 2014. "Similar But Not the Same. In Search of a Methodology in the Cold-War Communist Intelligence Studies." In *Need to Know: Eastern and Western Perspectives*, ed. W. Bułhak and T. Wegener Friis. Studies in Intelligence and Security Series 1, 19–44. Odense: Syddansk Universitetsforlag.

Bury, J. 2017. "Ochrona transmisji danych w sieciach teleinformatycznych służb specjalnych Polski Ludowej w latach siedemdziesiątych i osiemdziesiątych [Protecting Data Transmission in Telecommunication Networks of Special Services of the Polish People's Republic in the 1970s and 1980s]." In *High-tech za żelazną kurtyną. Elektronika, komputery i systemy sterowania w PRL*, ed. M. Sikora, 631–655. Warszawa-Katowice: Instytut Pamięci Narodowej – Komisja Ścigania Zbrodni przeciwko Narodowi Polskiemu.

Dąbrowski, F. 2017. "System informacyjny Departamentu III MSW: analiza informacji i prowadzenie dokumentacji działań operacyjnych [Information System of the Department III of the Ministry of Internal Affairs: Analysis of Information and Keeping Records of Operational Activities]." In *High-tech za żelazną kurtyną. Elektronika, komputery i systemy sterowania w PRL*, ed. M. Sikora, 551–567. Warszawa-Katowice: Instytut Pamięci Narodowej – Komisja Ścigania Zbrodni przeciwko Narodowi Polskiemu.

202   Franciszek Dąbrowski

Decree 1954: Dekret z dnia 7 grudnia 1954 r. o naczelnych organach administracji państwowej w zakresie spraw wewnętrznych i bezpieczeństwa publicznego [Decree of December 7, 1954 on Head Administration Units Dealing with Internal Affairs and Public Security].

Dictionary: Słownik terminów [Dictionary of the {archival} Terms], Inwentarz Archiwalny Instytutu Pamięci Narodowej. https://inwentarz.ipn.gov.pl/slownik.

Dziennik Ustaw PRL 1954, no. 54, pos. 269. http://isap.sejm.gov.pl/isap.nsf/DocDetails.xsp?id=WDU19540540269 (accessed May 28, 2021).

Dziurok, A., ed. 2004. *Metody pracy operacyjnej aparatu bezpieczeństwa wobec kościołów i związków wyznaniowych 1945–1989 [Security Apparatus Operative Methods of Work towards Churches and Religious Communities 1945–1989].* Warszawa: Instytut Pamięci Narodowej – Komisja Ścigania Zbrodni przeciwko Narodowi Polskiemu.

Dźwigał, M., and Skubisz, P., eds. 2017. *Piony śledcze aparatu bezpieczeństwa publicznego 1944–1990 [Investigative Units of Public Security Apparatus 1944–1990].* Szczecin: Instytut Pamięci Narodowej-Komisja Ścigania Zbrodni przeciwko Narodowi Polskiemu.

Engelmann, R., und Joestel, F. 2009. *Die Zentrale Auswertungs- und Informationsgruppe.* Berlin: Die Bundesbeauftragte für die Unterlagen des Staatssicherheitsdienstes der ehemaligen Deutschen Demokratischen Republik. www.bstu.de/informationen-zur-stasi/publikationen/publikation/die-zentrale-auswertungs-und-informationsgruppe/.

Hermański, S., Jusupović, A., and Wróblewski, T. 2013. "Cywilne organy bezpieczeństwa państwa 1956–1990 [Civilian Bodies of the State Security Apparatus 1956–1990]." In *Historyczno-prawna analiza struktur organów bezpieczeństwa państwa w Polsce Ludowej (1944–1990). Zbiór studiów. [Historical-legal Analysis of the State Security Structures in People's Poland (1944–1990). Collection of Studies]*, ed. A. Jusupović and R. Leśkiewicz, 111–163. Warszawa: Instytut Pamięci Narodowej – Komisja Ścigania Zbrodni przeciwko Narodowi Polskiemu. https://przystanekhistoria.pl/download/166/121170/analizastrukturorganowdointernetu.pdf.

Jedlitschka, K., and Springer, Ph., eds. 2015. *Das Gedächtnis der Staatssicherheit. Die Kartei- und Archivabteilung des MfS.* Göttingen: Vandenhoek & Ruprecht.

Jusupović, A., and Leśkiewicz, R., eds. 2013. *Historyczno-prawna analiza struktur organów bezpieczeństwa państwa w Polsce Ludowej (1944–1990). Zbiór studiów. [Historical-legal Analysis of the State Security Structures in People's Poland (1944–1990). Collection of Studies].* Warszawa: Instytut Pamięci Narodowej – Komisja Ścigania Zbrodni przeciwko Narodowi Polskiemu.|

Katzounov, V. 2020. "Bulgaria's Participation in the System of Joint Acquisition of Enemy Data (SOUD)." *Aparat represji w Polsce Ludowej 1944–1989* 1, no. 18: 447–456. https://doi.org/10.48261/ARPRL201816.

Komaniecka, M., ed. 2010. *Instrukcje pracy pionów pomocniczych Urzędu Bezpieczeństwa i Służby Bezpieczeństwa (1945–1989) [Proceedings' Instructions for the Auxiliary Branches of Department of Security and Security Service (1945–1989)].* Krakow: Instytut Pamięci Narodowej – Komisja Ścigania Zbrodni przeciwko Narodowi Polskiemu.

Komaniecka, M. 2011. "Struktura i normatywy pionu "W" i jego poprzedników (1945–1989) [Structures and Normative Acts of "W" Branch and Its Predecessors (1945–1989)]." *Aparat Represji w Polsce Ludowej 1944–1989* 1, no. 8–9: 179–198.

Komaniecka, M. 2017. "Informatyzacja Biura "B" MSW – koncepcje, realizacja, efekty [Informatization of the Bureau "B" of the Ministry of the Internal Affairs – Concepts, Implementation, Effects]." In *High-tech za żelazną kurtyną. Elektronika, komputery i systemy sterowania w PRL*, ed. M. Sikora, 591–610. Warszawa-Katowice: Instytut Pamięci Narodowej – Komisja Ścigania Zbrodni przeciwko Narodowi Polskiemu.

Komaniecka-Łyp, M., ed. 2017. *Ewidencja operacyjna i archiwum organów bezpieczeństwa PRL w latach 1944–1990. Zbiór normatywów [Operative Registry and Archives of Polish People's Republic Security Bodies in 1944–1990. The Collection of Normative Acts]*. Krakow Instytut Pamięci Narodowej – Komisja Ścigania Zbrodni przeciwko Narodowi Polskiemu.

Konopatzky, St. 2003. "Möglichkeiten und Grenzen der SIRA-Datenbanken." In *Das Gesicht dem Westen zu . . . DDR-Spionage gegen die Bundesrepublik Deutschland*, ed. G. Herbstritt and H. Müller-Enbergs, 112–132. Bremen: Ed. Temmen.

Konopatzky, St. 2019. *SIRA – System der Informationsrecherche der Hauptverwaltung A des Ministeriums für Staatssicherheit der DDR [SIRA – System of the Data Processing of the Hauptverwaltung A of the Ministry of State Security of GDR]*. Berlin: BStU.

Kozłowski, T. 2019. *Koniec imperium MSW. Transformacja organów bezpieczeństwa państwa 1989–1990 [The End of MSW Empire. Transformation of the State Security Bodies 1989–1990]*. Warsaw: Instytut Pamięci Narodowej – Komisja Ścigania Zbrodni przeciwko Narodowi Polskiemu.

Kwaśniak, M. 2014. "Elektroniczne bazy danych Służby Bezpieczeństwa [Electronic Databases of the Security Service]." *Przegląd Archiwalny Instytutu Pamięci Narodowej* 7: 55–70. https://ipn.gov.pl/par/tomy-archiwalne/89,Tom-72014.html.

Lucht, R., ed. 2015. *Das Archiv der Stasi. Begriffe*. Göttingen: Vandenhoek & Ruprecht.

Maćkowiak, B., Myszkier, A., and Safader, B. 2017. *Polskie komputery rodziły się w ELWRO we Wrocławiu. Rola Wrocławskich Zakładów Elektronicznych ELWRO w rozwoju informatyki w Polsce [Polish Computers were Born in ELWRO in Wrocław. The Role of the Wrocław Electronic Works ELWRO in Development of Information Technology in Poland]*. Wrocław: Archiwum Państwowe we Wrocławiu. https://historiainformatyki.pl/historia/dokument.php?nonav=&nrar=2&nrzesp=2&sygn=II%2F1%2F13&handle=1547.

Musiał, F. 2015. *Podręcznik bezpieki. Teoria pracy operacyjnej Służby Bezpieczeństwa w świetle wydawnictw resortowych Ministerstwa Spraw Wewnętrznych PRL (1970–1989) [Security Manual. Theory of the Operative Work of the Security Service in the Publications of the Ministry of the Internal Affairs of the Polish People's Republic (1970–1989)]*. Krakow: Instytut Pamięci Narodowej – Komisja Ścigania Zbrodni przeciwko Narodowi Polskiemu, Avalon.

Osek, R., and Grabowiecki, M. 2010. "Próba dokonania bilansu współpracy KGB – SB w latach 1970–1990 [An Attempt of Report on Cooperation KGB – Security Service in 1970–1990]." *Przegląd Bezpieczeństwa Wewnętrznego* 3: 149–173. www.abw.gov.pl/pl/pbw/publikacje/przeglad-bezpieczenstw-3/702,Przeglad-Bezpieczenstwa-Wewnetrznego-3-2010.html.

Paweł, P., ed. 2008. *Aparat bezpieczeństwa w Polsce. Kadra kierownicza. T. 3. 1975–1990 [Security Apparatus in Poland. Leadership Cadre. Vol. 3. 1975–1990]*. Warszawa: Instytut Pamięci Narodowej – Komisja Ścigania Zbrodni przeciwko Narodowi Polskiemu. https://przystanekhistoria.pl/pa2/biblioteka-cyfrowa/publikacje/23746,Aparat-bezpieczenstwa-w-Polsce-Kadra-kierownicza-tom-III-19751990.html.

Piotrowski, P., ed. 2006. *Aparat bezpieczeństwa w Polsce. Kadra kierownicza. T. 2. 1956–1975 [Security Apparatus in Poland. Leadership Cadre. Vol. 2. 1956–1975]*. Warszawa: Instytut Pamięci Narodowej – Komisja Ścigania Zbrodni przeciwko Narodowi Polskiemu. https://przystanekhistoria.pl/pa2/tematy/aparat-bezpieczenstwa/36979,Aparat-bezpieczenstwa-w-Polsce-Kadra-kierownicza-tom-II-1956-1975.html.

"Połączony System Ewidencji Danych o Przeciwniku (PSED) [Unified Registry System of Data concerning Enemy (PSED [SOUD])]". In *Współpraca SB MSW PRL z KGB ZSRR*

204   *Franciszek Dąbrowski*

w latach 1970–1990. Próba bilansu [*Cooperation of Security Service of the Ministry of Internal Affairs of Polish People's Republic with KGB USSR in 1970–1990. Attempt of resume*], ed. Z. Nawrocki et alii. 2013, 99–118. Emów: Agencja Bezpieczeństwa Wewnętrznego.

Rokicki, K., ed. 2007. *Departament X MBP: wzorce, struktury, działanie* [*Department X of the Ministry of Public Security: Patterns, Structures, Activities*]. Warszawa: Instytut Pamięci Narodowej – Komisja Ścigania Zbrodni przeciwko Narodowi Polskiemu.

Ruzikowski, T., ed. 2004. *Instrukcje pracy operacyjnej aparatu bezpieczeństwa 1945–1989* [*Instructions for the Operative Work of Security Apparatus 1945–1989*]. Warsaw: Instytut Pamięci Narodowej-Komisja Badania Zbrodni przeciwko Narodowi Polskiemu. https://ipn.gov.pl/pl/publikacje/ksiazki/12275,Instrukcje-pracy-operacyjnej-aparatu-bezpieczenstwa-19451989.html.

Ruzikowski, T. 2010. "Zarys historii Zintegrowanego (Zautomatyzowanego) Systemu Kartotek Operacyjnych resortu spraw wewnętrznych [Outline History of the Integrated (Automated) Operating File System of the Internal Affairs Department]." *Przegląd Archiwalny Instytutu Pamięci Narodowej* 3: 79–116. https://ipn.gov.pl/par/tomy-archiwalne/85,Tom-32010.html.

Sawicki, W. 2016. *Zintegrowany System Kartotek Operacyjnych Służby Bezpieczeństwa PRL* [the lecture delivered during the conference *Colloquia Jerzy Skowronek dedicata: Difficult issues of history and archives*, 2016]. https://colloquia2016.conrego.pl/files/referaty/Wojciech_Sawicki.pdf.

Schovánek, R., and Žáček, P. 2015. "Lustrace v evidencích bezpečnostních složek. Od evidence zájmových osob až k zákonu o účastnících odboje a odporu proti komunismu. [The Inspection of the Card Index Resources of Security Services. From the Registry of Persons of Interest to the Law on the Members of Resistance and Opposition to Communism]." *Vyjádření úcty a vděčnosti. 2. sborník o protikomunistickém odboji* 2, Prague: Ministerstvo obrany České republiky – VHÚ Praha: 35–72. www.csds.cz/cs/g6/5343-DS.html.

Stola, D. 2012. *Kraj bez wyjścia? Migracje z Polski 1949–1989* [*A Country with No Exit? International Migrations from Poland, 1949–1989*]. Warszawa: Instytut Pamięci Narodowej – Komisja Ścigania Zbrodni przeciwko Narodowi Polskiemu, Instytut Studiów Politycznych Polskiej Akademii Nauk.

Szwagrzyk, K., ed. 2005. *Aparat bezpieczeństwa w Polsce. Kadra kierownicza. T. 1. 1944–1956* [*Security apparatus in Poland. Leadership cadre. Vol. 1. 1944–1956*]. Warszawa: Instytut Pamięci Narodowej – Komisja Ścigania Zbrodni przeciwko Narodowi Polskiemu.

Terlecki, R. 2007. *Miecz i tarcza komunizmu: historia aparatu bezpieczeństwa w Polsce 1944–1990* [*Sword and Shield of Communism: History of the Security Apparatus in Poland 1944–1990*]. Cracow: Wydawnictwo Literackie.

Tomek, P. 2008. *Systém sjednocené evidence poznatků o nepříteli (v československých podmínkách)* [*System of the Integrated Registry of Data Concerning Enemy (in Czechoslovak Sources)*]. Prague: Ústav pro studium totalitních režimů.

Wegmann, B., and Tanzscher, M. 1996. *SOUD – Das geheimdienstliche Datennetz des östlichen Bündnissystems*. Berlin: Die Bundesbeauftragte für die Unterlagen des Staatssicherheitsdienstes der ehemaligen Deutschen Demokratischen Republik [Reihe B: Analysen und Berichte Nr. 1/1996]. www.bstu.de/informationen-zur-stasi/publikationen/publikation/soud/.

Zając, E. 2006. "Ślad pozostaje w aktach. Wybrane zagadnienia dotyczące funkcjonowania ewidencji operacyjnej w latach 1962–1989 [The Trace is in the Records. Selected

Solid modernity 205

Problems of Operative Registry Functioning in 1962–1989]." *Biuletyn Instytutu Pamięci Narodowej* 1–2, no. 60–61: 21–36. https://przystanekhistoria.pl/pa2/biblioteka-cyfrowa/biuletyn-ipn/biuletyn-ipn-2001-2011/24475,nr-1-22006.html.

Zając, E. 2010. "Polska w Połączonym Systemie Ewidencji Danych o Przeciwniku (PSED) – próba rekonstrukcji [Poland in SOUD – An Attempt of Reconstruction]." In *Ofiary imperium. Imperia jako ofiary. 44 spojrzenia. Imperial Victims/Empires as Victims. 44 Views*, ed. A. Nowak, 543–555. Warszawa: Instytut Pamięci Narodowej – Komisja Ścigania Zbrodni przeciwko Narodowi Polskiemu, Instytut Historii Polskiej Akademii Nauk.

Zieliński, A. 2010. "Przykłady dokumentacji wytworzonej przez pion ewidencji operacyjnej SB w latach 1972–1990 i jej wykorzystanie do badań naukowych [The Specimens of Records Produced by Operative Registry Units of Security Service in 1972–1990 and Its Use in Research]." *Przegląd Archiwalny Instytutu Pamięci Narodowej* 3: 147–168. https://ipn.gov.pl/par/tomy-archiwalne/85,Tom-32010.html.

Zieliński, A. 2012. "Utworzenie Departamentu X Komitetu do spraw Bezpieczeństwa Publicznego [Forming of the Department X of the Committee for the Public Security]." In *Archiwalia komunistycznego aparatu represji – zagadnienia źródłoznawcze*, ed. F. Musiał, 153–198. Kraków: Instytut Pamięci Narodowej – Komisja Ścigania Zbrodni przeciwko Narodowi Polskiemu.

10 Eliminating the human factor?

Perceptions of digital computers at the German domestic intelligence service

Christopher Kirchberg

Introduction

Although the century had not yet drawn to a close, a book published in 1999 appeared to offer a comprehensive and conclusive explanation of world events, as it bore the ambitious German title *So war es . . . Mein Leben im 20. Jahrhundert* (*That is how it was . . . My Life in the 20th Century*). While the ostentatious-sounding first part of the title suggested a historiographical tour-de-force with a grand narrative, the second part reveals that it was an autobiography, made exceptional by its author, Hans-Joachim Postel. Although most individuals who write their memoirs tend to be convinced that they have a very special story to tell, this autobiography is noteworthy for the sole reason that it was penned by a former German intelligence officer. But Postel did not belong to the group of former presidents of intelligence agencies, who sometimes provided a retrospective interpretation of their time in office for posterity[1] – he was merely a mid-level employee, who eventually rose in the ranks and became an officer later in his career. His book thus provides surprisingly candid insights into the arcane world of intelligence, along with unfamiliar interpretations of internal developments.

Hans-Joachim Postel was born in 1925 near Wałbrzych (Valbrich) in Lower Silesia, which became part of Poland after the Second World War. He completed an apprenticeship as a farmhand after leaving school and joined the German Air Force (*Luftwaffe*) in 1943. Having worked as a policeman and a criminal investigator in the early post-war years in West Germany near the Ruhr area, he subsequently entered the ranks of the BfV, the domestic intelligence service of the Federal Republic of Germany. As a 25-year-old, he began his career in the Evaluation Department – one of three main departments of the agency at that time[2] – where he analysed "news about radical right-wing parties and organizations; international fascism."[3] His recollections of the almost 35 years he spent working for the intelligence service make up the bulk of his autobiography, which also included some anecdotes from his personal life.

Remaining faithful to the dramatic title of his book, Postel presented himself as a maverick and great moderniser of the *Bundesamt*, who, as a nerdy workaholic, almost single-handedly advanced the digitisation of the intelligence service and brought it "out of the information technology Middle Ages and into the modern era."[4]

DOI: 10.4324/9781003147329-11

Figure 10.1 Cover of Postel's autobiography published in 1999.

Source: Image of the cover of Postel's biography. It shows a photo of Postel sitting in an aeroplane during a business trip to the United States in the 1970s.

Despite being a simple "administrative officer" without academic degree, he portrayed himself as a far-sighted pioneer in order to gain recognition from his colleagues and superiors, mainly on the basis of autodidactically acquired IT skills.

Initially, the *Bundesamt* was located on the top floor of a store for office furniture, while Postel's evaluation department was situated in the attic of a building

208   *Christopher Kirchberg*

that housed a shipping company. Despite operating under relatively primitive conditions in its early years, the BfV was nevertheless shaped by the spirit and organisational culture of a German government agency, where collegial cooperation was characterised by rigid hierarchies oriented towards status; promotions were possible only within the narrow corset of official titles and pay grades.[5] Within this context, Postel was not an ideal fit due to his lack of formal education, with no high school diploma or university degree to his name. This mainly affected his employment status, as Postel was formally a salaried employee (*Angestellter*) in the midst of civil servants (*Beamte*) assigned to similar or higher-ranking positions. Here, the technological modernisation of the intelligence service presented itself as an opportunity for Postel to advance his own career. Accordingly, his autobiography followed a narrative based on a challenge-response model: Postel repeatedly articulated (analogue) problems of information processing that he encountered in his daily work within the intelligence service, for which he could then present modern technological solutions. Once these solutions themselves gave rise to new challenges, Postel once again provided what he saw as an appropriate response. According to his memoirs, Postel's integral role in the overall process of digitisation allowed him to climb the career ladder from a simple analyst and outsider to the position of section chief; owing to his technical expertise, he ostensibly became a figurehead of the *Bundesamt*.[6]

Thus, Postel's autobiography refers to two significant developments within the *Bundesamt* from its founding until the early 1980s, when he left the service: the digitisation and professionalisation of the intelligence service – and their mutual dependencies. By analysing how Postel sought to present himself in his memoirs and juxtaposing this narrative with official archival records, this paper will demonstrate how Postel's arguments and the solutions he proposed not only digitised the *Bundesamt*, but also professionalised the agency at the same time – they also allowed him to climb the career ladder in the process. By focusing on the connection between digitisation und professionalisation, the following questions are examined: What did analogue information processing in the intelligence service look like in practical terms when Postel began working for the *Bundesamt*? How did Postel present digitisation as viable solution for problems encountered in the field of information processing – and how did he come to define these problems himself? Finally, how did digitisation transform work and the role of humans in information processing beyond Postel's own career, and what were the (unintended) consequences of these developments?

Using Postel's personal perspective and interpretation as a point of departure, these questions will be answered in three separate chapters: first, the status quo of analogue information processing in the *Bundesamt* is examined on the basis of the inherent limitations of analogue data processing techniques, as they were perceived, identified, and problematised by Postel himself. Second, the decision for and the reasoning behind using and configuring the computer system will be examined by using the example of a business trip that Postel took to the United States and how he cast himself in the role of an expert. Third, newly emerging (and unexpected) problems of digitisation encountered after implementation, and

Eliminating the human factor? 209

the changing ratio of work processes performed by humans on the one hand and computers on the other come into focus before concluding with a summary of this chapter's main findings.

In the process, I will be exploring the thesis that Postel's interpretations and stylisations of his own image as an expert were the main drivers behind the incipient computerisation of internal information processing techniques in the BfV – however, contrary to what Postel had promised his own superiors, digitisation did not result in simplification and greater independence from human influences. Rather, it led to further complications regarding internal work practices and information processing until the end of the 1970s, mainly because – as I argue – these remained highly dependent on the human factor.

Postel's lucky "punch"? (Perceived) limitations of internal analogue information processing and the proposed solution of Hollerith technology

As the central domestic intelligence service of the Federal Republic of Germany, the BfV was established in November 1950. Hans-Joachim Postel joined the *Bundesamt* within weeks of its initial founding. Shortly after the end of the Second World War, two experiences featured prominently in the discussions among the Western Allies about how the security architecture in occupied Germany was to be organised. What decisively shaped the establishment of security authorities in the Federal Republic of Germany was the maxim that no powerful new secret service such as the Gestapo in Germany under National Socialist rule should be allowed to emerge in West Germany; moreover, domestic and foreign intelligence activities should be separated based on the British model.[7] Accordingly, the *Bundesamt* was founded as an intelligence service without executive power, complemented by the so-called *Landesämter für Verfassungsschutz* (State Offices) in each federal state. Its main task was the "collection and evaluation of information, intelligence and documents on efforts aimed at the abolition, change or disruption of the constitutional order in the federal territory or in a federal state."[8] In doing so, the *Bundesamt*, which had initially taken up its work in 1950 with completely empty filing cabinets, collected information from public sources (such as newspapers and other press) or surveillance measures, which was gathered in case files maintained by the evaluation department. In his memoirs, Postel described the rudimentary conditions under which these activities were performed, especially in the early days, and his personal opinions on the matter:

> On two shelves were some folders labeled "Left", "Right" and "Zone". This was a rough division with the meanings "left-wing radicalism", "right-wing radicalism" and "Soviet zone". The few written documents were only filed according to the dates of the documents, i.e. without any further factual classification. Under these circumstances, retrieving relevant correspondence for the future was naturally difficult. . . . Since some of the already existing *Landesämter für Verfassungsschutz* were already working more efficiently,

210 *Christopher Kirchberg*

> a more orderly process of conducting business was needed in the BfV as quickly as possible. I soon realised that Dr. Nollau [the chief analyst at that time, C.K.]..., the former lawyer, seemed to neglect organizational problems. I saw this as a good opportunity for me to influence organizational questions at an early stage.[9]

Beyond the description of early information management in the *Bundesamt*, the quote from Postel's memoirs testifies to his view of the early years of the BfV and his self-image.[10] Obviously, he was concerned with elevating his own status as an expert in organisational matters – especially in contrast to the lawyers who were superior to him, which features as a recurring theme throughout his autobiography. This may also be the reason why Postel voiced his disapproval of the organisational logic described in the passage quoted above, which corresponded primarily to legal requirements by arranging incoming information according to case files, supplemented by a content registry. In retrospect, Postel highlighted the practical problems since "the growing abundance of files and findings made it necessary to make the most important facts available for immediate access at the workstation of the clerk, without having to physically consult the complete files stored in a central location." As his own work was affected by these unsatisfactory conditions, he "suggested that . . . so-called working card files be set up in the individual units for meaningful and evaluated brief information from the files."[11]

However, as Postel wrote in his memoirs, his proposals were not implemented by him personally, but instead by a higher-ranking colleague – likely to his personal dismay. This notwithstanding, his ideas met with approval within the intelligence service.[12] Over the course of the 1950s, a system of two main card indexes emerged: on the one hand, there were the working card files in the individual departments, which contained detailed knowledge about persons and referred to several, often separately filed cases about specific individuals. On the other hand, the *Bundesamt* had tracing files like the *Personenzentralkartei* (Person Central File, PZK), which either referred to these working card files or contained information about individual cases. However, since the space for information to be entered on the index cards of the PZK was limited, multiple tracing files were often created for one and the same person, thereby immensely increasing the volume of documents comprising this particular index. In general, this analogue system helped to systematise and to objectivise incoming information, in addition to organising the retrieval process.[13] As a result, the file search tool became a separate search option by means of individual categories recorded on the index cards.[14]

While internal information processing practices diversified in the early years of the *Bundesamt*, there was a general shift in the threat perceptions of the young Federal Republic from (former) National Socialists to Communists against the backdrop of the emerging Cold War context.[15] This was accompanied by new tasks for the intelligence apparatus, which led to the hiring of more personnel and a rapid increase in collected information by the *Bundesamt* at the same time: in the late 1950s, the intelligence service compiled 250,000 new index cards with details about persons under observation – which included individuals who were

Eliminating the human factor? 211

involved in extremist (right and left) organisations or working in security-sensitive areas – per year.[16] For the services themselves, every additional piece of information could potentially be relevant for their knowledge about suspected persons,[17] however the processing of incoming findings and the rapid retrieval of relevant information using analogue index cards apparently became an obstacle – at least in the eyes of some intelligence officers: for instance, the former president of the *Bundesamt*, Günther Nollau,[18] described in his autobiography how search queries using the index card technique sometimes took up to a week to be processed, since the intelligence service had over a million tracing files in its holdings. Furthermore, cross-references to other sources were arranged in a rather complicated manner.[19]

Although it is difficult to reconstruct the degree of importance that the agency attached to the problem of analogue information processing in general at the time, this represented a rather unsatisfactory situation for an intelligence service dependent on (rapidly accessible) information. It certainly did not escape the attention of Hans-Joachim Postel: in the wake of the agency's growth in personnel and tasks, he identified information processing as a special field of activity. As I argue, his framing of this issue as a problem for which he, as an expert, presented (simple) technical solutions, would come to decisively shape the trajectory of his career in the *Bundesamt*.

As Postel unequivocally states in his memoirs, he became one of the first employees in the *Bundesamt* who attempted to improve the ostensibly insufficient information processing – most certainly in an effort to overcome his controversial and tenuous position within the organisation. Despite already performing the duties of a section chief (*Referatsgruppenleiter*), he had long been denied a promotion and appropriate recognition, such as in the form of an adequate classification in the collective bargaining agreement, as he describes in detail in his memoirs.[20] Eventually, Postel filed a lawsuit against the *Bundesamt* in 1955 in an effort to gain this recognition, and ultimately succeeded with an out-of-court settlement guaranteeing him the required classification two years later.[21]

However, even though Postel achieved financial success with this lawsuit, he retained the status of a simple employee in the midst of many civil servants in high positions in the German intelligence service.[22] Hence, he continued to fight for recognition within what he himself described in his memoirs as the conservative staff of the *Bundesamt*, where formal education and party membership, rather than professional skills and abilities, played a decisive role when it came to promotions.[23] Subscribing to this (German) status-oriented mindset, Postel devoted himself to information processing since it obviously represented a suitable field within which to distinguish himself as someone who was highly interested in questions pertaining to information management, and familiar with cutting edge solutions to problems in this field.

Within the *Bundesamt* itself, however, these problems of internal information processing were presumably not perceived as ranging among the most pressing issues of the day, at least among senior officials. The public image of the intelligence service had been tarnished in the wake of numerous scandalised practices and missteps, human shortcomings and breaches of trust. For example, during

212 *Christopher Kirchberg*

the so-called Vulkan affair in 1953, West German counterintelligence had been misled by false information provided by a Stasi agent who had fled the country; a year later, in turn, the president of the *Bundesamt* Otto John fled to East German under circumstances that remain shrouded in mystery to this day.[24] In addition to the efforts to improve the reputation of the intelligence service, these affairs and the problems behind them probably also influenced internal debates, which certainly did not escape Postel's attention.[25] In the late 1950s, to draw attention to the disadvantages of intelligence information processing, he sought to exploit what he perceived as the core of the problem underlying these scandals, namely the unreliability of human beings, in an effort to bolster his own argument:

> Over the past years, the practice had been established to transfer employees who are no longer usable elsewhere to the *Zentralkartei* [the Central File Department of the *Bundesamt*, C.K.]. The staff is overaged (average age 45 years), partly ill (war-disabled). Tensions arising from unequal payment for similar tasks affect the working atmosphere. All of this has had a negative effect on individual performance as well as on the file as a whole, which damaged its reputation.[26]

Hence, Postel argued that the perceived problem of internal information processing at the BfV was not limited to the index card system that was in use up to that point, but also to the "human factor": in the late 1950s, he viewed his colleagues from the *Zentralkartei* and their inadequacies as a liability, rather than an asset, for the agency and its work. A vicious cycle was to blame for this; the central file was obviously held in low esteem, with mainly low-skilled and poorly-motivated staff working here – this in turn produced poor results, which themselves did little to improve its standing within the agency.

This was precisely where Postel, who had risen to the position of assistant consultant (*Hilfsreferent*) in the meantime, recognised a niche with which to distinguish himself from the staff of the *Zentralkartei* and to present a solution that would make it possible to break out of this cycle.[27] Therefore, Postel was less concerned with the reliability and adequate work results of individual colleagues:

> In the stress of everyday work life, the intellectual capacity of the card index employees proved to be too limited to reliably recognise, correct and properly allocate the various deficiencies of the often fragmentary and/or incorrect data gained by the intelligence service.[28]

In his view, this was the problem of the human element within the *Zentralkartei*, which itself was already considered to be a professional purgatory that impaired efficient work.

Thus, Postel shifted the focus onto data entry as the main problem of manual information processing, where human errors in transmission made it difficult to clearly categorise and quickly or reliably search for collected information. With punch card technology, Postel was able to present a promising, ostensibly easy

Eliminating the human factor? 213

and quick solution with which to overcome the inherent disadvantages of manual (analogue) information processing methods.

At that time, collected information was entered into a card file in at least one of several different indexes of the *Bundesamt*. These pre-formatted card files for persons, objects or characteristics contained empty fields for hard facts, such as names or addresses, and often there was additional space to fill in further (more or less) important details. When an employee tried to (re)locate this person or related information at a later date, he had to search through thousands of index cards, many of which contained incorrect or incomplete data. Since punch card technology promised a remedy for this by means of unambiguous entries (a hole that indicated "yes" or "no"), Postel could present it as an ideal way to solve the "human" disadvantage of slow information retrieval and low productivity by rationalising the information processing activities.[29] The fact that the system not only promised more rapid information processing, but also reduced manpower requirements in the *Zentralkartei* probably convinced the decision-makers, who had high hopes for rationalisation processes, not least because there was a notorious shortage of personnel at the *Bundesamt*.[30]

At this point, the intelligence service had fallen into an unquestioned vicious cycle, in which newly perceived dangers and new tasks led to an increase in the volume of information, to which the leadership responded with the hiring of additional personnel. However, more employees, if indeed they could be hired at all because of lacking qualifications or security concerns, tended to increase the volume of information even further. Additional personnel thus posed a new problem, especially since the employees brought inadequacies such as human error or other factors undermining reliability with them to the agency. Here, the technical solution propagated by Postel promised a way out.

But by presenting a solution based on new technologies, he simultaneously created a new unforeseen problem: to prevent human error in information processing by reducing the influence of his employees in the process, punch card technology required a renewed adaptation of the logic of the information to be recorded. While information from the files was summarised with the help of the card indexes in the early years, punch cards now became the main frame of reference for information-gathering:

> For data acquisition, as an intermediate storage [medium, C.K.] for transferring to punched cards and as an aid for the exchange of card indexes, uniform forms (*Lochbelege*) are used. The specialist departments of the BfV are responsible for the evaluation of the files. . . . They transfer the information to be indexed onto the punched documents. . . . The data are . . . manually translated into the specified machine language and entered into punch cards.[31]

In practice, this meant that the complete flow of information needed to be adapted to the new forms, which were also used by the *Landesämter* and other intelligence services. Thereby, a negotiation process was set into motion that lasted for several years. In the early stages, the degree to which the supposed advantages of punch

214   *Christopher Kirchberg*

card technology had a noticeable impact in everyday work processes was limited. In addition, the transformation process was delayed for a long time due to personnel shortages. Hence, when it came to implementing the promise of needing fewer employees for information processing, precisely these employees were a bottleneck during the transfer of 1 million card indexes to the new punch card format.[32]

Beyond this, however, not only the transformation was problematic, but it also created new dependencies in and of itself: while the *Bundesamt* was guided by Postel's arguments, Postel himself was influenced by the International Business Machines Corporation (IBM). Founded on Hollerith's patents, IBM had established itself as the market leader for punch cards in the 1950s and was also prominently represented on the German market due to its aggressive and successful marketing in Europe, which apparently also caught Postel's attention.[33] By arguing that there was no viable German competitor to the punch-card machines from the United States in the post-war period,[34] Postel was able to convince the head office to buy IBM machines in 1959 – with far-reaching consequences for the internal information processing. From 1960 onwards the punch card system was successively built up and put into operation. This immensely accelerated the search for persons and members of organisations in the fields in which it came to be used. This was due to two advantages of the punch card system: first, the coding of the information enabled electro-mechanical search queries, which usually provided the requested information within a few minutes. Second, the punch card system automatically sorted out cards that were no longer needed and could be destroyed, which helped free the information assets from unnecessary clutter that had prolonged search queries.[35] Beyond the mere rationalisation of information processing, the new format now also allowed for cross-sectional evaluations such as queries for certain characteristics like memberships in organisations. This potentially helped uncover links between persons or organisations and thus helped to expand the knowledge of the intelligence service: using mere references to case files on observed persons or organisations, intelligence officers could now build new suspicious cases by cross-referencing extracted individual pieces of information.[36]

Aside from these accompanying changes in the realm of knowledge production, the punch card system also affected the working practises for the staff in the *Zentralkartei* of the *Bundesamt*, as Postel claimed according to the official records:

> As a result of the mechanization of the card indexes labour productivity per employee . . . increased by 60%. The numerous new tasks could only be fulfilled because the personnel requirements for the existing work were considerably reduced by mechanization.[37]

What Postel failed to mention here, however, is that a lengthy process of conversion, replete with transmission work and adjustments, preceded these "accomplishments of rationalization." With the implementation of the step-by-step transfer of the most important card indexes onto punch cards, the tasks of the employees in the central file system changed: the staff now had to sort the incoming findings as preliminary work, prepare the information for transfer to punch cards by encoding

Eliminating the human factor? 215

them, press the punch cards and fill out documents for queries. All of these tasks required additional training for the employees, including for the operation of the new machines. Apart from these general effects on the personnel situation in terms of higher qualification requirements, the extensive conversion to punch card technology also came to represent a veritable "lucky punch" for Hans-Joachim Postel: by transforming internal information processing practices, the ordinary administrative officer became chief of the "Information Technology" unit and therefore a proven expert for information processing.[38] So, the introduction of the Hollerith technique was a career boost for him and brought him a certain recognition inside the agency.[39]

Beyond these changes regarding the personnel situation, i.e. the question of human influences, higher qualifications and Postel's rise in the ranks, the introduction of the new technology inadvertently led to at least two further developments. In order to be utilised properly, the entire organisational framework for the storage of information needed to be restructured and standardised, which was not limited to the *Bundesamt* itself. To make optimal use of the punch cards, the exchange of information between the central (federal) *Bundesamt* and the individual *Landesämter für Verfassungsschutz* had to be improved. For this purpose, the *Bundesamt* was authorised to establish and operate the so-called "Zentrale Hinweiskartei der Nachrichtendienste" (Central Index of the Intelligence Services, ZKN) in 1965 – based on punch card technology. This centralisation of intelligence information led to an expansion of the *Bundesamt's* authority. While this generally elevated the importance of the *Bundesamt* within the Federal Republic's security architecture, it also led to a further increase in the volume of information to be processed by the domestic intelligence service due to a general expansion of tasks for the intelligence apparatus.[40] Thus it fed into the contemporary discourse of a perceived flood of information, which remains in vogue to this day.[41] Punch card technology was supposed to help cope with the mountains of information, but *nolens volens* it generated new volumes of data, which soon led to new problems.

Thus, Postel had identified a window of opportunity and drawn attention to the man-made problems of information processing. Along with accelerating the pace of processing and also improving its quality by changing the storage logic, it also led to new tasks for the employees – and to Postel's own promotion. However, these changes were accompanied by unintended consequences, which, however, did not lead to an interruption of the transformation, although – according to Postel – the limits of Hollerith technology in processing large amounts of data would already become apparent a few years after its introduction.

Postel and the promised land: the digitisation of information processing between American hardware and German software

While information processing in the *Bundesamt* had been gradually modernised through the introduction of punch card machines since the early 1960s, Postel pushed ahead with plans for a new technical transformation: that of electronic data

216 *Christopher Kirchberg*

processing (EDP). One reason for this was the successful application of the new technology by security serves and law enforcement in the United States. Due to the *Bundesamt's* transatlantic ties and its role within the Western security architecture in the Cold War context,[42] two employees were able to closely observe the possible applications and the development of the new technology. Postel and a colleague travelled to the United States just one year after the introduction of the ZKN and the comprehensive use of punch cards within the *Ämter für Verfassungsschutz*:

> In the spring of 1966, . . . a trip to the USA followed. It was an initiative of the CIA and was to lead to selected destinations in Washington DC, New York City and upstate New York. Again, my section chief took part in this trip, for whom it was also the first trip to the US. Until then, the US had been primarily the destination of our office leadership. The invitation was preceded by a visit to Cologne by the head of the CIA's information system in Langley near Washington, DC. He was primarily interested in our broad application of the Hollerith technique for action analysis and sociological studies in the field of counterintelligence.[43]

This business trip, which Postel passionately recounted in his autobiography – appropriately his book is prefaced by a photograph of him on one of his trips to United States (Figure 10.1) – was indeed remarkable: Not only due to the adventurous journey with the *Bundeswehr* (the Federal Defense Forces of Germany) via the Azores (Terceira) and McGuire Air Force Base in the state of New Jersey, which Postel described in detail, but also because it highlights the specific context of technological developments in the Western hemisphere. Furthermore, the report of this trip reveals certain (culturally shaped) ideas in Postel's thinking. To what extent did these ideas and his trip to the United States inspire the more recent transformation, this time from punch card technology to EDP? How would Postel come to appropriate this trip as a means to cast himself in the role of an IT expert, thereby making the introduction of a computer system a reality? Finally, what problems did the transformation promise to solve in Postel's eyes, and which general developments provided the context for this?

Generally speaking, the punch card technology proved to be of disadvantage for information processing in the intelligence service context in several respects: first, their limited storage space of 10×80 characters soon turned out to be too small, and information could only be entered onto the punched cards in abbreviated form. Second, the mechanised information processing was pushed to the limits of its reading capabilities in the mid-1960s when the volume of stored intelligence information grew by several tens of thousands of cards per year. Third, the electromechanical technology became increasingly uneconomical, since it only partially fulfilled the function Postel had promised, namely that fewer employees would be needed for information processing. On the one hand, the results of mechanical information processing had still depended on human groundwork, which still led to errors. On the other hand, new punch card machines needed for further tasks required additional (higher-salaried) employees for their operation.

Eliminating the human factor? 217

These problems became increasingly urgent from the mid-1960s onwards, when processes of social and political change also became a challenge for the *Bundesamt*. After the construction of the Berlin Wall and the Cuban missile crisis, the hot phase of the Cold War subsided, giving way to a period of détente.[44] Yet the simultaneously forming student protests and the emergence of the New Left, initially categorised by the German security authorities as "radical left,"[45] led to new targets for observation and more work for the intelligence services, including the surveillance of students at universities in West Germany.[46] These new tasks intensified the problem of personnel and information growth up to 27 per cent in 1967[47] already described – a problem not only for intelligence agencies, but administrative bodies in general.

In this case, the changing threat perception presented a new window of opportunity for Postel in his quest to advance his idea of digitisation, as the problems of punch card technology became apparent to his own superiors against the backdrop of increasing volumes of information. At the same time, Postel's visions benefited from another general development.

Since the end of the 1940s, cybernetics had risen to become a leading science in the Western hemisphere due to its promising control theory, which paved the way for the triumphant ascent of computer technology that would eventually reach West Germany in the 1960s.[48] Simultaneously, contemporary observers diagnosed a "technological gap" in Western Europe: American accomplishments in the fields of space or nuclear technology – and now also in the field of EDP – reinforced this view in West German debates and led to various efforts geared towards closing this "gap."[49]

On the one hand, this (contradictory) discursive mood provided the backdrop for the first of several business trips by Postel and his colleague Werner Smoydzin, the future deputy director of the *Bundesamt*, whose purpose it was "to study electronic data processing."[50] During their almost two-week trip, the two Germans held, among other things, meetings with representatives of the CIA to discuss general questions pertaining to the organisation and tasks of their American partners, but also the use of modern EDP systems. They also had appointments with the FBI, discussed the use of EDP at the New York State Police, and paid a visit to the production facilities and laboratories of IBM to gain an impression of future technical developments. While the trip to the United States provided Postel with arguments and plans to promote the use of EDP in the *Bundesamt*, the American partner services pursued other goals beyond the provision of technical development assistance to the Germans. Presumably, the main interest of the American colleagues was a close exchange of data, for example, on communists. Accordingly, the report of the trip mentioned a "joint program for recording the legal foreign travel of Soviet citizens." In fact, a subsequent transfer of information from the so-called EGIS (East-German Intelligence Services) database by the *Bundesamt* occurred at the end of the 1960s.[51]

On the other hand, the contemporary debates about emerging EDP techniques also shaped Postel's view of the different (information technology) developments on both sides of the Atlantic. In contrast to these reasons indicated in the official

218   *Christopher Kirchberg*

files, however, Postel prepared the ground for a different interpretation, as implied in the previously cited quote: supposedly, the high standards and the achievements of analogue data processing based on punch card technology had aroused the Americans' curiosity about the accomplishments of the *Bundesamt* (and Postel in particular), and ultimately led to an invitation being extended to the two German intelligence officers.[52] Postel's memoirs indicate that this business trip sparked his enthusiasm and admiration for the United States, which he visited for the first time. Concurrently, however, his descriptions of this and subsequent trips implicitly also refer to a culturally charged contrast between an "idealistic" German worldview and American pragmatism. While the United States with its modern, technological achievements, particularly in the field of EDP, represented the promised land of technical progress, Postel, who was obviously influenced by contemporary debates among German techno-experts like Horst Futh,[53] felt a certain sense of superiority due to his German intellectual solutions for information processing, owing to two achievements: on the basis of his supposedly high level of mechanical information processing using the Hollerith technology (mentioned in his quote at the beginning of this chapter), and because of his ideas in the field of name searching, which he presented as superior to American solutions.

Postel claimed that he had been working on the problem of how to process similar sounding but differently spelled or incorrectly recorded names since the early 1960s. In order to standardise the encoding of names in the process of transferring them to punch cards, Postel developed a phonetic system with which to record and retrieve incomplete or even misspelled names. While this was initially a pressing problem, especially for intelligence services interested in tracking and identifying suspects with the smallest possible error margin, it became a general challenge for the digitisation of data: in the wake of EDP's expansion from the United States to Germany, corporations and even government organisations now faced the prospect of having to digitise large quantities of personal names.[54]

Against this backdrop, Postel successfully published his ideas in two papers at the end of the 1960s. The first paper with the title "Organisation und Verarbeitung biographischer Daten bei phonetischer Namensdarstellung"[55] ("Organization and Processing of Biographical Data in Phonetic Name Representation") was published in the German journal *Bürotechnik + Automation* (*Office Technology + Automation*), an "independent journal for electronic data processing"[56] in the Federal Republic at the time. In 1969, a second, similar paper appeared in the company magazine *IBM-Nachrichten* (*IBM News*), as the topic was also discussed by IT-businesses.[57] Here, Postel presented his automated processing system, which he dubbed Cologne Phonetics and dealt with fragmented or differently spelled names. This phonetic system was based on a reduction of names to their phonetic root by substituting consonants and deleting vowels as far as possible. Postel's considerations, however, were not only applicable to German names but also to Slavic, Spanish or English ones, since "Braun" or "Brown" became "BRN" in both cases, for example.

To emphasise the German provenance of his system, he clearly distinguished his phonetic system from other, American ones in both articles. Postel drew attention

Eliminating the human factor? 219

to the fact that other phonetic systems known at the time, such as the Russel Soundex System developed in the United States or the Chicago Title and Trust Company Index, which was used by the CIA,[58] required many special rules.[59] Conversely, Cologne Phonetics promised to forgo these to a large extent, which made the system suitable for automatic application without human intervention.[60] By using his sophisticated phonetic program, the intelligence service computer should be able to handle the conversion of names and automate the entire information process at the same time by searching for phonetic matches of first names or surnames between searched and stored data.[61] Thus, his phonetic system promised to utilise the technical equipment to overcome the error-prone human collection of information (for example by agents through wiretapping measures) and its acquisition for information processing. According to Postel, these supposed advantages of the system also caught the CIA's attention. While the *Bundesamt* sold the "employee invention" of Cologne Phonetics to numerous other users outside the intelligence community, such as government agencies and business corporations in the course of the 1970s and 1980s due to its practicability, the CIA was not included in this list of customers.[62]

Thus, Postel presented his "German" ideas – or "software" – with his experiences of American technical developments ("hardware") to tout EDP as a modern solution for the internal informational problems that his own superiors found convincing.[63] Thereby, he sought to strengthen ties with allied security intelligence services overseas while simultaneously making a national contribution to overcoming technological backwardness.

In the end, the *Bundesamt* began to implement an EDP system called NADIS ("Nachrichtendienstliches Informationssystem," Intelligence Information System) in the late 1960s, which was initially based on IBM system 360–40. Obviously, previous use of the punch card technology played a role in the decision to select IBM computers. However, beyond that, it is not exactly clear whether IBM's own sales strategy was particularly effective or whether Postel's American colleagues pushed for compatibility with US-based computer systems (in order to incorporate databases maintained by the CIA, such as EGIS). In any case, the *Bundesamt* decided against the adoption of a German-based solution, even though companies like Siemens began to offer equipment with comparable computational power in the late 1960s and German products were partially funded by the West German government.[64] While the hardware came from the United States, Postel and his colleagues developed their own software for NADIS – for security reasons, technical support provided by a (German) IBM sales manager was limited[65] – and began with the complex implementation and introduction of NADIS. After a test-run lasting several months, the transfer of data and staff training, the computer system NADIS was put into operation in a first phase of expansion in February 1971. The commissioning rationalised and accelerated the search for information to a considerable degree, and fundamentally transformed data processing activities. By using Postel's Cologne Phonetics, the computer overcame difficulties in the acquisition of personal names, avoided transmission errors in the storage process, and improved queries for personal data by displaying similar matches.

220 *Christopher Kirchberg*

Thus, in the mid-1960s, after successfully implementing punch card technology, Postel saw an opportunity to further modernise information processing by introducing an EDP system. This occurred against the background of two significant developments at the end of the 1960s: On the one hand, a euphoric discourse about technology now also gained currency among German authorities, as it highlighted the potential of EDP within their own organisations. On the other hand, student protests and the emerging New Left changed the threat perception of the intelligence service and the volume of information that it handled. Within this context, solutions that originated from Postel's "German mind," such as the Cologne phonetics, initially enabled him to gather arguments in the United States for the implementation of the computer system and thus to cast himself in the role of a worldly IT expert within the Federal Office, where he finally put NADIS into operation around the turn of the decade. Even though Postel had achieved his original goal of initiating the digitisation and automation of information processing in the *Bundesamt* while cementing his own status as an expert, problems remained. On the structural-organisational level, for example, digitisation was far from complete despite the commissioning of NADIS, and Postel's aim of ridding information processing of "human" obstacles was by no means fully accomplished, as will be shown below.

Postel's persistent problems: new human dependencies within the context of internal information processing at the BfV

Several weeks after the commissioning of the NADIS system, the "*Amtsleitertagung*" (Heads of Office Conference), a gathering of all presidents of the domestic intelligence agencies in the Federal Republic and representatives of the Ministry of the Interior took place in May 1971. Whereas the (domestic) political situation was usually discussed or agreements on cooperation were negotiated, this time, Postel was invited and made a major appearance.

> Above all, this [the successful commissioning of NADIS, C.K.] means real-time processing, i.e. the immediate response to inquiries by machines in dialogue mode. As a result, the number of employees could be reduced. In the meantime, the individual departments of the BfV have also begun to use decentralised input via screen. This shortens the response time and time-consuming manual work becomes obsolete.[66]

With an unmistakeable sense of pride, Postel reported that the first stage of configuration had since been in operation for several months, and he emphasised how computerisation accelerated the queries and further limited human influence on information processing. By focusing on the first years since the introduction of the new computer system, this section will investigate how computerisation enabled new forms of work, the new problems that arose from the use of computers, and the (unintended) consequences of digitisation for employees and the *Bundesamt* – many of which ran counter to Postel's own predictions.

Eliminating the human factor?   221

According to contemporary interpretations prevalent among personnel in the security services, digitisation promised to eliminate blind spots in the reservoirs of knowledge that had been the result of (human) transmission errors, and make the stored information (and even the knowledge derived from it) more condensed, centralised and (apparently) more objective through the rational use of EDP.[67] This nurtured the assumption, still widely held today, that more and better connected information would increase knowledge about suspicious individuals and groups and thus invariably improve security.[68] In one field in particular, this consideration and new, data-driven forms of evaluation seemingly led to successes for the *Bundesamt*: since the computerised search for spies was narrowed down to specific characteristics that exposed the agents, NADIS was propagandistically presented as a "spy hunter" tool, which had helped to expose several foreign agents from the East through cross-sectional evaluations of its databases in the mid-1970s.[69]

Despite these accomplishments, however, NADIS also confronted the *Bundesamt* with new problems. As a result of other dependencies that emerged in the wake of digitisation, the computerised search for potential suspects did not always run smoothly at the *Bundesamt* either. On the one hand, human employees sometimes called in sick or committed errors due to lapses in concentration; on the other hand, the computer system sometimes crashed without any prior warning, especially in the early years.[70] This posed new challenges for the processes of knowledge production. In his autobiography, Postel highlighted these challenges by using the example of the attacks by the Palestinian terrorist organisation Black September on the Israeli team during the Olympic Games in Munich on September 5, 1972, which led to the deaths of 17 people:

> Now, events followed in quick succession, we received the extended order to vet all Arab or ostensibly Arab persons in air and rail traffic as well as other alleged supporters of the terrorists in the country at short notice. In day and night operations . . . we achieved that, for example, no aircraft took off in Germany until relevant persons on board were vetted by NADIS and the Federal Border Guard. This also applied to cross-border rail traffic. I do not forget the stress when we received urgent requests for information from the Federal Border Guard at Cologne/Wahn Airport, but the computer system had to be restarted because it broke down, which was time-consuming. . . . In the end we were able to respond in time.[71]

Even though Postel ultimately sought to retroactively portray the system crash as a success story, this excerpt draws attention to a general problem of the computer system. This particular crash by no means the only one, and NADIS boasted failure rates of up to 20 per cent in the early 1970s. Internally, however, this was not levelled as a point of criticism against EDP; the chosen path was not called into question but retained. This decision was driven by the contemporary belief in technology – at least among certain adherents such as Postel, who envisioned a technical but expensive response to this new challenge: it was not until the mid-1970s that the intelligence service expanded the system with a second central unit, which

222   *Christopher Kirchberg*

made it a full duplex system that was less prone to crashes.[72] This notwithstanding, additional problems and unexpected challenges associated with digitisation remained. In fact, the expansion of the hardware equipment was the reason for new problems and carried unintended consequences in its wake.

Work was further rationalised and accelerated through the use of the computer system, and the electronic information processing required less personnel. However, this was only one side of the coin when it came to the relationship between the computer and the employee. On the other side, higher-ranking personnel who used the system for their analyses required extensive training. This in turn had an effect on the processing of information. At the same time, due to "intensive training, longer practice and greater familiarity of the staff with the system," the quality of produced knowledge and the computer system itself "led to a more qualified use of the procedure (more cross-sectional inquiries. . . , careful formulation and logging of queries and results)," as Postel stated in 1976. "This also causes increased internal processing effort. . . . It is therefore requested . . . to approve the increase of the main memory of both processors to 1.5 MB . . . because of the justified larger main memory requirement."[73]

This statement by Postel, which cited higher usage rates instead of security reasons to justify the expansion of the computer facility, shows two things. First and foremost, the successful use of the computer system produced assumed constraints that highlighted an interdependence of higher usage and greater computer performance. Second, Postel's concern demonstrates that the new technology evidently also generated new forms of knowledge within the intelligence service. Through the technological and terminological know-how regarding the concrete functioning of NADIS, Postel secured a kind of hegemonic knowledge that made him virtually irreplaceable for the *Bundesamt*.

But the reason for the need for more powerful computers was not only based on a more extensive use by the employees, as the development of the phonetic system demonstrates. Already in the early 1970s, Postel had updated his phonetic search tool, which was employed under the name "Cologne Phonetics 1973." This adaptation indicates at least two things. The addition of Arabic names to this new version reflects a shift in threat perceptions of the domestic secret service, which had been shaped by international terrorism since the aforementioned 1972 attacks during the Olympic Games. But the fact that at least several months passed between the emergence of new threats and the use of updated software highlights another problem that accompanied computerisation. This point was by no means limited to software programs alone – the database structure also had to be adapted to new threats; new risks often required the addition of new features to be captured. The counterterrorism file "Persons and Experiences on Terrorism," abbreviated PET, which was created in reaction to the climax of left-wing extremist terrorism by the Red Army Faction (RAF) in the Federal Republic, provides a case in point: while the terrorist attacks peaked in the already mentioned "German Autumn" of 1977, it would take until 1978 for the database to become operational.[74] While standardised search processes were massively accelerated by digitisation, as demonstrated by the previously cited example of the exposing of foreign agents, NADIS was only

Eliminating the human factor? 223

able to react to new threats with a considerable time lag. This was because new tasks did not merely depend on software engineering: in addition to faster computing capacities and larger storage space, which led to unexpected and high costs, the need for well-trained personnel also increased. The Information Technology Unit, which had been newly created in the late 1960s, was upgraded to a central department – this also carried another promotion for Postel in its wake. By 1976, more than 100 employees were already involved in the operation and development of the IT system. Rather than leading to a reduction of personnel in the BfV, which Postel had originally promised when he touted the introduction of punch cards, there was a shift towards better trained and higher-ranking departments. This contributed to increased professionalisation and greater demand for IT experts, such as system analysts and programmers, as well as new, comparatively simpler jobs like data typists or employees for data preparation and collection at the same time.[75] Thus, in 1969, a total of 27 people were employed in the *Zentralkartei*, almost two-thirds of whom performed rudimentary tasks as selectors or assistants.[76] Following the implementation of NADIS, there were more than 100 personnel in this area by mid-1976; however, the number of low-ranking employees in the simple service (*Einfacher Dienst*) remained unchanged, whereas more than half of all personnel were employed in the middle service (*Mittlerer Dienst*) and more than a third were in the higher or senior service (*Gehobener und Höherer Dienst*).[77]

In addition to the *Bundesamt's* general difficulties in finding suitable employees who met the high security requirements, it competed with business corporations and other government agencies who also sought to recruit and retain IT experts:[78] "For example, the BFV lost 30% of its programmers during the establishment of the Fee Collection Centre of the Public Broadcasting Companies in the Federal Republic of Germany [*Gebühreneinzugszentrale* (GEZ), C.K.] in Cologne."[79] This was an obstacle which would also negatively affect knowledge production in the *Bundesamt*: "The lack of personnel in the area of programming has repeatedly led to the fact that many technically justified machine evaluations could either not be produced at all or not within a timely manner."[80]

The use of the computer system had thus reduced the direct influence of employees on information processing in the agency, especially in the field of information acquisition and queries, through programs such as Cologne Phonetics. At the same time, however, the complexity of NADIS increased its reliance on employees who programmed, maintained or operated the system, which above all required higher qualifications on the part of the employees.[81] This circumstance obviously led to new people-based problems exacerbated by the already strained personnel situation. Once the new system had been established, abandoning it was not considered to be a viable option. In addition to these problems inherent in the system, the data protection provisions that emerged in the Federal Republic of Germany towards the end of the 1970s, which foresaw strict deletion requirements for the intelligence services, did not lead to dramatic changes in this regard, although they certainly deprived the system of its foundation. Neither the existence of the system, nor Postel himself, who had led the *Bundesamt* into this new spiral of dependency, were called into question, however: NADIS remains in use to this day, and apart

224   *Christopher Kirchberg*

from advancing Postel's own career, it has made data processing a key component of intelligence work, in which NADIS "plays a central role"[82] today. Simultaneously, the *Bundesamt* experienced a boost in professionalisation with regard to the agency's staff and their level of qualification – not only for Postel himself.[83]

Conclusion

When Postel left the *Bundesamt* in 1985 after 35 years due to ill health, the West German intelligence service and the way it operated had changed fundamentally since its foundation. Its tasks had become more diversified, the agency had grown considerably in terms of personnel and its duties, and internal processes and methodology underwent technological modernisation. The Hollerith technique represented an important first step in this regard, followed by the computerised information system NADIS, whose development and establishment is inseparably linked to Hans-Joachim Postel's career. By devoting himself to the field of information processing, which was supposed to have a niche existence, and by initiating changes with his enthusiasm for questions of organisation and technology, he was able to work his way up the career ladder from a simple employee to a unit chief, who apparently also made a name for himself beyond the agency through his publications. In the process, he followed a modernisation paradigm and constructed a challenge and response model. In accordance with this model, contemporary information processing problems were framed in such a way that he could present supposedly simple and inevitable modern technical solutions in the transition from analogue index card technology to electromechanical punch card technology and then to EDP, while changing the logic of information from qualitative files to quantitative data at the same time. However, these changes led to unforeseen path dependencies but rarely to the kind of comprehensive solution which he had envisioned. Thus, the *Bundesamt* did not achieve greater independence from human influences or employees in information processing, which he either concealed or promised to overcome with new technical solutions. Rather, these solutions inadvertently led to a professionalisation of the staff in terms of their tasks and qualifications – from typists to IT experts.

Postel proved to be adept at reading the contemporary mood in the *Bundesamt*, which allowed him to climb the career ladder against all odds, in an agency where the chances of promotion to high-ranking positions for personnel who were not formally trained lawyers were severely limited, by advancing the modernisation of information processing. However, this ability and intuition increasingly eluded him near the end of his career: caught in his rigid mindset, he was unable to comprehend the public demands for data protection at the end of the 1970s, which he saw as the end of all digital modernisation efforts – either because of the data protection regulations that supposedly hampered the further development of NADIS in the beginning 1980s[84] or because of insecurities regarding his personal status. In what surely represented an attempt to reassure both himself and the reader of his autobiography about his achievements throughout his ostensibly stellar career, his memoirs also included a letter from Franz Natusch, a long-time companion of

Eliminating the human factor? 225

Postel's and the president of the *Verfassungsschutz* in Berlin at that time. The letter served to underscore Postel's undeniable importance for, and key role within, the *Bundesamt*: "In our service, you facilitated the breakthrough of modern working methodology; indeed, you ultimately created it. That this working methodology has considerably increased the effectiveness of the Bundesamt is something that no one can seriously deny today." Moving beyond this biased interpretation, this essay has sought to arrive at a more complex and nuanced understanding of Postel's legacy. Rather than representing an unequivocal success story, the computer system and other changes instituted by Postel evoked entirely new problems, complexities, and new dependencies on (highly educated) human employees, which by no means ended with Postel's leave from the BfV in the mid-1980s.

Notes

1 For the German case see Nollau, *Das Amt*. I thank the editors Rüdiger Bergien, Debora Gerstenberger and especially Constantin Goschler, for important comments and helpful remarks, as well as Yvonne Hilges, Jan Kellershohn, Stefan Pulte, and Jens Wegener, who proofread the article.
2 The other two departments at that time were "Personnel and Administration" and "Information Collection."
3 See attachment to letter from Bundesamt für Verfassungsschatz to Bundesminister des Innern, subject: Personalwirtschaftliche Maßnahmen beim Bundesamt für Verfassungsschutz, 1–16–1957, Personalblatt Hans-Joachim Postel, 84, in: Bundesarchiv B 106 202278.
4 Postel, *So war es*, 86. This and all subsequent quotations from Postel's memoir are the author's translations.
5 At the same time, the intelligence service lacked a common "agency spirit" in the early years, which may have further encouraged competitive thinking. See Goschler and Wala, *„ Keine Neue Gestapo,"* 152.
6 In 1980, for example, he was awarded the Order of Merit of the Federal Republic of Germany, see: Verleihung des Verdienstordens der Bundesrepublik Deutschland 1981, Ministerialblatt (MBl. NRW.) 27:541. <https://recht.nrw.de/lmi/owa/br_mbl_show_pdf?p_jahr=1981&p_nr=27> (last accessed July 6, 2021).
7 See for example Goschler and Wala, *„ Keine Neue Gestapo,"* 15. On the history of the British domestic intelligence service MI5, see Andrew, *The Defence of the Realm*.
8 Gesetz über die Zusammenarbeit des Bundes und der Länder in Angelegenheiten des Verfassungsschutzes vom 27.09.1950 (Law on the Cooperation of the Federal Government and the Länder in Matters of Verfassungsschutz from 9–27–1950), § 3, Bundesgesetzblatt, No. 42 (1950), 682. <www.bgbl.de/xaver/bgbl/start.xav?start=//*%5B@attr_id=%27bgbl150s0682a.pdf%27%5D__bgbl__%2F%2F*%5B%40attr_id%3D%27bgbl150s0682a.pdf%27%5D__1605179450069> (last accessed July 6, 2021).
9 Postel, *So war es*, 56.
10 Ibid., 56.
11 Ibid., 62–63.
12 Ibid., 63.
13 The problems caused by the decontextualization of information during the transfer to card files were not discussed at all, nor was any thought given to the fact that this made the accuracy of the information on the card files all the more significant.
14 Bericht über Organisation, Umfang und Personalbedarf der bestehenden Karteien des BfV (report on the organization, scope and staffing requirements of the BfV's existing indexes), 2–28–1959, 4, in: Bundesarchiv B 443 5157.

226 *Christopher Kirchberg*

15 See Frei and Rigoll, *Der Antikommunismus in seiner Epoche*. This development has to be viewed within the transatlantic context of American McCarthyism, cf. Schrecker, *Many Are the Crimes*.

16 Bericht über Organisation, Umfang und Personalbedarf der bestehenden Karteien des BfV (report on the organization, scope and staffing requirements of the BfV's existing indexes), 2–28–1959, 19, in: Bundesarchiv B 443 5157.

17 Radu, Einleitung: Spionage, Geheimhaltung und Öffentlichkeit, 17.

18 Schrübbers entered the Bundesamt in 1950 and served as its president from 1972 to 1975.

19 Nollau, *Das Amt*, 236–237.

20 Postel, *So war es*, 66–67.

21 See Postel, *So war es*, 66–68.

22 In the 1950s, for example, the *Bundesamt* was mainly staffed with civil servants and only a few salaried employees were entrusted with higher-level tasks. See Goschler and Wala, „ *Keine Neue Gestapo*," 65.

23 Cf. Postel, *So war es*, 65–66.

24 For the Vulkan affair, see Goschler and Wala, „ *Keine Neue Gestapo*," 337–338. On the mysterious circumstances of John's crossing of the border and his life in general, see Hett and Wala, *Otto John: Patriot oder Verräter*.

25 In October 1961, the Bundesamt hired Friedrich Ernst Berghoff as its first full-time public relations officer, see Goschler and Wala, „ *Keine Neue Gestapo*," 199.

26 Ibid., 13–14.

27 Postel, *So war es*, 72.

28 Ibid., 86.

29 Vorschlag für die Umstellung der Karteien des BfV auf die Elektronische Datenverarbeitung (EDV) (proposal for the conversion of the BfV's files to electronic data processing (EDP)), 5–1–1967, 8, in: Bundesarchiv B 443 2821.

30 Goschler and Wala, „ *Keine Neue Gestapo*," 335.

31 Vorschlag für die Umstellung der Karteien des BfV auf die Elektronische Datenverarbeitung (EDV) (proposal for the conversion of the BfV's files to electronic data processing (EDP)), 5–1–1967, 7, in: Bundesarchiv B 443 2821.

32 Postel, *So war es*, 87.

33 Cf. Schlombs, *Productivity Machines*.

34 Schuhmann, Der Traum vom perfekten Unternehmen. Die Computerisierung der Arbeitswelt in der Bundesrepublik Deutschland (1950er- bis 1980er-Jahre), 241.

35 Karteianweisung und Auswertungsplan (card instruction and evaluation plan, undated), 11, in: Bundesarchiv B 443/2795.

36 Postel, Organisation und Aufgaben der automatisierten Informationsverarbeitung in den Behörden für Verfassungsschutz, 125–132, 128.

37 Vorschlag für die Umstellung der Karteien des BfV auf die Elektronische Datenverarbeitung (EDV) (proposal for the conversion of the BfV's files to electronic data processing (EDP)), 5–1–1967, 8, in: Bundesarchiv B 443 2821.

38 Postel, *So war es*, 98.

39 Ibid., 88.

40 For job growth and the expansion of the intelligence service's authorities, see Goschler and Wala, „ *Keine Neue Gestapo*," 294–301.

41 See Gugerli, Informationsflut.

42 See Goschler and Wala, „ *Keine Neue Gestapo,* " 334–336.

43 Postel, *So war es*, 99.

44 For example, new perspectives on the Cold War and its "fever curves" are offered by Reichherzer, Droit and Hansen, *Den Kalten Krieg vermessen: Über Reichweite und Alternativen einer binären Ordnungsvorstellung*.

45 Protokoll über die Amtsleitertagung am 2. und 3. September 1969 (minutes of the meeting of heads of office on 2 and 3 September 1969), 9–18–1969, 8, in: Bundesarchiv B 443 2517.

Eliminating the human factor? 227

46 See Bundesministerium des Innern, ed., 1967: Verfassungsschutz und SDS. In *Innere Sicherheit. Informationen zu Fragen des Staatsschutzes*, 11.

47 See Schreiben des Bundesamtes an das Innenministerium, Betreff: Umstellung der Karteien des BfV auf die elektronische Datenverarbeitung (EDV) (letter from the Bundesamt to the Ministry of the Interior, subject: Conversion of the BfV's files to electronic data processing (EDP), 3–28–1968, 5, in: Bundesarchiv B 443 2822.

48 For example with regard to developments in Western Germany: Kasper, *Wie der Sozialstaat digital wurde*, 40–41; In general see e.g.: Galison, The Ontology of the Enemy: Norbert Wiener and the Cybernetic Vision.

49 See Leimbach, *Geschichte der Softwarebranche*, 182–191.

50 Title of the mission report, 6–10–1966, in: Bundesarchiv B 2819.

51 See Schreiben des Bundesamtes an das Innenministerium, Betreff: Umstellung der Karteien des BfV auf die elektronische Datenverarbeitung (EDV) (letter from the Bundesamt to the Ministry of the Interior, subject: Conversion of the BfV's files to electronic data processing (EDP), 3–28–1968, 5, in: Bundesarchiv B 443 2822.

52 Postel, *So war es*, 99f.

53 His autobiography reveals that Postel became familiar with the subject of EDP primarily through books by Horst Futh: Futh, *Elektronische Datenverarbeitungsanlagen*.

54 Bösch provides a concise overview of current research on computerisation in the Federal Republic of Germany: Bösch, *Wege in die Digitale Gesellschaft*.

55 Postel, Die Kölner Phonetik (1968)

56 See the subtitle of the journal *Bürotechnik + Automation*.

57 Postel, Die Kölner Phonetik (1969).

58 See Grskovich, "Automating Name Searches."

59 National Archives and Records Administration. 2007. The Soundex Indexing System. <www.archives.gov/research/census/soundex> (last accessed March 31, 2021).

60 Postel, Die Kölner Phonetik (1969), 928.

61 Ibid., 928–929.

62 For early requests see: Entwurf eines Schreibens vom Bundesamt an den Bundesminister des Innern, Betreff: Veräußerung von Nutzungsrechten; hier: Kölner Phonetik, 7–14–1970, in: Bundesarchiv B 443 2825; For an overview of sales of the phonetic system see Bundesarchiv B 443 647 Kölner Phonetik.

63 Schreiben des Bundesministers des Innern an das Bundesamt für Verfassungsschutz, Betreff: Umstellung der Karteien des BfV auf die elektronische Datenverarbeitung, 1–10–1968, in: Bundesarchiv B 443 2822.

64 Fleischhack, *Eine Welt im Datenrausch*, 35–36.

65 Postel, *So war es*, 93.

66 Protokoll über die Amtsleitertagung am 4. und 5. Mai 1971 (Minutes of the meeting of heads of office on 4 and 5 May 1971), 6–2–1971, 3–4, in: Bundesarchiv B 443 2523.

67 See for example the ideas of Horst Herold, at the time head of the federal criminal police office: Herold, *Polizeiliche Informationsverarbeitung als Basis der Prävention*, 23–35.

68 The extent of this tendency to collect as much data as possible was most recently criticised by Edward Snowden's revelations about the NSA: Greenwald, *No Place to Hide*.

69 See for example: Anonymus. 1977. Spionage: Große Abräume, *Der Spiegel*, 30 May; Schaake, E. 1976. Kommissar Nadis, die Geheimwaffe der Abwehr. Eifel Computer entlarvt Agenten in Sekundenschnelle, *Express*, 17 August; or: Zimmermann, H. 1976. „Raster" – die moderne Agentenfalle schnappt zu. Der Computer Nadis verschafft den Leuten von der Abwehr den vielfach entscheidenden Zeitvorteil – Beispiel aus der Praxis, *Münchner Merkur*, 15 November. Possibly, this was part a longer-term media campaign by the *Bundesamt*: All articles used the same information and quotations and uncritically joined in corresponding hymns of praise – which at least was unusual for *Der Spiegel* at that time.

228   *Christopher Kirchberg*

70   See for example Protokoll der Tagung der Planungsgruppe NADIS am 10. Juni 1976 (Minutes of the NADIS Planning Group Meeting, 10 June 1976), 7–7–1976, attachment, in: Bundesarchiv B 443 2839.

71   Postel, *So war es*, 123.

72   See Protokoll der Amtsleitertagung vom 24. und 25. April 1975 (Minutes of the meeting of the heads of office of 24 and 25 April 1972), 5–9–1975, 10, in: Bundesarchiv B 443 2662.

73   Schreiben des Bundesamtes für Verfassungsschutz an das Bundesministerium des Innern, Betreff: Haushaltswirksame Planungen des BfV für die Weiterentwicklung des NADIS im Rechnungsjahr 1977 (Letter from the Bundesamt für Verfassungsschutz to the Bundesministerium des Innern, subject: Budgetary plans of the BfV for the further development of the NADIS in fiscal year 1977), 5–5–1976, 8–10, in: Bundesarchiv B 106 102168.

74   Internes Schreiben von Abteilung ID an Abteilung Z, Betreff: Fortschreibung der Rahmenplanung der Aufgaben des BfV auf dem Gebiet der Informationsverarbeitung und Sachstandsbericht zum 1.1.1978 (Internal letter from Department ID to Department Z, Subject: Update of the framework planning of the tasks of the BfV in the field of information processing and status report as of 1.1.1978.), 1–16–1978, in: Bundesarchiv B 443 2844

75   Schreiben vom Bundesamt für Verfassungsschutz an das Bundesministerium des Innern, Betreff: Bestandsaufnahme über die EDV in der Bundesverwaltung, 1–8–1976 attached form, in: Bundesarchiv B 443 2838.

76   Vorschlag für die Umstellung der Karteien des BfV auf die Elektronische Datenverarbeitung (EDV), 5–1–1967, attached form, 100, in: Bundesarchiv B 443 2821.

77   See Schreiben des Bundesamtes an das Innenministerium, Betreff: Bestandsaufnahme der EDV in der Bundesverwaltung, 8.7.1976 (Letter from the Bundesamt to the Ministry of the Interior, Subject: Inventory of EDP in the Federal Administration, 7–8–1976, in: Bundesarchiv B 2838.

78   See Bericht über den Personalbedarf für NADIS im Bundesamt für Verfassungsschutz, Mai 1977 (See Report on Personnel Requirements for NADIS in the Bundesamt, May 1977, in: Bundesarchiv B 106 102170; and, as reference for the 103 employees working there: Schreiben vom Bundesamt für Verfassungsschutz an das Bundesministerium des Innern, Betreff: Bestandsaufnahme über die EDV in der Bundesverwaltung (Letter from the Bundesamt für Verfassungsschutz to the Federal Ministry of the Interior, Subject: Inventory of EDP in the Federal Administration, 8–7–1976 attached form, 100, in: Bundesarchiv B 443 2838.

79   Interner Bericht über den Personalbedarf für NADIS im Bundesamt für Verfassungsschutz (Internal report on staffing requirements for NADIS at the Bundesamt für Verfassungsschutz), 5–2–1977, in: Barch B 106 102170.

80   Interner Bericht über den Personalbedarf für NADIS im Bundesamt für Verfassungsschutz (Internal report on staffing requirements for NADIS at the Bundesamt für Verfassungsschutz), 5–2–1977, in: Barch B 106 102170.

81   For example, due to a lack of skilled personnel, NADIS operating hours had to be shortened on weekends in 1978: Schreiben des Bundesamtes für Verfassungsschutz an alle Landesbehörden für Verfassungsschutz, Betreff: Betriebszeit des Nachrichtendienstlichen Informationssystems (NADIS) (Letter from the Federal Office for the Bundesamt für Verfassungsschutz to all Landesbehörden für Verfassungsschutz, Subject: Operating hours of the Intelligence Information System (NADIS)), 6–12–1978, in: Bundesarchiv B 106 102170.

82   See: <www.verfassungsschutz.de/DE/verfassungsschutz/verfassungsschutzverbund/foederale-aufgabenteilung/foederale_aufgabenteilung_artikel.html> (last accessed May 4, 2021).

83   For example, an internal memo on NADIS states that computing has also "contributed to a much improved level of staff training.": Nachrichtendienstliches Informationssystem.

Eliminating the human factor? 229

Erläuterungen zur Personenzentral-Datei (PZD) Anwendungsstufe 3, ohne Datum (vermutlich 1978) (NADIS. Comments on the Person Central File (PZD) Application Level 3, undated (probably 1978)), in: Bundesarchiv B 106 119459.

84 At the end of 1979, for example, the state offices withdrew their support for a long-planned third expansion stage of NADIS. See: Sitzungsbericht der Sitzung des AK IV "Verfassungsschutz" der Arbeitsgemeinschaft der Innenministerien der Bundesländer am 4./5. Oktober 1979 (Report of the meeting of AK IV "Verfassungsschutz" (Working Group IV) of the Working Group of the Interior Ministries of the Länder on 4 and 5 October 1979), in: Bundesarchiv B 106/119459; Cf. also Postel, *So war es*, 157–158.

Bibliography

Andrew, C. M. 2012. *The Defence of the Realm: The Authorized History of MI5*. London: Penguin.

Bösch, F., ed. 2018. *Wege in die Digitale Gesellschaft: Computernutzung in der Bundesrepublik 1955–1990*. Geschichte der Gegenwart 20. Göttingen: Wallstein Verlag.

Fleischhack, J. 2016. *Eine Welt im Datenrausch: Computeranlagen Und Datenmengen als Gesellschaftliche Herausforderung in der Bundesrepublik Deutschland (1965–1975)*. Zürcher Beiträge zur Alltagskultur 22. Zürich: Chronos.

Frei, N., and Rigoll, D., eds. 2017. *Der Antikommunismus in seiner Epoche: Weltanschauung und Politik in Deutschland, Europa und den USA*. Jena Center Geschichte des 20. Jahrhunderts. Vorträge und Kolloquien 21. Göttingen: Wallstein Verlag.

Futh, H. 1966. *Elektronische Datenverarbeitungsanlagen*, 2nd edition. München and Wien: Oldenbourg.

Galison, P. 1994. The Ontology of the Enemy: Norbert Wiener and the Cybernetic Vision. *Critical Inquiry* 21, no. 1: 228–266.

Goschler, C., and Wala, M. 2015. *„Keine Neue Gestapo": Das Bundesamt Für Verfassungsschutz und die NS-Vergangenheit*. Reinbek: Rowohlt E-Book.

Greenwald, G. 2014. *No Place to Hide: Edward Snowden, the NSA and the Surveillance State*. New York: Metropolitan Books.

Grskovich, E. N. 1969. "Automating Name Searches." *Titel News. The Official Publication of the American Land Title Association* 48, no. 7: 10–12; 23. www.alta.org/title-news/1969/v48i07.pdf.

Gugerli, D. 2012. Nach uns die Informationsflut. Zur Pathologisierung soziotechnischen Wandels. *Nach Feierabend* 8: 141–147.

Herold, H. 1977. *Polizeiliche Informationsverarbeitung als Basis der Prävention*. In *Prävention und Strafrecht. Tagungsbericht der Deutschen Kriminologischen Gesellschaft vom 4. September 1976*. Hamburg and Heidelberg.

Hett, B. C., and Wala, M. 2019. *Otto John: Patriot oder Verräter: Eine deutsche Biographie*. Reinbek: Rowohlt.

Kasper, T. 2020. *Wie der Sozialstaat digital wurde: Die Computerisierung der Rentenversicherung im geteilten Deutschland*. Medien und Gesellschaftswandel im 20. Jahrhundert 13. Göttingen: Wallstein Verlag.

Leimbach, T. 2010. *Die Geschichte der Softwarebranche in Deutschland. Entwicklung und Anwendung von Informations- und Kommunikationstechnologie zwischen den 1950ern und heute*. PhD diss., LMU München.

Nollau, G. 1978. *Das Amt: 50 Jahre Zeuge der Geschichte*. München: Bertelsmann.

Postel, H.-J. 1968. Die Kölner Phonetik. Ein Verfahren zur Identifizierung von Personennamen auf der Grundlage der Gestaltanalyse. *Bürotechnik + Automation* 9: 568–575.

230   Christopher Kirchberg

Postel, H.-J. 1969. Die Kölner Phonetik. Ein Verfahren zur Identifizierung von Personennamen auf der Grundlage der Gestaltanalyse. *IBM-Nachrichten* 19: 925–931.

Postel, H.-J. 1972. Organisation und Aufgaben der automatisierten Informationsverarbeitung in den Behörden für Verfassungsschutz. In *Datenverarbeitung. Arbeitstagung des Bundeskriminalamtes Wiesbaden. Vom 13. März Bis 17. März. 1972*, ed. Bundeskriminalamt, 125–132. Wiesbaden.

Postel, H.-J. 1999. *So war es: Mein Leben im 20. Jahrhundert*. Meckenheim: Warlich.

Radu, R. 2015. Einleitung: Spionage, Geheimhaltung und Öffentlichkeit – Ein Spannungsfeld der Moderne. In *Kampf um Wissen: Spionage, Geheimhaltung und Öffentlichkeit 1870–1940*, ed. L. Medrow, D. Münzner, and R. Radu, 9–30. Paderborn: Ferdinand Schöningh.

Reichherzer, F., Droit, E., and Hansen, J., eds. 2018. *Den Kalten Krieg vermessen: Über Reichweite und Alternativen einer binären Ordnungsvorstellung*. Berlin and Boston: De Gruyter Oldenbourg.

Schlombs, C. 2019. *Productivity Machines: German Appropriations of American Technologies from Mass Production to Computer Automation*. History of Computing. Cambridge, MA: MIT Press.

Schrecker, E. 1998. *Many Are the Crimes: McCarthyism in America*. Princeton, NJ: Princeton University Press.

Schuhmann, A. 2012. Der Traum vom perfekten Unternehmen. Die Computerisierung der Arbeitswelt in der Bundesrepublik Deutschland (1950er- bis 1980er-Jahre). *Zeithistorische Forschungen/Studies in Contemporary History* 9: 231–256. https://doi.org/10.14765/ZZF.DOK-1596.

11 Global war academies

Intelligence schools during the civil-military dictatorship in Brazil

Samantha Viz Quadrat

Introduction

In Latin America, the second half of the twentieth century, and especially the period from the 1960s to the 1980s, can be characterised as a period of intense confrontation and political disputes. Dictatorships shaped the trajectories of most South American states, such as Paraguay (1954–1989), Brazil (1964–1985), Argentina (1966 and 1976–1983), Uruguay (1973–1985) and Chile (1973–1990). During those years, violence was one of the main features of political life. Torture and other forms of gross human rights violations became common practices of the state.

The Latin American national intelligence agencies played an important role both in the establishment and maintenance of the authoritarian regimes and in the oppression and torture of opponents (the so-called subversive elements).[1] In Brazil, one of the key features of the long-lasting civilian-military dictatorship (1964–1985) was the strong investment in a dual system of information and repression.[2] State actors also created a complex information system with a civil–military structure. The national Brazilian intelligence agency Serviço Nacional de Informações (SNI) was one of the most important institutions within this structure, and it took on the role of "kingmaker": two SNI directors (out of a total of six), Emilio Garrastazu Médici and João Baptista Figueiredo, later became presidents during the dictatorship. Although SNI had the status of a ministry and was staffed by civilian and Armed Forces personnel, it was conceived, organised and permanently managed by military personnel who were part of the group that held power throughout the dictatorship. Thus, military men set the direction at SNI and dominated the entire command structure.

Due to accusations of human rights violations and the identification of sites of repression, the memory of SNI has become strongly associated with political violence. The National Truth Commission stated in its final report, published in 2014, that "inside the so-called information community, SNI has revealed itself as the only department having defined roles, which were collecting, storing, analysing, protecting and diffusing information regarding the regime's opponents."[3] In the same report, the commission highlighted the presence of SNI agents in places where gross human rights violations happened.

DOI: 10.4324/9781003147329-12

232 *Samantha Viz Quadrat*

Investigating the role of SNI and its members must therefore certainly remain an urgent topic of investigation. However, historical research can and should now also go beyond the search for proof of gross human rights violations and for offenders. We need to know, for instance, how the Brazilian intelligence service machinery actually functioned during the dictatorship. One important topic is the education and the training of the members of the intelligence community. How the members of the information system actually obtained the theoretical and practical knowledge that they needed to carry out their actions is a topic that is still poorly understood and remains understudied.

The Brazilian dictatorship was one of the longest-lived in Latin America, being established in 1964 and ending in 1985. This period saw tremendous transformations all over the world. In Brazil, the authoritarian government became directly involved in the economy. The average annual growth of the GDP of close to 10 per cent between 1969 and 1973 was celebrated as the "Brazilian economic miracle." Some mega-projects were launched, such as the construction of a bridge between Rio de Janeiro and Niterói (1965–1974) and the "Transamazônica" road that was meant to connect the Atlantic to the Pacific. Television became the most important medium of information and entertainment. And in the field of education, postgraduate studies were developed and extended at Brazilian universities, even though at the same time many university teachers and students were being openly persecuted and excluded from the intellectual field (when they were not murdered or disappeared).

My guiding questions are: considering these important transformations, how did the authoritarian regime guarantee that its security systems and its members kept up to date, and what were the most important developments concerning the education and training of intelligence personnel? This chapter aims at analysing the authorities' strategies for the professionalisation of military and civilian staff active in intelligence and/or political repression as field agents and analysts, especially after the creation of the National School of Information (Escola Nacional de Informações, EsNI) within the structures of SNI in 1971.[4]

I will focus on trainings that were offered in Brazil and in other countries. The EsNI courses were meant to provide both basic education and preparation for the higher ranks. With my analysis, I aim to contribute answers to the volume's overall questions about the professionalisation of intelligence services. I will focus not so much on how certain intelligence knowledge was produced or processed by Brazilian agents but rather on how changing and transnationally circulating principles and convictions about how an intelligence agency should function were transformed into teaching material and then introduced into Brazilian intelligence.

The study of intelligence history is always difficult due to the uncertain and incomplete access to the sources. This holds especially true for the study of secret services under authoritarian regimes that evidently committed gross human rights violations. Therefore, I want to say a few words about the sources that constitute the basis for my analysis. In 1990, the first president elected through direct vote, Fernando Collor de Mello, extinguished SNI and its entire structure, including EsNI. However, since members of SNI and EsNI were public employees, they

Global war academies 233

remained at work at the Strategic Affairs Secretariat (SAE) established in 1991 and at the Brazilian Intelligence Agency Agencia Brasileira de Informações (ABIN) created in 1999. SNI's archive remained in the custody of these new institutions until parts of it were released and integrated into the holdings of the Brazilian National Archive by order of the chief of cabinet and later President Dilma Rousseff in 2005. When Rousseff launched the National Truth Commission in 2011, she also signed the Access to Information Law (No. 12.527), which further facilitated access to SNI's documentation.

Although we have a good collection of documents regarding EsNI's courses, most of what we know about the trainings comes from oral history projects that conduct interviews with (ex-)members of the military. Little documentation about the transition from ESG and the Army Centre for Studies and Staff (*Centro de Estudos e Pessoal do Exército*, CEP) to EsNI or about study trips abroad is open to the public or to researchers. Most of the material remains under the military's guard or under departments that substituted EsNI, absorbing the staff, the archive,[5] the library and the installations themselves, in Brasília.

With regard to the transformations that took place in the training and the education of the intelligence agents, it is possible to at least sketch the most important developments and processes on the basis of the available sources. My contribution will be divided into four sections. In the first section, I will provide a general overview of one of the most important developments within security policies: the increased internationalisation. Concretely, I will sketch how – in the face of the "global" threat of communism – national defence strategies transformed into international combat strategies from the 1950s on. In the second section, I will analyse processes of professionalisation and centralisation that were undertaken through and in the Brazilian Escola Superior de Guerra (ESG). The earliest trainings of this kind in Brazil took place here. The third section then discusses the professionals who were invited to study at EsNI as well as the courses that they took. In the fourth and final section, I will draw some conclusion about the importance of EsNI in the training of intelligence professionals in dictatorial Brazil. It will become clear that the courses offered at EsNI were an attempt to unify the training of the entire community, standardise the production of documents and consolidate the idea of a community responsible for the country's security.

The internationalisation of combat strategies in Cold War Latin America

With the end of the Second World War and the beginning of the Cold War, important transformations took place within the Latin American Armed Forces. The "wave" of military coups in the 1960s and 1970s fostered a new military conduct and a high level of politicisation. The members of the Armed Forces started to see themselves not only as militaries but also as administrators and political leaders. From their perspective, they not only had the *capacity* to intervene in political issues and to influence the country's destiny but also the *duty* to do so.

One of the main features was the creation of the concept of an "internal enemy." According to Joseph Comblin's analysis[6] and the publications of the generals

234   *Samantha Viz Quadrat*

Golbery do Couto e Silva[7] and Carlos de Meira Matos,[8] which can also be found in the course hand outs of ESG and EsNI and were reflected in public speeches by military personnel, the enemy to be defeated was no longer an army under a different flag or soldiers wearing a distinct uniform but rather an *idea*. The defeat of communism and communists was imperative, and it could no longer be done through "surgical interventions." Rather, the fight would have to take place in several spheres, including the military, political, economic and psychosocial spheres.

As a result, the Armed Forces increasingly intervened in the country's political life and invested heavily in information and security institutions. The Brazilian intelligence service SNI was the most expensive state organisation. It received huge amounts of money and continued to grow as its assignments broadened when the phase of harshest repression had passed. Ultimately, national development in all its facets became strictly linked to security. The DSN has also been pointed to as the main factor responsible for the tortures that took place during dictatorships. Undoubtedly, the concept of an "internal enemy" had a great impact on political violence.

Authors like Joseph Comblin have subsumed these transformations under the term *ideologia da segurança nacional* (national security ideology),[9] while Alfred Stepan has labelled them *novo profissionalismo* (new professionalism).[10] What is frequently overseen and remains understudied (in part because the term "national security doctrine" emphasises the national) is the fact that these processes went along with and even partly depended on an increased international circulation of theoretical and practical knowledge. If until then the Armed Forces had been concerned with the defence of national borders, this orientation now became outdated: in the new context of world politics and in the face of a supposedly global "communist threat," an internalisation of the enemy took place, and this in turn was addressed through an internationalisation of the fight against it. In other words, members of the security institutions assumed an internationalist posture of combating "subversion."

In the past decades, new publications have pointed out the strong French influence on the repression exerted by Brazilian authorities.[11] The concept of revolutionary war started to be studied in depth by the French military after the failed wars of "liberation" in Vietnam and Indochina and during the fighting in Algerian territory. In May 1958, the French government, through Defence Minister Jacques Chaban-Delmas, created the Centre of Training in Subversive Warfare. The most important manual at this school was *Modern Warfare*, written in 1964 by Colonel Roger Trinquier,[12] which justified torture as a weapon in anti-subversive wars.

The first Latin Americans to come into contact with the new doctrine were the Argentinians and Brazilians who studied at the Paris War College. In 1956, Colonel Carlos J. Rosas became deputy director at the Superior War College in Argentina. Rosas had been military attaché at the Argentinian embassy in Paris. There he became acquainted with the new French concepts of combat. Back in Argentina, and having assumed his job at the Argentinian Superior War College (Escuela Superior de Guerra), he sought to reformulate a series of concepts, courses and publications. He invited members of the French military – such as François Badie, Patrice de Naurois, Robert Bentresque and Jean Nougues – to give courses and/or some helpful advice at the School. He also reformed the institution's journal, which started to publish papers on revolutionary and atomic war and similar topics.[13]

The French influence was strong in Brazil, too. Brazilian military officers, just like the Argentinian ones, came into contact with French ideas and principles from the 1950s onwards. They had a strong influence in the 1964 civilian-military coup, as General Octávio Costa, who was head of the Assessoria Especial de Relações Públicas (AERP), the organ responsible for the dictatorship's official propaganda, assesses:

> A big injustice is committed when the inspiration for the 64 movement is assigned to the Americans. I think the French thought had a stronger influence. The war studied at the French schools was the insurrectional war, the revolutionary war. Since we never stopped sending students to the Paris War College, our officials came back with this material in hand, the whole French rationale on the subject. This has got in through our Superior War College, which applied the ideas to insurrectional and revolutionary wars, and started to identify in them the framework of our own potential war.[14]

General Octávio Costa also affirmed that there were testimonies from Portuguese soldiers about the war in Angola. All these experiences would have contributed greatly to the creation of a Brazilian revolutionary war doctrine, which would be fundamental to the fomentation of the coup of March 31, 1964, and to the organisation of the dictatorship itself in the country.[15] Colonel Adyr Fiúza de Castro corroborates this: "By the times of Juscelino Kubitschek we had already sent them to many places, especially to England and France, and above all to learn interrogation techniques."[16]

The lessons learned in France were apparently transformed into "Latin American" knowledge, which then started to circulate among the Armed Forces of this continent. In 1961, the First Inter-American Course on Counter-Revolutionary War was held. The course involved the presence of militaries from 14 countries, including Brazil and the United States.[17] At the opening ceremony, Brigadier General Carlos Turolo invoked the spirit of "international solidarity with the people in the Americas . . . [who are distant from] . . . imperious need for coordinating actions, detaining and combatting the common enemy, communism."[18]

Between August 31 and November 5, 1962, a course was organised for 60 officials from the five sections of the Army General Staff (Estado-Maior do Exército, EME). Twenty officials from the four directories in the Army and five officials from the Navy and the Air Force participated. The classes were held in the building of the Army General Staff in Rio de Janeiro. The course followed the same programme as the one that took place in Argentina, except for some minor adaptations to national issues.[19] Some lectures were given by officers that apparently had spent some time in Argentina. The course bibliography refers to notes taken at the First Inter-American Course for Counter-Revolutionary War – Superior War College – Buenos Aires – Argentina.[20]

236 Samantha Viz Quadrat

The course lectures were published in the book *Guerra Revolucionária* (*Revolutionary War*), 2nd Section of the Air Force General Staff (Mello 1962, 69). In the lecture given by Danilo da Cunha E. Mello, the lieutenant colonel calls attention to the fact that "revolutionary war is triggered, practically, in all countries in the world; it exists and is alive under the ground, because it is characterized by the dispute between two ideological worlds – eastern and western."[21] In an alarming tone, he asks:

> In Brazil, who is supposed to counteract revolutionary war? This is a question that we are not prepared to answer integrally, because we can assert that actions in this direction are performed by the armed forces, the church, different police forces from political and social orders, truly democratic political parties and more conservative classes.[22]

Thus, it is possible to state that French knowledge (together with US knowledge) as well as instructors made their way into the Brazilian military institutions. The knowledge was adapted and integrated into the curricula of Brazilian military schools. From there, this knowledge started to circulate within the subcontinent and also in "inter-American" meetings. This knowledge certainly changed the way Brazilian (and other Latin American) authorities identified and fought their political opponents.

The Escola Superior de Guerra – centralisation and standardisation of knowledge

The Brazilian Superior War College (Escola Superior de Guerra, ESG) pioneered the idea of offering courses for members of the intelligence community. Although ESG's "Division for Information and Counter-Information Affairs" was created only in 1963, the first course ESG offered was in 1959 (this particular one was reoffered only in 1965). Additionally, it promoted lectures and conferences with specialists in the area.

The courses offered by ESG taught the concept of information. It was assumed that a strong information system would strengthen the government. In detail, the courses taught how to write a report (the data without analysis) and how to transform it into information (the analysed data). The experiences of intelligence systems in other states such as the United States, the United Kingdom, Germany, the Soviet Union and others were also discussed. The trainings strongly emphasised the chain of command, the structure and the methodology of secret services and focused particularly on what could be useful in Brazil.

Working as a radiating hub for the DSN, ESG started to modify its regulation and the courses it offered in order to meet the changing needs of security and development.

> Therefore,
> The 1st Regulation established the Divisions for National Affairs, International Affairs and Military Affairs. The 2nd, the Divisions for Political Affairs,

Global war academies 237

Psychosocial Affairs, Economic Affairs and Military Affairs, which substitute the previous ones. The 3rd Regulation (17–3–61) adds two Divisions: Doctrinal Affairs and Scientific and Technological Affairs. Finally, Regulation 4–12–63 suppresses the last Division and creates two others: Mobilization and Logistics Affairs and Information and Counter-Information Affairs.[23]

In 1969, the information course syllabus was divided as follows:

Student Movement (1. National Organizations Study; 2. Student Movement Relationships in the country and abroad, as well as the consequences; 3. Recommendations for addressing the problem); General staff studies; General staff exercises; Special work; study and internship trip (at SNI).[24]

In order to obtain a better understanding of the military and civilian training provided by ESG, we should revisit some definitions and concepts determined by the College and accepted by all information media. According to ESG theoreticians, there are two phases in the process of obtaining information. The first corresponds to gathering *informes* by agents – one of the core elements of information. The second is the moment in which the gathered data are processed and elaborated, creating information.[25]

According to ESG manuals, there were three types of information concerning development or security:

1 Descriptive information (static): knowledge about mutable and immutable aspects of a nation (or nations);
2 Dynamic information (dynamic): knowledge about the current moment of a nation (or nations) (mobility of human events);
3 Estimative information (potential): knowledge about a nation's (or nations') future actions (possibilities and intentions).[26]

Another concept that needs to be examined is the definition of counter-information, which is "the knowledge obtained through reason and presented clearly and in due time, aiming at providing measures for protecting a police or the preparation and execution of a specific enterprise."[27]

Procedures for classifying a source and the processed information obtained from that source were also taught at ESG. A letter-number system was used to grade sources' reputation, with a letter from A to F and the information's veracity with a number from 1 to 6. Thus, the source received the following classification that was widely accepted by all intelligence departments in Brazil.:

A – absolutely reliable source; B – usually reliable source; C – reasonably reliable source; D – not always reliable source; E – not reliable source; F – the reliability of source cannot be judged."[28] According to general Adyr Fiúza de Castro, most of the sources were level C.[29] Another criterion regarded the likelihood of the information: "1 – report confirmed by other sources;

238   *Samantha Viz Quadrat*

2 – probably true report; 3 – possibly true report; 4 – doubtful report; 5 – unlikely report; 6 – the veracity of the report cannot be ascertained.[30]

The classified documents of all authoritarian regimes in Latin America point to the existence of classification systems for the reliability of informants. However, each country created its own table. Brazil stands out due to its very detailed scheme, most probably because of the strong financial and personnel investment in the intelligence sector. However, a common classification model which unified the documents that circulated among the agents of repression was applied in the context of "Operation Condor," the joint action by the dictatorships of the Southern Cone countries to persecute political opponents.[31]

The dissemination or diffusion of information was also an important topic at ESG. According to the textbooks, dissemination was a critical factor in processing information because a missing item could, for example, already exist in another file or have already been investigated by another group or institution. In order to avoid the loss of information, a specific pattern was to be followed: subject matter, origin, classification, diffusion, previous diffusion, attachments and references. The idea was to avoid the situation of two departments separately investing in efforts to achieve the same goal. However, it is important to point out that in spite of the intense exchange of information, there regularly were disputes among the various departments within the so-called information community.

As has become clear, the courses offered by ESG (especially the ones concerning intelligence information) resulted in a greater centralisation and also standardisation of intelligence knowledge. However, that was not enough for the state authorities. From 1967 on, there was an intensive discussion within high-ranking militaries about the creation of a school specialised in training intelligence agents. The first debates took place at the Army Centre for Studies and Staff (Centro de Estudos e Pessoal do Exército, CEP), located at the Duque de Caxias fort in the district of Leme in Rio de Janeiro.[32] Soon, the discussions about the urgent need for a school specifically for the training of intelligence staff would lead to a decision to create a new institution: the Escola Nacional de Informações (EsNI).

The Escola Nacional de Informações

As mentioned in the introduction, the Brazilian civilian-military dictatorship created a complex information and repression system to combat the internal enemy. The most important was the national intelligence service Serviço Nacional de Informações (SNI) under the command of General Golbery do Couto e Silva, created on June 13, 1964, through law 4.341.

SNI was the cornerstone of the Brazilian information system. It absorbed the structure of its predecessors, the Federal Service of Information and Counter-Information (Serviço Federal de Informação e Contra-Informação, SFICI) and the Information Coordination Board (Junta Coordenadora de Informações, JCI), including existing employees and collections. All other members of the National System of Information (SISNI) had to send the processed information to SNI, following the chain of command. Its structure consisted of a director, who could be civilian or military, the central agency in the capital Brasília, regional agencies, the EsNI, Security and Information Offices (ASIs) and National Security Divisions located at important institutions (DSIs). The regional agencies had a structure similar to the Brasília one and consisted of: director, strategic information section, internal security section and special operations section.

As a core institution of SISNI, SNI accumulated great power and became responsible for training militaries and civilians acting in the field of intelligence. On March 31, 1971, as the military regime completed seven years in power, the EsNI was created in Brasília. This aimed at further centralising and standardising activities. It would later acquire the monopoly in training the sector's professionals. According to its statutes, EsNI's goals were to "prepare civilians and military personnel to meet the needs and provide information and counter-information to the National Information Service; cooperate in the development of the national information doctrine and carry out research aimed at enhancing the performance of the National Information System activities" (Law n°68.448, 31 March 1971).

It also represented an attempt by the regime to standardise the training of both civilian and military personnel, acting both in Brazil and abroad,[33] within the so-called National Intelligence Plan. It was believed that this would have a domino effect that would reach from the production of documents to the formation of silence pacts on secret actions. Its director had to be an active military officer in the Armed Forces, more precisely a brigadier-general, brigadier or rear-admiral. This was not one of the highest ranks of the Brazilian military, but it was an opportunity to stand out in the national intelligence scene. The director was to be chosen by the president from a list of three formulated by the heads of SNI. As mentioned above, all heads of SNI as well as of EsNI were from the Army. This generated resentment, rivalries and accusations from the Navy and the Air Force about the Army's role in the intelligence community.

According to one of the SNI directors, General Carlos Alberto da Fontoura, the decisive incident in the creation of EsNI was the imprisonment and subsequent escape of an Air Force official, supposedly a communist. There had been no information pointing to his political militancy. Fontoura claims to have said in a meeting with Médici: "SNI has exhausted its knowledge. We are all amateurs. You were an amateur as well as chief of SNI, Golbery was an amateur, I am an amateur and the ones following me will be amateurs."[34] Médici then asked what the solution was and Fontoura presented the idea of a training school. Two days later, Médici authorised it. This was the concretisation of a long internal debate in the Brazilian Armed Forces.[35]

A working group was then tasked with presenting a project within 60 days. In the report available at the National Archive, we discover that from the day the group was set up, on 1 March 1971, only 6 meetings took place under the coordination of General Ênio Pinheiro and in the presence of representatives from the Presidency, the Armed Forces General Staff, ministries from the Air Force, the Army, the Navy, Justice, Exterior Relations, Planning and General Coordination. Ênio Pinheiro stated right at the beginning that the school would be based

240   *Samantha Viz Quadrat*

in Brasília and would fulfil SISNI needs and that budget resources were available for its creation. There was an agreement about the courses, which we will talk about later in the paper, and it was decided that three working subgroups would be created: one to write the statutes of creation and the mission, one to elaborate the school regulations, and one to decide about its physical structures and budgets. After that, they would debate curriculum and statutes.[36]

After everything had been approved by the Presidency, it was time to begin the most ambitious part of the project: building a space where the activities would develop. The entire construction in the South Police Sector in Brasília was executed in absolute secrecy by the company Novacap, the same company that had built the city of Brasília. There was concern about possible infiltration of the workers involved in the construction. This complicated the task of those involved in the project, such as engineers and architects, who could not have copies of the floor plan and usually had no access to information regarding the overall enterprise.[37] Instead of just one building, independent blocks were built, separated one from each other but interconnected with strictly controlled streets and walkways. The building complex included an underground shooting range designed and manufactured in the United States, conference auditoriums, spaces to simulate special actions, classrooms, a library, an archive, accommodations for students, cafeterias, informatics rooms, sports facilities, closed circuit TV, and a recording studio, to name just some of the facilities.

According to Ana Lagôa, EsNI was inaugurated in May of 1972 – very discreetly, but not without a ceremony. The inaugural class was presented by the SNI director at the time, General Carlos Alberto da Fontoura. In his forty-minute speech without any press attendance, Fontoura affirmed that the school was not for training spies, but to educate technical personnel to be able to act according to the National Information Plan.[38] The system had grown, and the time had arrived to professionalise those working in it.

In the year following its inauguration, EsNI absorbed the intelligence course previously given by ESG, including part of its "most specialized and skilled" professors on Brazilian soil, as well as its teaching material. Other departments, such as the 2nd sections and the Army Centre for Studies and Personnel, also saw part of their staff recruited by EsNI.

EsNI was, from its beginnings, acknowledged by and interconnected with partner institutions abroad. For the Brazilians, it was important to circulate within and to become acquainted with the North American civilian departments. In the first meetings that took place about the creation of EsNI, it had been decided that one of its main goals should be the integration of civilians and militaries.[39] Accordingly, EsNI's founding group was invited to attend courses in the United States, Germany, Israel, France and England. The first principal of the school, General Ênio Pinheiro, was invited by US president Richard Nixon. Accompanied by the frigate captain Sérgio Douerty, he absolved a six-month internship at the CIA and the FBI. Ênio Pinheiro revealed that they were hosted at the hotel Alban Tower in Washington D.C., and that the courses took place at the same site. Classes took place every morning. For security reasons, the Brazilian officials could leave the hotel only in the company of US colleagues, even on weekends. There were trips to some installations – such as listening posts – and to accompany in loco some actions of US services.

According to Lucas Figueiredo, during the courses Ênio Pinheiro participated in interrogation classes, where it was recommended that prisoners' clothes be completely removed in order to humiliate and undermine them. Pinheiro was taught that only three people should be present in the room: an interrogator asking questions, a second person taking notes of the answers and a third person remaining hidden behind a mirror. In its deposition, the Brazilian military says that he participated in many interrogation sessions in the United States and never forgot the sight of the exposed bodies. The interrogation techniques, along with other theoretical and practical knowledge, were successfully transferred from the United States to Brazil after the internship: the two Brazilians took notes of everything, produced reports and brought home documents that were later incorporated as didactic material at EsNI, with the approval of President Emílio Garrastazu Médici.[40]

Whereas Pinheiro and Douerty were sent to the United States, other military personnel were sent to Europe. In his deposition, Ênio Pinheiro stated that Moacir Coelho, from the Army, was sent to London, "official Ururaí" to Germany and "official Pacífico" to France. In his own words, "in England, Moacir Coelho stayed in a London fort, located on the Thames River. There was a school specially dedicated to the problem with Ireland. . . . The report he brought home is very impressive. We are violent? Because you don't know what they do out there! In Germany, there was no school, but 'devices' – as they called it, separated houses where they put the teams. Normally, the officials would bring their wives who, mandatorily, would take the course with their husbands – in order to avoid leakage through their wives. In France, it was different. The course was in the Sûreté Française, near Notre Dame – also not exactly a school."[41]

Still according to Ênio Pinheiro, EsNI trained the people who worked on the front line in operations as well as the "academics" who engaged in the information community on a more intellectual level and who could later occupy higher ranks.[42] Even the ministers and general-secretaries took two-day courses.[43] There is a consensus between contemporaries and historians that the main difference between the courses offered by ESG and those provided by EsNI lay precisely in the sort of knowledge and skills that they imparted. ESG was considered to be very theoretical. The teaching materials and hand outs which are now available at the ESG library reveal that its courses focused on the importance of the existence of an intelligence system, on the question of how they were structured in countries around the world and on the doctrine of national security as a way of thinking about the country and the government itself. The key idea was that there could be no development without security. In this sense, the existence of a system capable of predicting attacks on the government and informing the president so that he could take a decision that anticipated the opposition's actions was justified.

EsNI, on the other hand, is seen by the military itself as responsible for training field agents. When the confrontation with the government's opponents became stiffer, EsNI was assigned to offer more practical knowledge. As a result, ESG

242 *Samantha Viz Quadrat*

lost space and importance in this new structure. Receiving much more financial and material resources, EsNI took on an increasing amount of responsibility and began to foster the doctrine of national security, instilling it in field agents, be they civilian or military. Its teachers were also civilians and military personnel who had taken courses on intelligence in Brazil and abroad. Some were recruited from ESG or CEP because of their experience. They were also permanent faculty members, unlike at ESG. This allowed a greater intellectual investment in these teachers, who could also develop their own research in the area. The teachers who taught classes not directly related to intelligence, such as foreign languages, received training at EsNI itself.

EsNI offered courses for both civilian and military personnel, civilians being the majority. It received Brazilian students as well as foreigners, mostly from other Latin American countries. The exact number and the provenance of the foreigners remains a well-kept secret until today.[44] The students were selected based on recommendations by their superiors. Persons were selected who were considered reliable and capable of reinforcing the bonds within the information community. One innovation was certainly the acceptance of women at EsNI, both as students and as employees, mostly in the area of psychology.

According to two invitations to tender for EsNI instruction courses in 1974 and 1975,[45] in addition to a recommendation, candidates had to pass physical and psychological exams as well as exams in Brazilian history, Portuguese language and literature, and geography. Registration was at the candidate's own request, and after checking if he or she actually met the requirements, enrolment in one of the school courses was completed. However, not all men and women who worked in intelligence received the same training (as not all of them worked on the front line in the combat against political opponents and resistance movements). Rather, the courses were offered according to the position in the military hierarchy or the civilian sphere, academic curriculum, and age.

According to Ênio Pinheiro, the school trained "two types of persons, two products: one scholar, and another that works in the operations area. In Brazil there was a very difficult issue: secrecy. Secrecy was a difficult issue, especially within the family. The person who works with information cannot talk, cannot discuss job matters. The Brazilian talks a lot, and this is dangerous. However, we were able to make a selection and tell [the students] how the work should be done. An honour code was also developed, as well as a code of ethics for the staff."[46]

Consequently, EsNI offered three courses at different levels.[47] Course A (advanced studies) was directed towards military and civilian personnel that would occupy leadership and analytical positions. Recruitment was from the Armed Forces superior officers that had taken the General Staff and Command Course and from civilians with a college degree. Considered a sort of postgraduate degree, the course was held over 41 weeks and comprised two modules, A and B. Those who took Module B were dispensed from Module A. The curriculum included classes about Brazilian reality, situation analysis and chaos theory. The course literature list also included main references of the left, such as Carlos Marighella, Che Guevara, Karl Marx, Mao Zedong and so on.

Global war academies 243

Course B (fundamentals) on the other hand was aimed at civilian and military personnel who would occupy mid-level information positions or directorships at intermediary levels of the National Information System. This course was held over 20 weeks. The recruits were majors or captains, as well as civilians of an equivalent level. The course curriculum offered classes in sociology, history (with an emphasis on the history of communism, from its origins to the Cuban Revolution) and political science.

Those who would handle informants and write information reports were primarily trained in Course B. There was also a great concern with writing discipline, apparently one of the greatest challenges for EsNI. The students were taught to compose an *informe* in a clear and objective way, without adding their opinions. In order to do so, they would work with poorly written texts which were completely unclear with regard to content and message.

The lowest level was Course C (operations) that comprised two sub-courses: C1 and C2. C1 was addressed to captains and lieutenants, C2 to sergeants. The goal was to train staff for to lead information sections, as well as for the planning and direction of information operations. Sergeants in turn would be information agents. Broadly speaking, the course trained agents that would work "on the streets." The curriculum included techniques of surveillance and interrogation, wiretaps, recordings, disguise, infiltration and so forth. All classes took place from Monday to Friday, full-time. Students from all regions of the country, as well as foreigners, mostly from other Latin American countries, were housed in Brasília during the course's duration.

In addition to these three courses, EsNI offered internships in different areas:

> Information – analyst; analyst auxiliary; military attaché; military attaché auxiliary.
>   Counter-Information – counter-espionage; cryptology; cryptology auxiliary; adverse advertisement analysis; JID/CID and attaché relatives' security.
>   Operations – chief of operation sections; operation section deputy; parachutist information operation; interrogation; interrogation auxiliary; electronics; photography for agents; photography for laboratory technicians; authorities protection; photointerpretation; photointerpretation auxiliary.[48]

Foreign language courses (English, German, French, Dutch, Spanish, Russian, Chinese, Italian and Arabic) were also offered for all levels, with classes taking place in individual cabins and through correspondence (with books and cassette tapes). Additionally, all students had to participate in physical exercises and shooting training.

Carlos Alberto da Fontoura revealed in an interview that in a one-year period about 120 students were trained, some 75 per cent of whom were civilians. Almost one thousand students were trained over ten years.[49] Given the vast territorial expanse of Brazil this may seem little. However, the extensive SNI collections in the Brazilian National Archive demonstrate that EsNI courses and trainings produced rich documentations about different sectors of Brazilian society, such as universities, for example.

244   *Samantha Viz Quadrat*

All these courses and internships reflected the need to create a national intelligence doctrine in Brazil. As Andrade and Antunes show, this doctrine was consolidated in the "Manual on Intelligence," approved on 10 December 1976, which was centred on the following axes: intelligence, counterintelligence and operations. It is the main reference on intelligence activities in Brazil. It dealt with everything from the system's daily routine and bureaucracy, to the system's end-activities and the importance of its actions in decision-making.[50] This material, formulated at EsNI for the whole of SNI, is one of the main documents for those who wish to understand how the intelligence system in Brazil was structured and how this vision endured even in the early years of the return to democracy.

Conclusion

During the dictatorship, the Brazilian "information community" accumulated great power. The national intelligence service SNI, created right after the coup d'état in 1964, had a particularly strong influence on Brazilian politics. It was also the main body responsible for the spying on and the repression of citizens.

However, as I have shown, the power of SNI was not simply there at its creation, and still less could it rely on static patterns and procedures. Rather, the power and influence of the institution had to be secured through different techniques, and by dynamically reacting to certain requirements. One of the main techniques, it seems, was the training and education of the members of the intelligence community according to suitable and up-to-date sets of theoretical and practical knowledge.

In the first section, I have demonstrated that after the Second World War and under the banner of the Cold War spectre of communism, the notions of a "national threat" shifted. However, the "global" threat presented itself in various ways. The enemy did not wear a foreign uniform or wave the flag of another nation but embodied an idea (or a set of different ideas) which were to be fought. In this sense, although there was transnational training, the construction of the *internal enemy* corresponded more to the rivalries and political disputes of each state than necessarily to communism itself.

However specific the respective internal enemies might have looked like in the different Latin American states, the intelligence community in Brazil adapted the training of their people in a very transnational way, in order to cope with this new way of thinking about the enemies, to make them visible and to fight them. The construction of the figure of the opponents to be fought generated the debate on new ways to neutralise and even exterminate them. This is how the significant investment in information and repression that we have seen in Brazil, but also in states like Argentina and Chile, can be explained.

The courses on intelligence offered by ESG must already be interpreted as a project for *centralisation* and *standardisation* of certain sets of knowledge. However, they were not considered satisfactory, as opposition to the dictatorship grew and organised in different ways, including through revolutionary struggle. EsNI, created in 1971, aimed to intensify these processes of centralisation and standardisation.

Global war academies 245

At the same time, I have demonstrated that *internationalisation* also played a key role in the functioning of EsNI. Its members and leaders were constantly in touch with partner institutions in the United States and in Europe; knowledge was transferred from these regions to Brazil. From Brazil, this knowledge circulated further due to the fact that EsNI students came from other parts of Latin America. This had previously also been that case at ESG. Although the disputes and rivalries between the states in the region were not overcome in that period,[51] EsNI turned Brazil into a reference in the region and strengthened connections between the intelligence communities. Thus, it can be argued that the main strategy for keeping the Brazilian intelligence agency "up to date" was to obtain "international" theoretical and practical knowledge which was then used for the training of its own personnel. The professionalisation happened through centralisation and, above all, through internationalisation, that is through the international circulation of knowledge.

Furthermore, teaching was not unidirectional, from the Global North to the Global South. Brazilian military officers circulated through many states, imparting their knowledge. For example, they gave courses at the School of the Americas in Panama. Maintained by the United States, this school received students from all over the Americas and professors from Europe, the United States and Brazil. This clearly demonstrates the transnational character of the fight against the left between the 1960s and the 1980s.

What also emerges is that the persons in charge of the intelligence services in a "peripheral" state were indeed willing to learn from the "centres" (the United States and Europe). However, they also viewed their own institutions as "knowledge disseminators" – they themselves trained other Latin American students and in some cases students from the United States or Europe. They did not conceive of themselves as mere recipients of (foreign) knowledge, but also as producers and distributors.

This circulation of personnel and exchange of knowledge was fundamental to the formation of joint espionage and repression activities, such as the aforementioned Condor Plan (Operation Condor). Bonds of camaraderie were forged in these courses that often existed alongside the connections of the individual states and governments; these bonds of camaraderie were important when it came to pursuing enemies beyond national borders.

Notes

1 This paper results from the project *A violência transnacional e as ditaduras da América Latina: um estudo do SNI* (Transnational Violence and Dictatorships in Latin America: A Study Regarding SNI) funded by CNPq.
2 Antunes, *SNI & ABIN*; Fico, *Como eles agiam*; Quadrat, *Poder e informação*; Quadrat, *Repressão sem fronteiras*.
3 Brasil. Comissão Nacional da Verdade, *Relatório Vol. 1*.
4 Quadrat, *Preparação dos agentes*.
5 In the moment of transition to democracy, in the 1980's, documentation (archival material) from all regional SNI agencies were send to the EsNI in order to be centralized and protected there. The author has been researching about this phenomenon recently.
6 Comblin, *Ideologia da Segurança Nacional*.

246   *Samantha Viz Quadrat*

 7 Silva, *Geopolítica do Poder*; Silva, *Conjuntura política nacional*; Silva, *Geopolítica do Brasil*.
 8 Matos, *Geopolítica e Destino*.
 9 Comblin, *Ideologia da Segurança Nacional*.
10 Stepan, *Os militares*.
11 Martins Filho, *Tortura e ideologia*; Quadrat, *Repressão sem fronteiras*.
12 Trinquier, *Modern Warfare*.
13 López, *Seguridad nacional*.
14 D'Araujo et al., *Memória militar sobre 1964*, 78.
15 Ibid.
16 D'Araujo et al., *Memória militar sobre repressão*, 66.
17 Three Brazilian militaries have been sent, but I could identify only two, majors Paulo Campos Paiva and Walter Mesquita de Siqueira.
18 Anderson, *Che Guevara*, 598.
19 Martins Filho, *Tortura e ideologia*.
20 Mensário de Cultura Militar do EME, número especial, ano XV, outubro de 1962.
21 Mello, *Técnicas*, 69.
22 Ibid.
23 Oliveira, *Forças armadas*, 23.
24 Argolo, *Direita explosiva*, 320.
25 Escola Superior de Guerra. 1959. Curso de informações. Conceituação básica da informação [1ª parte] e Técnica de produção da informação [2ª parte]. Rio de Janeiro: ESG, 4.
26 Idem, 10.
27 Equipe do DAICI, *A contra-informação*, 3.
28 Carlos, *Serviços de inteligência*, 21.
29 D'Araujo et al., *Memória militar sobre 1964*, 47.
30 Carlos, *Serviços de inteligência*, 22.
31 Quadrat, *Repressão sem fronteiras*.
32 D'Araujo et al., *Memória Militar sobre a repressão*, 263.
33 Mansan, *Formação dos agentes*.
34 D'Araujo et al., *Memória Miltar sobre a repressão*, 94.
35 Ibid.
36 National Archive, BR_rjanrio_cnv_0_ere_00092_001925_2013_19.
37 D'Araujo et al., *Memória military sobre a repressão*, 133–134.
38 Lagôa, *SNI*, 64.
39 D'Araujo et al., *Memória mlitar sobre a repressão*, 134.
40 Figueiredo, *Ministério do Silêncio*, 223.
41 D'Araujo et al., *Memória mlitar sobre a repressão*, 135.
42 Ibid., 136.
43 Ibid., 138 and 139.
44 Some requests made by the authors to the archives of ABIN e ESG in order to obtain more detailed information about who participated in the courses were rejected.
45 It regards the processes 60273/73 (box 35321/000002) and 64250/74 (box 3533/000003). The documentation was consulted throughout the year of 2003. In both calls one may observe how important it is for the Exterior Relations Minister, not by chance those were years of intense contact with neighbor countries authoritarian governments and/ or espionage of Brazilians in exile in the continent and in Europe.
46 D'Araujo et al., *Memória militar sobre a repressão*, 136.
47 The information on recruitment and the courses offered by EsNI have been taken from: Lee, *implantação*, 29–31.
48 Lee, *Implantação*, 30–31.
49 D'Araujo et al., *Memória militar sobre a repressão*, 95.
50 Andrade, *Escola Nacional de Informações*; Antunes, *SNI e ABIN*.
51 Quadrat, *Repressão sem fronteiras*.

Global war academies   247

Bibliography

Alves, M. H. 1984. *Estado e oposição no Brasil (64–84)*. Petrópolis: Vozes.

Anderson, J. L. 1997. *Che Guevara: uma biografia*. Rio de Janeiro: Objetiva.

Andrade, F. de Oliveira. 2014. *A Escola Nacional de Informações: a formação dos agentes para a inteligência brasileira durante o regime militar*. Franca: Unesp.

Antunes, P. 2002. *SNI & ABIN. Uma leitura da atuação dos serviços secretos brasileiros ao longo do século XX*. Rio de Janeiro: FGV.

Araujo, M. C. D', Castro, Celso, and Soares, Gláúcio Ary Dillon. 1994. *Os anos de chumbo: a memória militar sobre a repressão*. Rio de Janeiro: Relume-Dumará.

Araujo, M. C. Soares D', Soares, Gláúcio Ary Dillon, and Castro, Celso, eds. 1994. *Visões do golpe: a memória militar sobre 1964*. Rio de Janeiro: Relume-Dumará.

Argolo, J., et al. 1996. *A direita explosiva no Brasil*. Rio de Janeiro: Mauad.

Ariquidiocese de São Paulo. 1985. *Brasil: Nunca Mais*. Petrópolis: Vozes.

Brasil. Comissão Nacional da Verdade. 2014. *Relatório Final*. Brasília: CNV.

Carlos, E. M. 1992. *Os serviços de inteligência: origem, organização e métodos de atuação*. Rio de Janeiro: ESG.

Comblin, J. 1980. *A ideologia da segurança nacional. O poder militar na América Latina*. Rio de Janeiro: Civilização Brasileira.

Escola Superior de Guerra. 1959. *Curso de informações. Conceituação básica da informação (1ª parte) e Técnica de produção da informação (2ª parte)*. Rio de Janeiro: ESG.

Escola Superior de Guerra/Divisão de Assuntos de Informações e Contra-Informações (DAICI). 1968. *A contra-informação: conceitos básicos*. Rio de Janeiro: ESG.

Fico, C. 2001. *Como eles agiam. Os subterrâneos da Ditadura Militar: espionagem e polícia política*. Rio de Janeiro: Record.

Figueiredo, L. 2005. *Ministério do Silêncio. A história do serviço secreto brasileiro de Washington Luís a Lula (1927–2005)*. Rio de Janeiro: Record.

Huggins, M. K. 1998. *Polícia e política. Relações Estados Unidos/América Latina*. São Paulo: Cortez.

Joiffily, M. 2013. *No centro da engrenagem*. Rio de Janeiro: Arquivo Nacional.

Lagôa, A. 1983. *SNI: como nasceu, como funciona*. São Paulo: Brasiliense.

Lee, L. da Silveira. 1980. *A implantação do quadro de pessoal militar da área de informações nas Forças Armadas do Brasil*. Rio de Janeiro, ESG.

López, E. 1987. *Seguridad Nacional y sedición militar*. Buenos Aires: Legasa.

Mansan, J. V. 2015. "A formação dos agentes de inteligência nos primórdios da Escola Nacional de Informações (Brasil, 1972)." In *Violência e sociedade em ditaduras ibero-americanas no século XX: Argentina, Brasil, Espanha e Portugal*, ed. J. Marco, H. G. da Silveira, and J. V. Mansan, 79–98. Porto Alegre: EDIPUCRS.

Martins Filho, J. R. 2009. "Tortura e ideologia: os militares brasileiros e a doutrina da guerre révolutionnaire (1959–1974)." In *Desarquivando a ditadura: memória e justiça no Brasil vol. 1*, ed. C. Santos, E. Teles, and J. de Almeida Teles, 179–203. São Paulo: Hucitec.

Mattos, C. de Meira. 1975. *Brasil: Geopolítica e Destino*. Rio de Janeiro: Olympio.

Mello, D. da Cunha E. 2015. "Técnicas Destrutivas e Construtivas." In EMAer. *Guerra Revolucionária*, 1962.

Oliveira, E. R. de. 1976. *As Forças Armadas: política e ideologia no Brasil (1964–1969)*. Petrópolis: Vozes.

Quadrat, S. 2000. *Poder e informação: o sistema de inteligência e o regime militar no Brasil*. Rio de Janeiro: IFCS/UFRJ.

Quadrat, S. 2005. *A repressão sem fronteiras*. Niterói: PPGH-UFF.

Quadrat, S. 2012. "A preparação dos agentes de informação e a ditadura civil-militar no Brasil." *Varia História* 28: 19–41.

Silva, G. do Couto e. 1967. *Geopolítica do Brasil*. Rio de Janeiro: José Olympio.

Silva, G. do Couto e. 1981. *Conjuntura política nacional*. Rio de Janeiro: José Olympio.

Silva, G. do Couto e. 2003. *Geopolítica e Poder*. Rio de Janeiro: UniverCidade.

Stepan, A. 1986. *Os militares: da abertura à Nova República*. Rio de Janeiro: Paz e Terra.

Trinquier, R. 1964. *Modern Warfare*. London: Pall Mall.

12 Intelligence for the masses

The annual reports on the protection of the constitution in West Germany between Cold War propaganda and government public relations

Marcel Schmeer

Introduction

Every summer a rather peculiar political ritual takes place on the stage of German domestic security, which seems to need at least some explanation to foreign observers. Usually in June or July, the acting Federal Minister of the Interior and the President of the German domestic intelligence service publicly introduce the proof of work of an organisation that is as industrious as it is controversial:[1] the BfV. The two high-level state officials present the so-called *Verfassungsschutzbericht* (Report on the Protection of the Constitution) for the previous year. These reports, as well as their respective counterparts on the level of the German federal states, can be described as media for the creation of transparency and are almost unique in the world.[2] They make the knowledge of intelligence available to and verifiable for the broader public in a well-orchestrated and scientifically prepared form.[3]

The reports nowadays include detailed threat evaluations referring to the current activities of the extreme right, extreme left, Islamic extremist circles, extremist efforts of "foreigners," intelligence activities, espionage and cyber-attacks on behalf of a foreign power as well as efforts for the security of "classified information" and "counter-sabotage" actions. Another section deals with the activities of the "Church of Scientology" which is classified as an anti-constitutional cult in Germany.[4] As an "early warning function," the listing of parties, organisations and other groups which are suspected of potentially democracy-threatening activity "is intended to give citizens the opportunity to identify and assess the anti-constitutional objectives in advance of the realization of the threat"[5] and to enable public debate on these issues. The public presentation of the reports – together with the annual publication of the Federal Criminal Statistics[6] – can be counted among the central public events in the field of domestic security communication in Germany. The findings of the BfV usually receive considerable attention in the domestic and foreign media landscape.[7]

From a historical, legal and democratic theoretical perspective, however, the *Verfassungsschutz* reports appear to be particularly in need of explanation and legitimation. When and why, and in what historical context did West German

DOI: 10.4324/9781003147329-13

250 Marcel Schmeer

politicians, members of security institutions and secret service practitioners decide to make this previously internal and secret threat knowledge public and to publish it in the form of an annual report? What is the legal basis for these reports on "efforts directed against the free democratic basic order"[8] – and what are the consequences of labelling parties, political splinter groups or other organisations "hostile to the constitution"?[9] Are the reports a mere democratic early warning system or, as some critics have argued, part of a repressive regime of arbitrary "censorship of opinions"?[10] Finally, from the perspective of the theory of democracy, the question arises as to the highly conflictive relationship between the veil of secrecy that coats the work of secret services and an influential democratic transparency imperative as it has emerged in western liberal democracies in the second half of the twentieth century.[11] How and why do democratically founded intelligence agencies have to dispense with the secrecy of specific information and knowledge in favour of a social claim to transparency, and thus pursue a "management of contradiction"[12] or "management of mistrust"[13] between these intricately connected spheres? And what exactly does it look like?

Departing from these observations and questions, this article traces how the *Verfassungsschutz* reports developed from a propagandistic tool born from the necessity of the inter-German system competition on the peak of the Cold War into an adequate security communicative medium within a fundamentally changing society that, at the same time, had to deal with new confusing and often asymmetrical threats in the age of left-wing terrorism.[14] Inspired by the assumption that intelligence services "not merely describe the world in which the state operates, but in fact actively 'create' that world,"[15] the *Verfassungsschutz* reports, as genuinely popularised intelligence knowledge, will be interpreted as a powerful tool that has shaped and continues to influence the security policy discourse as well as the media and social perception of "security," respectively the German "security culture."[16] In the course of the (security) history of the Federal Republic of Germany and against the background of an increasingly critical media sphere, the reports have become a central cause for discussion about threats to the democratic order, but also about the BfV itself – and it is reasonable to assume that these debates had, in turn, an impact on its organisational culture and observation logics in a variety of ways. With a view to the overall conception and central questions of this anthology, this contribution aims to shed more light on the transformation of intelligence knowledge while circulating between the spheres of secrecy and publicity. Thus, it is less about the basics of knowledge production by intelligence services, but rather about conventions and strategies of presenting this particular body of knowledge to the public, which are subject to historical change. The popularisation of intelligence knowledge, I contend, was intimately connected with the purpose of establishing public trust in this knowledge. Consequently, the reports underwent several processes of professionalisation and scientisation transforming them (and the knowledge provided in the reports) from an ideologically impregnated propaganda brochure into a very detailed report based on a comprehensive variety of quantitative and qualitative data with a claim to objectivity.

Intelligence for the masses 251

The research perspective outlined here benefits considerably from the methodological suggestions from the highly dynamic field of the "history of knowledge."[17] The popularisation of intelligence knowledge in the form of the *Verfassungsschutz* reports can be examined as part of a media-analytical dimension of the history of knowledge as delineated by Swiss historian Philipp Sarasin. According to him, "knowledge cannot exist without storage, transport and media of representation." Instead, Sarasin continues, knowledge is intensively "shaped by the logic of these media . . . because it always has to be formatted and . . . is always transformed during its way through the channels." In this context, Sarasin emphasises that "the corresponding formats and media act as filters that select, emphasize and suppress knowledge, change it and combine it with other stocks of knowledge."[18] These considerations allow us to conceptualise the popularisation of intelligence knowledge in the shape of annual reports as a particular form of media-supported "circulation of knowledge."[19] Following up on this, I argue that in the process of preparation for publication and after the final step into public circulation the genuinely ambiguous and, in a sense, "precarious"[20] *intelligence knowledge* is transformed into a rather unambiguous official, evidence-based and publicly available *threat knowledge* provided by the state itself.[21] It is only in this processed form that the knowledge of the guardians of the constitution can be received by a broader audience (interested citizens or the media) and thus also be critically scrutinised.

Based on the printed reports, government files, and sporadic media reports as historical sources, the core of this article examines the origins of the *Verfassungsschutz* reports in the shadow of the Cold War and the changes in reporting since the late 1960s. I will particularly focus on three periods in time: In a first step, I will briefly outline the vigorous political debates on the necessity of public use of intelligence knowledge in the context of the German-German "propaganda war," which ultimately marked the beginning of intelligence public relations in the Federal Republic and can be considered the hour of birth of the *Verfassungsschutz* reports. The second part focuses on the early reports and embeds them in a general history of the public relations work of the BfV during the early and mid-1960s. In the third section, I will discuss the changes in public relations under the influence of increasing transparency demands since the late 1960s. In this period, the *Verfassungsschutz* reports also changed fundamentally from a mere tool of persuasion into a rather deliberative, yet still highly contested source of information. I will conclude with some continuative thoughts on the significance of the *Verfassungsschutz* reports for the ambiguous "management of distrust" by the state and its secret services, their influence on the national security culture as well as their value as a source for contemporary historical research.

The birth of intelligence PR from the spirit of anti-communism

The perceived necessity of making intelligence knowledge publicly available was intimately linked to the "asymmetrically interwoven parallel history" of the competition between the liberal democratic system of the Federal Republic and

252 *Marcel Schmeer*

its socialist counterpart (and contrast foil), the German Democratic Republic (GDR).[22] At the same time, however, the intensive debates and political concepts surrounding the specific design of "militant democracy" (*wehrhafte Demokratie*) enshrined in the West German Basic Law since the 1950s must be taken into account and will be outlined in the following paragraphs.

Already during early debates on the Federal Constitutional Protection Act in June 1950, high-ranking state secretary Hans Ritter von Lex had referred to the multidimensional nature of the term *Verfassungsschutz*: In addition to the executive and legal measures to protect the constitution, he focused on a third form, which he considered "perhaps the most effective form of protection of the constitution in the long term." Von Lex understood it along the lines of what we would nowadays call civic education but interpreted it more paternalistically in the sense of a one-way educational measure provided by the government. He continued that although it was "in the nature of the democratic form of government that it unfolded little propaganda for itself," the increasing "disintegrating counter-propaganda of anti-democratic forces" made it necessary to inform the "broad masses objectively about the nature of democracy and its working methods." In the spirit of the concept of "militant democracy" laid down in the Basic Law, the state secretary stressed with regard to one of the "fathers of the constitution," the renowned expert in constitutional law Carlo Schmid, that it was incomprehensible that "democracy should always remain on the defensive."[23] Consequently, the young democracy had drawn its sharpest sword in this respect only a few years later against the Socialist Reich Party in October 1952 and the Communist Party of Germany (KPD) in August 1956 – the only parties to be banned by the Federal Constitutional Court until today.[24]

The positive dimension of *Verfassungsschutz* conceptualised as measures to consolidate the constitutional order, in contrast to a negative, rather repressive way of dealing with enemies of the constitution, was also represented by the first President of the BfV, Otto John. He explicitly linked it with the idea of educating West German citizens about the work of its newly established democratic secret services. He published articles and gave interviews in which he explained the conditions under which the office came into being, its organisational structures and its areas of responsibility. In addition, he tried to clear up what he considered to be popular misconceptions about the nature and tasks of the service he headed.[25] For John, this solicitation for a leap of faith was certainly unavoidable, because the public was highly sceptical about the new security organisations. This scepticism arose from the necessarily secret nature of intelligence work as well as the baleful experiences of the Nazi era, especially referring to the vicious Gestapo, the secret police formed at the core of the SS empire.[26] John vigorously defended his staff against comparisons of this kind and emphasised that his employees were not allowed to "adventure like Don Juan or Sherlock Holmes." Their major task, according to John, had to be "carried out just as soberly . . . as medical research for the prevention of a people's contamination."[27]

Organisationally, both the negative and positive connotations of protecting the constitutional order were placed under the jurisdiction of the Federal Ministry of

Intelligence for the masses 253

the Interior (BMI), which was responsible for the control of the Federal Police and the domestic intelligence service as well as the political education work entrusted to the Federal Centre for Homeland Service, founded in November 1952. The Federal Ministry for All-German Issues was ultimately responsible for all German-German affairs and was also intensively involved in propagandistic measures aimed at "the East."[28] Within Germany's federal system, the security architecture became even more complicated by the fact that almost all federal states maintained their own independent security services and civic education agencies. This strict institutional separation of "positive" and "negative" actions to protect the constitution was increasingly regarded as dysfunctional by leading domestic security politicians at the beginning of the 1960s.

The newly perceived need for coordination and cooperation was primarily due to the propagandistic campaign policies of the GDR against the Federal Republic. In several publications and show trials, these harsh campaigns were directed against the continuity of the administrative elites from the Third Reich to the early West German democracy, thus branding it as a refuge of old and new Nazis.[29] The campaigns found an initial starting point in a wave of anti-Semitic swastika smears which had its origin in the desecration of the synagogue in Cologne on Christmas Eve 1959.[30] These appalling events led to heated discussions at home and abroad, as well as to large demonstrations against the rise of right-wing extremism in the Federal Republic. In early January 1960, for example, some 40,000 mostly young people in West Berlin joined a silent march against "neo-Nazism, anti-Semitism and racial hatred."[31] In the following months, this development spurred a far-reaching political reaction.

At various conferences since the beginning of 1960, the interior ministers of the German states intensely debated the question of how the specific threat knowledge of the *Verfassungsschutz* authorities could be used effectively in public to oppose the GDR in this inter-German propaganda war. At the same time, they were looking for a more impactful way to bring the work and effectiveness of the German secret services closer to the public's attention. It was only at the conference of interior ministers in Hamburg in early 1961 that a package of measures for the *positiver Verfassungsschutz* (positive protection of the constitution) was eventually adopted and subsequently implemented.[32] The matter was perceived as urgent by the political decision-makers, as can be seen from the protocol of a meeting of a planning staff for the new concept in Bonn in June 1961. The state officials made intensive use of the same (epidemiological) imagery of an ideological contamination we have already observed in the case of Otto John and which can be considered remarkably influential in this early phase of the Cold War.[33] In their perception, "the East" was

> trying to flood the population in the Federal Republic with its propaganda. The repressive *Verfassungsschutz*, which was working well, was obviously not enough to counter the constant infiltration of ideological poison. Rather, it was necessary to immunize the population by, among other things, confronting the propaganda theses of the East with 'positive' ideas.[34]

254 *Marcel Schmeer*

After long debates and more than a year after the enormous outrage caused by the swastika smears in Cologne and several other cities, West German politicians had been able to agree on a swift reaction to the continuing propagandistic attacks from the GDR. The focus was on the question of the involvement of the Offices for the Protection of the Constitution and the search for suitable forms of public and journalistic exploitation of intelligence knowledge. The latter was to be implemented through intensive reporting and educational lectures, but also through mass media, especially feature and educational films.[35] In this context, for instance, Bremen's Interior Senator Adolf Ehlers estimated that about 90 per cent of the material collected by the secret services would be suitable for publication.[36] In addition, the Federal and State Agencies for the Protection of the Constitution were to set up their own departments for public relations. The erection of the Berlin Wall in August 1961 accelerated these dynamics even further. The BfV established its own PR department at the end of 1961. In the (rather short) period that followed, we can observe a fundamental change in the relationship between arcane politics and the public exploitation of intelligence knowledge in a heated Cold War climate.

Propaganda or public relations? Or, how to publish the knowledge of intelligence

Following these intensive debates, the Interior Ministers and Senators decided in late 1961 to commission the first *Verfassungsschutzbericht*. It was eventually published by the BMI in March 1962 on the basis of material compiled by the BfV and secret services of the German states under the bulky title "Experiences from the Observation and Defense of Right-Wing Radical and Anti-Semitic Tendencies" as a supplement to the weekly political newspaper *Das Parlament* edited by the Federal Centre for Homeland Service.[37] In view of the previously mentioned communist threat perceived at a political level, such a publication on right-wing extremism appears paradoxical at first glance.[38] The report, however, could in fact pursue two objectives at once: the "field report" was intended to simmer down the harsh press reactions, which still had not fallen silent after the anti-Semitic graffities of 1959/60 at home and among the Western partners.[39] On the other hand, it could be used to stage the effectiveness of German intelligence services in sufficiently dealing with the threat popularised in the reports.

In the end, the birth of the *Verfassungsschutz* reports was not a mere "consequence of the burden of the past"[40] but arose from the deeply anti-communist consensus of the Adenauer era as an "objective" propagandistic tool against the ongoing "anti-fascist" GDR campaigns against Bonn. The foreword to the 35-page brochure already placed the report in the context of this inter-German ideological debate that had intensified tremendously after the permanent division of the country had been manifested in a guarded concrete barrier:

> The year 1961 has confronted the population of the Federal Republic with a chain of political events. Ulbricht built the wall across Berlin, drove the terror

Intelligence for the masses   255

in Central Germany to its extreme and, in connection with it, intensified his efforts to slander the Federal Republic of Germany before the world.[41]

In seven sections, the report provided information on the manifestations of right-wing radicalism in Germany: argumentation strategies, right-wing radical and anti-Semitic incidents, the influences of international fascist streams, corresponding tendencies in Eastern immigrant groups, Eastern contacts of West German rightists, and state countermeasures in the field of the protection of the constitution. It is remarkable that anti-communist references were constantly woven into the presentation of the findings. The report stated, for example, that the true extent of right-wing radicalism in the Federal Republic was often overestimated, mainly due to numerous "false reports" that had "often been recognized as the agitation of the Communists."[42] According to the findings of the BfV, anti-Semitic and neo-Nazi incidents (such as swastika smearings), had shown a sharp decline in 1961 compared to the previous year. A detailed analysis revealed that this was primarily due to the significantly lower proportion of "non-politically motivated acts." But even in cases linked to "politically motivated perpetrators," which accounted for 44 per cent of all incidents, the guardians of the state almost exclusively spoke about acts conducted by "politically non-organized lone wolves."[43] In this observation logic, one could by no means speak of a strengthening of the organised right. In contrast, however, the report noted that "the Soviet bloc had not only used the anti-Semitic incidents for a worldwide defamation campaign against the Federal Republic of Germany but had even initiated such actions in the territory of the Federal Republic itself."[44] This statement was underscored by three copies of leaflets attached to the brochure, which the Ministry for State Security (the infamous *Stasi*) was accused of depositing in public places such as telephone booths. These "Soviet inflammatory writings" were signed with "greetings" from the *Waffen-SS* and contained explicitly anti-Semitic slogans.[45] The report concluded by stating that right-wing radicalism in the Federal Republic currently did not represent an acute threat, although the possibility of future radicalisation among the population, for example in the wake of an economic crisis, could by no means be ruled out.[46] Nevertheless, the report put the *Verfassungsschutz* agents in a heroic light: Despite the soothing scenario described here – in the form of popularised intelligence knowledge – the security authorities were staged as being in total control of the situation and, in the event of an increasing threat from right-wing extremists, would not only recognise this at an early stage but also fight it "with all constitutional means."[47]

The first report on the findings on "communist activities in the Federal Republic" was published in August 1965 for the reporting year 1964. The available sources do not reveal why this brochure was published three years after the initial report on the state of right-wing radicalism. However, it seems plausible to assume that the release of this report was deeply motivated by the claim to provide additional information about the ongoing dangers of communist activities in West Germany. The 36-page brochure intended to dismantle the dynamics of the concerted "communist attacks against the FDR" and to show the close ties between the Socialist

256 *Marcel Schmeer*

Unity Party of Germany (SED) and the KPD, which had been operating illegally in the West since 1956. The report set itself the task of revealing the "goals and tactics" of the communists, highlighting the leading role of the SED and presenting focal points of communist political activities in West Germany. In addition, the report contained information on communist activities among foreigners (the so-called "guest workers"), the organisational structure of the banned KPD and other "communist-influenced organizations," as well as a separate section on communist activities in West Berlin, inter-German travel and criminal proceedings in matters of state security.[48] In an overall evaluation, the report concluded that the KPD, out of illegality, had succeeded in igniting "a public discussion about the lifting of the party ban" and in "loosening up the aversion of a part of the population to the SBZ [Soviet Occupation Zone, M.S.] regime." However, despite the high idealistic and material expenditure, the overall security in the Federal Republic was perceived as not being seriously threatened – mainly because the communists had been prevented from "developing their propagandistic potential" by the watchful eyes of the guardians of the state.[49]

In comparison to its counterpart on right-wing extremism, the report on communist activities was richly illustrated and endowed with numerous diagrams and charts. In addition to several press collages with titles and headlines from various communist publications, an expressive sketch of the "reception area of the German Television Broadcasting Corporation" or various propagandistic measures by the Free German Trade Union Federation against West German companies and trade unions impressively illustrated the perceived widespread extent of communist agitation and infiltration efforts. This systematic visualisation of the threat also influenced the style of the later *Verfassungsschutz* reports. In the aforementioned example, we can observe very clearly what BMI officials in the early 1960s labelled an alarming "seepage of ideological poison" into the Federal Republic. As can be seen from the early reports, one central strategy of popularising the knowledge of intelligence was to generate an easily interpretable (graphic) image of the threat perceptions of the state.[50]

At this point, I want to embed the reports into the broader framework of threat communication and governmental PR of the early 1960s. As already mentioned, the BfV had set up its own public relations department at the end of 1961, where the relevant reports from its different branches came together. These findings were then edited in the BMI and revised for official publication. From the files I have examined, it is hardly possible to estimate exactly how and according to what aspects the intelligence knowledge was edited and formatted into publicly accessible information. It is to be assumed, however, that the conventional secrecy concerns on the one hand and political considerations on the other hand played a decisive role in this process.[51]

During the first half of the 1960s, the cooperation between the BfV and the department for public relations in the BMI was organised in a twofold structure. The BfV seemed to have a great deal of room to manoeuvre in terms of media relations and the production of suitable content. At the same time, the responsible officials within the BMI controlled the reporting system

Intelligence for the masses 257

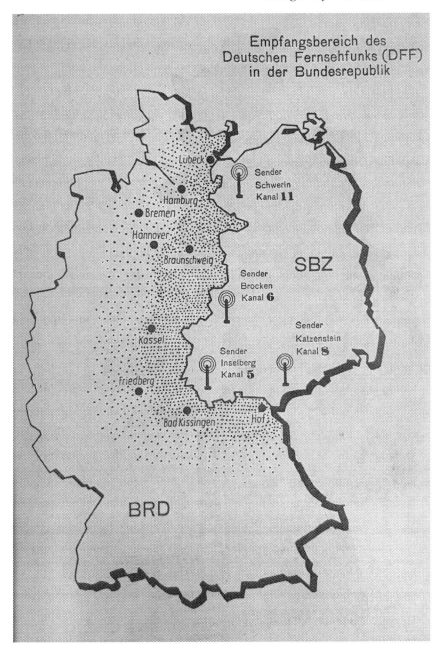

Figure 12.1 "Reception Area of the German Television Broadcasting Corporation in the Federal Republic" as published in the weekly journal *Aus Politik und Zeitgeschichte*.
Source: Anonymous, "Kommunistische Tätigkeit," 13.

258   *Marcel Schmeer*

and had the final authority in questions of publications et cetera. While the BfV focused almost exclusively on its own area of expertise, the Federal Ministry of the Interior attempted to provide a comprehensive panorama of the domestic security measures in the Federal Republic through various channels. Within this communicative ensemble, publications relevant to the intelligence services only made up one part of the picture. The PR experts within the BMI also developed security communication strategies with regard to the broad field of political education, the Federal Criminal Police Office or the Federal Border Guard. These efforts eventually led to the establishment of an official press bulletin titled "Domestic Security. Information on State Security Issues" that appeared regularly from 1966 to the 1980s.[52]

Within the BfV, the strictly anti-communist journalist and publicist Friedrich Ernst Berghoff was responsible for the public relations work. He mostly operated under his alias Hendrik van Bergh and had already attracted some attention as a journalist since the 1950s through several anti-communist publications and radio plays. This impassionate "spin doctor" of the Cold War took up his work for the BfV with zealous enthusiasm: He produced movie scripts and radio plays, published books on espionage issues and coordinated the overall cooperation with the BMI's public relations department. At the same time, other senior secret service employees, such as the later BfV president Günter Nollau, also published findings from their work for a broader audience.[53]

Taking on another area of responsibility, Berghoff operated as the contact person for journalists. Likewise, he carefully observed the national media landscape to gain a better sense of the BfV's public image. Nevertheless, he rather one-sidedly conceptualised the public as a mere resonating body for the anti-communist information policy of the guardians of the constitution. He saw the image of "his" agency in the public debate as distorted by many false accusations and sometimes maliciously misinterpreted by both politicians and journalists.[54] These observations point to the overarching question of the underlying principles of intelligence public relations in West Germany until the end of the 1960s. The actors involved were less concerned with a public dialogue about the organisational cultural foundations of intelligence knowledge or the observational logics and practical work of the service. Rather, PR activities centred on the propaganda-motivated distribution of intelligence knowledge according to a simple transmitter-receiver model. According to this reading, I contend, criticism of the BfV, for example in the wake of intelligence scandals, did not lead to a self-critical recalibration of its own activities and epistemological foundations of its work, but rather seems to have fostered a certain kind of organisational wagon-train mentality.

However, the hope of influencing the press for the mere purposes of circulating intelligence knowledge and thus fuelling the ideological competition between the blocs, as PR practitioners like Berghoff envisaged, was troublesome from the outset. The relationship between the media and the state had already changed significantly since the early 1960s. In a "time of affairs"[55] – such as the infamous Spiegel affair in 1962 or the telephone tapping affair in 1963 triggered by a whistleblower within the intelligence agency[56] – the BfV was increasingly scrutinised by a critical

Intelligence for the masses   259

(media) public, which emphatically formulated demands for transparency against the secret nature of the German domestic intelligence service. The popularised intelligence knowledge was now increasingly perceived as a potential resource of trust by political decision-makers who intended to give the BfV an image of transparency and reliability. An example of this attempt to restore confidence in the BfV is the publication of an anthology edited by the BMI in 1966. In its preface, Federal Minister Paul Lücke explained that he saw it as an important endeavour "to free this institution from the suspicion that its tasks and practices had to shun the light of publicity."[57] However, he continued, the work of the BfV would only be successful if the authorities could count on the public's trust. Lücke conceded that this was not an easy undertaking for any secret service in the West. The obligation of secrecy would probably never completely eliminate the "public's mistrust of exceeding the limits set by law and order." This basic mistrust of the abuse of power by state authorities, he added, was probably a "necessary characteristic of every democratic form of society." In the future, he concluded, the work of the domestic intelligence service had to be made "as transparent as possible for the individual citizen."[58]

His campaign for trust, however, was overshadowed by the ambivalence of transparency and secrecy: To the extent that Lücke made the promise of greater openness a concession to a more confident (media) public, he also admitted that the fundamental contradiction of a secret service in a democratic society was, at least for the time being, insoluble. In this respect, his contribution can also be interpreted as an early expression of a "mistrust management" that had now been more and more institutionalised by the political side. Politicians and the BfV became aware that the guardians of the state and observers of anti-constitutional activities – as well as their logics of observation – had become permanent subjects to critical scrutiny. However, the question of an adequate reaction to this "observation of the observers"[59] was still hanging in the balance. Berghoff's attempts, which can be described as state propaganda (the term "public relations" is misleading here), were based on the embittered bipolarity of the East-West conflict and seemed increasingly outdated in the now-enfolding era of détente.[60] In the same way, the domestic security authorities were confronted with a rapid diffusion of threats and a more ambiguous "image of the enemy"[61] in the aftermath of 1968: The competition between the political and ideological systems faded into the background of new menacing scenarios. Instead, the New Left and the rise of left-wing terrorism out of radical parts of the students movement a few years later were increasingly perceived as threats from within the heart of society.[62] Both developments made it urgent that the concepts, routines and practices of security and threat communication and thus the logics of popularising the knowledge of intelligence needed to be reconfigured under new auspices.

Professionalisation and democratisation?
Verfassungsschutz PR after 1968

At the end of the 1960s, the Federal Ministry of the Interior intervened more strongly than before in the public relations work of the *Verfassungsschutz*. A report from the PR department suggests that under Ernst Benda, who became the new

260   *Marcel Schmeer*

Minister of the Interior in early 1968, the Federal Office had been issued a "general ban . . . on publications" in the same year – the reasons for which remained unnamed.[63] It seems plausible, however, that the services of the valiant cold warrior Berghoff were no longer considered appropriate at this time. In any case, initial efforts were made under Benda to strengthen the control of government publications based on information from the BfV. This was accompanied by a centralisation, professionalisation and, to an extent, scientification of the most important publication organs of the BMI.[64]

Consequently, in August 1969 a "Field Report on Observations of the Offices for the Protection of the Constitution in 1968" was published in the BMI publication series *Zum Thema*, covering the former individual reports on right-wing and left-wing radicalism – and, in addition, "measures of counterespionage" – in one single volume. The preface to this first *Verfassungsschutz* report in today's form, presumably written by Benda himself, provides insights into the reasons for the merger of the reporting system:

> An overall view seems necessary in order to be able to better assess the stability of our democratic basic order and the dangers threatening it; it also contributes to the fact that the reader does not overestimate the threat of one extreme, which seems greater to him according to his own political standpoint, but underestimates the danger of the other. A democratic state can exist only if it is vigilant on all sides where danger is imminent and not only fends off attacks which seem to be more dangerous at the moment. Experience teaches that the chances of success of an attack are much greater if it is led from a direction from which it is not expected.[65]

On the one hand, we can observe a remarkable shift in the perception of threats by the BMI, which now officially ascribed the same potential danger to the right and to the "traditional" communist threat. A trigger for this was surely the success of the right-wing extremist National Democratic Party of Germany (NPD) in the state elections in Baden-Württemberg in April 1968. The "National Democrats" had achieved their greatest electoral success to date with 9.8 per cent of the valid votes, which was consequently mentioned right at the beginning of the 1968 report.[66] On the other hand, this equation of different political threats can also be understood as an offer of appeasement for those social forces that accused the BfV of being largely blind on the right eye or even of sympathising with fascist ideology – a common accusation until today.

Against the background of the apparently irreconcilable and often extremely violent clashes between the police and predominantly young protestors in the wake of 1968, however, the New Left also increasingly moved into the focus of the BfV. According to the 1968 report, they had been perceived as becoming more and more radical after the assassination attempt on student leader Rudi Dutschke in April 1968 with particular reference to the planning of violent actions by "radical circles" of the Socialist German Student Union.[67] The immediate threat posed by "traditional" communism, i.e. by the illegal KPD and the GDR, was perceived as

Intelligence for the masses 261

far less intimidating than at the beginning of the 1960s in view of the new complexity that the guardians of the constitution had to face now. With a total of 152 pages, the report was correspondingly more voluminous. 46 pages were dedicated to "right-wing extremist efforts" with a focus on the NPD and right-wing extremist publications. 58 pages were allotted to "communist and other left-wing extremist endeavors" which were strictly divided into "old" communism and the "New Left." Finally, 24 pages were devoted to counter-espionage measures. Overall, "society" and the potential threats it posed for the constitutional order rose to become a dominant theme in the security agencies in the years that followed.[68]

After the federal elections in September 1969, the new Federal Minister of the Interior Hans-Dietrich Genscher continued the course of his predecessor. Presumably because he did not want to burden the auspicious détente policy of the newly formed social-liberal government towards the GDR, he maintained the publication ban on the BfV and temporarily stopped the publication of the *Verfassungsschutz* reports. After a one-year pause, a 72-page document for the reporting years 1969 and 1970 was published in 1971 in the BMI's publication series *betrifft*. The revised report gave roughly equal space to right-wing and left-wing extremist endeavours. In addition, the report included assessments of "efforts by foreigners to endanger security." In the preface to the new volume, Genscher emphasised his ideal of maximum openness in the work of the protectors of the constitution:

> I consider it essential that the public knows what the Office for the Protection of the Constitution is doing. This authority collects information, of which only those are to be treated as secret, whose publication could lead to a threat to public security. But otherwise, the principle of maximum transparency applies to an authority which, by its nature as an intelligence service, stimulates the public's imagination and is therefore easily in danger of being demonized.[69]

The reports now also included a section on extremist groups of foreigners. This expansion of potential sources of threat was not, however, accompanied by an expansion of the disclosure of internal intelligence information. Genscher's frequently repeated promise of transparency was thus little more than rhetoric. In this sense, the minister also endeavoured to emphasise that the protection of the constitution was a task that "is incumbent on all democratic citizens." The BfV alone could never be sufficient if it were not backed by the "democratic commitment of the individual."[70]

The *Verfassungsschutz* reports, which were now completely overhauled in their presentation and style, can also be read as a source for a more intensive visualisation of threat scenarios compared to the 1960s. The increased use of photographs, newspaper collages and diagrams had a significant impact on transforming and thus reinforcing the rather diffuse intelligence knowledge in what was now perceived as an ever-increasingly complex security situation. A remarkable example of this can be found in the 1972 *Verfassungsschutz* report, where the danger posed by unscrupulous bomb attacks carried out by the Red Army Faction (RAF) in the course of its "May Offensive" was visually underscored by the depiction of a so-called "baby bomb" designed and built by notorious tinker and RAF supporter Dierk Hoff.[71] In the arrangement of the collage, this potentially fatal explosive weapon was placed next to pictures of the car of Karlsruhe Federal Judge Wolfgang Buddenberg, which was destroyed in an explosive attack in May 1972. Buddenberg's wife had been seriously injured in the attack. The "baby bomb," however, which a female terrorist could have placed inconspicuously under pretence of pregnancy, was never used, but apparently could be utilised formidably for threat communication in a generally tense security political climate to demonstrate the murderous determination of the left-wing terrorists.[72]

During the 1970s, the scope of the annual reports increased steadily, and the reporting system became more differentiated. From 1974 onwards, the Federal German state security authorities also abandoned the term "radicalism" in their public language use and replaced it with "extremism."[73] This alteration also affected the *Verfassungsschutz* reports. Federal Minister of the Interior Werner Maihofer (FDP) explained this decision in his foreword to the volume for the reporting year 1973 with the fact that "political activities or organizations are not anti-constitutional simply because they have a . . . 'radical' objective, an objective that goes to the root of a question." Instead, the term "extremism" was intended to explicitly describe anti-constitutional activities that were "directed against the . . . basic elements of our constitution, which is based on the rule

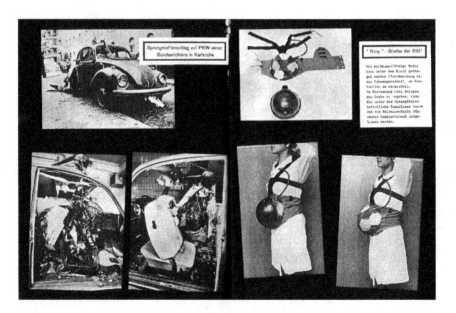

Figure 12.2 "Explosive attack on the car of a federal judge in Karlsruhe" and "RAF 'baby bomb'" as published by the German Ministry of the Interior in 1972.

Source: Bundesministerium des Innern, Verfassungsschutz 1972, unpaged.

Intelligence for the masses   263

of law and freedom."[74] The popularised intelligence knowledge subsequently became more and more diverse and has thus increased in complexity. The reports were published in scientific guise and during the 1980s increasingly took into account statistical and sociological findings.[75] It should only be briefly mentioned here that with the election of Helmut Kohl as chancellor and in the wake of the so-called "spiritual and moral turn" (*geistig-moralische Wende*) as well as new tensions between the Cold War superpowers, a change in the presentation of the reports also highlighted a change in the prioritisation of the observation logic of the guardians of the state. From the 1982 reporting year, the chapter dealing with "left-wing extremist efforts" was moved to the beginning of the reports. This position had previously been occupied by the threat portrayal of the extremist right. This order was only changed again in 1998 after the red-green coalition took office. Since then, and to this day, the reports on "right-wing extremist efforts" have taken first place in the order of the reports.[76] This seemingly marginal example shows how much the reports were embedded in major political developments and controversial (de-)securitisation processes.

As a further development in the 1970s, the Federal Constitutional Court established a broader legal framework for the reports in terms of constitutional law for the first time. In the 1968 report, Ernst Benda had still pointed out that the reporting was neither to be understood "as a political confrontation" with anti-constitutional forces nor "as a constitutional appreciation of the same."[77] Interestingly, it was not until 1975 that the Federal Constitutional Court first commented on the practice of the government reports in its resolution concerning the notorious *Radikalen-erlass* (Anti-Radical Decree) instituted in 1972 by the federal government and the state prime ministers.[78] According to the judges in Karlsruhe, it was, from a constitutional perspective, "unobjectionable and part of the political responsibility of the government that it presents its annual report on the development of anti-constitutional forces, groups and parties to parliament and the public." The constitutional judges added that a party was not protected from any disadvantages that might arise from such a mention in the *Verfassungsschutz* reports.[79] The right-wing extremist NPD had also filed a complaint against its nomination in the 1973 report. In a decision on the matter, the Constitutional Court reaffirmed its opinion and justified the assessment of the NPD as unconstitutional, stating that this exact phrasing in the *Verfassungsschutz* report constituted a "value judgement" issued by the Federal Minister of the Interior in order to protect the free democratic basic order – but without particular legal consequences attached to it. At the same time, the highest German judges also set limits for the reporting system and made clear that an arbitrary mention in the reports was by no means justified.[80]

Finally, a further development during the 1970s should be noted, which can be described as an overall transition within the West German security culture. The late 1960s saw the emergence of a security dispositive of *Innere Sicherheit* (domestic security), which implied "a new understanding of state and society, in which security can only be thought of in relation to freedoms and risks."[81] Old ideas of the authoritarian ideal of *Ruhe und Ordnung* (law and order) had become obsolete and it seemed necessary to political decision-makers to establish a new

264 Marcel Schmeer

basis for the relationship between secret services and (civil) society. Against this backdrop, security political actors took new paths, especially since the late 1960s in the state of Hesse. Here, the lawyer and former BfV employee Hans Joachim Schwagerl headed a rather unique department for secret service public relations in the Hessian Ministry of the Interior since 1968. He practiced what would later be officially called *informativer Verfassungsschutz* (informative *Verfassungsschutz*), which can be interpreted as a final departure from the propagandistic ideal of the Cold War. In the sense of civic education work, the population was to be assured of the sense of the existence of their state protection authorities through deliberative argumentation. To this end, Schwagerl gave lectures in schools, wrote newspaper articles and was the first guardian of the constitution to accept a (highly contested) teaching position at the University of Gießen.[82] In contrast to the image of a public sphere as a mere resonating body that was to be "immunized" against Soviet agitation, Schwagerl wanted to "lift the veil" of the arcane and perceived his audience as politically mature and critical democratic subjects that had to be convinced in political discourse. In this sense, Schwagerl believed that every citizen had to be enabled to protect or actively defend the democratic order:

> It is not the suppression of unconstitutional efforts, but rather their discovery, research into the causes and their elimination that constitute the ultimate meaning and purpose of the protection of the constitution. The highest learning goals of political education must be congruent with the goals of the protection of the constitution: securing the constitutional, social democracy by citizens who are able to criticize and be critical.[83]

The deliberative concept of *Verfassungsschutz durch Aufklärung* (*Verfassungsschutz* through education), which he decisively helped to elaborate, was to shape the relationship between the secret services and the public from the mid-1970s onwards.[84] This also had an impact on the popularisation of intelligence knowledge, which was now conceptualised as two different resources of knowledge: knowledge *about* the work of the services and the (processed) knowledge *of* the services. As a result of this concept, which was adopted by the federal and state interior ministers in December 1974, the *Landesämter für Verfassungsschutz* (Offices for the Protection of the Constitution in the states) began to publish their own reports in the second half of the 1970s.[85] These were intended to summarise the threat situations in the respective federal states and to provide citizens with transparency about the work of the services. The *Länder* reports differ considerably in their presentation and scope but allow interesting conclusions on different political threat assessments within German federalism and between different political camps.

Towards the end of the 1970s, the reports on the protection of the constitution as popularised intelligence knowledge had thus become significantly more professional, scientific and, in a sense, democratic than the propagandistically oriented brochures of the 1960s. They had evolved into an important and, to a degree, transparent media of democratic debate on domestic security issues. Similarly, it can be

Intelligence for the masses 265

assumed that the popularisation of intelligence knowledge and the public debates about it also had an impact on the services themselves, for example by questioning or recalibrating internal observation logics or by taking up current political, societal, or security-cultural dynamics of change. The circulation of knowledge between the spheres of publicity and secrecy is thus far more than a confidence-building measure. The *Verfassungsschutz* reports serve as a link between intelligence work and societal counter-observation, thereby enabling democratic control of the foundations of intelligence production. Nevertheless, quite a bit of information necessarily remains concealed by the veil of the arcane. Thus, an unresolvable transparency deficit remains the cause of an almost constitutive distrust in the BfV.

Conclusion: *Verfassungsschutz* reports, the knowledge of intelligence and historical research

This chapter traced the origins and further development of the reports on the protection of the constitution until the late 1970s in three steps, analysing the reports as a genuine form of popularisation of intelligence knowledge. As a first step, I reconstructed the debates on the public use of intelligence knowledge from the spirit of "militant democracy." Against the background of the ideological conflict with the GDR, political decision-makers and intelligence officials had agreed at the beginning of the 1960s to educate the population about the extent of communist agitation attempts by means of publishing intelligence knowledge. By doing so, they also wanted to correct the propagandised image of the Federal Republic as a refuge for old and new Nazis. In a second step, I investigated how exactly the popularisation of intelligence knowledge took place in the realm of the heated Cold War climate of the early 1960s. The concepts of the secret service and political PR practitioners were based on the assumption that the population should be "immunised" as far as possible against "ideological poison" from "the East" and used the findings of the protectors of the constitution to this end. This concept, as I have shown in the third step, increasingly turned out to be dysfunctional against the background of the détente period in the late 1960s. The reporting system was professionalised accordingly, and the reports were reconfigured as a social science-based medium of transparency within a discourse-oriented democratic debate on the potential dangers to the constitutional order from various sources. National security policy makers, intelligence practitioners as well as the critical (media) public henceforth considered the popularised intelligence knowledge as an important source of information in the field of domestic security issues within a liberal democracy – especially against the backdrop of a novel diffusion of dangers and risks.

As I have shown in this chapter, the reports of the Offices for the Protection of the Constitution, a rather unique form of government communication and popularised intelligence knowledge, hold great potential as a source for research in the broader fields of intelligence and security history. Against this backdrop, it is somewhat surprising that the reports have received little attention in historiographical analysis so far. Based on the findings outlined in this chapter, I will systematically identify three research perspectives on this particular source genre.

266   *Marcel Schmeer*

Firstly, the reports can be read in different historical contexts as a source of state perceptions of danger and the respective threat communication efforts. As historians, this allows us to trace a logic of perception that could be described as "seeing like a state" or, in this case, "seeing like an intelligence service" in reference to the work of James C. Scott.[86] The reports are an important element of discourse in the heated media and social controversies about problems of domestic security, which ultimately constitute the national "security culture" of Germany. Similarly, the reports, analysed in the *longue durée* of the Federal Republic's security history, allow conclusions to be drawn about the dynamics of large-scale political and social changes, (de-)securitisation efforts as well as various processes of professionalisation and scientisation within intelligence services as I have briefly sketched in this chapter. The knowledge of secret services has been, in a formatted form, the object of public debate, but on its way "through the channels" (Sarasin) this knowledge was also decisively politicised. In this process, the genuine secret service problem of an "indeterminacy of the enemy"[87] was clarified for public discourse, but at the same time always became a political point of contention.

Following on from this, the reports can, *secondly*, be interpreted with reference to the suggestions of a history of knowledge as a source for the construction of internal knowledge cultures in intelligence services, the circulation (and recalibration) of this knowledge between the various political institutions of domestic security in Germany, and ultimately the dynamics of processing this knowledge for publication as I have demonstrated in this contribution. Although it is in the very nature of intelligence history that our main research objects and the respective source material bear significant access constraints, a closer look at the *Verfassungsschutz* reports allows conclusions to be drawn about the basis of the circulation of secret knowledge and its impact both on debates about security policy and culture and the repercussions of these debates on the services themselves. Consequently, the popularisation of intelligence knowledge should not be understood as a unidirectional mode of communication. Quite the contrary, it can be assumed that heated debates about, for example, the naming of certain political groups, also influence the shape of the expert knowledge itself in the future with regard to presentation strategies, specific wording or other aspects. The seemingly trivial act of changing the order of threats in the structure of the reports under the Kohl administration might serve as an example for this. With a view to the recent German past, the debates about mentioning the Party of Democratic Socialism, the successor to the SED, in the reports of the 2000s or, even more recently, the right-wing populist Alternative for Germany as well as seemingly minor discussions about listing a far-left punk band in the state of Mecklenburg-West Pomerania equally provide interesting starting points for further considerations.[88] Following on from this, I would like to formulate the hypothesis that the BfV and its work itself are strongly shaped by the compulsion to publish parts of their specific intelligence knowledge. With a view to internal organisational-cultural dynamics, this raises the question of whether the reports, in their legitimising function, have a stabilising effect on the worldview of the guardians of the constitution. Do criticism and heated discussions about intelligence knowledge promote organisational change or do they rather perpetuate a wagon-train mentality within an intelligence service?

Thirdly – and this goes beyond the analysis of the reports themselves – intelligence public relations work should be interpreted as a specific mode of management of contradiction or mistrust. This points to the historical persistence of the fundamental contradiction between transparency and (state) arcana in liberal democracies and to the standing these societies assign to "their" secret services. This also touches on the fact that the role of secret services in (western) democracies has been an object of constant public (re-)negotiating, especially in the wake of changing threat constellations or media-fuelled secret service scandals. In this sense, it is far more than just a mere footnote that in 2020 the German Minister of the Interior Horst Seehofer – as Otto John had already done in the 1950s – placed the task of the BfV, interestingly enough in the middle of the global Covid19-pandemic, in the (semantic) proximity of immunology. The foreword of the *Verfassungsschutz* report for the year 2019 prominently states at the beginning: "The *Verfassungsschutz* is the immune system of our liberal society."[89] The question of how this immune system was set up and how the state publicly staged its work and the knowledge it produced remains a worthwhile endeavour for further intelligence and security history research.

Notes

1 Cf., for instance, the critical journalistic reviews of the *Chronique scandaleuse* of the *Verfassungsschutz*: Wessel, U. "Chronik einer Behörde. Spitzel, Wanzen, Bomben," *Die Zeit* 5/2012 and Prantl, H. "Wer schützt die Verfassung vor dem Verfassungsschutz," *Süddeutsche Zeitung*, 7 January 2012. The author would like to thank Marcus Böick, Julia Claire Catalano, Christopher Kirchberg, Lukas Mengelkamp and Martin Walter as well as the incredibly patient editors of this volume Rüdiger Bergien, Debora Gerstenberger and Constantin Goschler for numerous critical, but always very helpful and thought-provoking remarks on this contribution.

2 Although a similar reporting system exists in Austria, the Czech Republic, the Netherlands or Switzerland, these reports (*Verfassungsschutz-* or *Staatsschutzberichte* – the several designations are quite inconsistent) are difficult to compare with the German case in their sheer scope and political impact. Cf. Jesse, "Verfassungsschutzberichte des Bundes"; Jesse, "Verfassungsschutzberichte der Bundesländer"; Jesse, "Verfassungsschutzberichte des Landes Hessen," 39.

3 The current reports are available on the website of the Federal Office for the Protection of the Constitution. The State Offices for the Protection of the Constitution also offer their reports online for download: <www.verfassungsschutz.de/SiteGlobals/Forms/Suche/Publikationensuche_Formular.html> (last accessed March 15, 2021).

4 This refers to the issue of the annual reports for the reporting year 2019 published in July 2020, see Bundesministerium des Innern, für Bau und Heimat, *Verfassungsschutzbericht 2019*. All translations from German in this chapter are my own.

5 Möller, "Verfassungsschutzbericht im Licht der neueren Rechtsprechung," 305.

6 The *Polizeiliche Kriminalstatistik* (Federal Criminal Statistics) is compiled annually by the *Bundeskriminalamt* (Federal Criminal Police Office, BKA) based on figures from the 16 German *Länder*. The reports are also available online on the BKA website: <www.bka.de/DE/AktuelleInformationen/StatistikenLagebilder/PolizeilicheKriminalstatistik/pks_node.html> (last accessed March 15, 2021).

268 *Marcel Schmeer*

7 Cf., for instance, the comment on the *Verfassungsschutz* report for the reporting year 2019 by Esslinger, D. "Kriminalität von rechts ist viel gefährlicher als von links," *Süddeutsche Zeitung Online*, 9 July 2020 or the report "Das ist eine Schande für unser Land," *Frankfurter Allgemeine Zeitung Online*, 9 July 2020.

8 This terminology is used in the official language of the state authorities and refers to efforts to "abolish or invalidate one of the constitutional principles which are part of the free democratic basic order" according to the corresponding entry in the glossary on the BfV website: <www.verfassungsschutz.de/print/de/service/glossar/_lB> (last accessed August 2, 2020).

9 See Schwagerl, *Verfassungsschutz in der Bundesrepublik Deutschland*, 257–259.

10 Bertram, "Kommentar – Kollateralschäden einer 'wehrhaften Demokratie'?," 2967.

11 Cf. Schneider, *Transparenztraum*; Owetschkin, Berger, "Contested Transparencies: An Introduction"; Ritzi, "Das Geheimnis und die Demokratie."

12 I conceptualized "managing contradictions" in my (unpublished) 2015 master thesis (Ruhr-Universität Bochum) as an analytical tool to describe the oscillation between the spheres of secrecy and publicity in intelligence services.

13 On the conflictual relationship between mistrust and transparency within intelligence services see Goschler, "Intelligence, Mistrust and Transparency." For the original diagnosis of an increasing "transparency mania" that eventually would reduce politics to the mere "management of distrust" see the article by Krastev, I. "Der Transparenzwahn." *Eurozine*, 20 February 2014.

14 See Goschler and Wala, *Keine neue Gestapo*, 279.

15 Fry and Hochstein, "Epistemic Communities," 25.

16 Conze, "Security as a Culture." The political scientist Christopher Daase defines security culture as the "sum of beliefs, values and practices of institutions and individuals . . . that decide what is to be considered a threat and how and by what means this threat is to be confronted." See Daase, "Wandel der Sicherheitskultur," 9.

17 Cf. Sarasin, "Was ist Wissensgeschichte?"; Lässig, "The History of Knowledge"; Östling et al., "The History of Knowledge."

18 Sarasin, "Was ist Wissensgeschichte?," 168.

19 Östling et al., "The History of Knowledge," 17–26.

20 See the introduction to this volume by Bergien et al.

21 This, on a broader scale, also refers to the knowledge of the state and its transformations in the second half of the twentieth century. See, for instance, the contributions in Collin, Horstman, *Das Wissen des Staates*.

22 For this approach see Kleßmann, "Spaltung und Verflechtung."

23 See Hans Ritter von Lex, "Rede in der 65. Sitzung des Bundestages, June 1, 1950," StenBer., 2387; Carlo Schmid, "Grundsatzrede über das Grundgesetz im Parlamentarischen Rat, September 8, 1948," StenBer., 70 f.

24 See, for instance, Foschepoth, *Verfassungswidrig*.

25 For John's eventful biography see the recent study by Hett, Wala, *Otto John*; cf. John, *Zweimal kam ich heim*.

26 See, for example, John, *Zweimal kam ich heim*, 102.

27 Otto, John. "Das Bundesamt für Verfassungsschutz," *Das Parlament*, 22 October 1952.

28 See, for instance, Krämer, "Westdeutsche Propaganda."

29 Many of the accusations turned out to be true at a later point. The "findings" were first published in July 1965 in the notorious "Braunbuch" written by socialist politician Albert Norden. See Nationalrat der Nationalen Front des Demokratischen Deutschlands, ed., *Braunbuch*. For the campaigns against the FDR see Lemke, "Kampagnen gegen Bonn"; von Miquel, *Ahnden oder amnestieren?*, 27–70.

30 Cf. as a selection on the anti-Semitic wave of smears in the Federal Republic Schildt, "Schlafende Höllenhunde"; Kiani, "Zum politischen Umgang mit Antisemitismus."

31 According to the Berlin Senator of the Interior Joachim Lipschitz in an article for the DGB magazine "Freies Wort." The manuscript of 9 January 1960, can be found in LArch Berlin B Rep. 004, No. 158.

Intelligence for the masses 269

32 See "Auszug aus der Niederschrift der IMK in Hamburg am 2./3. Februar 1961, Maß-nahmen des positiven Verfassungsschutzes," 6, BArch, B 106/4274; cf. Schwagerl, *Verfassungsschutz in der Bundesrepublik Deutschland*, 240–242.
33 Cf. the articles in Creuzberger and Hoffmann, "Geistige Gefahr."
34 "Vermerk über die Besprechung mit den Innenministerien (Senatoren) der Länder am 8. Juni 1961 im Bundesministerium des Innern betr. "positiver Verfassungsschutz," 2, BArch, B 106/200111.
35 *BMI* Ministerial Director Rudolf Toyka, for instance, suggested during the same meeting to make use of the "political animated film . . . in the service of public relations." However, he added, the production of such a film might turn out very costly. In general, he remarked that it would be difficult to find a "form appropriate to the subject." Ibid., 10.
36 See "Auszug aus der Niederschrift der IMK in Kiel am 27./28. Mai, TOP 7 „Fortsetzung der Beratung über Fragen des Verfassungsschutzes," 22 f., BArch, B 106/4274.
37 Bundesministerium des Innern, *Erfahrungen aus der Beobachtung und Abwehr*; Anony-mous, "Bericht nach Erkenntnissen."
38 For the largely anti-communist political culture in the early Federal Republic and the political measures against the KPD see Kössler, "Grenzen der Demokratie."
39 The 1962 report was only one element in the federal government's crisis communica-tion strategy. As early as 1960, a documentation (white paper) was published which was dedicated to the topic: Bundesregierung, *Die antisemitischen und nazistischen Vorfälle*. Chancellor Konrad Adenauer had already made a statement on television on 16 January 1960 in which he called on the population to give the vandals a "caning" if they were caught red-handed. "Bulletin des Presse- und Informationsamts der Bundesregierung Nr. 11," 19 January 1960, 89.
40 Jesse, "Verfassungsschutzberichte des Bundes," 380.
41 Bundesministerium des Innern, *Erfahrungen aus der Beobachtung und Abwehr*, 1.
42 Ibid., 3.
43 Ibid., 22–23.
44 Ibid., 23.
45 Ibid., annex a.
46 Ibid., 34–35.
47 Ibid., 35.
48 Anonymous, "Kommunistische Tätigkeit."
49 Ibid., 36.
50 Ibid., 13–19 (especially the illustrations on 13 and 19).
51 Jesse, "Verfassungsschutzberichte des Bundes," 381.
52 Ibid., 334–336.
53 On Berghoff's work see the chapter about public relations within the BfV in Goschler, Wala, *Keine neue Gestapo*, 326–349.
54 See for instance Berghoff's sullen portrayal of the so-called telephone tapping affair in 1963 in a history of the Federal Office for the Protection of the Constitution written by himself. Bergh, *Köln 4731*, 197–231.
55 See von Hodenberg, *Konsens und Krise*, 326.
56 For the telephone tapping affair and its political and societal impacts see Goschler, Wala, „*Keine neue Gestapo*," 238–272.
57 Lücke, "Die Ämter für Verfassungsschutz," 9.
58 Ibid., 12.
59 Luhmann, "Beobachtung der Beobachter."
60 For the historical circumstances of the détente period see, for instance, the contributions in Bange, Villaume, *The Long Détente*.
61 Maddrell, *The Image of the Enemy*.
62 On these transformations and the emergence of new threat scenarios see Goschler, Wala, *Keine neue Gestapo*, 275–291.
63 See "Tätigkeitsbericht des Referats für Öffentlichkeitsarbeit im BfV für das Jahr 1968, 20. März 1969," 10, BArch, B 443/1619.

270 *Marcel Schmeer*

64 Goschler, Wala, *„ Keine neue Gestapo,"* 336–337.
65 Bundesministerium des Innern, *Verfassungsschutz 1968*, 3.
66 For the concerns also expressed in the media about the success of the NPD see, for instance, "Tut und tut," *Der Spiegel* 52/1968.
67 Bundesministerium des Innern, *Verfassungsschutz 1968*, 87–101, quote on page 97.
68 Goschler, Wala, *Keine neue Gestapo*, 298–299.
69 Bundesministerium des Innern, *Verfassungsschutz 1969/70*, 2.
70 Ibid., 3.
71 Gerhard Mauz, "Ich fand ihn eigentlich ganz nett," *Der Spiegel* 49/1977.
72 Bundesministerium des Innern, *Verfassungsschutz 1972*, unpaged.
73 On the meaning and different layers of the term "extremism" see Jaschke, *Politischer Extremismus*, especially 16–50; see also Goschler, Wala, *Keine neue Gestapo*, 303.
74 Bundesministerium des Innern, *Verfassungsschutz 1973*, 4.
75 Cf., for instance, the overall design, statistical and sociological data and rich illustrations in Bundesministerium des Innern, *betrifft: Verfassungsschutz '81*.
76 Cf. Bundesministerium des Innern, *Verfassungsschutzbericht 1983*. This was also the first time the reports were actually titled "*Verfassungsschutzbericht*"; Jesse, "Verfassungsschutzberichte des Bundes," 382.
77 Bundesministerium des Innern, *Verfassungsschutz 1968*, 3.
78 On the Anti-Radical Decree, see Rigoll, *Staatsschutz*, 335–456.
79 BVerfG, Beschluss vom 22. Mai 1975, Az. 2 BvL 13/73, BVerfGE 39, 334. (Extremistenbeschluss).
80 BVerfG, Beschluss vom 29. Oktober 1975, Az. 2 BvE 1/75, BVerfGE 40, 287. (Beschluss zur Erwähnung der NPD im Verfassungsschutzbericht).
81 Saupe, "Ruhe und Ordnung," 185.
82 See, for instance, the various newspaper articles on Schwagerl's work: "Schleier wegziehen," *Der Spiegel* 25/1972; Schwagerl, H. J. "Beobachter oder Überwacher? Der Verfassungsschutz darf keine Geheimpolizei sein," *Die Zeit*, 19 January 1973; "Hochschulen: An die Kette gelegt," *Der Spiegel* 18/1975.
83 Schwagerl, "Verfassungsschutz – vom geheimen Nachrichtendienst zur politischen Bildungsarbeit," 832.
84 Schwagerl, *Verfassungsschutz in der Bundesrepublik Deutschland*, 232–240.
85 Jesse, "Verfassungsschutzberichte des Bundes," 380–381.
86 Scott, *Seeing like a State*; Kirchberg, Schmeer, "The 'Traube Affair'," 180; for a fruitful application of Scott's suggestions on police history also see Weinhauer, "Zwischen organisatorischen Wandlungen und kulturellen Kontinuitäten."
87 Horn, *The Secret War*, 278.
88 See Jüttner, J. "Punkband Feine Sahne Fischfilet. Die Staatsfeinde," *Spiegel Online*, 5 November 2012. <www.spiegel.de/panorama/feine-sahne-fischfilet-im-verfassungss chutzbericht-mecklenburg-vorpommern-a-864974.html> (last accessed March 18, 2021); Balser, M. and von Bullion, C. "Superspeader von Hass und Gewalt," *Süddeutsche Zeitung*, 10 July 2020; for an overview on current studies on the intelligence history in Germany, see the articles in Großbölting, Kittel, *Welche "Wirklichkeit" und wessen "Wahrheit"?*. Cf. Bergien, "Geschichte der Nachrichtendienste."
89 Bundesministerium des Innern, für Bau und Heimat, *Verfassungsschutzbericht 2019*, 3.

Bibliography

Anonymous. 1962. "Bericht nach Erkenntnissen der Verfassungsschutzbehörden. Rechtsradikalismus in der Bundesrepublik. Ein Erfahrungsbericht." *Aus Politik und Zeitgeschichte. Beilage zur Wochenzeitung Das Parlament* 20: 241–252.
Anonymous. 1965. "Kommunistische Tätigkeit in der Bundesrepublik im Jahre 1964." *Aus Politik und Zeitgeschichte. Beilage zur Wochenzeitung Das Parlament* 33: 3–36.

Intelligence for the masses 271

Bange, O., and Villaume, P., eds. 2017. *The Long Détente: Changing Concepts of Security and Cooperation in Europe, 1950s–1980s*. Budapest and New York: CEU Press.

Bergien, R. 2021. "Geschichte der Nachrichtendienste/Intelligence History, Version: 1.0." *Docupedia-Zeitgeschichte*. http://docupedia.de/zg/Bergien_geschichte_der_nachrichtendienste_v1_de_2021.

Bertram, G. 2006. "Kommentar – Kollateralschäden einer 'wehrhaften Demokratie'?" *Neue Juristische Wochenschrift* 59, no. 41: 2967–2968.

Bundesministerium des Innern, ed. 1961. *Erfahrungen aus der Beobachtung und Abwehr rechtsradikaler und antisemitischer Tendenzen 1961*. Bonn.

Bundesministerium des Innern, ed. 1969. *Zum Thema. Hier: Verfassungsschutz 1968. Erfahrungsbericht über die Beobachtungen der Ämter für Verfassungsschutz im Jahre 1968*. Bonn.

Bundesministerium des Innern, ed. 1971. *betrifft: Verfassungsschutz 1969/70*. Bonn.

Bundesministerium des Innern, ed. 1973. *betrifft: Verfassungsschutz 1972*. Bonn.

Bundesministerium des Innern, ed. 1974. *betrifft: Verfassungsschutz 1973*. Bonn.

Bundesministerium des Innern, ed. 1982. *betrifft: Verfassungsschutz '81*. Bonn.

Bundesministerium des Innern, ed. 1983. *Verfassungsschutzbericht 1982*. Bonn.

Bundesministerium des Innern, für Bau und Heimat, ed. 2020. *Verfassungsschutzbericht 2019*. Berlin.

Bundesregierung, ed. 1960. *Die antisemitischen und nazistischen Vorfälle in der Zeit vom 25. Dezember 1959 bis zum 28. Januar 1960*. Bonn.

Collin, P., and Horstmann, T., eds. 2004. *Das Wissen des Staates. Geschichte, Theorie und Praxis*. Baden-Baden: Nomos.

Conze, E. 2006. "Security as a Culture: Reflections on a 'Modern Political History' of the Federal Republic of Germany." *GHI London Bulletin* 28, no. 1: 5–35.

Creuzberger, S., and Hoffmann, D., eds. 2014. *"Geistige Gefahr" und "Immunisierung der Gesellschaft." Antikommunismus und politische Kultur in der frühen Bundesrepublik*. München: De Gruyter Oldenbourg.

Daase, C. 2010. "Wandel der Sicherheitskultur." *Aus Politik und Zeitgeschichte. Beilage zur Wochenzeitung Das Parlament* 50: 9–16.

Foschepoth, J. 2017. *Verfassungswidrig! Das KPD-Verbot im Kalten Bürgerkrieg*. Göttingen: Vandenhoeck und Ruprecht.

Fry, M. G., and Hochstein, M. 1993. "Epistemic Communities: Intelligence Studies and International Relations." *Intelligence and National Security* 8, no. 3: 14–28.

Goschler, C. 2019. "Intelligence, Mistrust and Transparency. A Case Study of the German Office for the Protection of the Constitution." In *Contested Transparencies, Social Movements and the Public Sphere: Multi-Disciplinary Perspectives*, ed. S. Berger and D. Owetschkin, 153–171. Cham: Palgrave Macmillan.

Goschler, C., and Wala, M. 2015. *"Keine neue Gestapo." Das Bundesamt für Verfassungsschutz und die NS-Vergangenheit*. Reinbek bei Hamburg: Rowohlt.

Großbölting, T., and Kittel, S., eds. 2019. *Welche "Wirklichkeit" und wessen"Wahrheit"? Das Geheimdienstarchiv als Quelle und Medium der Wissensproduktion*. Göttingen: Vandenhoeck und Ruprecht.

Hett, B. C., and Wala, M. 2019. *Otto John. Patriot oder Verräter. Eine deutsche Biografie*. Reinbek bei Hamburg: Rowohlt.

Horn, E. 2013. *The Secret War: Treason, Espionage, and Modern Fiction*. Evanston: Northwestern University Press.

Jaschke, H.-G. 2006. *Politischer Extremismus*. Wiesbaden: Springer VS.

Jesse, E. 2006. "Verfassungsschutzberichte des Bundes und der Länder im Vergleich." In *Vergleichende Extremismusforschung*, ed. U. Backes and E. Jesse, 379–396. Baden-Baden: Nomos.

272 Marcel Schmeer

Jesse, E. 2008. "Die Verfassungsschutzberichte der Bundesländer. Deskription, Analyse, Vergleich." In *Jahrbuch Extremismus & Demokratie 19*, ed. U. Backes and E. Jesse, 13–34. Baden-Baden: Nomos.

Jesse, E. 2011. "Die Verfassungsschutzberichte des Landes Hessen im Vergleich." In *Verfassungsschutz in der freiheitlichen Demokratie. 60 Jahre Landesamt für Verfassungsschutz*, ed. Landesamt für Verfassungsschutz Hessen, 39–50. Wiesbaden.

John, O. 1969. *Zweimal kam ich heim. Vom Verschwörer zum Schützer der Verfassung.* Düsseldorf: Econ.

Kiani, S. 2008. "Zum politischen Umgang mit Antisemitismus in der Bundesrepublik. Die Schmierwelle im Winter 1959/60." In *Erfolgsgeschichte Bundesrepublik? Die Nachkriegsgesellschaft im langen Schatten des Nationalsozialismus*, ed. S. A. Glienke, V. Paulmann, and J. Perels, 115–145. Göttingen: Wallstein.

Kirchberg, C., and Schmeer, M. 2019. "The 'Traube Affair': Transparency as a Legitimation and Action Strategy Between Security, Surveillance and Privacy." In *Contested Transparencies, Social Movements and the Public Sphere. Multi-Disciplinary Perspectives*, ed. S. Berger and D. Owetschkin, 173–196. Cham: Palgrave Macmillan.

Kleßmann, C. 2006. "Spaltung und Verflechtung – Ein Konzept zur integrierten Nachkriegsgeschichte 1945 bis 1990." In *Teilung und Integration. Die doppelte deutsche Nachkriegsgeschichte als wissenschaftliches und didaktisches Problem*, ed. C. Kleßmann and P. Lautzas, 20–37. Bonn: Wochenschau Verlag.

Kössler, T. 2014. "Die Grenzen der Demokratie. Antikommunismus als politische und gesellschaftliche Praxis in der frühen Bundesrepublik." In *"Geistige Gefahr" und "Immunisierung der Gesellschaft." Antikommunismus und politische Kultur in der frühen Bundesrepublik*, ed. S. Creuzberger and D. Hoffmann, 229–250. München: De Gruyter Oldenbourg.

Krämer, S. I. 1997. "Westdeutsche Propaganda im Kalten Krieg. Organisationen und Akteure." In *Pressepolitik und Propaganda. Historische Studien vom Vormärz bis zum Kalten Krieg*, ed. J. Wilke, 333–371. Köln, Weimar, and Wien: Böhlau.

Lässig, S. 2016. "The History of Knowledge and the Expansion of the Historical Research Agenda." *Bulletin of the GHI Washington* 59: 29–58.

Lemke, M. 1993. "Kampagnen gegen Bonn. Die Systemkrise der DDR und die West-Propaganda der SED 1960–1963." *Vierteljahrshefte für Zeitgeschichte* 41, no. 2: 153–174.

Lücke, P. 1966. "Die Ämter für Verfassungsschutz in der Bundesrepublik Deutschland." In *Verfassungsschutz. Beiträge aus Wissenschaft und Praxis*, ed. Bundesministerium des Innern, 9–13. Köln: Heymann.

Luhmann, N. 1992. "Die Beobachtung der Beobachter im politischen System: Zur Theorie der öffentlichen Meinung." In *Öffentliche Meinung. Theorien, Methoden, Befunde. Beiträge zu Ehren von Elisabeth Noelle-Neumann*, ed. J. Wilke, 77–86. Freiburg: Verlag Karl Alber.

Maddrell, P., ed. 2015. *The Image of the Enemy: Intelligence Analysis of Adversaries since 1945*. Washington, DC: Georgetown University Press.

Möller, H. 2007. "Der Verfassungsschutzbericht im Licht der neueren Rechtsprechung." In *Festschrift zum 25-jährigen Bestehen der Schule für Verfassungsschutz und für Andreas Hübsch*, ed. A. Pfahl-Traughber and M. Rose-Stahl, 304–327. Brühl: Fachhochschule des Bundes für öffentliche Verwaltung. Fachbereich Öffentliche Sicherheit.

Nationalrat der Nationalen Front des Demokratischen Deutschlands, ed. 1968. *Braunbuch. Kriegs- und Naziverbrecher in der Bundesrepublik und in Westberlin*. Berlin: Staatsverlag der DDR.

Östling, J., Heidenblad, D. L., Sandmo, E., Hammar, A. N., and Nordberg, K. H. 2018. "The History of Knowledge and the Circulation of Knowledge. An Introduction." In *Circulation of Knowledge: Explorations in the History of Knowledge*, ed. J. Östling, D. L. Heidenblad, E. Sandmo, A. N. Hammar, and K. H. Nordberg, 9–33. Lund: Nordic Academic Press.

Owetschkin, D., and Berger, S. 2019. "Contested Transparencies: An Introduction." In *Contested Transparencies, Social Movements and the Public Sphere: Multi-Disciplinary Perspectives*, ed. S. Berger and D. Owetschkin, 1–32. Cham: Palgrave Macmillan.

Rigoll, D. 2013. *Staatsschutz in Westdeutschland. Von der Entnazifizierung zur Extremistenabwehr.* Göttingen: Wallstein.

Ritzi, C. 2017. "Das Geheimnis und die Demokratie. (In-)Transparenz als politische Herausforderung im digitalen Zeitalter." In *Staatsgeheimnisse. Arkanpolitik im Wandel der Zeiten*, ed. R. Voigt, 179–204. Wiesbaden: Springer VS.

Sarasin, P. 2011. "Was ist Wissensgeschichte?" *Internationales Archiv für Sozialgeschichte der deutschen Literatur* 36: 159–172. https://doi.org/10.1515/iasl.2011.010.

Saupe, A. 2010. "Von 'Ruhe und Ordnung' zur 'inneren Sicherheit'. Eine Historisierung gesellschaftlicher Dispositive." *Zeithistorische Forschungen/Studies in Contemporary History* 9, no. 2: 170–187. www.zeithistorische-forschungen.de/2-2010/id=4674.

Schildt, A. 2005. "Schlafende Höllenhunde. Reaktionen auf die antisemitische Schmierwelle 1959/60." In *Aus den Quellen. Beiträge zur deutsch-jüdischen Geschichte. Festschrift für Ina Lorenz zum 65. Geburtstag*, ed. A. Brämer, S. Schüler-Springorum, and M. Studemund-Halévy, 313–321. Hamburg: Dölling und Galitz.

Schneider, M. 2013. *Transparenztraum. Literatur, Politik, Medien und das Unmögliche*, Berlin: Matthes & Seitz.

Schwagerl, H. J. 1974. "Verfassungsschutz – vom geheimen Nachrichtendienst zur politischen Bildungsarbeit." *Die neue Gesellschaft* 21: 830–832.

Schwagerl, H. J. 1985. *Verfassungsschutz in der Bundesrepublik Deutschland.* Heidelberg: C.F. Müller.

Scott, J. C. 1998. *Seeing like a State: How Certain Schemes to Improve the Human Condition Have Failed.* New Haven, CT: Yale University Press.

van Bergh, H. 1981. *Köln 4713. Geschichte und Geschichten des Bundesamtes für Verfassungsschutz.* Würzburg: Naumann Verlag.

von Hodenberg, C. 2006. *Konsens und Krise. Eine Geschichte der westdeutschen Medienöffentlichkeit 1945–1973.* Göttingen: Wallstein.

von Miquel, M. 2004. *Ahnden oder amnestieren? Westdeutsche Justiz und Vergangenheitspolitik in den sechziger Jahren.* Göttingen: Wallstein.

Weinhauer, K. 2020. "Zwischen organisatorischen Wandlungen und kulturellen Kontinuitäten. Polizei, Jugendprotest und Demonstrationen in den 1960er bis 1980er Jahren." In *Polizei und Protest in der Bundesrepublik Deutschland*, ed. S. Mecking, 165–184. Wiesbaden: Springer VS.

Conclusion

Rüdiger Bergien, Debora Gerstenberger
and Constantin Goschler

One of the starting points of this volume was a change that took place in the self-perceptions and the external perceptions of intelligence and secret services in the decades after 1945. Regardless of the political system, the services seemed to become more oriented towards scientific methods and to place greater emphasis on the introduction of new technologies. On the eve of what contemporaries had been calling the "information society" since the 1970s, the services presented themselves to the outside world as more academic, more professional and more scientific. This change is illustrated by a cover of *Time* magazine from 1953: it portrays CIA Director Alan Dulles as an intellectual, presenting him with a suit, bow tie, pipe and silver-rimmed glasses. Dulles is contrasted with a figure in the background personifying the spy of bygone days through his cloak, dagger and large-brimmed fedora.[1] Accordingly, one of the initial questions of the volume was whether and to what extent these changing representations went beyond a communication strategy and popular images. The intention was to explore to what extent the actors, institutions and forms of intelligence knowledge changed. In addition, the volume examines to what extent analogies and divergences can be identified in a comparison between services of the West, the Soviet Bloc and the Global South.

The cover of *Time* magazine places the United States, which undoubtedly held a pre-eminent position in the Cold War world in economic and technological terms, at the centre of this development. The United States also played an essential role in the field of the scientisation and digitisation of intelligence services, although – or perhaps precisely because – the CIA, which was only founded in 1947, was a latecomer in the concert of traditional intelligence services. The contributions to this volume have shown, however, that it would be too simplistic to tell a story in which developments in other parts of the world were limited to a transfer or imitation of American technologies and methods of acquiring or dealing with intelligence knowledge. Rather, they show how important a transnational and global perspective is also in the field of the history of intelligence services in the Cold War world: both, within the alliance structures shaped by the East–West conflict and outside of them, there existed not only very different adaptations – including the circumvention of embargo rules – but also variations or alternatives to the US model. Above all, it has been shown time and again that knowledge is bound not

DOI: 10.4324/9781003147329-14

only to technology but above all to practices and thus to people, which is often forgotten, including in the current discussion about the power of algorithms and artificial intelligence.[2] In the end, computer technicians probably played a greater role in this history than scientists.[3]

Thus, a major yield of this volume is that it demystifies to some extent the wide-spread image of intelligence services in the Cold War world as shaped by science and computers. Both modernisation theory, to which the images of scientified and technologised intelligence services implicitly referred, and critique of modernity have produced their own myths: the two sociologists Zygmunt Bauman – himself a temporary employee of the Polish secret service after the Second World War – and David Lyon – the doyen of surveillance studies – diagnosed a transition from pan-optic surveillance in solid modernity to post-panoptic surveillance in the current liquid modernity.[4] At the same time, they follow the diagnosis of Manuel Castells, who described the de-territorialisation of power in his diagnosis of the "informa-tion society."[5] By contrast, the contributions in this volume show that, especially in the field of intelligence knowledge, nation-states continued to play an essential role, while technologies, data and practices flowed across borders, often chang-ing shape in the process. At the same time, the findings presented deny the image of a modernity inexorably marching forward; in our period of investigation, it appears neither solid nor fluid, but above all characterised by simultaneities of the non-simultaneous.

Intelligence and science

The contributions in this volume suggest that a rapprochement between intelli-gence and science first took place in the United States from the 1940s and 1950s onwards. The rise of Soviet studies as an academic discipline in the United States, to name just one example, was promoted considerably after 1945 by the US intel-ligence services (see Thomas Wolf). Analogously, with regard to information processing, an integration of technology companies into the field of "national security" becomes apparent. The investigative journalist James Bamford already spoke of a "crypto-industrial complex" with regard to the NSA at the end of the 1970s.[6] In the United States of the 1950s and 1960s, graduates of elite universities could be recruited by the CIA and other services without having to overcome fear of contact; top academics such as the information scientist Joseph Becker or the Sovietologist George T. Robinson switched back and forth between universities, intelligence services and research institutes. At the same time, the British services, MI5, MI6 as well as GCHQ, were able to recruit top graduates from the UK's elite universities, for whom serving in an intelligence agency was not a blemish on one's CV but a distinction.[7]

In contrast, although the West German Gehlen Organization of the late 1940s employed a "professors' group" of Eastern European academics, its management showed little interest in these scholars' professional expertise (see Thomas Wolf). The communist secret services also only developed an interest in science and research during the course of the 1960s. But even then, the reorientation of the

276   *Bergien/Gerstenberger/Goschler*

KGB under Yuri Andropov from 1969 did not carry this megalomaniac surveillance bureaucracy to a higher professional and analytical level. The broad-based academisation of KGB management cadres did not lead to a scientisation of secret police practice: what constituted scientificity at its core – universalism, reflectiveness, method orientation, critique – remained alien to the KGB until the end (see Evgenia Lezina). A directorate for intelligence analysis was not established in this secret police until the final crisis of the Soviet Union, but even then the analytical results remained modest.

However, this well-known narrative of the superiority of Western intelligence over the anti-intellectualism inherent in many dictatorships requires differentiation. On the one hand, scientisation also encountered limitations in the US intelligence community. Historians like Sherman Kent, who had shaped the development of US intelligence analysis in the 1950s and 1960s, faced anti-intellectualist resentment in the CIA's analysis branches. In the late 1970s, NIEs – "the gold standard in strategic intelligence knowledge production within the US Intelligence Community" – were sometimes dismissed in heated political discourse as "scientistic," that is disconnected from hard foreign policy realities (see Andreas Lutsch). Internally, there was already talk in the early 1960s that the "period of exhaustive, basic research within the DD/I [Deputy Department for Intelligence] has largely come to an end"[8] and that policy makers could be better served by more concise, shorter analyses produced with greater frequency. It fits into this picture that in the late 1960s the USAINTC thought it could dispense with any social science expertise in building databases aimed at identifying "riot indicators" in US metropolitan regions (see Jens Wegener). The phenomenon of militarisation of Western services such as the CIA in the context of the covert and hot wars of the Cold War can also be seen as a counter-trend.[9]

On the other hand, Western and Eastern European intelligence and secret services also moved towards science and scientific working methods. Thus, for instance, the new threat scenarios resulting from the political and social changes of the 1960s led to an acceptance of social science theories and methods in most Western services. Marcel Schmeer's chapter points out that the annual reports of the West German BfV in the 1970s made increasing use of social science terminology. The contents were underpinned with tables, graphs and charts; quantification and methodological reflection gained in importance. Regarding the communist Polish foreign intelligence service, Władysław Bułhak already spoke some years ago of a professionalisation of knowledge production and showed that, beginning in the 1960s, SB's information processing approached a pattern that was defined in the West as the "intelligence cycle" (and is still regarded there as an expression of an elaborate methodological consciousness).[10] Even in the Soviet KGB and in the East German Stasi, in the Brazilian SNI and in the Turkish MIT – despite all the limits on scientisation – there was at least an increasing awareness among management-level employees of belonging to an organisation that was essentially oriented towards information processing and knowledge production. The transformation of these services from power-asserting organisations to surveillance bureaucracies (analogous to their transformation from "hot" to

Conclusion 277

"cold" organisations in the sense of organisational sociology) is probably related to this basic trend.

Finally, the intelligence services and secret police can be traced to the rise of those "technoscientific experts" who assumed a key role in the course of the "scientification of the social and political"[11] – and again, the rise of these experts was not limited to the Western intelligence services. The information scientist Jospeh Becker in the CIA and the self-taught Hans-Joachim Postel in the West German BfV were matched by the engineer Stefan Paluch in the Polish SB, the mathematician Dieter Altdorfer in the Stasi[12] and similarly qualified people in the Latin American or Turkish secret services. They represented rationalities that were at least in tension with the core of intelligence organisational culture – compartmentalisation and secrecy. The traditional principle of need-to-know was not well suited to the increased possibilities for communicating knowledge. As many of the named experts in the West, the East and the South rose to leadership positions in the 1960s and 1970s, they hired personnel who would have had no place in an intelligence service as recently as the 1950s. Whether this made the services more civilian remains an open question. In any case, they became more heterogeneous, which caused considerable tension in their corporate culture.

Digitisation of intelligence agencies

Digitisation was a basic process of the developments examined in this volume. It affected all the services studied here and presented them with analogous challenges. There was undoubtedly considerable non-simultaneity: in the CIA, the first Imagery Intelligence (IMINT) EDP-applications were already up and running in the late 1950s, whereas the Polish SB and the Brazilian SNI did not launch their first computerised systems until 10 to 15 years later. Moreover, the resources that individual services were able to digitise varied widely. In 1974, the West German BND spent just under 12 million Deutschmarks (the equivalent of about 7 million US dollars) on the entire EDP – hardware, software and personnel costs.[13] In contrast, the CIA spent the gigantic sum of more than 40 million dollars on the development of a single programme – the SAFE analysis system.[14]

However, compared to these discrepancies, the similarities weigh more heavily. In the 1950s and 1960s, all the services under consideration in our volume were confronted with a phenomenon known as "information explosion." It was due as much to socio-technical change as to the character of the Cold War as an "information war." Moreover, travel across the Iron Curtain – against the backdrop of foreign policy détente – increased from the 1960s. At the same time, Western societies were threatened by new forms of political violence and by political extremism, while the regimes in Latin America, but also the military elites in Turkey, were under threat from the social consequences of rapid socio-economic change. They all "securitised" these threats as symptoms of the alleged advance of communism and used this to justify the expansion of technical surveillance systems.

In those years, EDP was initially perceived primarily as a means of mass data processing. From the perspective of intelligence and information services, it was therefore ideal for recording travel movements as well as fluid social (protest) in the Western world or political resistance movements in Latin America, analysing them and thus making them potentially controllable. Accordingly, one of the first EDP projects by the US intelligence services in the early 1960s was the Joint Soviet Travel Project. The KGB, the Stasi and the Polish SB also began their EDP rollouts by building travel databases. Similarly, major events such as the 1980 Moscow Olympics led to the establishment of new databases and query methods (see Evgenia Lezina). Against this background, Jens Wegener's interpretation of the early "security databases" as "spatial technology" that linked personal data with location-based data seems highly convincing. In fact, increasing mobility in all parts of the world did for intelligence processing what the extreme expansion in the emergence of technically mediated communications had done for signals intelligence: it was a driver of digitisation.

It is striking that the developmental steps were very similar in all the services under consideration. In the CIA and in the West German BfV, the Polish SB and the Brazilian SNI, the "automation" of information processing began *firstly* with existing paper indexes being converted into machine-readable formats that were initially stored on punch cards and later on magnetic tapes. The earliest electronic registers – the NADIS of the BfV or ZSKO of the Polish SB – characterised the practice of EDP use in the services well into the 1980s. The *second stage* consisted of the development of more complex databases that integrated different information sources. This represented a major step towards a form of intelligence knowledge that had not previously been accessible to the services. For example, the KGB's ESIOK integrated biographical data with information on political attitudes, financial circumstances, career paths, as well as "compromising material."

The tendency of "intelligence people" to store as much data as possible (see Jens Wegener) is evident across all systems. In the 1980s, however, this was still at the expense of system performance. Hardware that could not cope with the massive amount of data, as well as incorrectly entered data records, ensured that the revolution in knowledge production through these systems did not happen at that time. In contrast, the *third stage* of digitisation, the integration or networking of intelligence databases with external systems – in the case of the Polish SB with the population database PESEL, in the case of Brazil's SNI with Federal Police and vehicle databases – was more successful (see Franciszek Dąbrowski and Marcelo Vianna).

In view of these technical conditions, to what extent did EDP change the "knowledge of intelligence"? A noticeable difference was that more information was available much more quickly and for more users through the use of the information systems. For the state socialist regimes, this compression of information made it possible to keep the massive increase in East–West travel traffic in the 1980s under control to some extent (notwithstanding "input crises," like those experienced by the Polish "registration system of border movement" – SERP – in the late 1980s).

Another aspect is a certain standardisation of the information collected. The record structures for biographical entries usually only allowed the use of a fixed

Conclusion 279

set of terms to describe, for example, a person's appearance. Therefore, intelligence analysts in particular feared a loss of knowledge due to the introduction of computers, even though the corresponding paper files were still maintained almost everywhere. In the Brazilian intelligence service SNI, however, this loss of knowledge due to digitisation actually became an agenda. There the introduction of computers in 1978 soon led to the destruction of more than 90 per cent of the information that had previously been stored in paper form. It is possible that the SNI leadership wished to get rid of uncomfortable material from the time of the military dictatorship, of knowledge gained in a dubious manner and that might give rise to attacks against the secret service in the new political circumstances (see Debora Gerstenberger).

It is questionable to what extent intelligence knowledge production in the narrower sense – intelligence analysis – benefited from digitisation during the period under study. Marcelo Vianna's findings for the Brazilian SNI – "in general, the digitization process expanded the capacity for surveillance and data accumulation, without overcoming analytical information poverty" – can probably be applied to other services. However, the Polish EPIW – the information system of the foreign intelligence branch – was considered an efficient system, and in 1979, Jürgen von Alten, the former head of the West German BND's evaluation department, concluded that EDP had "contributed to problems and solutions in defence intelligence analysis (precisely where counting, measuring and listing is carried out) . . . that could not even be tackled before." On the other hand, von Alten did not see any useful application possibilities "so far" for political intelligence analysis.[15] To what extent the 40-million-dollar SAFE programme opened up new insights for CIA intelligence analysts remains to be investigated.

Another similarity in the digitisation of all the services considered here is that it was always about more than just the transfer of information into new storage formats or the installation of mainframes and data-viewing devices. As in other areas of government and society, the adoption of computers was coupled with a modernisation narrative. "In the future," CIA official Jessel told representatives of West German intelligence services in Bonn-Bad Godesberg in 1959, computers would be "part of the equipment of every powerful intelligence service."[16] Similarly, a new era literally began for the Brazilian SNI with the official introduction of EDP in December 1978, insofar as from then on a distinction was made between "old" information (produced before this date) and "new" information, which was presented as being of higher value. Just as SIGINT's high-tech collection systems – spy planes, satellites and so forth – had raised SIGINT's relevance from the point of view of decision-makers, the use of mainframes and databases meant an increase in relevance for non-SIGINT intelligence services.

Admittedly, the embedment of computerisation in a modernisation narrative also generated resistance. Even in the CIA, which was considered to be technology-savvy, there was repeated talk of severe disputes between the "computer people and everybody else" in the 1960s. Similar developments were found, for example, in the GDR, where the Stasi computer expert Dieter Atdorfer was removed from his position as head of the data processing department in the mid-1970s. Allegedly

280 *Bergien/Gerstenberger/Goschler*

this happened because he adhered to a "Siemens ideology," that is had relied too heavily on Western technology, but in fact it was probably because his initiatives began to disrupt the established Stasi surveillance bureaucracy.[17] What becomes visible here is that EDP and the modernisation of information processing embodied in it also represented a power resource that could challenge the power hierarchies within the secret services, which were often still military in character.

Circulation of knowledge in the field of intelligence

The contributions in this volume paint a multilayered picture of the changes in the circulation of knowledge as a result of scientisation and digitisation. For information processing in the US services, the quest for interagency compatibility was continuously hampered, as OCR mastermind Joseph Becker phrased it in 1961, by the fact that the "local or 'in house' needs of any one agency usually have priority over the needs of the other agencies"[18] – and a look at the "9/11" report shows that this problem was not eliminated by digitisation in the following decades.[19] Similarly, in the Polish SB (as in the East German Stasi), transfers between data repositories in different departments remained severely restricted due to security concerns despite the centralised structure of the communist secret police. In particular, the foreign intelligence divisions – the Polish Departament I MSW and the East German HV A – insisted not only on completely separate databases from the rest of the services but also on their own hardware equipment and computer centres.[20] EDP's ability to expand horizontal communication, perceived by contemporaries as revolutionary, thus in fact had only a limited effect on intelligence knowledge production in the 1970s and 1980s.

Here too, however, there is a "but." Several chapters show that the knowledge of the secret and intelligence services circulated beyond their organisational boundaries to a large extent – for example, their technical knowledge about EDP systems. The CIA, for example, transferred computer knowledge to its West German partner services the BND and the BfV, which was then passed on – with a good decade's delay and in an appropriated form – to Turkey's intelligence services (see Egemen Bezci). In the opposite direction, there was a transfer process of the phonetic system that Hans-Joachim Postel, responsible for the BfV's computerisation, had developed and had proudly presented to CIA employees on a trip to the United States in 1966 (see Christopher Kirchberg). Elsewhere, it could also be shown that EDP knowledge circulated across the Iron Curtain – that is, was transferred in both directions.[21] Taken together, this supports the idea that even in the field of secret intelligence the production of knowledge could have been a collaborative process.

In this context, the trips to the United States by Hans-Joachim Postel, Ebrulf Zuber and many other employees of other West German security agencies are also an example of a "tech-pilgrimage" through which not only technical knowledge but also elements of US intelligence culture were transferred. This and the discussion rounds that the CIA employee and EDP expert Jessel cultivated with his West German partners are further examples of what in recent political science perspectives on intelligence is conceived as transnational "epistemic communities." The

Conclusion 281

role of expert circles – composed of members of different national services, whose shared rationalities were able to bridge the national antagonisms – obviously rose in importance.[22]

Analysis of the development of intelligence education and training institutions in the Brazilian military dictatorship also provides remarkable insights into the transnationality of intelligence knowledge. In the ESG and EsNI institutions, the transmission of knowledge, a professionalisation through the standardisation of practices and the transfer of the "knowledge of violence" were closely intertwined. According to Samantha Viz Quadrat, EsNI primarily imparted encyclopaedic knowledge (albeit selected according to political criteria), practiced work techniques (writing "objective" reports) and history (of communism up to the Cuban Revolution). However, the school also taught interrogation techniques, including the use of physical violence, which the school's management personnel had learned during internships of several months at the CIA and the FBI. This finding fits in with recent research on the transnational character of Operation Condor, the notorious state terror network of Latin American military dictatorships.[23] And according to recently released CIA documents, representatives of West European intelligence services visited Buenos Aires in the fall of 1977 to find out if they could learn from the Condor network, as if they were considering a transnational European anti-terrorist network.[24] This indicates the existence of a further circulation of knowledge. Here, as in the case of the post-1945 Anglo-American SIGINT partnership, secret intelligence services – notwithstanding their role as guardians of the nation-state *arcana imperii*, proved remarkably open to an exchange of secret knowledge – always provided that this exchange promised to further broaden their information base. The differences between Western services and those operating in dictatorships, long emphasised in intelligence studies, apparently played only a negligible role in the practice of intelligence knowledge sharing.

Relations and communications with the political field

A final premise of the present contributions is that the knowledge of intelligence is not a form of knowledge that can be categorically separated from the field of the political (understood here in a comprehensive sense as influenced by structures of power and influence). On the contrary, the approach of the US services, to establish a "machine hegemony" over their partner services through the transfer of computer knowledge, was clearly politically motivated. Conversely, the temporary reluctance of BND employees to accept the computer knowledge offered by the CIA can also be interpreted as an effort to avoid becoming too dependent on the dominant partner. SNI's attempt to gain influence over the institutions and players in the IT industry in Brazil by building up technical expertise was also about national independence. According to Marcelo Vianna, the aim was to counter IBM's "uncomfortable dominance," which was equated with a technological dependence on the United States.

The introduction of EDP in the core areas of national security was, as can be seen throughout, part of a "technopolitics," the "strategic practice of designing and

282 *Bergien/Gerstenberger/Goschler*

using technology to enact political goals."[25] Incidentally, this was also true from an internal perspective: resistance to the introduction of EDP in the services is not explained solely by hostility to technology. It can also be explained by the – often accurate – perception that the digitisation of the organisation was accompanied by a redistribution of power resources. The much-lamented fragmentation of EDP deployment in most services – in 1979, an EDP expert at the BND spoke of being "stunned" by the "60 programmes in the service that are not interlinked"[26] – is largely due to this. Finally, domestic power struggles could hinder the professionalisation of intelligence services, as was the case in Turkey (see Egemen Bezci).

However, the most clearly political "output" of the intelligence services was "threat knowledge" (Marcel Schmeer), that is knowledge about (potential) internal and external threats. The contributions by Marcel Schmeer and Andreas Lutsch show the extent to which intelligence knowledge can be the subject of political appropriation as well as hostility in public discourse. Annual reports by the West German BfV on threats to internal security quickly became a fixture in political and mass media discourse – even though the BfV was at the same time subject to sometimes harsh media criticism and regular scandalisation. The "popularization" of intelligence knowledge was simultaneously part of a domestic political negotiation process over the question of what could be considered a threat and to what extent, of what should be confronted as a matter of priority (see Marcel Schmeer).

Attempts by intelligence services to use their knowledge in the political field, however, also had a downside: they could lead to this intelligence knowledge being publicly questioned. This concerned not only domestic issues, as in the example just mentioned, but also foreign policy issues, as Andreas Lutsch describes with reference to the CIA's strategic assessments of Soviet nuclear armament. For the time being, it remains open to what extent the question of the "scientific nature" of intelligence was generally a criterion in such political debates about the quality of intelligence knowledge or whether this was tied to democratic systems.

We are confident that the contributions in this volume are first and important steps on the way to a global history of intelligence knowledge in the Cold War world. In particular, we hope to be able to show how profitable it is to break up the often predominant national perspective on the history of secret services. Only in this way is it possible to answer more precisely which of the developments are specific and which are general in nature, and this of course extends far beyond the questions addressed here. Much remains for further research to do, and we hope that this volume will provide a stimulating basis for this future task.

Notes

1 <https://commons.wikimedia.org/wiki/File:Allen_Dulles-TIME-1953.jpg> (last accessed July 29, 2021).
2 See Gugerli, *Welt*.
3 Compare Ensmenger, *Computer Guys*.
4 Bauman and Lyon, *Liquid Surveillance*.
5 Castells, *Information Age*.
6 Bamford, *Puzzle Palace*.

Conclusion 283

7 Andrew, *Defence.*
8 The internal report continues: "The ponderous 200–300 page study, based on detailed analysis of all available materials, is no longer being written. The DD/I analyst's reports are now much briefer, their topics more circumscribed, and their chronological span more restricted." Chief, DD/I Automation Staff to Deputy Director, Intelligence: Computer Needs, Apr. 21, 1961. CIA CREST Database, Doc. ID. CIA-RDP83T00573R000500170003-9.
9 Carson, *Secret Wars.*
10 Bułhak, "Similar But Not the Same."
11 Martin Kohlrausch and Helmuth Trischler define technoscientific experts as "all manner of scientists . . . [but also] trained professionals who, while not scientists per se, drew on scientific principles in their work" and were often "able to convert their expertise into political and societal influence." Kohlrausch and Trischler, *Building Europe*, 8.
12 Bergien, "Programmieren," 9.
13 Estimate of financial outlay for UAbt IV E, 5/14/1974, BNDA 42297_OT, 4.
14 Project Safe. Feasibility of an Agency-wide Information System to Support the Analysts File Environment, October 1974. CIA CREST Database, Doc. ID. CIA-RDP79-00498A000400050049-9, here p. 15.
15 Alten, Jürgen from: [Erfahrungsbericht des früheren Leiters der Abt. III], 1977–78. Bundesarchiv, B 136/53585, p. 76 f.
16 Hans-Joachim Postel, ref. Neuordnung des Karteiwesens, here: Vortrag von Mr. Jessel (CIA) über die Erfahrungen bei der Anwendung des Hollerithverfahrens [. . .], 28.3.1959, BArch Koblenz, B 443, 2817, o.Bl. (p. 7).
17 Bergien, "Programmieren."
18 Joseph Becker (OCR): Ideas on Processing Information, 11 July 1961. CIA CREST Database, Doc. ID. CIA-RDP80B01139A000200080004-0, p. 3.
19 Zegart, *Spying Blind.*
20 Bergien, "Big Data."
21 Bergien, "Programmieren."
22 With regard to SIGINT: Kniep, "Eine nicht mehr ganz so geheime Welt."
23 See also Shiraz, "Drugs and Dirty Wars."
24 "European Spies Sought Lessons from Dictators' Brutal 'Operation Condor'," *The Guardian*, 16 April 2019. <www.theguardian.com/world/2019/apr/15/operation-condor-european-spies-dictators-cia-documents> (lats accessed June 9, 2021)
25 Hecht and Edwards, "Technopolitics of Cold War," 274.
26 Sturz, Friedrich [DN Seipold] to Präsident BND, 01.08.1979. BNDA, 4731_OT.

Bibliography

Bamford, J. 1983. *The Puzzle Palace: A Report on America's Most Secret Agency*, 32nd [print]. New York: Penguin Books
Bauman, Z., and Lyons, D. 2013. *Liquid Surveillance: A Conversation*. New York: John Wiley & Sons.
Bergien, R. 2017. "'Big Data' als Vision. Computereinführung und Organisationswandel in BKA und Staatssicherheit (1967–1989)." *Zeithistorische Forschungen/Studies in Contemporary History* 14, no. 2: 258–285.
Bergien, R. 2019. "Programmieren mit dem Klassenfeind. Die Stasi, Siemens und der Transfer von EDV-Wissen im Kalten Krieg." *Vierteljahrshefte für Zeitgeschichte* 67, no. 1: 1–30. https://doi.org/10.1515/vfzg-2019-0001.
Bułhak, W. 2014. "Similar But Not the Same. In Search of a Methodology in the Cold War Communist Intelligence Studies." In *Need to Know: Eastern and Western Perspectives*, 19–43. Odense: University Press of Southern Denmark.

Carson, A. M. 2018. *Secret Wars: Covert Conflict in International Politics*. Princeton, NJ and Oxford: Princeton University Press.

Castells, M. 1996–1998. *The Information Age: Economy, Society, and Culture*, 3 volumes. Oxford and Malden, MA: Blackwell

Ensmenger, N. 2010. *The Computer Boys Take Over: Computers, Programmers, and the Politics of Technical Expertise*. Cambridge, MA: MIT Press.

Gugerli, D. 2018. *Wie die Welt in den Computer kam. Zur Entstehung digitaler Wirklichkeit*. Frankfurt/Main: Suhrkamp.

Hecht, G., and Edwards, P. N. 2007. "The Technopolitics of Cold War. Toward a Transregional Perspective." *Essays on Global and Comparative History* (2007): 271–314.

Kniep, R. 2017. "Eine nicht mehr ganz so geheime Welt. Intelligence Services and Digitization from a Field Theory Perspective." Wissenschaftszentrum Berlin für Sozialforschung 2017. *WZB-Mitteilungen*, 155.

Kohlrausch, M., and Trischler, H. 2014. *Building Europe on Expertise: Innovators, Organizers, Networkers*, 1st edition. London: Palgrave Macmillan.

Shiraz, Z. 2013. "Drugs and Dirty Wars: Intelligence Cooperation in the Global South." *Third World Quarterly* 34, no. 10: 1749–1766. https://doi.org/10.1080/01436597.2013.851886.

Zegart, A. B. 2007. *Spying Blind: The CIA, the FBI, and the Origins of 911*. Princeton, NJ: Princeton University Press.

Index

Note: Numbers in *italics* indicate a figure.

ABIN *see* Agencia Brasileira de Informações
Abwehr (German military intelligence service of the Wehrmacht) 20
AC *see* Agência Central (AC), Brasília
Access to Information Law (No. 12.527) (Brazil) 233
ACE *see* Arquivos Cronológicos de Entrada
ACLU *see* American Civil Liberties Union
Adenauer, Konrad 254, 269n39
AERP *see* Assessoria Especial de Relações Públicas
Afghanistan: Soviet invasion of 42
Agencia Brasileira de Informações (ABIN) 233
Agência Central (AC) (Headquarter of the Brazilian intelligence Servico Nacional de Informacoes [SNI] in Brasilia) 143
Akins, James 91–92
Allen, George W. 89
Altaylı, Enver 178, 182n12
Alten, Jürgen von 279
Altdorfer, Dieter 277
American Civil Liberties Union (ACLU) 94–95, 97
Andropov, Yuri 1, 37–39, 42, 276
anti-communism 122–124, 175, 251–255, 258
Anti-Radical Degree (Germany) 263
anti-Semitism 21, 253–255
anti-Soviet activities 38–39, 45, 46
anti-war protestors (United States) 86, 92–93
APPD/RJ *see* Rio de Janeiro Association of Data Processing Professionals
Argentina: dictatorships 231; French ideas, contact with 235; information and repression 244; Paris embassy 234; Secretaría de Inteligencia (SIDE) 122; state terror 142; Superior War College 234

Army Centre for Studies and Staff (Brazil) *see* Centro de Estudos e Pessoal do Exército
Arquivo Geral (ARGE) (General Archive of the Brazilian Serviço Nacional de Informações) 145
Arquivos Cronológicos de Entrada (ACE) 126–127, *127*, 137n29
ARUANDA (public data network) 128, 156
ASIO KD *see* avtomatizirovannaya sistema informatsionnogo obespecheniya kontrrazvedyvatel'noi deyatel'nosti
ASOD *see* avtomatizirovannaya sistema obrabotki dannykh
Assessoria Especial de Relações Públicas (AERP)(Brazil) 235
Association of Data Processing Professionals *see* Rio de Janeiro Association of Data Processing Professionals
Ataöv, İhsan 173
Automated Information Processing Center (OBIUM) (Turkey) 176
Automatic Information Technology Units (OBI) (Turkey) 170
Automatyczny System Ewidencjonowania Zainteresowań Operacyjnych (EZOP) (Poland) 192, 193
Avakoum Zahov vs. 07 (Gulyashki) 1
avtomatizirovannaya sistema informatsionnogo obespecheniya kontrrazvedyvatel'noi deyatel'nosti (ASIO KD) 40, 47, 49; "Delta-Sverdlovsk" 60n77
avtomatizirovannaya sistema obrabotki dannykh (ASOD) 48–49

Badie, François 235
Bakatin, Vadim 52

286   Index

Bamford, James 275
Banco Nacional de Desenvolvimento
  Econômico (BNDE) 124
Baumgarten case 136n23
Baykal, Deniz 174
Becker, Joseph 104, 275, 277, 280
Beduk, Saffet Arıkan 181n58
Benda, Ernst 259–260, 263
Bentresque, Robert 235
Bergh, Hendrik van (alias of Berghoff,
  Friedrich Ernst) 258
Berghoff, Friedrich Ernst 258
Berlin: United States Embassy in 85;
  Verfassungsschutz in 225; West Berlin
  253, 256
Berlin Wall 217, 254
Bigalı, Burhanettin 176, 178
Biographical Data Survey (LDB) 126–127
Biuro "B" MSW (Bureau "B") 192
Biuro "C" MSW (Bureau "C") 185
Biuro Ewidencji Operacyjnej (BEO)
  (Bureau of the Operative Registry)
  MSW 198n8
Biuro Paszportowe MSW 195
Biuro Informatyki 190
BKA *see Bundeskriminalamt* (Federal
  Criminal Police Office, West Germany)
"black boxes," intelligence agencies as 6
Black Panther Party 88
Black Sea 172
Black September 221
Blakefield, William H. 90
BMI *see* Federal Ministry of the Interior
  (Germany)
BND *see* Bundesnachrichtendienst (West
  German Federal Intelligence Service)
Board of National Estimates (BNE)
  69–70, 79
Bonn 101, 253, 254
Bonn-Bad Godesberg 106, 279
Braunbuch 268n29
Brasil (Brazil): 1964 civilian-military
  dictatorship (Brazil) 12; authoritarian
  regime 12, 121; civilian-military
  dictatorship 124–126, 231–245, 281;
  "computerized era" 143; "economic
  miracle" 130; Federal Senate 156;
  Folha de São Paulo 153; informatics
  128–129, 133, 135; informatics policy
  123, 131; information technology sector
  121–135; "Manual on Intelligence"
  244; "political détente" (*distenção
  política*) 144–145, 159; secret service
  159; *see also* Comissão de Coordenação

das Atividades de Processamento
  Eletrônico (CAPRE); Serviço Nacional
  de Informações (SNI); Sistema Nacional
  de Informações (SISNI)
Brasília 143; Brazilian National Archives
  123; Central Agency of SNI 140,
  143–145, 147, 233, 239; EsNI 239, 243;
  South Police Sector 240
Brazilian Aeronautical Commission 137n34
Brazilian Computer Industry Association 131
Brazilian Computer Society 131
Brazilian Development Bank (Banco
  Nacional de Desenvolvimento
  Econômico, BNDE) 124
Brazilian Navy 124
Brízida, Joubert 133, 134, 136n25, 138n54
BRUSA agreement of 5 March 1946
  78n19
Brustolin, V. 137
Buddenberg, Wolfgang 262
Bundeskriminalamt (BKA) (Federal
  Criminal Police Office) (West Germany)
  106, 160n27, 177, 253, 258, 267n6
Bundesnachrichtendienst (BND) (Federal
  Intelligence Service) (West Germany)
  1, 19, 27–32, 101, 166, 277, 282; "ADP
  Briefings" 109, 113, 117n60; CIA and
  10, 102–115, 280–281; evaluation
  department 279; *see also* Alten, Jürgen
  von; Felfe, Heinz; Gehlen Intelligence
  Organization; Gehlen, Reinhard
Bundesamt für Verfassungsschutz (BfV)
  (Federal Office for the Protection of
  the Constitution) (West Germany) 12,
  26, 106, 112, 166; anti-Semitism and
  neo-Nazi activities in 1961, findings
  regarding 255; BMI and 254, 256;
  Postel at 206, 208–210, 212–213, 220–
  225; public relations (PR) department,
  establishment of 254, 256; *see also*
  John, Otto; *Verfassungsschutz* and
  Verfassungsschutzbericht (Report on the
  Protection of the Constitution)
Bundeswehr 216 (West German Armed
  Forces)
Bush, George 75

C3I (Command, Communication, Control
  and Intelligence) 171
CAPRE *see* Comissão de Coordenação
  das Atividades de Processamento
  Eletrônico (CAPRE) (Commission for
  Coordination of Electronic Processing
  Activities) (Brazil)

Index 287

Catholic University of Rio de Janeiro (PUCRIO) 125

Çayan, Mahir 172

CENIMAR military information centre (Brazil) 125

Central Intelligence Agency (CIA) (United States) 1, 20–26; Eastern European Division 109; West German intelligence and 101–120; *see also* CIG; DCI; DCDPO; DD/P; FBI; IBM; OCR; ONA; O/NE; OSS; RID; technopolitics

Central Intelligence Group (CIG) (United States) 69

Centre of Training in Subversive Warfare (Brazil) 234

Centro de Estudos e Pessoal do Exército (CEP) (Brazil) 233, 238

Centro de Informações da Aeronáutica (CISA) 125, *132*

Centro Tecnológico para Informática (CTI) (Brazil) 134

CEP *see* Centro de Estudos e Pessoal do Exército (CEP)

CEPAL *see* Comissão Econômica para a América Latina e o Caribe (Economic Commission for Latin America and the Caribbean) (Brazil)

Çeti, Bayram Turan 174–175

Chaban-Delvas, Jacques 234

Chebrikov, Viktor 53

Che Guevara, Ernesto 242

Chekism 53

Chekists 45; Kazakh SSR 50; Nalchik 51; terminology of 37

"Chekist science" 53, 54–55

Chile 122, 142, 231, 244

CHIVE (EDP Project at CIA) 104–105, 109

Chronological Archives of Entry *see* Arquivos Cronológicos de Entrada

CIA *see* Central Intelligence Agency (CIA) (United States)

CIE *see* Military Information Centres (CIE) (Brazil)

CIG *see* Central Intelligence Group (CIG) (United States)

CISA *see* Centro de Informações da Aeronáutica

"closed world" discourse 89, 124

CNPq *see* Conselho Nacional de Desenvolvimento Científico e Tecnológico

COBRA *see* Computadores Brasileiros

COCOM embargo 193, 196

CODIB *see* Committee on Documentation of the US Intelligence Board

Coelho, Moacir 241

Cold War: early 18–32, 88; *Bundesamt* and 210, 216, 217; détente 13, 217; German propaganda and 249–267; hot wars of 276; knowledge of intelligence agencies during 1–7, 275–276, 282; narratives of 92; "second" 42–43; Soviet Union and 72–77, 178; Turkish intelligence and 164–180; United States strategic intelligence during 65–78

Comissão de Coordenação das Atividades de Processamento Eletrônico (CAPRE) (Commission for Coordination of Electronic Processing Activities) (Brazil) 121, 130–135

Comissão Econômica para a América Latina e o Caribe (CEPAL) (Economic Commission for Latin America and the Caribbean) (Brazil) 131

Committee on Documentation of the US [United States] Intelligence Board (CODIB) 105

"Committee on the Present Danger" (CPD) (United States) 75, 76

Communist Party of China (CCP) 91

Communist Party of the Soviet Union (CPSU) 37; 22nd Congress 37; 24th Congress 41; Central Committee 38, 55; General Secretary 43; *Komsomol* 45; post-Stalin era 54

Communist dictatorships: East Europe 6

Communist security police: Poland 184–197

Computadores Brasileiros (COBRA) 125

Condor Network *see* Operation Condor

Conselho Nacional de Desenvolvimento Científico e Tecnológico (CNPq) 133

Continental Army Command (CONARC) 91, 92, 94

Cotrim Commission 133

Cotrim, Paulo 138n46

Counterintelligence (CI): BND 107–108, 110, 112; CIA 105, 112; EGIS (East German Intelligence Service) database 112; ESIOC's role in collecting 41–44, 46–47; Fifth Directorate for Ideological Counterintelligence (KGB) 39–40; Fourth Directorate (KGB) 42–43; KGB 9, 38–50, 52; "Manual on Intelligence" (Brazil) 244; Sixth Directorate (KGB) 43; security databases (United States) 86–87, 91, 93, 115; Soviet 38, 48; technology 10, 39; Transport Counterintelligence (KGB) 42–43; West German 54, 212; *see also* Directorates

288 *Index*

coup: Brazilian civilian-military 122, 131, 142, 235, 244; Cold War Latin America 233; Turkish military 11, 165–169, 172, 174–179
CPD *see* "Committee on the Present Danger"
Criminal Codes: Soviet 39
criminal intelligence 115
criminalisation of "anti-Soviet agitation" 39, 54
criminal police 11, 188, 195; *see also* *Bundeskriminalamt* (BKA) (Federal Criminal Police Office)
CTI *see* Centro Tecnológico para Informática
Cuban missile crisis 217
Cuban Revolution 243, 281
Cruz, Newton 153
Crypto AG cryptographic equipment 128, 137n35
crypto-industrial complex 275
Cyprus, 1974 Turkish military intervention of 169, 170, 171

Data Processing Company of São Paulo (PRODESP) (Brazil) 136n27
DCDPO *see* Directorate for Civil Disturbance Planning and Operations (United States)
DCI *see* Director of Central Intelligence
DD/P *see* Deputy Department of Plans (CIA) (United States)
Delta computers 48
Delta (code name for ESIOC) 41, 43, 44, 46, 47, 48, 51
Demirel, Süleyman 169
Departamento de Informática of the Escola Nacional de Informações (DI/EsNI) (Brazil) 150, 151
Departamento de Polícia Federal (Brazil) 156
Deputy Department of Plans (DD/P) (CIA) (United States) 103–106, 111
"Détente" (*distenção política*) (Brazil) 144–145, 159
détente (United States–Soviet relations) 13, 39–42, 75, 77, 217, 277
Dias, Ezequiel Pinto 131
Dickopf, Paulinus 106
DI/EsNI *see* Departamento de Informática of the Escola Nacional de Informações
DINA *see* Dirección de Inteligencia Nacional (Chile)
Dirección de Inteligencia Nacional (DINA) (Chile) 122

Directorate for Civil Disturbance Planning and Operations (DCDPO)(CIA)(United States) 90, 94
Directorate for Intelligence (DD/I) (CIA) (United States) 103–104, 276, 283n8
Directorate of Security (Turkey) *see* General Directorate of Security (Turkey)
Directorates (KGB): "A" 40, 46, 47; Analytical 52; counterintelligence 42, 49; Eighth Chief 56n27; Encryption and Decryption 56n27; establishment of 276; Fifth 39–40; "N" 41, 46, 47; Fourth 43; I&A 52; Inspection 50; Operational and Technical (O&T) 39, 57n27; regional 51; Scientific Operational 41; Second Chief 39–41; Sixteenth 57n27; Sixth 43; Sverdlovsk regional police (*militsiya*) 45; Third Chief 46
Director of Central Intelligence (DCI) (United States) 70, 75
dissidents 7, 125, 172
domestic intelligence 8; Brazil 142; Soviet 38; Turkey 165–166; United States 86
domestic intelligence service: Danish (PET) 15n56; German 12–13, 206–225, 253, 259; German (BfV) 26, 106, 263
domestic politics: Turkey 167, 174–175, 282
domestic security: Germany 2, 249, 258, 264–266
domestic spying (United States) 86
domestic subversion: Soviet Union 164
domestic surveillance 7; Poland 189, 192
domestic threats: United States 96
domestic turmoil: Turkey 169, 174
domestic uprisings 90
Dória Porto, José Rubens 138n53
Douerty, Sérgio 240, 241
Doutrina de Segurança Nacional (DSN) (Brazil)124, 135, 234, 236
DSN *see* Doutrina de Segurança Nacional (Brazil)
Dytz, Edison 128, 134, 137n36, 138n54
Dziak, John 37

Eastern Bloc 26, 30
Eastern Europe: communist dictatorships, end of 6; early Cold War 18–32; economies, knowledge of 27–30; energy sector 23; intelligence 276; National Socialist New Order 19; plans for the occupation of 20; scholars of 20–24; Soviet forces withdrawal from 46; United States research on 33n40
Eastern European Division, CIA 109

Index 289

Eastern European studies 25–26; associations 34n50; *see also Ostforschung*; "professor's group"
East German Intelligence Service (EGIS) database 112
ECHELON intelligence networks 85
Edinaya sistema informatsionnogo obespecheniya kontrrazvedki (ESIOC) (Unified Information Support System for Counterintelligence) 40–41, 43–49, 51, 278; "Delta" stage 44; four elements of data groupings 44; four major stages of 57n35; thematic list of information 44–45, 51
EDP *see* electronic data processing
EGIS (East German Intelligence Service) database *see* East German Intelligence Service database
Ehlers, Adolf 254
Eisenhower, Dwight D. 168
electronic data processing (EDP) 2, 10, 48, 277–282; American society, impact on 96; BND's use of 103, 108, 112–113, 277, 279, 282; *Bundesamt's* use of 216–221, 224; CIA's use of 101–103, 105–115, 280; Joint Soviet Travel Project's use of 278; Pentagon's use of 89, 91; Polish security police's use of 190–197
electronic reconnaissance *see* ELINT
Elektroniczne Przetwarzanie Informacji [Wywiadowczej] (EPI or EPIW) (Electronic [Intelligence] Data Processing) (Poland) 189, 191–197, 279
Elektroniczny System Ewidencji Faktów-Zagrożeń (ESFAZA) system (Poland) 192–194
Elektroniczny System Ewidencji Zainteresowań Operacyjnych (ESEZO) (Poland) 192–194
ELINT (electronic reconnaissance) 102, 109, 114, 167
EME *see* Estado-Maior do Exército
Emokhonov, Nikolai 46
Empresa Técnica de Consultoria e Projetos 147
Ervin, Sam J., Jr. 95
EPI or EPIW *see* Elektroniczne Przetwarzanie Informacji [Wywiadowczej] (EPI or EPIW) (Electronic [Intelligence] Data Processing) (Poland)
Escola Nacional de Informações (EsNI) (Brazil) 126, 146–147; Departamento

de Informática 150–151; courses delivered by 232–234; creation and purpose of 238–245; Dytz and 137n36; internationalization of 245; IT department 127, 157; "knowledge of violence" transmitted by 281; Medeiros as director 136n23; Mello's destruction of 232; SNI and 238–245
Escola Superior de Guerra (ESG) (Brazil) 124, 126, 233–238, 240–242, 244–245; Division for Information and Counter-Information Affairs 236; transmission of knowledge by 281
ESEZO *see* Elektroniczny System Ewidencji Zainteresowań Operacyjnych
ESFAZA system *see* Elektroniczny System Ewidencji Faktów-Zagrożeń system
ESG *see* Escola Superior de Guerra
ESIOC *see* Edinaya sistema informatsionnogo obespecheniya kontrrazvedki (Unified Information Support System for Counterintelligence)
EsNI *see* Escola Nacional de Informações
ESPIN domestic operative evaluative system (Poland) 192
espionage: BND counter-espionage 101; Brazil 12; communist foreign 6; GDR 110; joint 245; KGB counter-espionage 48; secrecy and 5; Soviet 7; technological 3; Western 193; West German 249
espionage to intelligence, transformation from 1, 105
Estado-Maior do Exército (EME) (Brazil) 235
Estado Novo 124
Evdokushin, Aleksandr 40
EZOP *see* Automatyczny System Ewidencjonowania Zainteresowań Operacyjnych

FACOM m360 computer 127
Fakel-U (outdoor surveillance) (Ukraine) 46
FBI *see* Federal Bureau of Investigations (FBI)
federal agencies (United States) 90, 95, 97
Federal Border Guard (Bundesgrenzschutz) (Germany) 221, 258
Federal Bureau of Investigations (FBI) (United States) 90; Bundesamt visit with 217; CIA and 166; EsNI internships at 240, 281; interagency biographical information network involving 105; National Crime Information Center 95; Watergate scandal 96, 97

290 *Index*

Federal Centre for Homeland Service (West Germany) 253
Federal Communications Commission (FCC) (United States) 137n34
Federal Constitutional Court (West Germany) 263
Federal Constitutional Protection Act (West Germany) 252
Federal Criminal Police Office (BKA) *see* Bundeskriminalamt (BKA) (Federal Criminal Police Office)
Federal Criminal Statistics (Germany) 249
Federal Data Processing Service *see* Serviço Federal de Processamento de Dados (SERPRO)
Federal Defense Forces of Germany *see* Bundeswehr
Federal elections of 1969 (West Germany) 261
Federal Foreign Office (West Germany) 27
Federal government: United States, surveillance powers of 94; West Germany/Social Democrats 113
Federal Intelligence Service (West Germany) *see* Bundesnachrichtendienst (BND)
Federal Institute for Eastern Studies (West Germany) 25–26
Federalism: German 264
Federal Minister of the Interior (West Germany) 249, 259, 261, 262, 263, 264
Federal Ministry for All-German Issues 253
Federal Ministry of the Interior (BMI) (West Germany) 253, 254, 256–261
Federal Office for the Protection of the Constitution (Germany) *see* Bundesamt für Verfassungsschutz, BfV)
Federal Police (Brazil) 126; databases 278; systems 128; *see also* Departamento de Polícia Federal
Federal Republic of Germany 20, 23–24; anti-communist political culture of 269n38; anti-Semitism in 268n30; German Democratic Republic (GDR) and 251–253; intelligence public relations by 251; Nazis harbored by 265; Turkish training in 178–179; right-wing radicalism in 255; security history of 250, 266; *see also* Bundesamt für Verfassungsschutz (BfV)
Federal Security Service (FSB) (Russia) *49*
Federal Senate (Brazil) 156

Federal Senate Data Centre (PRODASEN) (Brazil) 136n27; terminal 156
Federal Service of Information and Counter-Information (Brazil) *see* Serviço Federal de Informação e Contra-Informação (SFICI)
Federal University of Brasilia 136n15
Felfe, Heinz 101, 108, 110, 117n62
Ferranti 124
Ferris, John 102–103, 115n14
Fico, Carlos 125, 132, 142, 152–153
Fifth Directorate for Ideological Counterintelligence (KGB) 39–40
Figueiredo, João Baptista 126, 129, 133, 142, 144, 231
First Inter-American Course on Counter-Revolutionary War 235
Five Eyes alliance 78n19, 85
Five Year Plan (12th) (Russia) 53
Fontoura, Carlos Alberto da 239–240, 243
Ford, Gerald 75
Foucault, Michel 96, 167
Fourth Army (United States) 91, 94
Fourth Directorate (KGB) (Russia) 42–43
France 18; computer hardware from 196; interrogation techniques 235; nuclear energy 122
French military, influence on Brazil 234–236
Free German Trade Union Federation 256
Fregat surveillance system (Ukraine) 46, 57n35
Freyer, Hans 27

Gehlen, Reinhard 1, 22, 73, 106, 109; computerisation, interest in 101–102; departure of 113; prioritization of digitization 110; successors 101
Gehlen Intelligence Organization 20–31; CIA funding of 107; data processing 106–109; "professors' group" 20–25, 27, 31, 275
Geisel, Ernesto 129, 131, 133, 144
Gendarmerie Intelligence Command (Turkey) 166
Genelkurmay Elektronik Sistemler Komutanlığı (GES) (Turkey) 170
General Directorate of Security (Turkey) 164
General Staff Electronic Systems Command *see* Genelkurmay Elektronik Sistemler Komutanlığı
Genscher, Hans-Dietrich 261
"German Autumn" of 1977 (terrorist attacks) 222

Index 291

German Democratic Republic (GDR) 252; Altdorfer's role in 279; BND's espionage 110; centralized card indexes 188; Genscher's position on 261; IfO research on 25; microelectronics, ridiculing of 6; propagandistic campaign policies of 252–254; security police 199n31; "traditional" communism of 260; US technopower 10–11
German-German affairs 253
German Television Broadcasting Corporation 256, *257*
GES *see* Genelkurmay Elektronik Sistemler Komutanlığı
Gestapo (Nazi Germany) 209, 252
glasnost 38, 43
Glavny vychislitelny tsentr (GVTs) (KGB) (Main Computing Center) 48–49
Gorbachev, Mikhail 43
Government Communications Headquarters (GCHQ) (British) 102; base in Turkey 172–173; official history of computerisation (Ferris) 103; recruiting for 275
Grishanin, Gennady 50
GTE/I *see* Information Technology/Special Working Group
Gulyashki, Andrei 1
Günzel, Karl 27–28
GVTs *see* Glavny vychislitelny tsentr (GVTs) (KGB) (Main Computing Center)

Hamlet Evaluation System (HES) 89, 81
Helms, Richard 71
Hennessy, John J. 90
Hennessy Report 90
HES *see* Hamlet Evaluation System
Hollerith technology 209–216, 218, 224
Honeywell Bull G-118 computer/hardware system 196
Honeywell-Bull H-6030 and H-6040 computer/hardware system 195
human agents (spy network) 175
human capital 165, 168, 172, 178–179
human factor in intelligence collection 143; German domestic intelligence 206–225
human geography, technologies of 87
human informants 91, 143
human intelligence (HUMINT) 70, 167, 175, 179
human rights violations 6, 231–232
HUMINT *see* human intelligence (HUMINT)

IBM (International Business Machines Corporation) 105; CIA and 108–112, 114–115; communist security police in Poland's use of 195; dominance of Brazil market 124, 136n12; Postel and 214, 217; SNI and 140–142, 156; STAIRS software 127; Turkish intelligence's use of 176
IBM computer 101, 102; Brazil 126; Germany 107, 109; model 360/30 109; model 360/40 107; model 650 104; model 1401 91; model 1401/1410 104; model 3231 127; model 3270 140, *141*
IBM-Nachrichten 218
ICC/Coencisa company 132
identity cards 186, 193, 198n10
IfO *see* Institut für Ostforschung (IfO)
Informatics Centre of Ministry *see* Ośrodek Informatyki MSW
Information Technology Bureau *see* Biuro Informatyki
Information Technology/Special Working Group (GTE/I)(Brazil) 133, 138n47
Institute for Research on Turkish Culture *see* Türk Kültürünü Araştırma Enstitüsü (TKAE)
Institut für Deutsche Ostarbeit (IDO) (Institute for German Work in the East) 21
Institut für Ostforschung (IfO) (Institute for Eastern Studies) 22–26
Instituto Brasileiro de Geografia e Estatística (IBGE) 156
Institut zur Erforschung der Judenfrage (Institute for the Study of the Jewish Question) 21
Itamaraty 128, 129, 137, 138
Integrated System of the Operative Card Indexes *see* Zintegrowany System Kartotek Operacyjnych
International Traffic System (STI) 128
Iron Curtain 1, 178, 277, 280

Japan 69
JCI *see* Junta Coordenadora de Informações (Brazil)
JIC *see* Joint Intelligence Committee (United States)
John, Otto 252
Johnson, Harold K. 92
Johnson, Lyndon B. 71, 74, 90; "Great Society" program 96
Joint Intelligence Committee (JIC) (United States) 69
Joint Soviet Travel Program 112, 278

292　*Index*

Jordan, Paul 92
Jordan, Robert E. 90
Junta Coordenadora de Informações (JCI)
　(Brazil) 238

K-202 device 196
Kaufmann, Franz von ("Kreuzberg")
　107–111
Kennedy, John F. 73–74
Kharkhordin, Oleg 38
Kissinger, Henry 72, 76
Kızıldere incident 172–173
Klocke, Helmut 27–29, 34n50
Koch, Hans 20–21
Kohl, Helmut 263, 266
Komitet do spraw Bezpieczeństwa
　Publicznego (KdsBP) (Poland) 184
Komitet gosudarstvennoi bezopasnosti
　(KGB) (Russia) (Soviet Committee
　for State Security): Collegium 52;
　EDP and 278; Felfe as spy for 101,
　108, 110; intellectualization of 1,
　276; scientific and technological
　capacities, 1960s–1980s 37–55; *see also*
　Directorates; Glavny vychislitelny tsentr
　(GVTs) (KGB) (Main Computing Center)
Komsomol 45
Korean War (1950–1953) 69
Korolev, Valentin 48
"Kreuzberg" *see* Kaufmann, Franz von
　("Kreuzberg")
Kubitschek, Juscelino 124
Kurashvili, Boris 40

Lagôa, Ana 240
Laird v. Tatum 94–95
Lefebvre, Henri 86, 96
Leiberich, Otto 113, 115
Leonov, Nikolai 52
Lipschitz, Joachim 368n31
liquid modernity 275
Lithuania 45, 47; Trakai 50
Lourinha computer 124, 137n36
Loyola Reis, Antonio de 127, 134
Lücke, Paul 259
Luftwaffe (German Air Force) 206
Lviv massacre of 1941 20

MAGISTER subsystem (Poland) 193
Maihofer, Werner 262
Manual on Intelligence (Brazil) 244
Mao Zedong 242
March on the Pentagon (1967) 93
Marighella, Carlos 242

Markert, Werner 20, 21, 27, 28
Marshall, Andrew W. 76–77
Martins, Gílcio 131
Marx, Karl 242
Massachusetts Institute of Technology
　(MIT) (United States) 104
Matos, Carlos de Meira 234
McCarthyism 226n15
McCloy, John J. 74
McGhee, George 172
McGuire Air Force Base 216
McNamara, Robert S. 74–75, 89
Medeiros, Octavio Aguira de 126, 133, 136n23
Meder, Walter 22, 34n48
Médici, Emílio Garrastazu 142, 153, 231,
　239, 241
Meissner, Boris 22, 34n48, 178, 182n12
Mello, Danilo da Cunha E. 236
Mello, Fernando Collor de 232
Mello, Zey Bezerra de 160n39
Mera 100B device 196; Mera 9150 device
　196
Military Information Centres (CIE)
　(Brazil) 125
minicomputers 124, 131, 132; domestic
　manufacturing of 134; G-10 125
Ministerstwo Bezpieczeństwa Publicznego
　(MBP) (Ministry of Public Security)
　(Poland) 184, 187
Ministerstwo Spraw Wewnętrznych (MSW)
　(Poland) 184
Ministry of Foreign Affairs (Brazil) 123,
　128, 134
Ministry of Internal Affairs (Poland) *see*
　Ministerstwo Spraw Wewnętrznych
　(MSW) 184–197
Ministry of Public Security (MBP) *see*
　Ministerstwo Bezpieczeństwa Publicznego
MIT *see* Massachusetts Institute of
　Technology (United States)
MIT *see* National Intelligence
　Organization (Turkey)
modernisation theory 4, 87, 183, 275
Mossad (Israeli intelligence agency) 136n25
Motorola company 175–176
Motta, Jecy Serôa 145
MSW *see* Ministerstwo Spraw Wewnętrznych

NAACP *see* National Association for the
　Advancement of Colored People
Nachrichtendienstliches Informationssystem
　(NADIS) (Intelligence Agency
　Information System) (West Germany)
　12, 176, 219–224

Index 293

Nachtigall Battalion (Ukraine) 20
NADIS *see* Nachrichtendienstliches Informationssystem (NADIS)
National Association for the Advancement of Colored People (NAACP) 91
National Computer Training Programme (Brazil) 130
National Crime Information Center (FBI) (United States) 95
National Democratic Party of Germany (NPD) 260, 261, 263
National Information Plan (Brazil) 240
National Information System *see* Sistema Nacional de Informações
National Intelligence Estimates (NIEs) (United States) 65, 69–70, 75–76, 78, 276
National Intelligence Organization (MIT) (Turkey) 166, 168–180, 276
National Intelligence Plan (Brazil) 239
National Security Agency (NSA) (United States) 11, 102, 115, 170, 275; *see also* Snowden, Edward
National Security Council (MGK) (Turkey) 168
National Socialism (Germany) 18–21, 209–210
National System of Wanted and Prohibited People (SINPI) (Brazil) 128
National Truth Commission (Brazil) 144, 231, 233
NATO *see* North Atlantic Treaty Organization (NATO)
Naurois, Patrice de 235
Nelidov, Nikolai 50
Net Assessment (United States) 76–77
Neto, Octavio Gennari 127
NIEs *see* National Intelligence Estimates
NIIAI *see* Scientific Research Information and Analytical Institute
Nitze, Paul 75
Nixon, Richard 72, 240; Watergate scandal 95–96; use of CIA against rivals 85
NKVD *see* People's Commissariat of Internal Affairs
Nollau, Günter 258
Norden, Albert 268n29
North Atlantic Treaty Organization (NATO) 11, 73; Turkey as member 164–165, 167–170, 179
Nougues, Jean 235
NPD *see* National Democratic Party of Germany

nuclear and missile technology, Cold War period 92; nuclear annihilation 2; nuclear attack and armament: by Soviet Union 65, 282; nuclear armament 14, 282; nuclear energy 122, 129; nuclear force policy: Soviet Union 76; United States 75; nuclear power: Soviet Union as 74; nuclear proliferation and non-proliferation 69, 73

O&T *see* Operational and Technical Directorate (KGB)
Oberländer, Theodor 20, 21, 24
OBIUM *see* Automated Information Processing Center
OCR *see* Office for Central Reference
OEPI *see* Ośrodek Elektronicznego Przetwarzania Informacji
Office for Central Reference (OCR) (CIA) (United States) 103–106, 108, 110–111, 113, 280
Office of National Estimates (O/NE) (CIA) (United States) 68–75, 77
Office of Net Assessment (ONA) (CIA) (United States) 67, 76–77
Office of Strategic Services (OSS) (United States) 18–19; dissolving of 69; USSR division of 18, 25
oil 137
Oil Shock of 1973 128
OI MSW *see* Ośrodek Informatyki MSW
Olympic Games: 1972 Munich 221, 222; 1980 Moscow 42–43, 278
ONA *see* Office of Net Assessment (CIA) (United States)
O/NE *see* Office of National Estimates (CIA) (United States)
Operational and Technical Directorate (O&T) (KGB) (Russia) 39, 45, 57n27
Operation Condor 126, 136n6, 137n30, 238, 245, 281
Organisation of Ukrainian Nationalists (OUN) (Ukraine) 20
Ośrodek Elektronicznego Przetwarzania Informacji (OEPI) (Poland) 190
Ośrodek Informatyki MSW (OI MSW) (Poland) 190
OSS *see* Office of Strategic Services (United States)
Ostforschung (German research on Eastern Europe) 32n4, 18–32; knowledge about economies of Eastern Europe 27–30; re-establishment of 24–26; völkisch-nationalism of 31, 32n4; *see also* Institut für Ostforschung (IfO)

294 *Index*

Palestinian terrorist organization 221
Paluch, Stefan 192, 277
Paraguay 231
Paris War College 234
Pentagon (United States) 92–94; 1967 March on the Pentagon 93; McNamara's leadership of 89
People's Commissariat of Internal Affairs (NKVD) (Russia) 7
perestroika 38, 43, 52–53
Personenzentralkartei (Person Central File, PZK) (Germany) 210
Persons and Experiences on Terrorism (PET) (Germany) 222
PESEL system (People's Republic of Poland) 193–197, 278
PET (Danish domestic intelligence service) 15n56
PET *see* Persons and Experiences on Terrorism (Germany)
Pinheiro, Ênio 239–242
Pipes, Richard E. 75, 80n58
Pipia, Georgii 47
Poland: BND analyses of 29–30; communist security police 184–197; German rule in 21; Silesia 206
Poland Handbook 28
Polvo project *see Projeto Polvo*
Pontifícia Universidade Católica 147
Postel, Hans-Joachim 176, 206–225, 277, 280
Privacy Act of 1974 (United States) 97
PRODASEN *see* Federal Senate Data Centre (Brazil)
PRODESP *see* Data Processing Company of São Paulo (Brazil)
"Professors' group" (Gehlen Organization) 20–25, 27, 275
Projeto Polvo (Project Octopus) (Brazil) 128, 156
Prólogo Project (Brazil) 123, 128, *129*, 137n36
PUCRIO *see* Catholic University of Rio de Janeiro
Pullach, Germany, headquarters of the West German Federal Intelligence Service, 20, 23, 26–27, 101–102, 108, 111, 112
Pyatakov, Stanislav 51
Pyle, Christopher 85–86, 93–94, 96
PZK *see Personenzentralkartei* (Person Central File) (Germany)

Quantico, Virginia 97

Raborn, William F. 1
Radikalenerlass (Anti-Radical Decree) (West Germany) 263
Rauch, Georg von 22
Record Integration Division (RID)(CIA) (United States) 103–105
Red Army Faction (RAF) (Germany) 222
Redford, Robert 1
"registration system of border movement" (Poland) 278; *see also* System Ewidencji Ruchu Paszportowego, the Registration System of Border Movement (SERP)
Registro Nacional de Pessoas Naturais (RENAPE) (National Registry of Natural People) (Brazil) 128
Regnecentralen RC8000 system 196
Reid, Susan 39
Reis, Antonio de Loyola *see* Loyola Reis, Antonio de
RENAPE *see* Registro Nacional de Pessoas Naturais (National Registry of Natural People) (Brazil)
Republican People's Party (CHP) (Turkey) 174
Riad computers (series of general-purpose computers in the Soviet bloc) 195, 196
RID *see* Record Integration Division (RID) (CIA)
Riocentro attack 136n23
Rio de Janeiro: Army Centre for Studies and Staff 238; Army General Staff in 235; bridge to Niteroi 232
Rio de Janeiro Association of Data Processing Professionals (APPD/RJ) (Brazil) 131–132, *132*, 134, 135
Robinson, George T. 18, 24, 275
Robotron computers (GDR) 6
Rosas, Carlos J. 234
Rousseff, Dilma 233
Recht *und Ordnung* (law and order) 263

Sabis, Ali İhsan 168
SAFE programme (CIA) 277, 279
SARDI *see* Sistema de Arquivamento e Recuperação de Documentos para Informação
Sarney, José 121, 138n53
Sbornik KGB SSSR journal 40, 45, 51, 52, 54
SBZ *see* Soviet Occupation Zone
Schiller, Otto 20, 21, 34n48
Schreyer, Helmut 124, 136n14, 137n36
Schrübbers, Hubert 106

Index 295

Schwagerl, Hans Joachim 264
Scientific Research Information and
Analytical Institute (NIIAI) 40, 49,
56n27, 58n50
Scientific-Technological Revolution
(STR) 39
Scientology, Church of 249
SECOMU *see* Seminar on Computing at
the University
Secretaría de Inteligencia (SIDE)
(Argentina) 122
Secretaria Especial de Informática (SEI)
(Special Department for Informatics)
(Brazil) 122, 123, 134, 135
secret police: data processing and analysis
by 7, 50–54; Soviet 37, 38, 43, 50, 52,
54–55; *see also* communist security
police; KGB; SNI; Stasi
Seehofer, Horst 267
SEI *see* Secretaria Especial de Informática
SEKAMED subsystem (Poland) 193
Semi-Automatic Ground Environment
(SAGE) 89
Seminar on Computing at the University
(SECOMU) 130
SEOP subsystem (Poland) 193
Seraphim, Peter-Heinz 21, 24–26
SERP *see* System Ewidencji Ruchu
Paszportowego
SERPRO *see* Serviço Federal de
Processamento de Dados
SESTA subsystem (Poland) 193
Serviço Federal de Informação e Contra-
Informação (SFICI) 238
Serviço Federal de Processamento de
Dados (SERPRO) 125–126, 128,
131, 156
Serviço Nacional de Informações (SNI)
(Brazil) 1, 122, 140–159; 1970s
123–135; 239; Central Agency 145,
147, 150; condensation of data by
154–156; database networks *157*;
D files 149–150; directorate 148;
"Documentation, Telecommunications
and Information Technology Division
(D/7)" 147–148; elimination of data by
148–153; external databases 156–158;
IT politics, involvement in 142; "leaden
years" 144–145; modernisation of 11;
PNI, control of 134; regional agencies
(RA) 145, 147, 150; Secretaria Especial
de Informática (SEI) and 122, 123, 134,
135; Section 06 "Research and Archive"
(Pesquisa e Arquivo) 143, 147, 149

Shin Bet (Israeli intelligence agency))
136n25
Służba Bezpieczeństwa (SB) (Poland) 184
SIDE *see* Secretaría de Inteligencia
(Argentina)
Siemens 193, 195–196, 219, 280
signals intelligence (SIGINT) 72, 279;
GES for 176; non-SIGINT computer
104; postwar cooperation agreements'
roots in 78m19; Turkey and 167,
169–174, 176, 179; *see also* Five Eyes
SIGINT *see* signals intelligence
SIGINT bases: Turkey 169–171
SIGINT partnership, Anglo-American 281
Silva, Golbery do Couto e 234, 238
Silveira, Azeredo da 128
Sino-Soviet relations 69, 79n29
SINPI *see* National System of Wanted and
Prohibited People
SIO *see* sistemy informatsionnogo
obsluzhivaniya
SIRA system (East Germany) 192
Sistema de Arquivamento e Recuperação
de Documentos para Informação
(SARDI) (Brazil) 127–128
Sistema Nacional de Informações (SISNI)
(Brazil) 1, 123, 125–126, 128, 134,
238–240
Sixteenth Directorate 57n27
Sixth Directorate 43
Smoydzin, Werner 217
SNI *see* Serviço Nacional de Informações
Snowden, Edward 5, 85, 227n68
socialism and socialist regimes 172, 278;
Poland 184
Socialist German Student Union 260
Socialist Unity Party of Germany (SED)
256
SOUD system (joint data repository
of Communist foreign intelligence
services) 188, 196
Soviet Bloc 20, 28, 104; anti-Semitic
incidents used by 255; computer and
information systems 191, 195–196
Soviet Committee for State Security *see*
Komitet gosudarstvennoi bezopasnosti
(KGB)
Soviet-controlled Eastern Europe 29
Soviet Occupation Zone (SBZ) 256
Soviet Socialist Republic (SSR): Kazakh
50; Ukrainian 40, 46, 48, 50
Sovietologists 68, 275
Soviet Union 3–4, 169; Afghanistan,
invasion of 42; agitation by 264; Cold

296 Index

War and 72–77, 178; Communist Party 37; counterintelligence 48; Criminal Codes 39; Delta-Potok information block 47; dissidents 7; espionage 7; Fakel-U 46; final crisis of 276; Fort-67 46; Ftor-74 46; Gehlen Organization's interest in 21; IfO and 22–23, 25–26; "Joint Soviet Travel Program" 112, 278; Lithuania and 45; National Intelligence Estimate (NIE) regarding 65; nuclear armament 282; *perestroika* 43; post-Stalinist era 37–38; secret police 38, 50, 52, 54–55; Sino-Soviet relations 69, 79n29; Sixth Directorate 43; Stalin, death of 37; Third Chief Directorate 46; Turkey and 164, 165, 169–170, 175, 179; Ukraine and 46; United States and 67, 69, 72–77, 179; West Germany's research and intelligence regarding 18; *see also* Edinaya sistema informatsionnogo obespecheniya kontrrazvedki (ESIOC); KGB; USSR
Soviet studies (United States) 5, 18–19, 31, 178, 275
Soviet-style intelligence agencies 185
Soviet Occupation Zone of Germany 209
Special Department for Informatics *see* Secretaria Especial de Informática, Special Department for Informatics (Brazil)
SS-Hauptamt 110
SSI *see* Subseção de Informática (Brazil)
SSR *see* Soviet Socialist Republic
Stalin, Joseph 37
Stasi (East German Secret Police–*Staatssicherheit*) 276–280; F16 and F22 card indexes 199n26; historical analysis of 6; personal data on employees stored by 112; personal data of travelers stored by 7; "Soviet inflammatory writing" spread by 255 *Stasi-Unterlagenbehörde* (BStU) 198n4
Status of Forces Agreement, United States and Turkey 169
Stepan, Alfred 234
STI *see* International Traffic System
Strategic Affairs Secretariat (SAE) (Brazil) 233
Strauß, Franz Josef 74
Sturz, Friedrich 111, 113, 118n74
Subseção de Informática (SSI) (Brazil) 156
Sûreté Française 241
System Ewidencji Ruchu Paszportowego (SERP) (Poland) 193, 195, 278

S*istemy informatsionnogo obsluzhivaniya* (SIO) (Poland) 40

Tastaibekov, Kubash 50
Tatum, Arlo 94–95
Technical School of the Army/Military Institute of the Army (ETE/IME) (Brazil) 124, 137n36
Technological Institute of Aeronautics (ITA) (Brazil) 124, 131
technopolitics 281; CIA 103, 105–106, 109–110, 114; definition of term 102; knowledge transfer and 101–115; SIGINT and 170
Thematic List of Information (ESIOC) (Russia) 44–45, 51
Third Chief Directorate (KGB) 46; *see also* Directorates
Third Programme of the Communist Party of the Soviet Union 37, 39
Third Reich (Nazi Germany) 253
"threat knowledge" 282
Three Days of the Condor (film)(1975) 1
torture 6; Brazil 231, 234; DSN 234; SNI and SISNI 125, 128, 142, 144
Toyka, Rudolf 269n35
Trakai 50
Trinquier, Roger 234
Turkey: 1970s 174; ASALA attacks on 181n44; Cold War experience of 11, 167–168; foreign ministry 170; intelligence 11, 164–180, 280, 282; military elites 277; military intervention of 1960 167; Republican People's Party (CHP) 174; Soviet Union and 164, 165, 169–170, 175, 179
Turkish Armed Forces 170–171
Turkish General Staff Intelligence Branch 166, 169
Turkish National Intelligence Organization 166, 169, 174, 178
Turkish National Police Intelligence Bureau 166
Turkish People's Liberation Front 172–173
Türk Kültürünü Araştırma Enstitüsü (TKAE) (Institute for Research on Turkish Culture) 178
Turolo, Carlos 235
Tüzüner, Musa 177

"Ugly Duckling" computer 138n51
Ukraine 46; "Nachtigall Battalion," 20; SSR 40, 46, 48, 50

Index 297

Union of Soviet Socialist Republics (USSR) 21; collapse of 38; Council of Ministers 65n5; disloyalty inside 42; foreigners arriving and departing 41, 43, 46, 47; international relations, expansion of 40; military programs, budgetary impositions of 76–77; Sixth Directorate 43; seeking superiority over United States 75; subversive activities inside 44–45; *see also* KGB USSR Division (OSS) 18, 25

United States: 1967 summer of protests; Cold War, strategic intelligence during 65–78; security databases 78–97; intelligence community 22; Soviet Union and 67, 69, 72–77, 179; *see also* Central Intelligence Agency (CIA); Federal Bureau of Investigation (FBI); Johnson, Lyndon B. Kennedy, John F.; Kissinger, Henry; National Security Agency (NSA); Nixon, Richard; United States-Soviet relations

Uruguay 231

Urząd Bezpieczeństwa (UB) (Security Department)(Poland) 184

USAINTC *see* United States Army's Intelligence Command

United States Army (US Army) 20, 90–91, 96–97

United States Army's Intelligence Command (USAINTC) 86–87, 90–94; *see also* Blakefield, William H.; Jordan, Paul

United States Joint Chiefs of Staff (US Joint Chiefs) 69

United States Mutual Assistance Program to Turkey 170–172

United States Senate Judiciary Committee 95

United States-Soviet relations *see* détente

USSR *see* Union of Soviet Socialist Republics

Venturini, Danilo 129

Verfassungsschutzbericht (Report on the Protection of the Constitution) 225, 249–267; public relations (PR) after 1968 259–265

von Kaufmann *see* Kaufmann, Franz von ("Kreuzberg")

von Lex, Hans Ritter 252

Vulkan affair (West Germany) 212

Waffen-SS 110, 117n74, 255

"Walnut" reader-printer system (CIA) 104–105

Warsaw Pact 11, 196, 199n31

Watergate scandal (United States) 85, 95–97

Weber, Hilde *130*

Wessel, Gerhard 113

West German Federal Intelligence Service *see* Bundesnachrichtendienst (BND)

Wojska Ochrony Pogranicza (WOP) (Poland) 193

Working Group for Computer Applications (Brazil) 124

Yom Kippur War 136n25

Zakharov 187

Zakład Techniki Specjalnej (ZTS) (Poland) 190

ZAM-41 system (Poland) 190, 195, 196

Zentralkartei (Central File Department of the *Bundesamt*, C.K.) (Germany) 212, 213, 214, 223

Zentrale Hinweiskartei der Nachrichtendienste (ZKN) (Central Index of the Intelligence Services) (Germany) 215

Zentralstelle für das Chiffrierwesen (ZfCH) (Germany) 113

"Zezinho" (ITA) 124

Zintegrowany System Kartotek Operacyjnych (ZSKO) (Poland) 190–191, 193–195, 278

ZKN *see* "Zentrale Hinweiskartei der Nachrichtendienste" (Central Index of the Intelligence Services)

ZSKO *see* Zintegrowany System Kartotek Operacyjnych

ZTS *see* Zakład Techniki Specjalnej

Zuber, Ebrulf ("Ackermann") 107, 110–115, 280

Printed in the United States
by Baker & Taylor Publisher Services